M000169630

BECK

BEAUTIFUL MONSTROSITY

BECK

BEAUTIFUL MONSTROSITY

JULIAN PALACIOS

First published 2000 by Boxtree
an imprint of Macmillan Publishers Ltd
25 Eccleston Place London SW1W 9NF
Basingstoke and Oxford

www.macmillan.co.uk

Associated companies throughout the world

ISBN 0 7522 7143 1

Text copyright © Julian Palacios, 1999

The right of Julian Palacios to be identified as the author of this work has been asserted
by him in accordance with the Copyright, Designs and Patents Act 1988.

All rights reserved. No part of this publication may be reproduced, stored in or introduced
into a retrieval system, or transmitted, in any form, or by any means (electronic, mechanical,
photocopying, recording or otherwise) without the prior written permission of the
publisher. Any person who does any unauthorized act in relation to this publication
may be liable to criminal prosecution and civil claims for damages.

1 3 5 7 9 8 6 4 2

A CIP catalogue record for this book is available from the British Library.

Designed and typeset by Neal Townsend
Printed by Mackays of Chatham plc

All photographs © Retna Pictures Limited

This book is sold subject to the condition that it shall not, by way of trade or otherwise, be
lent, re-sold, hired out, or otherwise circulated without the publisher's prior consent in
any form of binding or cover other than that in which it is published and without a similar
condition including this acondition being imposed on the subsequent purchaser.

Dedications spoil books; so I'll keep mine short.
When I heard Beck, I heard a door open.

This book is dedicated to all those who work at night.

ACKNOWLEDGEMENTS

Rachel (soul mate, patience incarnate, great beauty), Hugo/Barbara (parents, moral support), Ryan/Kate (friends, giggling souls of shamalama), Erin Buxton (comic relief and green eyes), Matt 'Orangejazz' Wellins (proof that there are those who don't agree with television), M&M (for Scattergories and Sepultura), Mojo's coffee house (sustenance and 4 a.m. reveries), Austin (where some people celebrate their failure, others coast, some become yuppies and others refuse to buy into any scheme, even ones that might help them…bless you all). Thanks to Dennis Campa, Harry and Debbie (for extreme hospitality) and good old Ben and Virginia. Also, to all the punks, geeks, freaks, Goths, indie snobs, alienated frat. kids, starving sorority sisters, people who dance to Brazilian records at midnight, people who have a clue, people who have no clue. I thank Radical Action Network, for proving that tree huggers and bongo players actually serve some purpose in life. I salute the Seattle protesters and remember the Poll Tax rioters. I thank the proto-yuppies and their sponsorship of tanning salons, bistros, consumer goods stores, and their cell-phone powered, four-wheel drive, and power shifting mindless consumption. I would like to thank proponents of ultra-capitalism, who waste resources, like people, and who forfeit the future for profit today. Are you watching television or is television watching you? I want to thank everyone who reaches 30 and is not bitter. Thanks to real souls, like Timothy 'Speed' Levitch, Harmony Korine, Chloe Sevigny, Beck, Roger Manning and others who shrugged off the deadweight and in refusing to give in to the dehumanising aspects of American culture, are outlining a new aesthetic based on empathy, excellence and acceptance of both horror and humour. I want to say thanks to the writers for the music rags who didn't lie to me during the 1980s: Simon Reynolds, Ian Watson, Jon Savage, and Barney Hoskyns. But most of all I want to thank people, especially young people, who don't give in to cynicism or despair and laugh as they give two fingers to the world forever.

CONTENTS

INTRODUCTION

Everything is in a state of flux, including the status quo.
Robert Byrne, *Writing Rackets*, Lyle Stuart Publishing, 1969

March 1946. Private Al Hansen, a 19-year-old American soldier, stands in line, waiting to jump out of a plane. As part of the invading army, paratrooper Hansen and the 508th Parachute Infantry Regiment (known as the Red Devils by the German Luftwaffe, who are mightily impressed with their daring-do and bravado) are going to police the dregs of the extinguished war.

One by one they parachute out of the door of a B-29 Superfortress. Ice cold winds whip through the metallic hull of the plane. Their parachutes open like spores over the incredibly green fields of Germany, bitter winds alternate with the warming sun as spring comes around. Once on the ground, the officers shout orders that echo off the bullet-stripped village buildings. The Red Devils are parachuting into the ruins of what was once Europe's most progressive culture. With muddy boots, worn from basic training and fighting across Europe, the regiment make their way into Frankfurt, which resembles nothing so much as a honeycomb, with shattered walls and windows caving in amidst powdery fine dust coating tons of brick and twisted wires. The detritus lies all around as the soldiers tramp down the mud banks and through the ghostly cathedral-like shells of buildings.

The regiment requisition abandoned houses in Hedderheim, a suburb of Frankfurt. In the chaos of the closing days of the war, dodging the black marketeers, wandering refugees, demobilised German soldiers and locals trying to pick up the pieces, Al Hansen surveys the ruins of Frankfurt. The young man from Queens, the immigrant-filled borough of New York City, marvels at the destruction. The firebombing of Frankfurt has reduced centuries of history to dust and boiled lakes. A frisson goes up and down his spine and he looks at the houses, some totally intact, as if by chance operation, in the midst of utter ruination. It all seems so arbitrary, a throw of the dice. Hansen later recalled his stunned impressions of the destruction wrought on Germany's defeated cities in his *Notes On A Mini-Retrospective*: 'The devastation in Frankfurt, Köln and Berlin from aerial bombing was awesome; a surreal, lunar landscape of skeletal buildings, ruins, bomb craters and mounds of rubble.'[1]

Hansen's regiment found themselves a makeshift camp in a bomb-blasted house. The doors on their floor opened onto a straight five-storey drop down to the ground; against a wall in one room, hanging right at the precipice, stood an upright piano. 'It was just a few centimetres from the edge,' Hansen recalled. Day by day the young paratrooper grew obsessed with the piano's parlous state: 'I thought about it while drinking and eating. I thought about it while fucking. I thought about it while jumping out of aeroplanes, while shooting machine guns, while on guard duty.'[2]

One night, after the final reveille, and when all the other soldiers had fallen asleep on their cots, Hansen snuck out of their room, and put his hand on the piano. He pushed it a hair's breadth; the entire floor groaned as if about to give way. He jumped back. He pushed a little more, a little more. The piano teetered on the edge, about to fall, each second of anticipation sending an electrical current coursing through Hansen's blood. And finally, off it went. The piano fell five storeys and hit the ground with an unbelievable crash: 'Tsccchwauuuuuuuuuuuungha!'

'The sound of it and the whole experience was the starting point for Al's interest in performance,'[3] Hansen's grandson Beck explained some fifty years later. Al called the toppling of that piano his first piece and later re-created it at the Happenings Fluxus Show at the Kunstverein in Köln, Germany, in 1969.

§

1   Hansen, Al. *Notes On A Mini-Retrospective*, Kölnisches Stadt Museum, 1995

2   McCormick, Carlo. 'Interview with Beck Hansen', *Playing With Matches*, Smart Art Press/Plug In Editions, 1998

3   Smith, Ethan. 'Re: Fluxology – Beck And Yoko Ono Sound Off On Found Art, Family Ties, And Flying Pianos', *New York* magazine, 21 September 1998

1

MYSTIC REGULATION
AT THE GRAND OLE OPRY

Please don't tell what train I'm on
So they won't know where I've gone.
'Freight Train' by **Elizabeth Cotton**

24 March 1997
Nashville, Tennessee

This afternoon Beck is taking a walk through the Country Hall Of Fame Museum. It is noontime, and very quiet. All the tourists are downtown on Broadway with melting popsicles running down their hands, eating nachos or treading the wooden boards of record stores which stock three hundred and sixty Minnie Pearl albums. All the black and white photos of broken down shacks and gaunt, serious farmers only serve to remind one what the heart source of the music is, and to never forget it. Lefty Frizzell was born in an oil field behind an oil well and his music was hobo music, mountain music. The fallen stars of country, dead from drunkenness or barbiturates, car wrecks or plane crashes, are remembered in this place. And those country tears were not crocodile tears: Hank Williams must have sat shell-shocked many times, thinking about where Audrey was that night, and with whom. A song like 'Your Cheating Heart' is coloured with real pain.

Beck walks past the pictures that trace country's increasing adoption of gaudiness and glitter, the stars whose music was heard from taxicabs in Indonesia to bars in Glasgow; Dolly Parton's ten-thousand-watt capped teeth glittering on television at the new Opry, a massive auditorium somewhere out past the blinking lights of Nashville, far from the studios where a thousand top session men toiled in anonymity. And all the while Willie Nelson, Waylon Jennings and Johnny Cash kept it outlawed and real. Lots of junk, lots of treasures, sometimes both one and the same, all under glass cases and under lights. And there at the end of it all is Hank Williams' car.

This is not just any old Hank Williams car. It is the 1952 Cadillac in which, just shy of midnight on New Year's Eve that same year, Hank died of an overdose, curled up in the back seat on a freezing cold night, the last four lines he ever wrote on a small scrap of paper, held so tightly that it had to be pried from his hand. It read: 'We met, we lived and dear we loved, then comes that fatal day, the love that felt so dear fades far away.' His driver, Charles Carr, drove him nearly 300 miles before he realized his boss's long-suffering heart had finally failed. Hank was 29 years old. Where do you go when you reach the end of the road?

The history of country is, of course, the mirror image of the history of another American music, that of black America, which is still as startling to most white Americans as looking into a mirror and seeing a different face. The blues stems from something else completely. The Scottish-Irish roots of country are thousands of miles from the outback land of Dahomey and

Ghana, where storytellers wandered from village to village, playing instruments and reciting history in long, memorized stretches. But the blues is a music of pain and regeneration, as is country. 'The blues is connected to a tradition, and has all these other levels and dimensions to it,' Beck once noted: 'the Biblical side and the religious side, the African roots, and elements of English balladry, and characters and stories from that tradition. It's a rich music.'[1] The blues was born out of sanctity and sacrilege, a carnal version of the holy hymns sung in black churches. It was moulded and made on whorehouse pianos with players like Jelly Roll Morton playing ragtime accompaniment to the carnality that is never far from the surface of the blues. It was an attempt to branch out from the modal and into a rigid scale that can be played forever, its subtle variations ever changing. Omnivorous by nature, blues references pure African music and adopts European instruments, taking European scales and bending two notes to give it flavour, emotion and a cultural stamp. 'That's what I love about the blues,' Beck told the *Shambhala Sun* in September 1999, 'a lot of those refrains were spread out in a lot of different people's songs. They would take verses from different things and assemble them. They just become a part of you and then they just come out. I've done that a few times. It just becomes unconscious if you're playing that music long enough... [I] got really heavy into the old music, from the Carter Family to all the blues stuff, and the field recordings. Became fascinated by it... We'd just sit, listening for hours, trying to figure out how to do this stuff. And wrestled with it for five, six years.'[2]

Son House, the Delta bluesman, cited field hollers and singing as the roots of the blues: call and response, extending back to Africa, through the fields and the church. Black music thrives on communication between audience and performer; it's the magic element. In the classical European tradition, music is passively observed; it's almost joy by proxy, with the musician reaching rapture and the listener vicariously thrilling to that rapture.

It is fitting that Beck has covered 'John Hardy' and 'Stagger Lee'. It is fitting that he most admires the white country singer Jimmie Rodgers who yodelled his way through the black blues, and Mississippi John Hurt, the black Mississippi bluesman, whose favourite musician was Jimmie Rodgers. Beck is straddling the line of two worlds that seem so far apart. White music and black music are an ocean apart, and not since the turn of the century have these two worlds been anywhere near each other, except for in the rapid dawning of rock and roll, where country and blues collided. This union and schism oscillate at intervals, sometimes forty or more years apart, both tied to rapid industrialization and migration. During the advent of the gramophone, it was often difficult to distinguish which artist was white and which was black. The advent of the record itself widened the schism, separating white and black music into marketable categories. The dividing of genres has long been a form of racism. It was Englishmen who took black blues and white country blues and reconfigured them and sent the finished product back to America. In America, we are often blind to our own heritage, and this blindness is to our profound detriment.

Far beyond the Mississippi Delta, or the hills of Appalachia, Beck is also in the forefront of cutting-edge international pop music, slotting in nicely with the likes of Japan's Cornelius and England's Stereolab. He has played harmonica on albums by Japanese pop sensation Kahimi Karie, performed with American country icons Willie Nelson and Emmylou Harris, and bridged the gap between hip-hop and pop. He has collaborated with hip-pop visionary (so visionary he is blinded by it at times) Carl Stephenson, the Jon Spencer Blues Explosion, rapper Kool Keith and electro-folkist Beth Orton. He has worked with producer teams the Dust Brothers and the Bong Load squad of Rothrock and Schnapf; he has covered songs by Skip James, Son House, Skip Spence, Mississippi John Hurt, and Jimmie Rodgers. He ties into that underside of American folklorica of lonesome innovators going it alone, entertainers and song and dance men.

9 p.m.

Well, this is it, the Grand Old Opry in Nashville, Tennessee. This is the shrine of country music, the place where all the backwoods twangers and hayseed mirabli make it or break it. This is where Hank Williams became a star, only to be asked to leave, in the last throes of his brokenhearted drunken dissipation. Beneath the famed feather backdrop and the announcers whose phantoms now announced fixed dates with the vanished past, when Johnny Cash and Jimmie Rodgers, Hank Snow and George Jones held their radio-bound audience on WSM in thrall. And the Grand Old Opry is also where the Byrds, with Gram Parsons, had introduced their 'Sweethearts of the Rodeo' country set in February 1968 to a thoroughly conservative audience that was sceptical, to say the least, of long hair rockers displaying a fondness for country music. After a refurbishment of the sort that seeks to preserve but often destroys the charm of a building, the Grand Ole Opry has been transformed into a theatre with carpeted stairwells and pleasant, bland lights in beige hues chosen by interior designers to highlight old posters with wondrous names.

The Ryman Auditorium, as the Opry is officially known, is the latest stop on Beck's whirlwind jaunt through the United States and the world. He is touring in support of *Odelay*, a most remarkable album of cut and paste artistry, loving pastiche, long loping grooves and devilishly beguiling lyrics. The touring band is solid, in contrast to the ragtag band of holy amateurs that bewildered the Lollapalooza audience just two years before. Beck's show this time around has taken a quantum leap forward in presentation, with its tribute-pastiche of the soul revues of lore and evoking the participatory hip-hop block parties that were as popular in the late 1970s as the Ryman's country radio shows had been in theirs.

The audience, mostly teenagers, file in, freshly scrubbed and self-aware, milling around the lobby and stairs and talking in polite tones, ignoring the country relics posted on the walls. This is a sell out show and the sense of anticipation among the gathering throngs is palpable. People glance at each other, as if to see just who else would have come down to see Beck. There are those who knew Beck as a wacky iconoclast who did a novelty song called 'Loser'. To others, *Odelay* has become the soundtrack to a springtime of illicit beer drinking on back lawns in the South, amid the smell of fresh mown grass and sterilized, antiseptic suburbs. Sprinkled among the crowds are indie fans, dressed in the retro fashions that have been recycled to the point at which their original cultural subset has been long forgotten. Here and there, people in their thirties look bewildered to find themselves in such a young group. They have heard Beck in their cars on the way to work, on National Public Radio, where dulcet-toned radio jocks sprinkle him in alongside Lucinda Williams or the Indigo Girls, and have become charmed by his offbeat weirdness.

All and sundry begin to fill the august auditorium, with its pews of oak, buffed and finished to lacklustre perfection, arranged in a half-octagonal configuration facing the stage, grandly draped in velvet curtains. Rising in two tiers, the hard wooden seats make it feel more like a church than the setting for a rock and roll show. The stained glass overlooking the stage only serves to heighten the effect. The crowd is dressed well, with nary a ripped jean or an untucked shirt among them. The air of mild affluence engendered by recent economic prosperity is shown by their middle-class accoutrements: cellular phones, brandished for no ostensible purpose, clean white trainers costing more than most Third World workers' annual salaries, Levi's jeans and ironed T-shirts.

Swedish pop band the Cardigans, led by the lissom and lovely singer Nina Persson take the stage, with the all-male Nordic instrumentalists seemingly hell bent on derailing their thin gossamer pop into a mutated metal hybrid. They sing 'Iron Man' by Black Sabbath and inoffensive pop tunes beefed up with power chords, making for an interesting juxtaposition. They obligingly play their current hit, 'Lovefool', with its meagre lyrics celebrating female witlessness. The only untoward moment occurs when a strange lad with a Cheshire Cat grin appears between bassist Magnus Sveningsson and drummer Bengt Lagergerg, popping and jerking in breakdance movements to their juggernaut rhythm. The Swedes smile, puzzled but tolerant at the intrusion. Is he taking the piss? Who is he? In fact, it's a member of Beck's band, sent like the emissary of chaos into a calculated and somewhat boring 30-minute set. He waves his arms in robotic fashion, seemingly double-jointed and soon all eyes are riveted on him. Giggles erupt from the bevy of twelve- and thirteen-year-olds already out of their pews and crushed to the front of the mahogany stage despite the admonitions of the besuited ushers, with their walkie talkies, ill-fitting beige pants and sweaty brows.

Seeing the breakdancing fool on stage gives me the oddest feeling, as if I had been stuck in a time warp without realizing it for the past hour. The whole scene feels like 1960s America right before the Beatles arrived and changed all the rules, or a Blackpool theatre in the late 1950s where fresh-faced British teens await the Nabob of Sob, Johnny Ray. But the breakdancer is like an emissary from another place entirely, a jester in a tepid court, the facsimile of soul in a very ordinary event. The Cardigans bang to a close and exit, the lights dim and roadies mull in the semi-darkness, rolling amplifiers away and winding cables up with meaty paws.

During the break, my mind keeps returning to the history of this home of country music. I think of the WSM Barn Dance radio show, with the Carter Family taking the bus to Studio B of WSM, in the old National Life & Accident Insurance Building, first home of the Opry, to sing 'Keep On The Sunny Side' in 1928. I try to imagine the two girls, Sara and her sister-in-law Maybelle, harmonizing pure and sweet on 'Will the Circle Be Unbroken' as Sara's solemn husband Alvin P. Carter plays the guitar with righteous force and fervour and sings in low rumbling thunder, all of them shaking under the hot lights for a fitful audience who could make or break them. I can picture Sara's trembling fingers stroking her autoharp while Maybelle picks the bass line on a Gibson L-5 guitar that dwarfs her small frame. The Carter Family seem like phantoms of an America now paved under and denuded by television, cars, trailer homes, violence and apathy.

The auditorium feels like church and court house, theatre and circus, museum and music hall. And it is all those things; make it or break it in Nashville or take the train home. It was once a church, through which travelling revival preachers of the 19th century had stormed, demonizing the saloons a block away on Broadway to an auditorium full of the faithful, fanning themselves in the heat with fans bought wholesale from a funeral parlour. The windows seem as old as time itself.

Smokey Hormel, in a three-button mod suit and slicked-back lounge lizard hair ambles to his guitar as cheers rustle through the hall like small waves. The drummer, Joey Waronker, takes his seat at the stool, sharp and professional, rolling his wrists and clutching Bonham sticks. Bassist Justin Meldal-Johnsen plugs in and DJ Swamp follows, assuming his place behind the fabled twin Technics turntables and mixer. Theo Mondle, keyboardist, settles in behind his Moogs and a battle-worn Fender Rhodes piano (are those things indestructible?). I am almost certain turntables have never been onstage at the Ryman before.

Bam! All the lights go on at once and the stage is bathed in harsh electric white light, startling everyone on my pew. The bone-breaking riff to 'Devil's Haircut' kicks off and Beck dashes in, not as small as one would have thought, and vibrating head to toe with visible energy, grabbing the mike off the stand just like a revival minister, ready to testify damnation or salvation. Everyone jumps to their feet.

His voice crackles with laconic intensity, voiding the febrile overture awkwardness. It's as if he's dropped in from the sky with an urgent message that he has to relay to us, the assembled throng. He stares out into the auditorium, pointing and pivoting on his heels. He is dressed like a cross between the louche, unshaven panache of Serge Gainsbourg and the Nudie suit rhinestone grandeur of George Jones.

He shakes, he shimmies. The band break into co-ordinated dance moves, hopping up and down in a late 20th century approximation of the Ubangi stomp. What is immediately impressive is how tight the band is, seasoned professionals to the man, on cue, in tune and in time. How far Beck has come from his scuffling days, his steady rambling days, shambling to the mike at New York or Los Angeles coffee bars, singing his songs to indifferent audiences, big blue eyes blinking under the lights. Here is someone in control and confident, declaiming and shouting. His words ring out like shattered poetry, obeying their own internal logic and always hinting at something that remains unarticulated but hints at plain truths. Following the old maxim that people always scrutinize what they don't quite understand, the audience takes in scattered phrases: 'Everywhere I look there's a devil in waiting.' How many of them know he is invoking the spirit of Stagger Lee, the murderous gambler who stalked the rough house bars of the barely settled frontier?

Beck and his band toy with the songs, treating them irreverently, sometimes following what seems to be either a backing tape or just samples spun with liquid ease by DJ Swamp. Occasionally they abandon the song's recorded structure completely, venturing into a bit of freeform jazz or funk. The band is seasoned like a Broadway fajita, charred on the outside, tender on the inside. My girlfriend Anja and I dance, but we and the teenies up front are the only ones; everyone else just stares. Jesus, the guy is packed full of vigour and spark!

Nina Persson watches Beck from the wings, as he does trouser-bursting splits and kicks. Persson stands theatrically in the wings, arm across her breasts, tapping a cigarette, hip slung to the right, smoke trailing up in slow, undulating waves in the spotlights. She stands in cool European repose, studying Beck. At the front of the stage a young Swedish photographer, with short cropped hair and octagonal glasses, black turtle neck and beige jodhpurs – the very essence of European intellectual cool – is snapping away, pausing occasionally to study Beck and smile. I laugh when I realize Beck has come all the way from media post-grunge moppet to sex symbol.

He runs through a selection of his songs in quick progression, never pausing or faltering. He sings 'Hotwax', voice cracking every now and then, a side effect of so many gigs in so many places on so many lousy public address systems. At the halfway point, the band retreat into the wings and the lights switch to a solitary spotlight hovering over the fevered tangle of unkempt hair as Beck steps to the lip of the stage. His smallest fans reach out to touch him. Armed only with a harmonica he breaks out into some full-bore Sonny Terry-style harp playing. Damn me if he isn't an apparition lifted from the Delta and dropped into the citadel of country. It is electrifying and confusing in equal measure, as a quick look around me confirms. People try to clap along with his frenetic, uneven beat as he lets loose squalls of harmonica and shouts out the words to 'One Foot in the Grave', his foot stamping like a metronome on the hallowed stage. He exhorts the audience to participate, and they try. Should they take this ride with him? He seems so febrile, on the verge of something even he isn't sure he can channel.

The rawness of his voice and his harmonica, tag-teaming each other to ever greater heights, is shocking in its looseness. No effort has been made to smooth out the rough edges that pop pundits, record label A&R men and cursed radio programmers strive to eradicate. Beck shouts himself hoarse between harmonica blasts, his voice over-amplified until the stained-glass windows shake with dissonance. 'I never rocked the pews before,' he wisecracks in an aside that garners a ripple of laughter, followed by a shouted 'Clap your hands!' Crazed he is, with a vocal quality somewhere between a rabbinical cantor intoning the Torah and Yamataka eYe of the

Japanese noise band the Boredoms. There is something almost frightening about the intensity of Beck's solo spot under the lights, standing alone. He has to get through, to communicate, shouting with something approaching desperation.

'You got to REGULATE!' he exhorts, getting half the audience to respond to his shouted plea. Beck's regulation seems something almost mystic, a means by which to decode the puzzles he is presenting, urging his audience to work their way into a new mode of thinking. To submit to flux and turn off the static; the static that pervades modern culture. 'YOU KNOW THAT FEAR, WHEN YOU GET UP IN THE MORNING, THAT'S ONE FOOT IN THE GRAVE, BABY. YOU KNOW WHAT YOU GOT TO DO TO GET OVER THAT FEAR, YOU GOT TO REGULATE!' With much effort he finally manages to get nearly everyone to chant along with him.

The gut bucket country blues ends and he exhales, a hoarse, theatrical sigh that sweeps through the congested pews, where everyone stands but no one seemed to know what to do. I've never seen an audience so utterly fixated on a performer before, watching to see what he would do next and looking for clues, both tense and delighted. Despite the set lists taped to the stage, Beck and the band give off the vibe that the script will be abandoned at any moment.

He leaves for the wings and the audience crane their necks following him. His heels crack the boards where so many rambling phantoms have alighted for a moment. He returns with a Martin acoustic guitar and intones calmly about the Ryman's illustrious past and how he had grown up enamoured of old-time country and blues, namechecking the Singing Brakeman Jimmie Rodgers, and Fred McDowell, making note of the latter's finger-picking prowess. He plays an acoustic set comprising 'Jack-Ass', 'Rowboat', Rodgers' 'Waiting On A Train' and 'I Get Lonesome'. Around about this time comes the first sign of discord, as some young malcontents, drunk on smuggled beer, shout abuse from behind us, insinuating Beck was not what he said he was, that he was that worst of all interlopers in the South: 'Carpetbagger!'

But Beck, if he notices the catcalls at all, ignores them. He continues to strum quiet, plaintive folk and country, delving a bit deeper into his repertoire to evoke the yodels of Rodgers and the gritty flavour of back roads, cotton plantations and trains leading to fixed destinations to nowhere but back on themselves. Through the music comes a sense of a blessed and cursed land that still surprises outsiders with its curious manners and charm so out of place in the fast-edit future of strip malls, videos and conspicuous consumption that increasingly make up the American landscape. It's the South of moss-shrouded plantation houses, levees where thieves roamed, the tar paper shacks of the black sharecropper and the Devil waiting at the crossroads. The juke joints and firewater moonshine distilled in the hills of Kentucky, the Appalachian songs with their traces of 17th-century Scottish ballads. It's the cut-throats and card cheats on the Mississippi, the gentlemen of the Crescent City, New Orleans, drinking to their own success, the Madames and the mad spinsters, the murderers and the minstrels, the roving medicine shows of the early 1900s. Scott Joplin fingering ragtime licks on a broken down piano, XFM broadcasting across the Mexican border. The genteel homes of mysterious Savanna where debauchery is done on the sly. Suffocating summertime heat and kudzu vines choking fields, cotton bales and sweaty farmhands, farmers with taciturn faces and leather-bound Bibles cracked at the spine. Boo Radley and Atticus Finch, and Faulkner's never-ending sentences. The whips of slavery, the water hoses and lunch counters and back seats on the bus of Jim Crow, the gospel churches. The mandolins and guitars, the radios beaming out of Memphis, Elvis' stillborn twin in Gladys' hands. The mud, water, fire and rain and sun of the South.

The audience settle back into their pews, and I marvel at the rapt attention paid by the worshipful pre-pubescents up front. That they should sit and listen to someone playing songs beloved of their grandparents seems utterly alien to me; America's richest musical heritage is so often consigned to the dustbin of history by those besotted with the illusions of progress. The songs of the Singing Brakeman had no relevance to their lives until someone shook them and said, 'Here, look, these are fantastic living, breathing songs'. These are folk songs that are burnished by age and people playing them until they constitute true history, the history of plain people in motion, stasis, joy and pain, the maudlin despair of drunkenness and adultery, travel and escape, and most of all, transcendence.

By reclaiming those vital pieces of music and restaging them in this church of country music, Beck is trying to preserve the fruitful traditions of Southern music in a modern context, to put these people in touch with their own culture in a tantalizing array of country-inflected songs. The rest of the audience, not used to slow music, absorbs the lesson suspiciously. What was he trying to prove? When would he play 'Loser' or 'Where It's At' with its sing-along chorus of 'two turntables and a microphone', something that was tangible to them? (Even if the song's refrain of 'Ooo la la Sassoon', refers to designer jeans stitched and worn and torn before they were born, is as oblique as any of Rodgers' blue yodels.)

The band returns, the lights flash on and Beck barnstorms through six more numbers, the audience taking it in as a spectacle that, in the words of one Beck fan, they knew they liked but were not sure exactly why. My girlfriend Anja and I are still the only ones dancing, except for the teenies whom Beck addresses with loving grace – 'My freaks, my freaks are in full effect.' While so many others stand with arms folded and passively observe the spectacle, those kids are actively engaged in the participatory ethic which underpins Beck's shows. In the call and response sections, it is they who are here to represent. They apparently understand and grasp intuitively what the rest of us are trying to puzzle through using logic. Beck seems to realize they are his prime constituency, the ones who get it without questioning why. His music reaches them viscerally and raw, without being filtered through the media who so often seek to paint him as a wacky novelty act, a goof, an error in the spectrum of predictable acts that go through the required motions, cash in and sell out with a flash of a pen on a corporate contract.

A giant board of flashing lights – you might call it a Diskobox – pulses irregularly to the beat of the music, and Beck's DJ Swamp drops in all manner of samples that had never been cleared for inclusion on *Odelay*. They are the fruits of the eclectic record collection of *Odelay* co-producers, the Dust Brothers. A sample of Barbie, the doll epitomizing the vacuous nature of America's chosen iconography, is dropped into the mix; her silicone voice chirps, 'Let's get together and eat ice-cream!' The lights flash off, casting the auditorium into near darkness as Beck and his band freeze in place, heads bowed, while a few bars of Franz Schubert's Unfinished Symphony No. 9 in B Minor, blast through the speakers. There is so much to communicate, and so little time to do it in. The feeling of this being a band on the run, one step ahead of irony and categorization, is all too palpable. One can sense the tour bus with its engine idling, ready to whisk them off over to Raleigh, North Carolina for tomorrow's performance.

Beck and band slip into a mesmerizing rendition of 'Derelict', the haunting essraj-laced number that evokes black skies over Bombay, and send a hush through the house. The drones seem to make the audience restless and uneasy. Indeed, there is something foreign about Beck's stage presentation; it reminds me of his grandfather, the artist Al Hansen's happenings, with all the props assembled as if to highlight and deride any presumed talismanic significance. The Diskobox is crude and primitive, blinking erratically, but its place on the stage elevates it to the status of a totem. The vibe the band give off is a copy of a copy of a copy until it is original. Like a Michigan garage band learning ? and the Mysterians' '96 Tears' from a knock-off Mexican Sixties compilation of garage bands. In Beck's phrase, they were 'doing it to it'.

For me, the magic moment that encapsulates Beck's performance comes during an incendiary 'High 5 (Rock The Catskills)' as Beck shouts out the verses with all the maniacal fervour of Luigi Russolo winding his Futurist noise machines. He is dancing like a Jajoukan Pan at the height of his ecstasy, rubbing a soft-shoe at the lip of the stage. He shakes his slight hips with such vigour you pray he won't fall into the pit. Then comes the Zen moment – a low-lying bank of monitors jut out from the stage at an angle, directly in the line of Beck's gyrations. Beck leaps backwards over the monitors, as nimble as Nijinsky, without a glance, chicken-scratching riffs Jimmy Nolan-style on his guitar. That strikes me like nothing else in his performance. I'm amazed at how sure-footed he is, how he doesn't trip and how he is up there with all the confidence, humour and aplomb so conspicuous by its absence in so much of our generation. It is liberating to see someone shake off the cloak of apathy, the numbness of cynicism. It isn't that he is infallible, but just that he is human, talented and doing it, not just thinking or talking about it. And most importantly, he is succeeding.

Beck and the band withdraw into the wings as DJ Swamp steps to the fore. Swamp, an Ohio native, is working on serious inspiration. He deftly uses scratches and the cross fader to construct a collage from heavy metal classics, such as the famed riff from Deep Purple's 'Smoke On The Water'. The audience gasp as he drags the needle back and forth, using the cross fader as an instrument in its own right. This is probably the first time most of the audience have actually witnessed turntable techniques up close, showing the artistry and co-ordination that belie hip-hop's detractors.

The band returns with a grand encore of 'Where It's At'. The performance is playful and forceful, acoustic and bombastic – always alternating between twin poles of opposite polarities until the chaos is peeled back to reveal a small pulsing fractal of perfect order at the centre. That is to say, Beck, and whatever fevered processes in his mind have engendered this barnstorming show.

Laura, a young fan who is there that night, drags her friend around to the back and waits for one hour and 30 minutes to meet Beck. When he finally ambles out the steel doors, they crowd in to say hello. 'At first I thought he was high,' Laura recalled later, 'but after standing close for a while I decided that he was just really tired... He looks really good close up. One thing I noticed was that he had really nice hands. They were really soft and smooth and thin, really gorgeous, so if he ever flops in the music business, he can always get rich by being a hand model.'[3]

1   Babcock, Jay. 'Beck', *Huh*, July 1996

2   Ginsberg, Allen. 'A Beat/Slacker Transgenerational Meeting Of Minds', *Shambhala Sun*, 27 September 1999

3   Slo-Jam Central Website. http://earth.vol.com/~debber/beck/mainpg2.html

2

THE END OF THE PARTY LINE:
BECK'S GRANDPARENTS

Back in the day...

Audrey Ostlin Hansen, Beck's maternal grandmother, whom he never met, was a Greenwich Village bohemian at a time when the term actually held some cachet, implied some risk and involved cutting links with the straight world. She had opted out of the world of her hometown in the State of New Jersey to be, at various times, an actress, model, poet and general *bon vivant*. Audrey came from Eastern European Jewish stock. Known to her friends as 'Nikki', she was truly ahead of her time, wandering through Washington Square with dyed green hair in the 1950s.

Audrey was the belle of the bohemian ball in those freewheeling days in downtown New York City, a pixie-sized fireball of intensity. Her friend Daniel List remembered her fondly: 'What a great spirit she had been back in the days of the old Waldorf Cafeteria on Sixth Avenue. At that time, we all lived together in lofts this side of the Bowery... It was pretty hot stuff, and quite usual for someone to produce a real joint of 'gage' like the musicians used on 52nd Street – but our scene was booze, the cheaper the better, and Charlie Parker. It was a red wine world and fundamentally pretty harmless.'[1]

It was a different world then, populated by the same milieu that Jack Kerouac, LeRoi Jones, Diane DiPrima and Allen Ginsberg circulated in and out of, sharing the same cold water flats and hot bebop 78s. This was the world of 52nd Street jazz clubs like the Royal Roost and Birdland where Charlie Parker played the saxophone he perpetually had in hock at the pawnshop, where Miles Davis blew hot and then cool. The squares marched by in their grey flannel suits, hats and ties, oblivious or hostile to the freaks and eccentrics on the pavement. The Beats scribbled in notebooks dug out of rucksacks at the Café Figaro on MacDougal Street, old-style Italian cafés with steam shrouding the mirrors. A world where the neon glare of all-night cafeterias contrasted with rain-slicked dirty streets, where Herbert Huncke scribbled a few words on paper between heists and scams, hustles and fixes. The nights were Benzedrine-fuelled odysseys of elliptical conversation that took in the straight world and fixed a squinted eye of disdain on it. And the ever-present threat of world destruction by the atom bomb added a pinch of tetchy restlessness to the brew. It was a world of hard-drinking abstract expressionist painters such as Jackson Pollock lurching out of the San Remo bar and the Cedar Tavern, the sky black and scattered conversations drifting around fire escapes and the billows of subway steam hatches. And also where homosexuals enjoyed their own clandestine company in apartments overlooking chain link gardens. Audrey was a part of this furtive world of free spirits roaming crooked streets.

Her daughter Bibbe remembered: 'Audrey was a dancer on the *Perry Como Show* – the one who did the Thumbalina dance. And she was in those old commercials that were done live. One of the famous ones was the one she goofed up, where the girl comes onscreen in elegant profile and gets her cigarette lit. Then she turns to the camera to exhale and coughs half a lung out. She could be very silly and fun.'[2]

Al Hansen, now an artist living on Bleeker Street, met Audrey in the Village and theirs was a full-on bohemian romance, full of circumlocutions and verbal badinage conducted between Houston Street and 14th, amidst the tight ellipses that drew them into each other's orbit. They first locked eyes at the Waldorf cafeteria, where the all-night bohemians congregated round coffee. 'Al met his first wife, Audrey, in 1950 in New York,' Beck later recalled. 'She was doing a cabaret act and she'd painted herself green and dyed her hair green. She walked into a cafeteria with two black guys dressed as eunuchs, and Al took one look at her and said "That's the woman I'm marrying."'[3]

They married, producing a lovely daughter, Bibbe, then split and Audrey started hanging out at society nightclubs such as the 21, the Pompeii Club, the Stork Club, mixing with lowlife and gangsters. Bibbe remembered her mother in scattered, vivid images – sitting up in bed in a lilac satin dress, with a record playing off the gramophone, instructing four gangsters in music appreciation. But Audrey found herself spiralling deeper into the world of the 'scurves' (Daniel List's phrase), taking refuge with those she should have escaped had she had the strength. By the time the 1960s rolled in, and bohemia had been repackaged for the masses by the media in the aftermath of the phenomenal success of Kerouac's *On the Road*, the Village had become for her both a hiding place and a watershed of tears.

Audrey ended up living at a Bank Street brownstone, where she lived with a cast of angels and no-hopers, a rundown Village flophouse filled with eccentrics, drug addicts and dubious personages of all shades and stripes. The original Auntie Mame (Marion Tanner) presided, living in a room chock-a-block with the ephemera of her scattered, ebullient life. She took a liking to Audrey, perhaps seeing a bit of herself in her, a bright spirit trying to keep her chin up despite bad circumstances. While at Bank Street, Audrey wrote short feverish poems, including a series called 'BROAD SONGS' from July of 1964 through October 1965. The poems, wistful and jaded, are filled with longing for things she knew she wouldn't have for much longer, not least of which was her daughter. In a poem entitled 'Lament' Audrey writes with devastating clarity of:

> *The longmade beds*
> *Of lonely, unmade broads.*

Tanner moved to Bierer House, a halfway house in Chelsea, where she worked and lived. She urged Audrey to apply for entrance, which she did, successfully. Audrey slowly began to get her life back together. She cut out the vices and enlisted in a rehab program, seeing a shrink at Greenwich House, a counselling centre on 14th Street. As she got things together a bit more, she started to teach a poetry workshop there. Her old enthusiasm and vibrancy returned in time; such an indomitable spirit was she, and so well liked by her fellow patients and the program directors, that she was offered a position as an assistant case worker. She was the first patient ever asked to act in that capacity. She reported for her first day with a great smile, eager to help. A snooty lady behind the desk, one of those people whose job it is to make people wait, told her to wait in the reception room. Audrey waited and waited. She felt ill, her hands trembling. A few minutes later she keeled over with a great sigh. By the time they got her to St Vincent's Hospital she was dead on arrival. It was August 1968 and she was gone much too soon at thirty-seven, 'a great broad' in her daughter Bibbe's estimation.

Back in White Plains, Audrey was laid to rest. Al Hansen stood next to her estranged brother, with a dozen others, mostly friends from the Village. It had been a sunny day as the funeral cortege wound its way up to the burial site, but as soon as the ceremonial handful of earth was dropped on Audrey's casket, the sky crackled with thunder, the clouds split at the seams and rain poured down. Some bright spark had brought along an umbrella and popped it open: it was bright, vivid green, as bright and vivid a shade as Audrey had been when she skipped down the streets of the Village in her doe-skin slippers. You could almost hear her laughter pealing from somewhere far away. 'It was really very poetic,' Daniel List wrote in her obituary for the *Village Voice*. 'Audrey would have loved it.'[4]

Alfred Earl Hansen, Beck's grandfather, was born on 5 October 1927 in the New York City borough of Queens. Hansen was born in a year when a quantum leap into the future seemed to be happening; the Roaring Twenties flourished and America was in its ascendance as a bastion of all that was progressive and new. Writing at the end of his life, Hansen noted that 1927 was the year of Fritz Lang's dystopian vision of the future, *Metropolis*, as well as that of the first 'talkie' film *The Jazz Singer*. Most significantly, 'Lucky Lindy' Lindbergh, the aviator, traversed the ocean in a silver plane, bringing the far-flung continents closer together. The epic journey was a symbolic reversal of Columbus' European expedition of 1492: from now on it would be the New World that would close the gaps in exploration. Phonographs and radios were becoming widespread enough for jazz, which had barely begun thirty years before, to be heard everywhere from Buenos Aires to Berlin.

In one of his beautifully illustrated and hand-lettered books – staccato lettering, slashes and short sharp lines – which he kept throughout his life, Al Hansen recalled: 'My grandfather Nicholas Alfred Hansen was sailing as a cabin boy on a big schooner out of Larvik, Norway. He shipped out at fourteen years. Old Nick Hansen Sr. liked cigars, whiskey, boats and women. My fifteen- or sixteen-year-old grandfather got fed up with the brutal captain of the schooner and one night jumped ship in Port Newark, New Jersey.' 'I grew up with the sense that our family had a really rich history,' Beck later revealed. 'I knew Al's father; he lived into his nineties; and he was a tough World War I vet who ran a garage and was heavy into motorcycles.'[5]

Al recalled being 'educated publicly from an early age in the ways of filling stations, Norwegian sea-families and heavy machinery.'[6] His childhood friend Jimmy Breslin, today a New York institution via his newspaper column, remembered some of the unique domestic arrangements of the Hansen household: 'Al's father operated a crane that he rolled home in each night. He kept it in the side yard of Al's house. The boom was high in the air. Al and I grew up with the shadow of manual labour falling across the bed each morning.'[7] As a child Al was awestruck on one occasion at the sight of his mother Katherine doodling a swan while talking on the phone. Soon, he himself evinced a talent for drawing, a prodigious gift for depicting figures with a few flashes of a pencil nub on the back of a piece of paper. By the time Al was enrolled in school he already could read and write: 'I felt like a one-eyed person in the land of the blind!'[8]

On his first day at school, Al was astonished to discover that his fellow classmates could neither read nor spell. Raising his hand, he told the teacher that he needed to use the bathroom. Slipping out of class, Al found his way downstairs to the boiler room and sat for a while with the janitor, who gave him a pickle from his lunch. Thereafter, he simply walked out of school. Later in the day, his mother explained to him that he had to go every day and stay! He dragged his heels and cried all the way to school the next morning.

In the 1940s, 'Jimbo' Breslin, Al and Al's kid brother Gordon would half-run, half-walk down Jamaica Avenue, under the shadow of the thundering El, the elevated subway that roared over the avenue, with its rickety iron supports that looked like they were going to give at any minute. The kids would get penny candy at Irving Worship's candy and news stand and go to see

Snow White And The Seven Dwarfs at the ornate Valencia Theatre. 'We remembered every scene,' Breslin recalled later. 'Al could draw the faces and stumpy bodies with great speed. He started making dwarfs in his cellar, and the two of us begged for puppets as holiday gifts. Between his hands and the gifts he had enough dwarfs to put on a puppet show in his cellar.'[9]

The trio drew up their own newspaper, the *Daily Flash* and sold them to their neighbours; the dentist and the Italian barber always bought a copy. As they got a little bit older, Al, Gordon and Jimbo would make their way on the subway to Manhattan, with its soot-stained monolithic building facades and canyons of chrome, glass and steel. Crossing on the Queensboro Bridge, over the sprawling hospitals and old jails on Welfare Island, the panoply of Manhattan would spread from one end of the horizon to the other, a massive monument to motion. In the piers, enormous ocean liners were being stripped and fitted for wartime duty. Billows of smoke puffed up the railings of the bridge from tugboats ushering ships through the East River, horns blasting. Coal barges and the Circle Line ferry passed below. Hansen's point of entry into Manhattan was at the foot of the bridge, 59th Street, where the click clack of heels on concrete echoed and passengers disembarked and embarked at speed onto the subway stations, with their wrought-iron porticoes. Yellow taxis with bulbous hoods and long windows, reflecting hazy sunlight and the faces of passers-by, all streaming in different directions. Small wonder that Hansen would later be driven to create collages, for Manhattan was the ultimate collage, a larger-than-life rendering of human aspirations, with the failures hidden in the cracks. Manhattan was an illusion cast in concrete and glass.

Hansen's teenage years were a blur of zoot suits, swing dancing and frivolity fanned by the cataclysmic war across the ocean. When World War II broke out, he was too young to enlist until near the end, when he joined the army and made the crossing by boat to Le Havre. An eternity of water later, they steamed in toward land. Al was struck by the derelict hulls of torpedoed ships in the harbour, like the bleached bones of whale skeletons. Welcome to Europe.

During 1946 Al and his cronies in the 508th Parachute Infantry Regiment, wound their way through Frankfurt where Hansen listened in fascination to the sound of that shattering piano echoing across the wasted city. In 1948, honourably discharged, Al began his education back in New York at the Art Student's League on West 57th Street. It was his point of entry into the downtown art scene centred around expansive, cold lofts and small roving galleries and exhibitions. Blissfully unaware of the avant-garde, he constantly sketched, working on what he called his 'weird art'. Al spent his time in cafés, drawing, writing and reading, his mind fast and feverish with Dali-esque images, grotesquerie and fantastical reflections of what he saw around him, such as an image of nuns scurrying across the street in the shadow of the triangular Flatiron Building, their habits fluttering in strong wind. The sci-fi magazines and newspapers he sent his drawings to turned them down, finding them too idiosyncratic and, well...*weird*.

He began to run into a generous assortment of Greenwich Village bohemians, artists and freaks, not least of which was Audrey. They chased each other down the winding streets of the Village, running into each other at odd hours of the day and night at 24-hour cafeterias and Automats or Bowery lofts that artists were beginning to turn into studios. Shortly after marrying, the couple moved into a little shack on the roof of a building on Bleeker Street, in the heart of Greenwich Village; it was freezing in the winter and burning in the summer. Their daughter Bibbe Ann was born soon after.

The marriage broke up much too soon and Hansen, at a loose end, re-joined the Air Force for a time, living in insufferably hot barracks down South. He drew constantly, but paid no mind to establishing himself as a commercial artist, other than to produce the odd dabble for the newspaper at the base: 'I did some small paintings using glue and sawdust to create an uneven textured surface. Fortunately none of them exist today.'[10]

Al did manage to win a scholarship to the highly selective Cooper Union Art School in New York City, but was unable to get out of the Air Force in time to attend. On his return to New York, he found a straight job at McGraw–Hill uptown, doing commercial art and graphic design. Meantime, he continued his studies at the Pratt Institute and Brooklyn College. When his second wife Marvyne enrolled in a course at the New School For Social Research, he chanced across an intriguing course in her prospectus. And so, in 1956, Hansen had the good fortune to join the Experimental Music class taught by John Cage, the pre-eminent avant-garde theoretician and composer in America at the time.

'So, you can't read or write music and you don't play any instrument?' Cage asked Hansen. 'No,' came the reply. Hansen was the only non-musician there, and Cage was dazzled by his audacity in joining. Cage, then struggling to rid his students of their accrued learning, responded, 'We'll get along fine.'* Hansen was hardly a dilettante, though; Beck affirmed, 'Al's sensibility was fairly well developed by the time he met Cage.'[11] Hansen was involved in theatre groups, read radical literature and eagerly consumed the films of the Nouvelle Vague, the French New Wave of François Truffaut, Claude Chabrol and Jean-Luc Godard. Cage, in turn, was America's leading avant-garde composer and theorizer, and one who had made a vital connection between music and accidents. Using his readings of Zen Buddhist texts and the Chinese Oracle the I-Ching, Cage began to try to incorporate silence, chaos, randomness and chance into his compositions. His scores would contain scripted chaos, a small pocket of room for the unexpected to occur. Cage is best known in popular culture for his piece '4'33"', which is nothing more than someone sitting at a piano for four minutes and thirty-three seconds in silence. But, of course, it's not silence at all: the piece works as a mirror, with the audience becoming the performer. Beck acknowledged the paradox, in an interview with Belgium's *Humo* magazine, commenting, 'Silence is the only perfect noise.'[12] The coughs, rustling of papers, shifting in seats and maybe laughter of the audience makes up the content of the piece. In his attempt to remove the artist from art, Cage composed over one hundred pieces on the basis of flipping a coin. In 1949 John Cage and partner Merce Cunningham would perform at Juilliard with students like Miles Davis sitting in the audience. Cage would play prepared piano and Merce Cunningham would dance.**

John Cage made a great point of the lack of silence by highlighting the sounds overlooked in everyday life, thus making life a constant symphony; the use of everyday sounds would become even more prominent in *Musique Concrète*. Thanks to modern technology composers were able to record the sounds of cicadas in small fishing villages or the sounds of a man going for a walk. *Musique Concrète* comes from a long, diverse history, dating back even before Cage. Composers such as George Antheil, with *Ballet Mechanique*, incorporated aeroplane propellers, anvils and saws, into their compositions. More influential though was Luigi Russolo, whose manifesto, 'The Art Of Noise', would influence everything from classical music to techno. Yet the men credited with the invention of *Musique Concrète* were Pierre Schaeffer and his apprentice Pierre Henry, who built a studio in 1948, loaded with tape recorders, phonographs, and various other machines, and the intention to create a new form of sound.

By now Hansen had more or less made the move downtown full time and was fully integrated

---

★ Cage would remain a fan of Hansen right up until his own death in 1992. In an interview with journalist Ellsworth Snyder, he made a point of namechecking Hansen, asking, 'In our discussion, why have we not heard the name of Al Hansen?'

★★ Davis, beguiled, would leave class and go up to his other class, the afterhours jams at Milton's Playhouse in Harlem. There, along with Dizzy Gillespie and Charlie Parker, Davis would work on the relentless defining of bebop's radical parameters.

into a small core of proto-Fluxus folk enrolled in Cage's class, including future Fluxus luminaries George Brecht, Toshi Ichiyanagi and Allan Kaprow, a link to the so-called 'Rutgers Group' at Rutgers University in New Jersey. The latter was a wild and electric bunch which included Roy Lichtenstein, George Segal, Geoffrey Hendricks, Robert Watts, Lucas Samaras, and Robert Whitman. From 1957 to 1963, they all helped foment the bubbling stew of Happenings, Pop Art, and Fluxus. In the late Fifties the Beat poetry boom also fuelled the artistic zeitgeist, and Hansen would watch poet Kenneth Rexroth reciting to a jazz backdrop at the Five Spot on Third Avenue. Kerouac and Ginsberg often dropped by for a moment in between their itinerant wanderings.

Hansen, Claes Oldenburg and Jim Dine found a refuge at the Judson Church in Greenwich Village where the kindly and progressive padre, Reverend Moody, encouraged them to stage theatre, performances, exhibitions and whatever else they could think of. Jim Dine one night staged a happening called *Car Crash* in which, dressed in a silver suit, with clownish make-up, he gesticulated to the audience mutely, projecting a frustrated inability to communicate. He went to a nearby chalkboard and, using big pastel-coloured chalk, tried to scribble out his message on the board, but so feverish were his attempts that the chalk crumbled before he could write. Hansen, in the audience, wept at the poignancy of the piece, of Dine's frustrated efforts to reach the spectator. Leaving the performance, Dick Higgins also had wet eyes. Hansen was ready to commiserate with him on their shared experience, when it became apparent that Higgins' tears were tears of laughter. 'Wasn't that funny? It was so funny!' he exclaimed.

With the impetus from performances like these, Hansen's creativity began surging right past the Abstract Expressionism that ruled the Village art scene so ruthlessly at the time. Hansen was constantly trying to expand the perceived limitations of what artwork should be – he stuck geometric stickers on canvas, painted letters on an armchair, and took newspaper fonts and pasted them into new configurations, a constant drive to take things violently out of context and create new meanings for them. He began scavenging interesting rubbish from gutters, bins and rubble-strewn lots to make his sculptures and collages.

'I had been picking up objects from the street and from trash cans; the urban detritus and scraps of decay that Kurt Schwitters used in his collages,' Hansen recalled of this period. 'Schwitters was very important to me. Above all he was a master composer in the way he placed objects in relation to each other. I had several boxes and packages of this stuff and I decided to do a series of collages exploring the possibilities that would come up. So much of it was Schwitters like material that I decided to un-compose it, that is, instead of composing and melding them into unified wholes, I would put them together in a way that jarred, that made apparent that they did not go together.'[13] *

At the time, Hansen also took a number of jobs helping half-delinquent and half-maddened youngsters, and would take them along to his classes. He saw no distinction between his day job and his art work, classes or anything else in his life. He called his studio flat the Third Rail Gallery Of Current Art, and opened it to the public in 1962: 'The third rail is the one that supplies

---

* Schwitters, a favourite of both Al and Beck, was a brilliant artist who worked on the fringes of Dada in Germany in the 1920s. He built collages that paid special attention to the mechanical – gears and bits of machines interspersed amidst numbers and words cut from newspapers, arranged with a sharply developed sense of composition. He grouped all his art under the name *Merz*, a name culled from a scrap of shredded paper from the Commerzbank. Schwitters also built a very elegant column in one corner of his room which extended from floor to ceiling; he dubbed it the *Merzbow*, and worked on it for years. When he reached the top of his ceiling, he evicted the tenants upstairs, hammered a hole through the ceiling and continued building the column all the way to the top of the house.

electricity for trains. Touch it and you fry die.'[14] Another favoured spot was the Epitome on Bleecker Street, where Hansen performed his recitation of an 'An Incomplete Requiem for W.C. Fields' in 1958, and where Dick Higgins began doing his whimsical performance pieces stressing humour and lampooning the formality of high art. Hansen read the text with projectors flashing spliced film on him, using a flashlight handed to him by artist Larry Poons to decipher the text. Higgins would sit at a table on the stage, put on gloves, take a book out of a briefcase, take off his gloves, put the book back in the briefcase, stand up and walk out the door of the café.

Other artists were quick to label these performances neo-Dada, echoing the riotous absurdity of the Cabaret Voltaire in 1916, held in the back room of a tavern at Spiegelgasse 1 in Zurich. Primeval happenings and confrontational performance art were the hallmarks of the Cabaret Voltaire, with Tristan Tzara declaiming violent poetry alongside outlandish theatrics that provoked the audiences to attack the performers. Accomplished artist John Heartfield would fashion photomontages, shredding images, text and photos into collages that actually better reflect both Beck and Al's artistic sensibility than Cubism. But Hansen, Kaprow and others outgrew the neo-Dada tag, and it was clear that a new aesthetic was being outlined, a progression from the Surrealism and Dada which inspired it. Beck later commented 'Dada was all about the connected disconnectedness of our lives, the nonsensical nature of our lives. It's in flagrant disregard of reality in creating your own parameters.'[15]

Happenings, which Hansen played a substantial role in disseminating and producing, were an extension of Alfred Jarry, Dada, the Cabaret Voltaire, the Bauhaus, the Black Mountain College of Art and the New York avant-garde. Happenings were like a three-dimensional abstract painting and taking part in one was the equivalent of stepping inside the work, surrounding yourself with the work. As Hansen put it, artists were increasingly dissatisfied with working in two dimensions or the three dimensions of sculpture and wanted to work in a way that would address time and space. Happenings finally took stock of performance and sought to get it off the stage and into the audience, surrounding them, breaking the Greek code of observed performance and extending it into an all-surrounding experience. Fluxus sought to make both audience and performer look at the nature of performance itself and question it. So whether it was John Cale, later of the Velvet Underground, performing Erik Satie's 'Vexations' 432 times at Carnegie Hall in tandem with others, or Yves Klein slithering naked, coated in paint, across a bolt of paper, they were trying to splinter the notion of what constituted an event. Happenings were ultimately open-ended events emphasizing spontaneity and a degree of chance. The potential for chaos was always there, giving an edge to the proceedings. The lack of a scripted outcome made for a delicious prospect: anything could happen!* This spirit of spontaneity and chance was something Beck later embraced: 'I have a lot of general attachments to Fluxus, embracing that Dada [and] anti-reason.'[16] 'I believe in the philosophy of flux. There

23

---

* John Cage: 'It was at Black Mountain College that I made what is sometimes said to be the first happening. The audience was seated in four isometric triangular sections, the apexes of which touched a small square performance area that they faced and that led through the aisles between them to the large performance area that surrounded them. Disparate activities, dancing by Merce Cunningham, the exhibition of paintings and the playing of a Victrola by Robert Rauschenberg, the reading of his poetry by Charles Olson or hers by M.C. Richards from the top of a ladder outside the audience, the piano playing of David Tudor, my own reading of a lecture that included silences from the top of another ladder outside the audience, all took place within chance-determined periods of time within the overall time of my lecture. It was later that summer that I was delighted to find in America's first synagogue in Newport, Rhode Island, that the congregation was seated in the same way, facing itself.' ('An Autobiographical Statement', Kyoto, Japan, November 1989.)

are so many elements flying in so many different directions that you really have to go with what feels right instinctively. The nature of the universe is fairly whimsical and nonsensical. In the most sombre, beatific peacefulness there's complete chaos and maniacal laughter. Music that doesn't reflect that is boring.'[17]

Inspired by Allan Kaprow's 'Happening Environment', held at the Hansa Gallery in 1958, Hansen founded the Audio Visual Group together with future fellow Fluxartist Dick Higgins, to provide a vehicle for their early happenings, which consisted largely of multi-screen projections and proto-Pop Art sculpture. Hansen's 'The Hep Amazon' a motorized sculpture of a woman, was exhibited at the Below Zero show at the Reuben Gallery in Manhattan in 1959. The Reuben shows were a direct outgrowth of the feverish conversations stretching late into the night which Hansen had with classmates from Cage's class. When a friend commented that his scattered works had no identifiable stamp that said 'Al Hansen', Hansen seized upon the image of the Venus of Willendorf, the ancient fertility idol sculpted in stone. Its monumental hips and breasts fascinated him, and he set about sculpting his own versions of the statuette with matchsticks, glue, cigarettes, silver foil and anything and everything else that came to hand. He would remake the image in a thousand guises, always different and always changing. Toward the end of his life, he crafted Venuses with bits of toilet paper rolls, cut and fitted to perfection, windswept and slight, locked in a painter's box.

The Venus, a presumed fertility doll was discovered in the Palaeolithic version of a rubbish dump in Austria in 1908. Twenty-three thousand years old, the Venus celebrates an extreme feminine fertility. One wonders if women looked like waifs then too, or whether there was mass starvation at the time, because the doll, carved from limestone, takes femininity to its illogical extreme. One can only marvel at the enormous breasts, hips and pudenda. Feminists have adopted the sculpture as their own, and a popular T-shirt was born which bore the snickering legend 'must be Venus Envy'.

A discussion with a friend about the ubiquity of Hershey's chocolate bars sparked Hansen into starting to make Venus collages from the wrappers, cutting them up and rearranging the letters to spell 'her' and 'she' and pasting them to board and canvas. 'In New York, on the Lower East Side, there were candy stores frequented by junkies. Junkies eat lots of candy, lots of chocolate, and Hershey Bar wrappers would be all over the sidewalk.'[18] Hansen's Hershey Bar wrapper collages and paintings were a lifelong passion, and he debuted them in public at a one-man show at the New York Six gallery. 'He did the Hershey label series for years,' Beck remembered. 'The other thing he used a lot were cigarette butts. And he did all the Venus figures made out of cigarette butts, or candy bar wrappers or matchsticks or anything he found.'[19] Al's debt to Kurt Schwitters' collages of rubbish and leftovers was evident.

In 1961 Hansen was the unintentional curator of what he dubbed a Walking Show, which consisted of the paintings he had left in a friend's house, and which had been stolen by junkies, who walked up and down the Bowery selling them. At the Judson Memorial Church, Hansen, Claes Oldenburg and Jim Dine all worked on multi-room happenings. The most notable of these was the Ray Gun Spex, in March 1960, which featured Claes Oldenburg dressed like a mummy, Dick Higgins orchestrating happenings within happenings, Stan VanDerBeek filming in 16mm, Hansen projecting film cut-ups of W.C. Fields, paratroopers and clips of teenagers dancing to rock and roll.

One very memorable happening was held in the backyard of Al's house, the great rambling Brooklyn house at 104 Hall Street with stamped pattern tin ceiling, exposed water pipes and sheaves of paper spilling off overloaded shelves. Al and recruits from the Pratt Institute close by had constructed a huge figure of a man out of framing wood and cardboard. Nearby was a bed where two artists kissed languidly, all part of the performance. Artist Larry Poons sat in the belly of the wood and cardboard man and read aloud from a Dada book, while eleven-year-old Bibbe walked around with a candle on a plate, looking like a ghost, humming pop tunes. On the roof were two of Hansen's collaborators: Cynthia Mailman, doing a belly dance in her leotards while Chinatown Powers played a series of records on a portable record player. Al recalled, 'People read poetry from the bushes in the garden, and there were large sheets of plastic on which words were spray painted on.' The happening took a turn towards the chaotic when Cynthia took a spill and fell through a skylight, fifteen feet down to the living room of the house. As she howled in pain, no one was sure whether or not the incident had been staged as part of the happening. Eventually, police and ambulances showed up, with neighbours, who had been watching the spectacle in curiosity, wondering what all this was. The artists continued with the happening, with Dick Higgins reciting poems by Tristan Tzara while Poons read counterpoint from the Dada book. Bibbe circled one of the policemen with her candle, smirking and singing Dionne Warwick tunes. Hansen, well pleased, noted 'It was a fine bit of mayhem and quite abstract.'[20] Hansen would perform pieces such as 'McLuhan Megillah' and 'Hi Ho Bibbe' at Judson Memorial Church, Café Au Go Go, and Circle in the Square. On 14 March 1960 at the Living Theatre, Hansen was at the Concert of New Music performing 'Bibbe's Tao', which involved a script for two automobiles and flashing headlamps. Sometimes his very ubiquity made him invisible; people assumed he was always at hand.

By now Hansen had hooked up with the hopped up heads of Fluxus, who were piloted (in the way that an out of control tank is piloted) by George Maciunas, the Lithuanian renegade graphic designer whose colour blindness influenced a whole new look in typography. Maciunas crystallized loose trends happening in downtown New York's art scene, and developed the concept of Fluxus in 1962, as 'a fusion of Spike Jones, vaudeville, gag, children's games and Duchamp.'[21] Maciunas recognized a commonality between a group of artists that had been branching out from Cage since the middle of the 1950s, including Al Hansen. He was smart enough to see that disparate artists and musicians, including LaMonte Young and Tony Conrad, were aiming in vaguely the same direction, as part of a reaction against European classicism. This was fundamentally the same direction the Dada and Surrealist movements had been going in, which is to say, everywhere at once, and sometimes nowhere as well. Maciunas put out a zine and called it *Fluxus*, thereby giving the loose movement a name. The first exhibition under that new title was the 'Fluxus International Festspiele', in Wiesbaden, West Germany in September 1962. It put a name on events which had been germinating for several years; just a few weeks before at the *Neo-Dada In Der Musik* event in Düsseldorf, where performance artist Nam June Paik, in a piece entitled 'One for Violin' solemnly took the stage in Düsseldorf, took out a violin from its case, resined the bow, and adjusted it to his chin. The audience waited patiently. Without warning, Paik took the violin and smashed it to bits. Performance over. A ripple of uneasy laughter rippled through the spectators.

One notable and perhaps surprising aspect of Fluxus was the cosmopolitan nature of the crowd of artists it was composed of. Artists from Japan, Korea, Germany and the United States were all present and accounted for, including Nam June Paik, Yoko Ono, Dick Higgins and Al Hansen. Hansen remarked with great satisfaction that the pioneering happenings that he and Kaprow, Dine, Red Grooms and the rest had been engaged in were paralleled by similar developments in other countries, quite unbeknownst to them. Nam June Paik and Wolf Vostell had also been extrapolating from Schwitters and crafting sculpture from trash in Germany in the late Fifties. In Japan the Gutai Group experimented with paint, paper and ink, using their bodies as the brushes, a reflection of the work of French artist Yves Klein. These myriad streams from Germany, Japan and New York all seemed to indicate, if anything, a pan-global restlessness with established art and a desire to craft a new means of transcending it. Thus, Ben Vautier took to signing anything he could with his first name, quietly determined to void the notion of high art one signature at a time, turning everything he could lay his hands on into art.

As well as being rife with foreigners, there were also women in Fluxus – anathema to the rigours of macho Abstract Expressionism. Alison Knowles, Takako Saito, Shigeko Kubota and Mieko Shiomi and Yoko Ono were all significant figures in the movement. Knowles devised a terrific performance art piece which involved only one thing: making a salad and serving it. In fact, to call Fluxus a movement is to do its anti-establishment impulses a disservice. 'Fluxus was a very loosely organized movement,' Yoko Ono stated recently.' Fluxus didn't *want* to formalize things. It wasn't like twenty artists got together and said, "Well, now. What shall we do? Shall we create this movement?"' [22]

It was Dick Higgins who articulated the concept of 'Intermedia', which referred to the concept of Fluxus' activities existing in the gaps between painting, music, typography and performance. Mail art, concrete poetry, experimental cinema, dance theatre, conceptual art, performance art and happenings all co-existed in the same sphere, sometimes harmoniously, at other times rubbing against each with friction, causing wavelets of innovation. Looking back at those heady days almost forty years later, Fluxartist Ken Friedman, wrote 'the radical contribution Fluxus made was to suggest there is no boundary to be erased.' [23] Clearly, this was a lesson not lost on Al's grandson Beck, who came to view the movement as a valiant attempt to make art tumble off its pedestal: 'Fluxus is more reflective of life. As formal art in the last half of this century became less a part of our daily lives, Fluxus reflected how we were oriented in our society.' [24]

One of the movement's most important features, and something which again emerged as a major factor in Beck's own music, was that it retained a fine, self-deprecating sense of humour. Fluxus was a species of solemn fun; its unincorporated members would sit outside the galleries they showed in, at a table hastily set up on the sidewalk, in their bowler hats and oddly formal clothes, brushing their teeth in a mock-ceremonial seriousness and arousing curious laughs from passers-by. The artists would perform on Village sidewalks, one playing the violin, the other tying the violinist up with string. Their old world art antagonism seemed as archaic as it was modern, and their jokes were a sly smile which cracked their bohemian cool. The Fluxites also evinced a strong interest in product, and the fetishization of products. They produced irregular catalogues, boxes, packages and prints, reflecting a preoccupation reminiscent of the intricately wrapped gifts common to Japanese culture. Fluxus, in some sense, worked as a cataloguing of the artist's effects, his or her discarded papers, mailing tubes, interesting junk, packaging.

Al Hansen was an integral influence working at the edges of the movement, an early inspiration, though his name is strangely absent from the lavish books that are published these days about Fluxus. He actively participated in the Fluxus Anti-Musik Festival in Düsseldorf in March 1963, but if you look through the pictures of that era, you see him in the background, like a phantom presence. In the art world, where ego provides much of the impetus that makes some artists persevere, Hansen wasn't interested in achieving fame. But there he was, always in the periphery and if not in the thick of it, then close by. Flashes of photographs come by: Al with Warhol and Jonas Mekas, John Lennon and Yoko Ono and participating in the epochal Ray Gun Spex Show. In 1965 his landmark book, *A Primer of Happenings and Time/Space Art*, was published by Dick Higgins' Something Else Press; it is cited as a classic text today in the field of performance art.

Hansen's motto was 'Art Always Wins' and though a few of Hansen's contemporaries, as well as collectors and curators, denied him a place in the Fluxus pantheon, labelling him a 'beatnik', dilettante and worse, Hansen was a vital and electric artist. It was a case of being 'more Fluxus than thou', with all the contemptible snobbery of the art world. In the end, it was those who hocked their ass better than others, to a large extent, who won the day, and Hansen didn't seem driven to try. Art historian Kristine Stiles remembers a painful incident in 1982, at the 20th anniversary commemoration of the first Fluxus fest at Wiesbaden in Germany: fluxartist George Brecht refused to take the stage until Hansen stood down, as Hansen 'wasn't Fluxus'. Hansen shrugged, and obliged.

In the words of a Fluxus leaflet, he was true to their original goal of artists who 'forgo all pretension toward significance'. Hansen was, however, an artist's artist, known to those who mattered among the new wave of artists in the Fifties and Sixties, including his mentor John Cage, Jasper Johns, and Robert Rauschenberg, who praised him. Claes Oldenburg observed, 'Al was an outsider playing by rules he made up himself. But even if you questioned his sense of form, you couldn't resist his energy, humour and his love of art, all of which he generously shared with others.'[25] Yoko Ono agreed, 'Al would share anything with anyone. His work was very well known amongst us. Al was very Fluxus; he was innately rebellious.'[26]

In June 1968, Al paid a visit to Andy Warhol's Factory. He ran into a very crazed Valerie Solanis coming out of the lift; she didn't respond to his greeting. When Al walked into the studio he found Warhol on the floor with two bullets in his gut. 'He actually ran into Valerie Solanis as she was on her way out of the Factory from shooting Warhol,' Beck marvelled later. 'He made a book about it called *Why Shoot Andy Warhol?* It's really beautiful. He actually came up with the name for the Velvet Underground. It was a few weeks before their first gig, and they were calling themselves Falling Spikes and desperately looking for a better name. Al had this semi-pornographic book called *The Velvet Underground*, and he was having lunch with their manager one day, and he said, "Well, this is a good name. Why don't you use it?" The manager ended up taking credit for the whole thing and said it was "his" book.'[27] Warhol's Exploding Plastic Inevitable, the multimedia show he arranged which included the Velvets, was at least partly indebted to Al's own multimedia shows, which preceded the EPI and were very similar in feel. Hansen never took umbrage at others using his ideas; often he was perversely amused by it, as if the car he had bought had been driven off by someone else.

After Warhol was shot by Solanis – a psychotic feminist and an alarmingly original writer – things changed in the art world: paranoia took over and things got streamlined and primed for making more money. The Factory was no longer a place where layabouts, heiresses, speed-freaks and slumming rock stars could congregate; now there was a secretary with an appointment book. Warhol hid himself somewhere behind buffed and polished double doors in a new Factory on Union Square.

Hansen had no genius for self-publicity, and merits only one mention in Andy Warhol's Sixties *roman à clef*, *POPism*. Warhol drolly relates how Al's silver Hershey wrapper backgrounds on his collages mesmerized the amphetamine freaks who loved the glitter of sharp white lights on reflective surfaces, seeing the world in black and white terms. Hansen was much more than a diversion for the A-heads, though. Hansen's happenings were riotous events which, as all good happenings should, left little to be collected for documentation; he was interested in total involvement in the event itself, not in securing a record for posterity. For Hansen, there was no delineation between his collage work and his happenings, which he called 'collage theatre'. Hansen's anarchistic instincts were strong; his happenings were hardly designed for posterity, and neither was the bulk of his career. He was simply too busy creating and doing.

Hansen was that most unrecognized of artists, the catalyst. 'He was this presence; he got people excited about that scene,' Beck acknowledged. 'Every scene has someone like that.'[28] It was fitting that he ended his days an instructor, always on the go and always patient, if at times irascible, with younger minds. Hansen spent 1967 to 1974 teaching at Rutgers University, across the river from New York City (but an aesthetic light year away) in Newark, New Jersey. Nineteen-seventy found him at Parsons School of Design, instructing young artists. However, he still hadn't found his niche, and he ventured on restlessly. During these years, Hansen the Elder made several trips to see his daughter and grandsons in California, showing up at the their house on Lanewood Avenue in Hollywood in 1975. He left as quickly as he had alighted, but returned the following year and stayed for a two-year stretch in a garage out back. During his time in Hollywood he worked on his collages, managing punk bands, including the Screamers and the Controllers, produced a punk zine with Bibbe and acted bit parts in several movies. After her father awakened her to the punk scene, Bibbe readily became a convert and soon had young punks crashing on the couch. She took photos of the bands for Al, including the Germs, the Dils and the Screamers. 'Al was very interested in that energy, and in the multi-media possibilities that the punk scene offered,' Beck recalled later. 'I think his attraction to it was the rawness of it, the intensity.'[29]

His only regret was that he didn't have enough money to buy Hershey's chocolate bars: 'In Los Angeles, not being able to afford to buy them, I looked around for something equally invaluable, throwaway, worthless and I discovered, from a large bowl ashtray on my side porch studio, cigarette butts and burnt matchsticks. I also made Venus figures fashioned from burnt paper matches. At one time, when Beck and Channing must have been eight and six years old, I gave each of us a plastic shopping bag and we scoured Sunset Boulevard from La Brea west almost to Fairfax and back again east to Yucca. The three shopping bags full of cigarette were all the art materials I needed. All I had to buy was glue.'[30] By 1979 Hansen's boot heels began to itch again and he was off to New Jersey and on to Europe. A spell in 1979 at an Eskimo Art School in the evocatively named burg of Nuuk Godthab in the icy wastes of Greenland was followed by more itinerant wanderings. And everywhere he continued to make his trademark Venuses, always scanning the gutters and alleyway dumpsters for interesting trash. The world was his collage.

But despite his artistic disposition and the distances that it led him to cover, Al never completely cut himself off from his family. Jimmy Breslin remembered, with some satisfaction, 'When Al's father was ill in Brookhaven, on Long Island, the family decided that they couldn't count on him. But he came back for two years and nursed the man until he died. Showed them all.'[31] After that Hansen returned to Europe, where he had enjoyed growing appreciation and sporadic successes with each successive visit, though money, as ever, was tight. However, he found a refuge when he returned to Köln for the Art Fair. In retrospect it seems strange for Hansen to have returned to Germany, his point of entry into the art world, the site of his piano drop so many years before. Like Frankfurt, Köln was as unrecognizable as the city would have been in 1945 to those who lived there before the wars. It was a sprawling metropolis that approached Los Angeles-sized proportions, yet with a strong funding push by the government for artists.*

A tourney of teaching during 1988 at the Hochschule für Bildende Kunst in Hamburg

---

* Bibbe cites it as the premier art city of the world. Indeed, it is a bubbling font of artistic activities. The Ultimate Akademie continues to this day, and exceptionally creative bands such as Mouse on Mars have emerged from the city in recent years.

reiterated for Hansen that this was where he wanted to be. The German government actually had something in the way of support for the arts, and Köln bustled with artistic mayhem, funded by public hands. 'I hadn't been to Köln for seven or eight years and in the Bahnhof several people smiled, waved and said, "Hi, Al!"', he remembered with affection, years later. 'I began to realize that Köln was some kind of artist heaven.'[32] By 1987 Hansen had cemented his vision to the point that he founded the 'Ultimate Akademie' with collaborator Lisa Cieslik, in Köln.

The Ultimate Akademie opened in August 1987 at Mozartstrasse, a studio space that Cieslik and Hansen refurbished. Soon artists were clamouring for them to exhibit their work, asking them to come to their studios to select appropriate works. Hansen pointedly told them to choose the works themselves, and the artists, surprised and delighted, began to throw themselves into organizing events, classes and exhibitions at the Akademie. It is testament to Hansen's perseverance and altruism that the Akademie continues to this day, with hundreds of exhibitions and alumni. Not alumni in the traditional sense, but artists, many of them young, many of them Neapolitans, who were inspired by the *eminence grise* who would work late into the cold Köln nights under a solitary light, listening to the records of his youth, armed only with glue, cigarette butts, paper and his own inimitable magic.

On 21 June 1995, Al Hansen died in Köln. In his obituary for his old pal, Jimmy Breslin beautifully recorded Al's determined creativity and penchant for the non-conventional: 'Al tried every day to put something bright and different into the lives of people trying desperately to live like each other.'[33] In 1996 there was a retrospective of his work at the Kölnisches Stadt Museum in Germany. Two years later, Beck paid tribute to his grandfather in the *Los Angeles Times*: 'Having spent time with Al in Europe I know how respected he is there, and he's definitely been given short shrift in America. There's a conspiracy here to control the history of Fluxus and Al tends to get marginalized in Fluxus shows organized here [...] Al had no interest in the spoils of a successful career in art, and he didn't stand for a lot of the bull that walks in that world, the gaming and intrigues [...] In a way, he was innocent, which is something that must run in our family; we're so worldly in some ways and completely clueless in others. For most of his life Al wore leather pants and big boots, and it wasn't until he was in his fifties that he started wearing a proper suit. It took him forty years to realize he'd get more shows if he was presentable.'[34] Contrary to the slacker status that was lazily bestowed on him in the light of 'Loser''s success, Beck's self-motivation should be evident to even those with the most casual interest in his work, and it's a quality that he feels most definitely runs in the family. 'I was never formally tutored by Al,' he told the *Los Angeles Times* in May 1998, 'but he transmitted an optimism to me. That side of the family is very industrious and has a lot of spirit, and although Al went through some unbelievable things, he kept pushing on. The most valuable thing I learned from him was a certain work ethic, and to be persistent in what you're doing. Al tooled away making art for decades, and there were never any trumpets blaring.'[35] 'There's some fundamental kinship in how I approach what I do and however Al was operating', Beck told Carlo McCormick,' the desire and that need to reflect the dynamic of energy in art, [...] an intuition beyond a convention or structure.'[36]

'You worship junk and garbage?' Al asked himself in a 1976 self-interview. 'No,' he wrote back, 'I arrange it so it can be worshipped.'[37]

1   List, Daniel. 'Bibbe's Ma, Audrey', *Village Voice*, 15 August 1968

2   Bibbe Hansen interview With Vaginal Davis, *Index* magazine, November–December 1999

3   McKenna, Kristine. 'Beck's First Sampling', *Los Angeles Times*, 3 May 1998

4   List, Daniel. 'Bibbe's Ma, Audrey', *Village Voice*, 15 August 1968

5   McKenna, Kristine. 'Beck's First Sampling', *Los Angeles Times*, 3 May 1998

6   Hansen, Al. 'An Incomplete Requiem for W.C. Fields', Great Bear Pamphlets, 1966

7   Breslin, Jimmy. 'The Happening Of A Lifetime', *Newsday*, July 1995

8   Hansen, Al. *Notes On A Mini-Retrospective*, Kölnisches Stadt Museum, 1995

9   Breslin, Jimmy. 'The Happening Of A Lifetime', *Newsday*, July 1995

10 Hansen, Al. *Notes On A Mini-Retrospective*, Kölnisches Stadt Museum, 1995

11 McKenna, Kristine. 'Beck's First Sampling', *Los Angeles Times*, 3 May 1998

12 Interview with Beck, *Humo* magazine (Belgium), 14 December 1999

13 Hansen, Al. *Notes On A Mini-Retrospective*, Kölnisches Stadt Museum, 1995

14 Hansen, Al. *Notes On A Mini-Retrospective*, Kölnisches Stadt Museum, 1995

15 Kim, Jae-Ha. 'Pop's Golden Boy; Beck On Mantras, Dadaism And Fame', *Chicago Sun-Times*, 30 July 1997

16 'Super Beck: "Loser", Artist, Rock Star, Genius', *UHF* # 10, July–August 1996

17 Wiederhorn, Jon. 'The Many Faces of Beck', *Guitar*, January 1999

18 Hansen, Al. *Notes On A Mini-Retrospective*, Kölnisches Stadt Museum, 1995

19 Ginsberg, Allen. 'A Beat/Slacker Transgenerational Meeting Of Minds', *Shambhala Sun*, 27 September 1999

20 Hansen, Al. *A Primer of Happenings and Time/Space Art*, Something Else Press, 1965

21 Kellein, Thomas. *Fluxus*, Thames and Hudson, 1995

22 Smith, Ethan. 'Re: Fluxology – Beck And Yoko Ono Sound Off On Found Art, Family Ties, And Flying Pianos',
    New York magazine, 21 September 1998

23 Friedman, Ken. 'The Twelve Criteria of Fluxus', *Lund Art Press* magazine, Vol. 1, No. 4, Summer–Autumn 1990

24 Smith, Ethan. 'Re: Fluxology – Beck And Yoko Ono Sound Off On Found Art, Family Ties, And Flying Pianos',
    New York magazine, 21 September 1998

25 McKenna, Kristine. 'Beck's First Sampling', *Los Angeles Times*, 3 May 1998

26 Smith, Ethan. 'Re: Fluxology – Beck And Yoko Ono Sound Off On Found Art, Family Ties, And Flying Pianos',
    New York magazine, 21 September 1998

27 Smith, Ethan. 'Re: Fluxology – Beck And Yoko Ono Sound Off On Found Art, Family Ties, And Flying Pianos',
    New York magazine, 21 September 1998

28 'The Evolution Of Golden Boy Beck', *Paper* magazine, July–August 1996, www.papermag.com/magazine/beck

29 Hoskyns, Barney. *World Art Magazine*, Issue 19, Autumn 1999

30 Hansen, Al. *Notes On A Mini-Retrospective*, Kölnisches Stadt Museum, 1995

31 Breslin, Jimmy. 'The Happening Of A Lifetime', *Newsday*, July 1995

32 Hansen, Al. *Notes On A Mini-Retrospective*, Kölnisches Stadt Museum, 1995

33 Breslin, Jimmy. 'The Happening Of A Lifetime', *Newsday*, July 1995

34 McKenna, Kristine. 'Beck's First Sampling', *Los Angeles Times*, 3 May 1998

35 McKenna, Kristine. 'Beck's First Sampling', *Los Angeles Times*, 3 May 1998

36 McCormick, Carlo. Interview With Beck Hansen. *Playing With Matches*. Smart Art Press/Plug In Editions, 1998

37 Hansen, Al. *Questions And Answers*, Al Hansen Archive Text, 1976

3

A RAINY DAY IN LOS ANGELES

Bibbe accompanied her father on his jaunts through the Village art world. Like Chaplin and the Kid, they wandered through the denizens of bohemia, both innocents amidst so much guile and careerism. Hansen dedicated his 'An Incomplete Requiem For W.C. Fields' to Bibbe, with the words, 'To Bibbe, who in so many ways is just like me'. Artist Carolee Schneemann remembered going to Hansen happenings where a five-year-old Bibbe would be asleep on a massive pile of coats. Bibbe was bounced around a bit between her parents, living on and off with Audrey. 'I spent my first couple of years in an all black community in Nova Scotia called Africa Town,' she told *Index* magazine in late 1999. 'The old matriarch was a wonderful woman named Old Rose, and I was left in her care for the first several years of my life. I sort of went between her and Chickie Lantini, who was this gay woman who slept at the foot of my mother's bed. She took care of me. She was a bartender at a dyke bar, and she worshipped my mother.'[1]

Throughout her childhood, Bibbe hung out with her father at places like Andy Warhol's notorious Factory and Max's Kansas City and from 1964 to 1966 would hang at the first Factory independently of her father. Bibbe, then all of thirteen years old, appeared in Andy Warhol's film *Prison*, sharing the screen with the unwitting tragedienne Edie Sedgwick. There are scattered photos of her that show up in the flood of books on Warhol's Factory. There she is in Billy Name's (née Linich) book, her small and perfect features radiating in contrast to her melancholy and self-aware expression. She's there again in Stephen Shore's book of Factory photographs, *The Velvet Years: 1965–67* (Thunder's Mouth Press, 1995) sitting amidst tape recorders, silver-painted walls and painting supplies, smoking a cigarette, staring off into a corner, sitting next to an equally distracted Billy Name.* She told *Index* magazine, 'I made several films with Andy. The first was *Prison*, when I was thirteen. Andy was wonderful, he made an enormous impression on me and set a certain tone that has followed me all my life... in a world that was very exclusive and standoffish, he was very welcoming, even though I was just a child.' Bibbe found a soul mate in Warhol waif Edie Sedgwick, who gave her beauty tips: 'We'd do speed and play with cosmetics for hours.' She also starred in Warhol's *10 Beautiful Girls* and the self-explanatory *10 More Beautiful Girls*. 'I also did Andy Warhol's *L'avventura*, which takes place at the L'avventura restaurant on second avenue. We'd be hanging out and somebody would say, "Let's go to dinner," and in most circles they would have dumped the kid, but not Andy. Of course I was going along.'[2]

A native New Yorker, Bibbe was the daughter of working-class intellectuals, an artist father and a poetess mother, which gave her a formidable pedigree – not in money or social status, but in artistic richness. Bibbe: 'I grew up in an environment with lots of different artistic disciplines happening simultaneously. My father was working with dance companies, designing stage sets,

31

---

* Billy Name/Linich was the Factory's photographer/major who painted the Factory silver. He left the Factory in 1971 after many years of dedicated service, leaving only a note reading: 'I'm fine, just gone.'

doing happenings, making paintings, collages and experimental music with John Cage; culturally, it was very rich.'[3] In addition to performing from a very tender age in her father's happenings, Bibbe performed in summer stock theatre in upstate New York.

Bibbe took modern dance lessons from Lucinda Childs, whom Al paid in collages. Her partner in dance was Jan Kerouac, daughter of the Beats' tarnished patron saint; the two lived together for a while. 'We ran around the city getting into incredible amounts of trouble – drugs, scams, you name it,' Bibbe later told *Index* magazine. 'It's a shame so many adorable people, people I've loved so much, gave their lives to all that. I'm lucky to be a survivor; I was in and out of reform school. I was beyond out of control. My father would give me a couple of dollars to go to the store, and I wouldn't come back for three weeks. I was also in trouble with the law. There was some dicey stuff – a big drug bust and a few sex scandals. They eventually locked me up for a very long time (in 1968).'[4]

Immediately after her mother's death, Bibbe escaped reform school to the Virgin Islands, only returning once she had reached eighteen, the American age of consent, and could safely return without being thrust back into the bedlam of the reformatory. After a brutal winter in New York City Bibbe made her determined way to the sunnier climes of Los Angeles. Making quick connections with vital young musicians and artists, she performed in an avant-garde mime-ballet-play by Bill McKinley. The accompanying music quartet had a handsome viola player; a serious but affable lad by the name of David Campbell.

They couldn't have come from more different backgrounds. The son of a Presbyterian minister, Campbell was a prodigy on the violin. He later switched to the viola, and played in a germinal quartet as a teenager in Seattle with one of the founders of Kronos Quartet. As a teenager, Campbell also became the protégé of Sir William Primrose, who pioneered the viola as a solo instrument. David left Seattle, and the strictures of a conservative and religious family, for something more exciting and moved to New York at the tail end of the Sixties to attend the Manhattan School of Music. Campbell began playing with Leopold Stokowski's American Symphony but he found himself getting restless with classical music, and so dropped everything to venture out to Los Angeles. There he found himself accompanying the cast of the play with a striking young woman reciting her lines in rehearsals. Campbell took quite a shine to Bibbe, studying her over the score sheets on their stand. He pursued Bibbe, who was touched by his sincerity and determination.

After a simple wedding ceremony in Los Angeles they were off, ostensibly to Paris, to pursue *la vie boheme* and an internship with a blind cellist, with both viola and violin in tow. But dire finances would beach them back in New York where they would share skimpy dinners and talk late into the night. David wanted to break out of the classical mould and began looking for release from the strictures of the symphony. Bluegrass music, with its string friendly tonalities and structures, seemed the best choice. When Bibbe discovered she was pregnant the couple began making plans to return to California, eager to flee the bleakness of Hell's Kitchen, where they were living a broke and dead-end existence. The couple were far from hippie wastrels however, and were determined to move forward. 'I was never a hippie,' Bibbe maintained. 'I went from beatnik to mod to punk to international cultural bourgeoisie with no stops in between.'[5] Their son Beck was born Bek David Campbell in a house in Pico-Union in Los Angeles on 8 July 1970, just one minute shy of noon. 'My parents lived in a rooming house near downtown Los Angeles,' Beck recalled nearly thirty years later. 'They were very young. My mom was eighteen or nineteen when they had me. Then, later on, we moved to Hollywood and lived just off of Hollywood Boulevard. It wasn't a privileged situation. What I'm doing now is pretty sweet for my family, because there's been a lot of struggle for a long, long time.'[6]

Around the time Beck was born, David Campbell and his friend Geoff Levin, used to go to Westwood with other friends and busk on the sidewalk for the audiences lined up to see films at the various movie theatres. Their repertoire was largely bluegrass, and they would play Bill Monroe and Flatt and Scruggs songs with Campbell playing violin and Levin on guitar.

'David was just a musician for hire, he played violin,' Beck remembered in 1997. 'I heard him play here and there, but it wasn't like I went into the living room and people were jamming or anything. I just remember that he was always working. I liked what he played, but it wasn't like I went out and picked up an instrument and started playing myself. It wasn't until a lot later that I picked up an instrument.'[7]

Campbell soon tired of busking to support his family but attempts to break into session work failed. At that time string sections in Los Angeles consisted of men in their fifties, a tightly bound cabal of studio pros who had a tight grip on the market of arranging and playing on major label record sessions. Campbell started his own string section of young men and women in their twenties, and set himself up as a contractor. The introduction of women musicians was a breakthrough. Until then female session players in the Los Angeles music scene were few; only exceptional players like Carol Kaye were grudgingly allowed into the game. With this new, young, diverse and talented group of session players, Campbell made an immediate niche for himself with the stars of the Californian singer-songwriter boom who felt they could relate better personally and professionally to his string squadron. Campbell's players could translate the stars' ideas into string arrangements free of the schmaltz of the old studio men. Before long, he was the number one string contractor in L.A. Arranging was the next logical step. Campbell started arranging for artists such as Carole King, which led to work with Peter Asher, (onetime member of British pop sensation Peter and Gordon) arranging gigs with Rita Coolidge and Kris Kristofferson, James Taylor, Carly Simon, Jackson Brown and Linda Ronstadt. He would eventually also score beautiful string arrangements for Beck's albums, as well as accompanying him to the Grammies in 1997. Campbell lent his skills to an album of Scientology's™ deceased arch-thetan L. Ron Hubbard's questionable compositions.

At the end of the 1970s, Al and Bibbe, were fired up by the electric possibilities of punk rock and so, surprisingly, was David. He did pro-bono duty for several punk bands, producing them in the punk style and ensuring the needles stayed well in the red and tape was threaded through the reels. Through Al, David hooked up with the punk band The Controllers and produced their debut single. He also produced some demos for the power pop band the Quick, and also started arranging a film score for Dutch filmmaker Rene Daalder's film on the Screamers, another seminal L.A. punk band managed by Al Hansen.

Throughout the late seventies and into the early 1980s, Campbell worked tirelessly, late into the night, as the whims of bands demanded. In his youngest years, as his father established himself as an arranger in the music industry, the young Beck Hansen grew up around the Pico Union area on 9th Street and River, then later down by MacArthur Park before moving to Hollywood. Pico Hill, as it was colloquially known, was in Beck's words, 'A very un-stimulating environment. There's not a lot of natural beauty there, and not a lot of interesting architecture. Besides some rag-tag, thrown-together aesthetic, there's no contingent character, just lots of bits and pieces. So it was a place where you really either tune out or you engage your own imagination and create your own interior landscape.'[8] Bibbe had another son, Channing, in 1972, and pursued a career as an actress and artist while holding down work in an office. She founded a theatre company, acted in 'B' movies and participated in the local punk scene as musician, and *documenteur*. Beck recalled Bibbe as a 'totally free-form mom. A chain-smoking, make-your-own-dinner mom.'[9] Bibbe would later open and operate a fantastic café with partner

Sean Carillo, a hotbed for art, coffee and multi-cultural bohemian activities of all shades and stripes. She played rhythm guitar in Black Fag, the outrageous multicultural, pan-sexual band. In later years she would become something of a doyenne in Silverlake, L.A.'s bohemian neighbourhood. Never abandoning her own artistic inclinations she continues to be involved in photography and theatre; the fleeting Warhol connection is probably the least interesting thing about her.

As David Campbell became a successful arranger the family moved to a house on Lanewood between Hollywood Boulevard and Sunset Boulevard before Marlon Brando's old house in Laurel Canyon, a maze of staircases up and down the house. Bibbe remembered this period as one during which she sought a traditional life: 'I did for a little while; I wanted to know what it was like. I was a Hollywood wife back then. Married to Beck and Channing's dad, David Campbell. I always had a wild streak, but I was in wild recovery living with my staid husband – a wonderful musician, arranger and composer [...] I had my own children and things were very calm for me for about five or six years.'[10]

The record industry slump in the early Eighties and the increasing reliance on synthesizers made traditional arranging outmoded; synth programmers turned arrangements into aerodyne, lifeless washes of perfectly synched digital rubbish. It would have dire effects on the Campbell family finances.

Beck's first talents manifested themselves in a precocious knack for picking up language. He learned how to rhyme at the age of five by computing the formula himself, with typically methodical and logically sound reasoning: 'Two words that sound the same, and you put them at the end of the line. It's this perfect formula; all the questions of the universe.'[11] His first couplet was unintentionally hilarious, rousing the adults to howling laughter: '"Want a pickle? Get a nickel! Or you can pull down your pants and do the hot dog dance." At the time, I didn't really get what I was saying.'[12] (Beck would later use a variant of this on Odelay's 'Lord Only Knows'.) Clearly the discovery of his ability to manipulate language to his own ends made an enormous impression on the youngster: 'I remember driving around in the car with Al about that same time. I was just getting into words, just learning how to read, and I remember him teaching me how to rhyme. I thought that was the greatest thing. You could make words lock together.'[13]

Before long, Bek became Beck. 'When I first started school, when I was four or five, the administrators and the teachers, and the certifiers, the paper-registrating people of the world, gave it to me. I don't think they could deal with B-e-k. It would always become B-e-c-k, and I got tired of saying "No, B-e-k." So I just went with it. Somehow it gave a little more weight. I thought maybe as a small kid with a name that small I was going to float away anyway.'[14]

Beck grew up in the post-industrial wasteland of Los Angeles, alternating with summers spent in the Bible-belt of Kansas, with his paternal grandparents. Being good-hearted Christian folk, they prevailed upon Beck to follow the path of Christ; he declined to. The five-year-old Beck seems to have felt adrift in both worlds, though, and his sense of being an outsider, viewing the world from its perimeters, would influence his music later on. Certainly, the church music and hymns Beck heard growing up had an impact on his songwriting later with biblical phrases appearing in his more down-home style folk. The Mahalia Jackson-style renditions of 'Down Low' clearly registered with him, the seesaw between spirituality and secularity, sin and sanctity evident even then. Beck's appreciation of the music always seems sincere and surprisingly unromantic. In his concerts the core of the show for some time remained a solo harmonica and voice rendition of 'One Foot In The Grave', powered by fiery sermon-style declaiming and singing. 'That music influenced me a lot, but not consciously. There's something biblical and awkward and great about all those lyrics,'[15] he told *Rolling Stone* in 1994. Moreover, the declamatory tone and the inspired use of language to conscious effect resonated in a secular context for the adult Beck: 'It's not really for the religious content, just the way the preacher would sermonise the rhythm. The building up of the preaching, I hear that in Chuck D or Ice Cube.'[16]

Bibbe had a strong desire to inculcate Beck and his younger brother Channing with self-determination and this paid off, teaching them both a lot about the confidence that coping for yourself can inspire. 'Both my parents were very non-controlling,' he told the *Daily Telegraph* in 1997. 'They were young when they had me, so they just let me do things. They weren't the kind of parents who were behind your back telling you what to do, or where to go every minute, making you neurotic. It can be empowering, because it's about self-realization and not something drilled into you. I think a lot of people my age have a hard time becoming adults. They had to raise themselves and figure out a lot of things themselves. It takes them well into their thirties before they get it all worked out, whereas forty or fifty years ago, by the time you were twenty you were an adult male, you were raised.'[17]

When *Star Wars* was released in 1977, Beck became obsessed with the panoply of Jedi knights, wookies, Jawas and stormtroopers, as did most of the kids his age. Beck worked his way through the trilogy as it came out, watching it fifty times. Cinema was an escape for Beck. It's fitting that Hollywood is perched at the westernmost edge of the New World, its eye the last frontier. An early Beck cinematic influence, and something of an epiphany when he saw it, was the 1959 French film *The 400 Blows* by François Truffaut. In later life Beck would use elements from this New Wave classic in his video for 'Devil's Haircut' which he devised in conjunction with director Mark Romanek. The film relates the tale of a thirteen-year-old boy trying to find his way in the world only to realize how difficult that really is and, particularly, how bizarre adults are. Another early influence was the 1969 John Schlesinger film *Midnight Cowboy*, the story of a Texas cowboy-turned-hustler (Jon Voight) and his consumptive sidekick Ratso Rizzo, played memorably by Dustin Hoffman. Both films are notable for their protagonists, what Leonard Cohen would have called 'beautiful losers'; innocents adrift in the big city, separated from family and home.

Another central influence on Beck's evolving cosmology at this time was the intermittent appearance of his grandfather, Al Hansen. Showing up completely unannounced, Al, bedecked in black sombrero, with wiry grey hair, maniacal eyes and a sly grin, would stay for a few months and then dash back to New York or Europe, always chasing his muse. Beck recalled of his first meeting with Al, 'I was about six or seven. We were hearing for months that he was coming [...] We were consumed by the whole unfolding comedy/tragedy of his life. He finally showed up around dawn one morning, and he gave me a big kiss on the head and an African machete. I remember being so stunned that an adult would give a child such a dangerous thing, but right there was a sort of trust. I immediately found several large boxes to destroy, and got that out of my system.'[18]

When Beck was seven, Al moved into the garage behind David and Bibbe's house and stayed for two years. 'As far as ideas and looking at things in different ways, my grandfather was amazing,' Beck acknowledged. 'I learned a lot from his speech and the way he talked. He had the whole 1940s jazz/hipster talk. He was a zoot-suiter in the 1940s.'[19]

Rooting around in the basement one day, Al found an old plastic rocking horse of Beck's covered in dust. He offered the bewildered Beck five dollars for it. A couple of days later, Beck had the shock of his life when he discovered what had happened to his childhood toy. Al had decapitated it, spray-painted it silver and glued cigarette butts over it. 'I was horrified but also electrified at the possibility of taking something that was useless and turning it into a beautiful monstrosity.'[20] The effect was somewhat akin to a revelation to the young Beck; Al's unfettered artistic imagination had found a kindred spirit: 'He opened the possibility of taking something that wasn't obvious – something that anybody would normally pass by without thinking twice about it – and transforming it into something artistic. One of his grand statements was that he was an alchemist; he could turn shit into gold.'[21] Al also recruited Beck and Channing to collect cigarette butts which he then formed into a ribald Venus of Willendorf with the aid of glue and not a little mad glee. Beck, then all of eight years old, was suitably impressed with the old gent and his mystifying ways. Making art out of rubbish seemed to make perfect sense to Beck, living as he did at what seemed the ends of the earth, where the rubbish of Los Angeles' dozen or so cultures was available for the picking. Suddenly, being an artist didn't require expensive paints or canvas, and Beck began making sporadic drawings and collages, though nothing he took too seriously.

School was bewildering at best for Beck, who gained his first exposure to performance in a second grade play, a version of *Winnie The Pooh*. It was a disaster, though. 'I used to shy away from being put on the spot at all'. In a curious incident that provides a glimpse into how Beck viewed the world, he did an unintentional deconstruction on the play's script, walking to the front of the stage, and reciting his line, 'The donkey goes Eeyore'. The audience laughed so hard Beck was frozen. 'I thought they were laughing at me, as though I was the fool, and that really turned me off performing,' he told the *Daily Telegraph*'s David Thomas in 1997.

In 1982, aged twelve, Beck returned to Los Angeles from the last of his summers spent at his grandparents' house in Kansas, ending his oscillations between the two homes. Bibbe and David had set up household near Hollywood, and Bibbe raised Beck and Channing, holding down a day job as a secretary and working on art in her spare time. Beck's father was busy with an ever-increasing workload as arranger for major label recording artists. Of the odd duality of Kansas and Los Angeles, Bibbe and grandparents, permissiveness and religious rigidity, Beck noted, 'I don't think anybody's had a conventional upbringing. Our parents were part of the generation where music was exploding and everybody was experimenting with drugs. The whole "Leave It to Beaver" idea of the family never existed for us. It's something on TV.'[22] But influential though his artistic and unconventional parents were, the young Beck already had enough about him to mark him out as an individual.

Beck's experience of school in California was a frustrating one, especially for an artistic child who had already demonstrated an interest in language. 'I was a kid who was in love with the idea of books even before I could read them,' he told the *Daily Telegraph* in 1997. 'The education system in America depends on where you grow up. In my part of Los Angeles, it was completely backward. I remember being in an English class, aware of being taught the same thing year after year. It never went anywhere and there was nothing interesting. But I knew there were interesting things out there and I knew there were possibilities.'[23] He had few friends, and frequently wandered the halls of his school in a daze, feeling out of place and bored with the repetitious and unimaginative lessons. Moreover, the threat of being beaten up in the high stakes of violence endemic in American high school education was a very real worry. 'The local high school was one of the worst in the country', he later reflected. 'It had a gun security check, metal detectors at the entrances – this was in the 1980s. Besides, walking the three blocks to the bus stop just to go to anywhere was already little sketchy. I was pretty much chased all the time.'[24] Beck left school at fourteen, completing junior high, and never returned, to his later regret: 'I envy my friends that got to go to college. I thought maybe I would work for a few years and save money to go to college, but that never worked out. I went to New York instead and was playing music. I thought I would eventually go back to school, but I never have.'[25]

Always a voracious reader, Beck substituted his school education for a steady diet of books, anything from Westerns to newspapers, soaking in everything he read. He also read good literature, by choice rather than by duress. The strength of Beck's autodidact education lay in his free use of variegated influences to create something original and new, untainted by the bland fare on offer at American high schools. And though he regretted leaving school early, it was probably the best thing that could have happened to him. Beck would try to get out of the house as much as possible, heading to the library. He loved reading about the history of the Old West, the imagery of which would lace later songs such as 'Fourteen Rivers Fourteen Floods', or the spoken aside at the end of 'Modesto' with its images of sand, mule, wagon, sourdough and lard. Cormac McCarthy's allegorical Westerns made a big impression; the books dwell in a zone where honour, escape, fatalism and transcendence converge with edgy results.

Whilst taking extension classes at L.A.'s City College, Beck met a Los Angeles poet called Wanda Coleman and her husband, a professor at L.A.'s City College. The two provided Beck with an informal, alternative education in the arts that would serve him well. Coleman encouraged Beck to develop his writing and poetry, introducing him also to the warmth of Afro-American culture that, for the most part, white Americans are too colour-blind to appreciate. When Beck started a band of poets called Youthless with his brother Channing, cousin Scoli Acosta and several friends, Wanda became a great champion of the kids, writing about them in the *L.A. Weekly* and having them on her and Austin's poetry radio show on KPFK. Youthless read at the emerging poetry readings held in coffee houses. Like the all-ages punk clubs, the coffee houses were a sanctuary for young creative souls, adrift in a city without much to offer them. A documentary on L.A. poets by film maker Sophie Rachmuhl for French TV featured Wanda Coleman, Marisela Norte, Charles Bukowski, Jack Grape, Dr. Mongo and the Youthless kids. It included their poetry readings, their handmade magazine, videos and super-8s, music and also performances and happenings. Beck did most of the mechanical work of Youthless from paste-up to copying, collating and stapling. He also hand-delivered it to stores on 'consignment' and solicited subscriptions and donations from family friends

The long shadows of the New York downtown arts scene loomed large in Beck's family, and as he grew older he began to understand more about that world. When he was sixteen he found a copy of the Velvet Underground's 1967 debut *The Velvet Underground & Nico* in the stack of his mother's LPs. Bibbe noticed his discovery, and told Beck that she'd known the people who had made the record. Beck asked his mother to tell him more and Bibbe described what it had been like to be part of the Factory scene.

Already the possessor of an inquisitive, artistic mind, the teenage Beck couldn't help but be receptive to the extremes of L.A.'s culture – as dizzyingly diverse as the elements in one of his grandfather's collages – and draw inspiration from them for his own artworks and music. The city hummed with a broad diversity of immigrant cultures, taking in Vietnam, El Salvador, Mexico, but it was also an overpopulated, smog-ridden, sprawling testament to bad town planning and excess, with a sketchy blend of hedonism and violence. Perhaps for all of those reasons, it was the perfect place for Beck Hansen to grow up: 'Los Angeles is a desert, in a lot of ways, in more ways than one. So the idea is it's all makeshift. That goes into a lot of my songs, but I love it here. I go out all over the place, but I still totally dig Los Angeles. It's such a blank slate, a generic city: you can make it whatever you want. Neighbourhoods are transformed overnight. You'll have some white middle-class suburb, and within seven years it's the biggest Chinese population outside of China. I dig that.'[26]

Los Angeles is a city where fame is the prime commodity. It's the constant, what oil is to Brunei and jangle-noise indie pop to New Zealand. It's an education in sleaze, from the starlets in the clubs with the silicone breasts, watched by lotharios of dubious repute, to the casting calls that resemble cattle herds at slaughter time. From the clichéd image of buses from the Midwest

37

disgorging starry-eyed would-bes, to the phantom-like apparitions that haunt Hollywood Boulevard bitter with disappointment, fame rules here; its intrigues and vagaries reward the few at the expense of the many. The famous waving at their legion of fans contained behind velvet ropes, the hoi polloi with disposable cameras ablaze, feed a media culture built on ever shorter term profits, and ever increasing disposability. In America entertainers are the aristocracy. The dividing line between the movies, music, television and reality is blurry, with those pasty-faced, sugar-coated false gods inhabiting a Valhalla simultaneously far away and uncomfortably ubiquitous.

Los Angeles is also a beautiful city half hating and half loving itself, where the rusted columns over the Venice Beach market cast shadows on transients, steroid enhanced body cults, sadly shifting migrants. It's the perfection of Greek food on Sunset at 8 p.m., or leafing through magazines bought at the outdoor newsstand; it's the bracing air as one walks fifteen feet from a parked car to the ocean. And under all the illusions and failed schemes, temples to self-fulfilment and stucco castles of vainglory, lies fear. A strong feral whiff of dreams built on stilts over fault lines, with the ever-impending earthquake rumbling below.

To deny the impact that that city has had on you as one of its citizens, is also to deny your own roots. 'The West Coast becomes a part of you,' Beck observed in 1997. 'I grew up hating it. Sometimes it has this feeling of a deserted place; there's millions and millions of people, but they are all in their cars and houses. As an adult, I came to realize it was a part of me. If you hate it, you end up hating a part of yourself. So eventually I was reconciled with the fact that this is me whether I like it or not. It's like the family you grew up in; you don't agree with how it is, but it's your family.'[27] The glittering wreck of Hollywood Boulevard formed the backdrop for Beck's childhood wanderings. Schwab's Pharmacy, where Lana Turner was discovered, demurely sipping a soda, was gone. The Taft Hotel above remained, but its dank hallways and faded upholstery held few clues to its old glory. The elegant cinemas were demolished or became porno theatres. Beck used to walk up and down the Boulevard, where a few vestiges remained.

'Our house on Lanewood was quite a nice old house actually though in a rather strange neighbourhood,' Bibbe told Beck fanzine *Cyanide Breathmint*. 'The street was lined with old tall pine trees but it was located between La Brea and Highland and Hollywood Boulevard and Sunset Boulevard. Hookers and punks; tourists and trolls. There was Tiny Naylor's, a drive-in hamburger place, and Arthur J's on La Brea; up on Hollywood were the Chinese Theatre, the Gold Cup and the Masque; all were within walking distance. The house itself was a perfect replica of a turn-of-the-century upstate New York house, white with green shutters.'[28] Beck remembered, 'There was Ali Baba's, a Middle Eastern restaurant with belly dancers, and on top of it was a two- to three-storey statue of Ali Baba. Then in the early 1980s, all that was suddenly gone. The developers came in and tore it all down and turned it into giant condominiums and block apartments. I remember seeing Los Angeles just transformed within a couple years. All of a sudden there was mini-malls everywhere. The 1980s came and conquered, and it erased a lot of the heritage of the city. It's not the same city at all.'[29]

Beck, from a young age, cast a withering eye on the vanities of the city, with its visions of extending its citizens beyond their frailties. To him, there was something bizarre about how ten miles in any direction would take you into another zone – where language, colour, culture erected unsteady signs as if to stake a claim in the midst of so much impermanence. Beck told Norwegian newspaper *Dagbladet*, 'Los Angeles is full of foolish, tragic and scary people. Especially the rich people, living in their glass bubble. The city has disgusting sides, and I have tried to enter the sexuality, confusion and decadence. Los Angeles is in many ways a pathetic city without a soul.'[30]

1 Bibbe Hansen interview with Vaginal Davis. *Index* magazine, November–December 1999

2 Bibbe Hansen interview with Vaginal Davis. *Index* magazine, November–December 1999

3 McKenna, Kristine. 'Beck's First Sampling', *Los Angeles Times*, 3 May 1998

4 Bibbe Hansen interview with Vaginal Davis. *Index* magazine, November–December 1999

5 Bibbe Hansen interview with Vaginal Davis. *Index* magazine, November–December 1999

6 Kemp, Mark. 'Where It's At Now', *Rolling Stone*, 17 April 1997

7 Kemp, Mark. 'Where It's At Now', *Rolling Stone*, 17 April 1997

8 Gladstone, Eric. 'Musical Mutations', *Ray Gun* magazine, January 1999

9 Grob, Julie. 'Beck', *Thora-zine*, May 1994. www.eden.com/thora-zine

10 Bibbe Hansen Interview with Vaginal Davis. *Index* magazine, November–December 1999

11 Browne, David. 'Beck In The High Life', *Entertainment Weekly*, 14 February 1997

12 Browne, David. 'Beck In The High Life', *Entertainment Weekly*, 14 February 1997

13 Ginsberg, Allen. 'A Beat/Slacker Transgenerational Meeting Of Minds', *Shambhala Sun*, 27 September 1999

14 Bornemann, Tim. 'Beck Meets Squeegee', 2 April 1997. Slo-Jam website. squeegee@frontier.wilpaterson.edu

15 Wild, David. 'Beck', *Rolling Stone*, 21 April 1995

16 Rubin, Mike. 'Subterranean Homeboy Blues', *Spin*, July 1994

17 Thomas, David. 'It's Good To Be Beck Hansen, Musical Genius', *Daily Telegraph*, 10 May 1997

18 Hoskyns, Barney. *World Art Magazine*, issue 19, Autumn 1999

19 Ginsberg, Allen. 'A Beat/Slacker Transgenerational Meeting Of Minds', *Shambhala Sun*, 27 September 1999

20 'Super Beck: "Loser", Artist, Rock Star, Genius', *UHF* # 10, July–August 1996

21 Johnson, Calvin. 'Calvin Talks to Beck, Beck Talks Back to the Rocket', *The Rocket*, January-February 1997

22 The Evolution of Golden Boy Beck, *Paper* magazine, July-August 1996, www.papermag.com/magazine/beck

23 Thomas, David. 'It's Good To Be Beck Hansen, Musical Genius', *Daily Telegraph*, 10 May 1997

24 Schoemer, Karen. 'The Last Boy Wonder', *Elle* magazine, December 1999

25 Kemp, Mark. 'Where It's At Now', *Rolling Stone*, 17 April 1997

26 Sessions At West 54th Street, 6 September 1997, www.sessionsatwest54th.com/

27 Porter, Charlie. 'Beck To The Future', *The Times*, 25–31 October 1997

28 *Cyanide Breathmint* fanzine, 1995

29 Kemp, Mark. 'Where It's At Now', *Rolling Stone*, 17 April 1997

30 *Dagbladet*, December 1999, www.dagbladet.no

4

KANSAS TO KOREATOWN

'I take no credit for Beck's creativity,' Bibbe told the *Los Angeles Times* in May 1998, 'he came into the world with it, and I recognized early on that he was gifted. But I did create a [creative] environment for him. Beck's father is a musician, I worked in film, photography and in bands, and when Beck was a child Al lived with us. He used to sit in the backyard making art, and because he was involved in L.A.'s punk scene, there were always people at the house playing guitars.'[1]

The Los Angeles punk explosion briefly flourished at the end of the Seventies and early Eighties, mutating into hardcore, as witnessed in the 1983 film *The Decline Of Western Civilization* directed by Penelope Spheeris. Both Bibbe and Al were galvanized by punk, coming as it did at the end of the spurious wreckage of California's singer-songwriter period. Both were involved in the scene and befriended many of the young Hollywood punks who created a vibe which distantly mirrored the initial punk explosion in Britain. Bibbe more or less held an open-house for young punks who dropped in on broken-down van tours and, in the time-honoured tradition of punk, needed a place to crash for the night. On Bibbe's part it was both sympathy and empathy. 'Punk was the best thing I'd heard in years,' she enthused over a decade later, 'So there was always a peanut butter-and-jam sandwich and a couch.'[2] One of those who found a couch to sleep on for a night or two was Darby Crash (a.k.a. Bobby Pyn), a child of a splintered Los Angeles family and the singer and lyricist of the Germs. Crash held forth at the mike with a dazed, drugged and moronic countenance, baiting the punters and often getting a bottle in the head for his trouble, but his lyrics were sharp, concise and full of articulate rage.

Al Hansen was also invigorated by punk's simultaneously nihilist and idealistic ethos, even going as far as to manage punk bands the Screamers and the Controllers. Bibbe and Al also collaborated on a punk zine, and attended shows at the Masque on Hollywood Boulevard, seeing bands Beck would later describe as 'infamous Los Angeles punk-terrorist bands. Al loved that world; the aesthetic, the attitude. I definitely remember them around the house.'[3] Kid Spike of the Controllers recalled, 'Al used to call me Marty Mongoloid and said if I ever read a book I could become a truly dangerous person. He taught me to carry a notebook and write things down; lyrics, appointments, poems. I've lost just about everything I've ever acquired in my life but I have about fifty boxes of these notebooks and I still carry one to this day.'[4] Despite the punk milieu at home, Beck's first album, purchased at the age of twelve, was the soundtrack to the abominable rollerskating epic *Xanadu*, featuring the clarion pipes of Olivia Newton-John.

Bibbe and David split when Beck was fourteen. David, in a scenario more common than not to modern-day America, was out of the picture for most of Beck's teenage years. A true rapprochement didn't happen until Beck and his brother Channing were well into their early adulthood; Beck took on his mother's maiden name after his parents divorced. Soon after the separation Bibbe met a teenage artist named Sean Carillo, a Chicano born in El Paso, Texas, whose family was originally from Chihuahua, Mexico. 'When I met Bibbe I was just this teenage kid,' Sean told *Index* magazine. 'She already knew everything about me and the Chicano art

movement at the time. She knew where we came from, what we were about. She knew her shit.'
For her part, Bibbe abandoned the traditional family life that she'd had for the past six years: 'I
gave it all up for love, I've always been like that.'[5] They married the following year, and Beck
gained a stepfather who was committed to his art and proved to be a strong positive influence on
Beck. Years later, Beck would take pride in the fact that his family had such diverse cultural
background: 'Half my family is Mexican. Even now I feel more comfortable being around
Mexican people than anyone else; it's the way of life that was around me growing up. It's very
natural with them. I can feel out of place with other people, but not with them.'[6]

At the outset things were hard for the new couple, along with Channing and Beck. They
moved back near downtown and Pico/Union and Koreatown. It was a rough neighbourhood,
where Beck used to get chased by local villains. One night when Bibbe was home alone, a
gangster tried to break in through the front door with a crowbar. Later, during the L.A. riots the
whole neighbourhood got torched except for the houses on their block. The one-room
apartment in a Salvadoran neighbourhood, close to Koreatown; the lack of space meant that
Beck slept in a sleeping bag under the kitchen table sometimes. 'It was a little rough,' Beck
acknowledged wryly in later years. 'By the time I was a teenager, we were living on the edge of
things [...] It was an impoverished childhood, but it was rich in other ways [...] Everyone was
outside all the time, there were mariachi bands, animals running down the middle of the street.'[7]
To escape the claustrophobia at home, Beck would spend days in his local library. He used to
carry a slightly torn bag on his shoulder, with a dictionary and heavy library books weighing him
down, but lightening the load on his mind. Wandering around Los Angeles, on foot or by bus,
he navigated the shadeless crumbling sidewalks. Sometimes he would walk up in the hills ringing
the city, boots kicking up dust, looking down on the smog choked city below. With no television
in the house, he was forced to rely on his own imagination for entertainment, and in time would
develop the keen perception needed for seeing through façades. Beck touched on L.A.'s
distinctive landscape in an interview with *Details*: 'On most days, the way the light is diffused
through the smog creates this blinding whiteness. You get the feeling you're on an island – you
can't see for more than two blocks. Then when it rains or the wind blows, there's a revelation
and you can see all these giant mountains.'[8]

Beck's musical education was, if not self-taught, then self-motivated. He grew up listening to
Bibbe's eclectic LPs – film soundtracks by Henry Mancini, James Bond soundtracks by John
Barry and records by Brazilian bossa nova composer Antonio Carlos Jobim featured prominently.
In later years Beck would delve further into orchestration and arrangement, stirred by memories
of the structure underlying these early records. He took to tinkling on a piano at the home of one
of his mother's friends. He and his friend Mike Boito would play piano and keyboards, or even
improvise over muzak; Boito would later play on Beck's albums and tour with him before forming
part of the exceptional Silverlake band Brazzaville. The way that muzak transformed pop hits into
saccharine shadows of their former selves fascinated Beck. 'We'd play muzak stations,' he told *Spin*
in 1999, '"cause they were pop songs but they were all instrumental, so it was like karaoke. Me and
my friend Mike, we didn't know the lyrics, so we'd make up our own.'[9] 'Mike Boito was the
archetypal thirteen-year-old jazz piano prodigy,' Beck recalled. 'I used to play with him all the
time but I veered off into more of a Professor Longhair thing. I can hang a little Booker T if
necessary, but I prefer to keep with the blues.'[10]

But any hope of a future in music seemed far-fetched to the young Hansen. 'I always wanted
to play music as a kid, play guitar, but it just seemed impossible to me,' he told *Time* in 1997. 'You
would turn on the radio, and they'd be playing Huey Lewis or some super-produced 1980s
music. That music, it was so professional – there didn't seem any way to be able to do that.'[11] By

41

1985, the beefed-up rock music of Huey Lewis and the News, with its bogus inflated choruses stressing a false sense of superherodom, was in the ascendant. It was the perfect soundtrack for a soulless decade, notable only for rampant neo-conservatism, and a senile president with good speechwriters and a persona ready-made for television. School funding was cut and benefits for the young and elderly were slashed. Everywhere greed was extolled in the media, whether covertly or overtly, as the means to achieve a stake in the New America. Inevitably, the line between rich and poor widened: the rich made more money and the poor sank deeper into AIDS, crack, crime and homelessness. In the midst of this was the music, superproduced and big and empty, stripped of meaning or worth, paralleling the hollowness of a culture ever more beholden to a mass media powered by aggressive advertising.

In popular culture, being vacuous became art: hair was crimped, teased and blown out into ludicrous styles, or else shellacked into place with mousse specially tested on animals. Designer labels were hyped into conferring some status onto the bearer, with blue jeans, then sneakers becoming the new mark of belonging to a supposed elite existing nowhere other than on a Madison Avenue drawing board. Metal music took a mild transvestitism and cloaked it, bizarrely, in super machismo. That the excesses of the decade invite premature nostalgia is comical. In the light of this, Beck's 'Loser' was a perfectly valid ironic joke, puncturing the invincibility of the Eighties with self-deprecation.

One day, in 1985, fifteen-year-old Beck Hansen experienced a moment of musical epiphany via a form of music that had long become part of the very fabric of America. He was at a friend's house and was rummaging through his friend's father's albums, when he found an album with a close-up of an old man's wrinkled face on it. Beck laughed at the bizarre cover. The man on the cover was sweating intensely, with huge rheumy eyes radiating a soulful languor. It was a Sixties' re-issue of a Mississippi John Hurt LP, complete with psychedelic lettering designed to appeal to hippie students who had gotten hip to folk and country blues. Amazingly, it was still sealed in its original plastic wrapping, albeit covered with dust. Realizing that no one would miss it, Beck popped the album into his shoulder bag. 'I was fascinated by the cover – this old, kind, wrinkled face sweating,' he recalled over a decade later. 'It was the antithesis of something you'd see on some airbrushed Eighties album cover. I was attracted to that; I thought something was going on.'[12]

Beck took it home and put it on the beat-up record player in his room. A wave of dislocation hit from the first notes, a crusty recording from 1928 taken directly from old shellac 78s. Then he felt awe, wonder, puzzlement as he heard Hurt sing about that mean old Stagger Lee. 'I was going to return it, but I didn't,' he told *Spin* magazine in 1994. 'I loved the droning sound, the open tunings, the spare, beat-down tone. And his voice was so full. Hurt just went through so much shit, and it came across [as] really, really amazing.'[13] The effect was little short of a revelation, as Beck realized the power of music to communicate something genuine, something real. 'I was looking for something more honest in music. This was 1985, the height of the artificial synth pop, no-personality, drum-machine, zero-charisma music period – music influenced by greed and materialism. When I found the blues it was like, this is what I am.'[14]

A gifted musician, Mississippi John Hurt recorded just thirteen songs in Memphis during February and a cold New York December of 1928 for the Okeh label, only seven of which were issued, before drifting back into obscurity. A farmhand who was spotted by a talent scout, Hurt was already thirty-five when he boarded the train to New York. He spent most of his life working in the fields, and his folk blues were shaped by the reality of his mundane life, as hard and plain as callused hands on a plough. His slim output was revered by Greenwich Village folkies of the 1960s. Folk blues enthusiast Tom Hoskins sought him out in 1963 and Hurt was persuaded to play in public, becoming a full-time performer in his old age, but retaining a mastery of complex chords and highly stylized finger-picking that made him a favourite on the folk revival circuit. His charming manner and gentle voice made him famous in his twilight years. Hurt's repertoire was much the same as it had been in the late Twenties, when he would play purely for his own enjoyment or at friend's parties. Beck's interest in Hurt is particularly noteworthy in the light of the fact that Hurt played his own curious hybrid of the country-blues, bred largely in isolation and without any formal training whatsoever, allowing him to preserve and develop his idiosyncrasies. Hurt also played the guitar and phrased words in a way unusual for black bluesmen, his style more in line with white country; his favourite musician was reputed to be Jimmie Rodgers. Beck seems to have been attracted to bluesmen and country singers who strove, intentionally or not, to break the stylistic colour barrier, the crossover artists in a time when such a thing was almost heretical.

Jimmie Rodgers played his own variant of the black blues, what writer Nolan Portfield called 'the soul-weary but stoic lover'. Beck would in time play covers of Rodgers' 'Peach Pickin' Time In Georgia' and 'Waitin' On A Train', complete with the yodels that launched Rodgers to fame. Rodgers' yodels are a curious thing, a trait which some writers believe he adopted from blues singers doing a vaudeville take on Alpine yodels. It's impossible to pinpoint the origins of such matters, but it is evident that the exchange of musical ideas between black and white was a lot more open-ended than one might imagine, despite the strictures of institutionalized racism prevalent throughout the South. A reviewer at the time described Rodgers as 'a white man gone black'.[15] Like Beck, it appears Rodgers was hardly lifting from contemporary black music, but doing his own idiosyncratic blend of whatever struck him, whether black or white. It was fitting that he once cut sides with Louis Armstrong, who liked him tremendously, on trumpet.

Born in the depths of Mississippi in 1897, Rodgers worked on the railways for a period, always carrying his guitar; his cohorts nicknamed him the 'Singing Brakeman'. Until he developed tuberculosis, Rodgers travelled the length of the country, from the Delta to Chicago. It was likely that he had ample opportunity to play and learn blues tunes, rags, reels, spirituals, gospel songs, Latin tunes and Broadway hits; a rich cross section of American music of the time. Rodgers joined up with a minstrel show, of the sort that would wear blackface and perform pastiche blues at fairs and fetes. In 1927 he was discovered by Ralph Peer, who travelled the country for record label Victor, looking for new material and artists.

With the proliferation of gramophones and 78s, country and blues became more and more of a commercial proposition, and scouts like Peer were dispatched to find musicians for their 'hillbilly' and 'race' records. This marked the advent of modern country music, with Rodgers soon laying down the million-selling 'Blue Yodel'. Rodgers became immensely popular in the 1920s, and was a sharply dressed guy with a great smile and winning stage presence; seeing him in rare film reels sheds light on his great charisma. He would dress in a straw hat, well cut-suit and bow tie, distancing himself from the hillbilly image Victor wanted him to capitalize on, but the music was never far from his heart.

Amazingly, Peer found both Rodgers and the Carter Family in the same week. The Carter Family – Alvin Pleasant Carter, his wife Sara and her cousin Maybelle – auditioned for Peer in Asheville, Virginia on the recommendation of the local Victor records dealer. He had heard Sara's high, keening voice that perfectly captured the isolation and beauty of the hills, a music descended from Scottish border ballads hundreds of years old, a distillation of church hymns and sentimental songs distributed on old sheet music. 'As soon as I heard Sara's voice, that was it,' Peer remembered years later, 'I knew it was going to be wonderful.'[16] By their second session, the Carter Family, with A.P. playing bass lines on his Martin guitar, Sara playing the autoharp and

43

Maybelle playing crisp, clear lines on her Gibson, was in fine fettle. They laid down the basic core of country music, the first instalments in a serialized version of the canon that extends to this day: 'Weeping Willow', hauntingly beautiful, 'Keep On The Sunny Side' and 'Anchored In Love', which displayed Sara's unusual prowess on both guitar and vocals to its fullest. They closed the session with their quintessential tune, 'Wildwood Flower'.

As Beck began searching for more traditional folk and blues music, he began finding treasures like these left and right. There were enough friends of the family who had been into folk in the Sixties to ensure a steady stream of nuggets. Beck quickly got together a small but impressive collection of scuffed LPs by the Carter Family, Jimmy Rodgers, Fred McDowell and Sleepy John Estes. He was particularly drawn to country blues and started thumbing through the library records looking for obscurities by Mance Lipscomb, Furry Lewis and Leadbelly. Beck was intrigued by songs like 'Stagolee' and 'John Hardy', stories of murderers and outlaws, told and retold in dozens of ways. John Hardy was a desperate little man who murdered another man over a twenty-five cent gambling stake and was hung in 1894, unwittingly becoming immortalized in song for his deed. Likewise, Stagger Lee (a.k.a. Stag-o-Lee, Stagolee and a host of variants), who murdered Billy Lyons in a gambling dispute in a St. Louis barroom at the turn of the century.

Beck listened in wonderment to people such as Mance Lipscomb, the Texas guitarist and singer who not only played blues but had memorized over 350 songs for whatever occasion he might be called on to play at, ranging from ballads to rags. Lipscomb was born in the closing days of the 19th century, in Brazos County, Texas. His career was farming, and music was initially just a sideline. His trade ultimately became his songs, though, and he produced a staggering quantity during his lifetime. Like many songwriters of that era, Lipscomb wrote in a variety of genres. The divisions between blues, folk, country, ballads and boogies was ephemeral at best, echoing the Texas rivers that reached their final destination regardless of their meandering course. Lipscomb played at tar paper shacks and beer halls in Navasota, Texas for well over half a century before being discovered. (Funny that one can produce a lifetime of music and still be 'discovered' way down the line.) He eventually became a fixture on the folk circuit and his 'Blues In G' was recorded at the 1965 Newport Folk Festival, the same event at which an electrified Bob Dylan nearly got his wires cut by overzealous folk purists.

One striking feature of the country blues is its pacing: songs that go on for seven to ten minutes at a stretch, and the relative lack of chordal progression produces an almost meditative effect on the listener. It's difficult to discern what exactly is being said, and it feels like music existing outside of the modern world, in a time when listeners would let it wash over them rather than have it pre-packaged and served up as a finished product. That it was a music of transcendence from a world of very limited opportunities shines through.

Beck got hold of a Son House album and was amazed at how forceful his delivery was. Born Eddie James House in Lyon, Mississippi, Son House grew up in Tallulah, Louisiana. He took off to New Orleans, where he shined shoes, including Louis Armstrong's. Son's father played tuba in a brass band so waltzes were in the background of his music somewhere, but he hated them, preferring the four-part harmonies of church music. Inspired by the slide guitar just beginning to become widely popular in the Delta, House began playing at the age of twenty-six. Son House is unique among the bluesmen for his sense of drama, a mastery of delivery that is shocking to see, in film clips from his 're-discovery' in the Sixties. He grits his teeth, leans back and not so much sings as unleashes the blues, his hand restless across the strings of a National, with slide shivering up and down the neck; his guitar playing is staggering for both its rawness and its conciseness. House only recorded ten sides for Paramount in 1930 before fading off the map of popular culture until he began playing again in the Sixties. One of the most indestructible of bluesmen, he lived into his eighties. Beck has covered his 'John the Revelator' and ' (Don't You Mind) People Grinnin' In Your Face' throughout his career, in the acoustic sections of his concerts or, memorably, in two radio sessions. Like 'One Foot In The Grave', these songs form the bedrock of his musical roots, songs with unshakable conviction.

Another favourite of Beck's was Nehemiah 'Skip' James, the taciturn country blues author of 'Jesus Is A Mighty Good Leader', which Beck would reinterpret on *One Foot In The Grave*. Beck also did a splendid cover of James' 'Devil Got My Woman', one of the bleakest blues ever written. James had begun playing songs he heard amongst the current of folk tunes that ran through the Delta, neither clearly white or black, but often hillbilly tunes turned blues or the other way around. An example was 'Drunken Spree', which the young James heard a fiddler named Green McCloud playing, and which inspired him to pick up a guitar, tune it to A, and strum it out on his first session. In his superb biography, Stephen Calt noted that James learned an open E minor tuning from some black soldiers from the Bahamas, and began writing the bulk of his own tunes in this weird, chiming key.

'Devil Got My Woman', the true life story of his young wife running off with his best friend, is appropriately bitter and devastating. 'Hard Time Killing Floor Blues' is another classic blues tune, reinterpreted later by Jimi Hendrix in a version that perfectly evokes the knife-on-steel-strings slide and alienation of James' original. '22-20 Blues', written and performed in one fell swoop, features James playing jagged, angular piano, a remarkable sound, with James not so much playing as stabbing and gliding over the keys. Unable to launch a successful career when the Depression hit in the Thirties, James became a minister. It is hard to imagine someone less suited to preach the good book than the mealy-mouthed and mean James, but if the passion he channelled into his music is any indication, he was probably able to carry it off without too much effort. One of the bluesmen sought out by folk researchers in the Sixties, James played the new folk blues circuit but played the songs of his youth with an offhanded disdain. It was too little too late.

Above all, Beck was hooked on Mississippi John Hurt, and swiftly began pounding out rudimentary blues scales and singing in a nasal, Woody Guthrie-like voice. The deep, articulate cantor-like voice that would give his white boy blues its own distinct flavour would come later. Beck's world soon shrunk to a room at home full of Delta blues LPs scrounged from the library or bought cheap in bargain bins. Charley Patton and Blind Willie Johnson soon augmented Mississippi John Hurt. Woody Guthrie followed soon after, broadening the young Beck's audio palette to include folk and traditional country and western. For contemporary music, he would tune into local college station KXLU, listening to the indie rock and scattered oddities they played at night.

He worked his way studiously through the bins at the libraries, surprised that he was the only one interested in the folk and country and blues albums. He'd take home mint copies of Leadbelly, Washington Phillips and Woody Guthrie's *Dustbowl Ballads* that he'd learn note for note, one ear close to the shitty Sears turntable speakers. He would hunt down grizzled blues freaks with drinking problems and skin ailments, who would tell him about Blind Lemon Jefferson and how he had asked that his grave be kept clean. Blind Blake, Blind Willie Johnson and Blind Lemon Jefferson – amidst all that sightlessness was this deep resonant music that defied two-dollar record player needles, the screaming downstairs or the noise from the kitchen and TV in the living room. It was an escape route, but also a world which seemed to jibe with Beck's soul. 'Leadbelly, the most powerful 12-string player,' he marvelled. 'You can't copy his music, you can't even play it, because it's coming from hands that are three times bigger than

45

normal hands.'[17] (In truth Beck, although slight in height, possessed large hands of his own, perfect for fingering chords stretched across the fretboard that other people would find painful.)

Leadbelly began his career with a jail sentence for murder, it was served out in the notorious Angola penitentiary in Louisiana, a hellish plantation of misery, with chain gangs broiling in the hot sun, breaking rocks in striped pyjamas. It was there that folklorists John and Alan Lomax recorded Leadbelly in 1933 for their series of music for the Library of Congress. With a powerful voice and superb 12-string technique, Leadbelly had a vast repertoire of songs he'd written, so many of which went on to become standards. Leadbelly would perform 'Goodnight Irene' and 'The Midnight Special' for guards and prisoners, indicating he had achieved full proficiency by the time the Lomaxes found him. The Lomaxes helped him gain his release and Leadbelly is one of the few musicians mentioned here to sustain a profitable career right up until his death in 1949.

Slide guitar, in which anything from a knife blade to a broken beer bottle neck is used to glide, slur and accentuate notes on a guitar, came from an unlikely source. In *Country: The Twisted Roots of Rock and Roll*, Nick Tosches traces the origins of slide to Hawaii, where a student in Oahu slid a comb across the strings of a guitar in 1894 and never stopped. By 1903, blues pioneer W.C. Handy saw someone on a street corner doing the same thing with a knife blade. One of the earliest recorded slide blues was the 1927 'Jack O'Diamond Blues' by Blind Lemon Jefferson. Tosches, with his usual commendable lack of delicacy, described Jefferson as 'a grotesque creature who cared for nothing but whiskey and sex.'[18] The earliest country song to use a variant of slide, Frank Hutchinson's 'Worried Blues', was recorded a scant few months later, showing how progressions ran neck and neck, with little importance placed on the colour bar. Stylistically similar, the main difference was Hutchinson played his guitar flat on his lap, in the Hawaiian style as opposed to Jefferson holding his upright in the familiar Spanish mode. Jefferson's emphasis lay more in singing, with his rhythm occasionally erratic, and an oddly compelling counterpoint to his vocals the majority of the time.

The warmth of the music gave Beck the first inkling that playing music was possible, that it was something someone like him, an impoverished average kid, could play. In 1998 he observed to MTV, 'Most rock music has roots in that music [but] a lot of the punk and late Seventies, Eighties rock was a reaction against the hippie re-interpretation of the blues and folk so a lot of it was bastardized. But if you go back to Leadbelly or Son House, they still rock. I found a beautiful strangeness in a lot of that music.'[19] He found a wretched guitar that the family cat had actually vomited a hairball into. It was missing several strings and was woefully out of tune, but Beck had found the tool that would transcend him from his mundane realities. One of the first songs he taught himself, picking out the chords with difficulty, was the country classic 'John Hardy'. The complexity of the country blues, with its rolls and finger-picking, quickly became apparent. But Beck was patient, and after work he would spend hours behind closed doors working it out. 'I'd never heard anything like that,' he told *Rolling Stone*. 'This wasn't some hippie guy finger picking in the 1970s, singing about rainbows. This was the real stuff. I stopped everything for six months and was in my room finger-picking until I got it right.'[20] His enthusiasm for the blues and country, and his almost wilful ignorance of more recent popular music, made for some curious blind spots in Beck's musical knowledge: 'I'm pretty ignorant of Seventies and Eighties music, a friend of mine or my girlfriend will start singing and they're expecting me to chime in at any time, and I've never heard the song.'[21]

His early nylon-strung instrument served for his apprenticeship, but in due course Beck managed to save up enough cash to get himself an old Gibson, identical to the model that Woody Guthrie played. 'It didn't sound good when I tried to play a pop song – it sounded good when I tried to play a folk song, so I got into that kind of music. I wasn't conscious of this at the time, of course, but in retrospect I realize that I gravitated towards music that was a relic from another time, music that had substance, whereas everything else around me was phoney.'[22] One great inspiration was folk group Koerner, Ray and Glover, regarded by many as the punks of the folk scene. Both Beck and his brother Channing were particularly impressed by the sheer abandon with which they made music, the way they put real rock and roll energy into their folk: 'A lot of the music from that period was very respectful, almost too tasteful and quaint. They were just so raucous. That really appealed to me at the time. They were these kids playing with abandon, and they played really well. They made no apologies, whereas everyone else in that scene seemed apologetic.'[23] Until his early twenties, country and delta blues absorbed Beck, and formed the backbone of his musical education. Moreover, that old and definitively American working-class music was the key for Beck's later discovery of hip-hop. 'I was totally lost in that music [...] It's how I learned to play the guitar. Lots of ragtime, reels, spirituals and Professor Longhair and Dr John. That was my world growing up.'[24]

Dr John and his mentor Professor Longhair epitomized the faded grandeur and *laissez-faire* attitude of New Orleans, the flavour of the city at the end of the Mississippi River, a musical gumbo stew of an inordinate number of rich flavours. Beck's 'O Maria' on *Mutations* displays the New Orleans influence to full effect, with its distinctive after-the-beat accent and blaring New Orleans horns echoing the funeral procession marches of the Crescent City. The remnants of the French *bon temps* music, the spice of the Caribbean, the meat of the blues and the cauldron of country all play a prominent role in making the sound of a city that is both terminus and point of entry. In later years Beck would increasingly bring horns into his music, recruiting a saxophonist, David Ralickie, and trumpet player, childhood friend David Brown, and taking them on tour, dubbing them the Brass Menagerie. The name is a play on 'Glass Menagerie', the name of the glass animals which Tennessee Williams' heroine Laura, a shy and crippled girl, collected in the play of the same name, evoking that mysterious and insular world that curves like a river around Beck's music. It was a sample from a cover of Dr John's 'I Walk on Guided Splinters' by Johnny Jenkins on the 1970 album *Ton Ton Macoute!* that would give 'Loser' its louche air.*

The New Orleans sound is a distillation of a confluence of different influences, not least of which was the African music brought to the docks by slave ships in the 17th, 18th and 19th centuries. Here was the last point where pure strains of African music were heard before tribal identity was shattered by the maelstrom of slavery. Many slaves could understand their counterparts from other African tribes even less than they could their English-speaking masters. But their music survived as their sole link to the Old World, and slaves quickly began to reassemble the fragments of their culture via new instruments, including fiddles, on which black musicians began evincing such talent that their masters would have them play at their parties in starched uniforms and powdered wigs. African-Americans brought the jangling plucked sonorities of the banjo to America, an instrument with roots deep in Afro culture.

The very essence of the New Orleans stew is culled from those old-time drummers in Congo Square, the marking point of the black diaspora, where all African cultures were disassembled and had to find new means of reassembly, including musically. Using Western instruments, they evolved a scale of their own and introduced the soul-satisfying, gut-wrenching blue note – two misplaced notes in a correct European scale, but the very essence of black music. The blue notes hearken back to something essential in music that has been nearly lost – the fact that our Western

---

* Though the sample is listed in *Mellow Gold*'s credits, and it sounds like it's all over 'Loser', Beck maintains it wasn't a sample of Dr John at all.

scale squeezes all the true tones into an even spectrum that doesn't need to be re-tweaked every time one changes octaves.

African music is commentary on commentary, perpetual and non-linear, akin to the way West African conversations circle in on a point rather than shoot right to the heart of the matter, which is considered rude and senseless. They don't call the talking drum of the Yoruba tribe a talking drum for no good reason: in their culture, rhythm is not only a means of communication but a vital connection to culture, tribal identity and society.

The true tonalities of so-called primitive music, audible in Bulgarian field songs or Andean folk or Pygmy chants, have an emotional power that is well nigh devastating. What stroked the ear as atonal at first becomes, in time, more pleasing and natural feeling. It permeates Appalachian music and everything from sea shanties to the music of the Gullah on the islands off the coast of South Carolina. Harry Partch, an American composer of this century, spent a lifetime building instruments that could reflect that sweeping spectrum of 'just intonation' – handmade instruments with a forty-three-note micro-tonal scale. Black music has instead opted for the simple bending of two notes to plug us back into that lost and true music. It is almost a bittersweet memory of the eternally splintered music of Africa, a vestigial remnant of a lost world, lost culture, lost identity.

Many cultures choose to use a five-note, pentatonic scale, voiding out the two semi-sour notes that complete our Western chromatic scale. There is a meditative quality in the pentatonic scale. In Bali, for example, the pentatonic scale is played up and down through the octaves, perceptually ascending and falling like tropical rain on a tin roof. Likewise, the Scottish and Irish ballads brought over by poor white immigrants to the New World remained almost intact in far mountain hamlets. These are still living traces of a musical tradition culled from a forgotten past that persist to this day, making for a fascinating vision of a vanished past. Delving into this music, Beck admits, 'is escapist in a way, which is dangerous, which is how I eventually embraced a lot of other music, but there is this need, this ache to have something a little more real, a little more human. Just the way it sounds, the way it feels a little more time-worn, just like an old car is nicer to drive than some new factory-fresh Hyundai. It's got character in that way, it's easy, because the character's all there for you. There's something sickening about that. Ultimately people wouldn't be doing that if there wasn't a loss in substance of things.' [25]

'Funk', as it was envisaged by the black American performers of the Sixties and Seventies, meant letting your hair out. It meant celebrating all the things that traditionally held black people back from making it the white world. It was an embracing of their culture rather than a denial of it, and as such it was revolutionary. The loud clothes, conversation and vibrancy that Afro-Americans are stereotyped for became a badge of pride rather than a blot. Afro hairdos were cultivated into huge symbols of Afro-centricism, witness Sixties radical Angela Davis' monumental 'fro from that time. In music, everyone from Jelly Roll Morton to the Bar-Keys to Funkadelic took all the gut-bucket, southern fried, loose, flared bell bottoms and down-home humour, loud laughter, absurdity and beauty and pathos of the black experience in America and turned it into an art form.

Beck's white boy funk draws on similar impulses, taking all the odd bits that make him unique and amplifying them. Beck's closest British counterpart would be Jarvis Cocker of Pulp, who once memorably stated, 'If you have big feet, wear big shoes'. The crux of it all is to make your weaknesses into your strengths, and thereby to discover, paradoxically, that your 'weaknesses' were your strengths all along, creating a free and untrammelled flow of originality.

Funk and R&B became deeply entrenched in Beck's urban folk. 'It comes from being eleven years old on a Saturday night hanging out on Hollywood Boulevard with all the break dancers [...] That music's everywhere. It's urban music. I grew up around downtown Los Angeles, so that's the music you heard.'[26] Beck, his younger brother Channing and sundry friends would risk getting beaten up to attend block parties in East Los Angeles where rap music blasted out of makeshift speakers – two turntables and a microphone to rock the joint – and call and response bounced from MC to audience. Aged eleven or twelve, they would taperecord the MCs rapping over the DJs' beats, then go home and imitate them. Years later Beck would listen to these tapes for inspiration, and a reaffirmation of that rush he felt then.

The heart and soul of funk was the second line, what Dr John remembers in his autobiography as 'a syncopated percussion beat in 2/4 with double-time accents that can be played a million different ways.'[27] Descended from New Orleans' sombre then joyous funeral marches, the second line would break down as dancers and percussionists marched down the hot and humid streets of the Third Ward, priming themselves for Mardi Gras.

Part of Beck's intense identification with the blues and country was that they seemed like realistic role models, instead of the amped-up rock heroes of the day. 'I identified with them because they just said something to me. I was a small, skinny guy. If I was a strapping handsome brute then I would identify with something else. You tend to be attracted to the things you can relate to, people who were outsiders. Real working-class people respected Woody Guthrie, he was an outcast to the corporate music industry in America, and that was very rare at that time. He was very brave: he took chances. You don't see many brave people any more in music.'[28] With an insatiable appetite for the raw and rustic roots of any music, Beck forsook the Fifties and Sixties folk stylings of Pete Seeger and Woody Guthrie's son Arlo, gravitating instead towards the period in folk music from the Twenties and Thirties: 'they held melody paramount. People often ask me if I'm influenced by Dylan and the Stones, and I say, well, I truly am not. I was into the people that influenced those Sixties guys: Woody Guthrie, Blind Lemon Jefferson, Mississippi Fred McDowell. Folk and blues.'[29] Dust bowl ballads probably meant more to a scuffling Beck than Arlo's tales of drug smuggling or Seeger's sometimes saccharine songs, not to mention the inflated bombast of Eighties pop music: 'Hearing Woody Guthrie, it's like "Oh, that's guitar." He's just talking. He's just a person.'[30]

Woody Guthrie's *Bound For Glory* should be assigned reading in every American high school, but it will never happen. The book expertly reveals the real America, a strange place of dreams made and unmade constantly, and the vastness of the country with its thousands of contradictions and wandering minds. Guthrie is believed to have written over a thousand songs in a career tragically cut short by Huntington's chorea, a nerve debilitating disease that crippled his body and impaired his speech. Though Guthrie was essentially a one-man troubadour, he also played in bluegrass bands and folk combos and jammed and recorded with everyone from Leadbelly to Sonny Terry. But there was more to Guthrie than just the social and political commentator: '[he] wrote just as many personal things, sexual material, songs about UFOs,' Beck observed. 'He wasn't just the Okie by the side of the road, or John Steinbeck's roadside sage. Woody Guthrie was aware of certain cultural phenomenon beyond the time we place him in.'[31] Beck later paid tribute with his 'Woody Guthrie Song', commenting, 'Guthrie was bringing out some honest human natural communication in a time when a lot of that was suppressed.'[32]

Beck, like Bob Dylan before him, became fixated with Guthrie and entertained thoughts of fleeing to the imagined folk mecca of New York City. Also in common with Dylan, Beck was Jewish, a race more often than not outsiders to every American dream; author Eric Weisbard writes about creative Jews 'nurturing fantasy universes as a way of escaping the alienation of being a stranger in a strange land.'[33] The identification with renegade Guthrie, a card-carrying Communist in the worst days of McCarthyism, a hobo in the Depression, a mystic rider of the rails, held great cachet with both Dylan and Beck in their youth. Yet Guthrie's vagabond playing

49

and travelling seemed the province of myth, not something a lower-working-class kid from Los Angeles could pursue. And in a country where blues legend Muddy Waters was working as a house painter at the end of the 1970s, Beck was probably right. Beck's dreary day jobs would provide him plenty of fodder for his later songs, but the sheer monotony of driving a forklift at a warehouse in South Central, or working moving furniture paled next to romantic visions of Woody Guthrie hobo train riding and composing restlessly rambling blues epics.

Through Guthrie's albums on Smithsonian-Folkways, Beck also got his first exposure to another of his central influences, Sonny Terry. Born Saunders Tedell in North Carolina, Sonny Terry was almost totally blind. He spent his early years playing on street corners and achieved great fluency on harp, as well as a singing style that was so visceral he soon found himself playing with everyone from Woody Guthrie to Blind Boy Fuller. Terry sung a capella falsettos, including a standout 'Mountain Blues' at the 1938 'Spirituals to Swing' concert held at Carnegie Hall, but it was for his harmonica skills that he is best remembered. Terry's playing is all over Woody Guthrie's albums, as well as those of everyone from the Reverend Gary Davis to Leadbelly. He was a master of the harp, blowing harmonica solos that seemed to be the purest expression of soul, just breath exhaled into notes. Together with his partner, guitarist Brownie McGhee, Terry played all over America from 1939 onwards. The duo would play ramshackle Los Angeles clubs in the 1950s which, like a drumstick on the chitlin circuit, were the last remnants of the once vital Central Avenue jazz and R&B scene. The stamping foot of Sonny Terry and the metronomic tapping shoe of John Lee Hooker made a strong impression on the young Beck: 'Before I had a drum machine I had my foot. I would just stomp the thing.'[34]

Though he didn't travel the country as an outlaw musician, Beck lived through his teenage years in Hollywood as something of an outsider. He was one of the two white teenagers (the other being his brother) in a neighbourhood which resounded to the sounds of ranchera music and hip-hop, and as a result felt little in common with the white culture of America's suburbs. By the same token, he couldn't fit in with the Salvadorian or Korean gangs in the area: 'to them I was the *güero*, the weird white kid.'[35] Their poverty meant that he couldn't have a Bar Mitzvah as a child, though he attended Hebrew classes for some time and enjoyed Passover, not only because it was his first experience of getting drunk but also because Bibbe's non-Jewish friends would turn up, and brought a party atmosphere along with them. He later used a Passover prayer in his 'Little Drum Machine Boy' jam, a Hanukkah interpretation of surely the most vile of all Christmas songs, 'The Little Drummer Boy'. Despite the social misery around him, and its attendant degradation, Beck felt a genuine communal spirit existed in the ghetto. 'A lot of drugs, a lot of refugees from the Central American wars. It wasn't the safest place, but it was definitely a community. I remember walking to the bus in the morning to go to school and there'd be roosters and chickens running through the street and mariachis passed out on the sidewalk. There was an anarchy there in the neighbourhood, but still, it was a neighbourhood. It's east of South Central.'[36]

Hip-hop wasn't played so much as performed, the antithesis of the head-nodding, arms-folded indie rock shows. Call and response, extending back to Africa, through the fields and church, is a vital ingredient in the funk stew. Black music thrives on communication between audience and performer – it's the magic element – whereas in the classical European tradition, music is passively observed. It's almost joy by proxy, with the musician reaching rapture and the listener vicariously thrilling to that rapture. Small wonder that Beck's ears were caught by hip-hop.

In the very early Eighties, rap was an entirely novel sound, fusing sampled beats of R&B with cut-up scratches and samples. Sound was layered, and a re-investigation of black American music was carried out by the DJs working their way through the strata like archaeologists, uncovering tracks by Parliament–Funkadelic, James Brown, Sly Stone, Bobby Byrd and myriad less well-known talents. This dissection and reassembly of the heart source of black rhythm was an invisible procedure to most white ears, unschooled as they were in the source material. It was a radical de- and re-construction of music, and now stands as one of the most important developments in modern music. The eclectic roots of rap are almost forgotten today, when hip-hop has become ever more stagnant and motionless, the beats staccato and nightmarish, a music of warfare and revenge. But the earliest DJs threw anything that had a good breakbeat into the mix, and that included albums by German electronic pioneers Kraftwerk, or some long rhythmic workout on an English prog rock album. Supplanting the musician by the record, hip-hop sought to collage found rhythms into-one-tone poem of continuous motion.

In the late Seventies Afrika Bambaataa, a young Bronx DJ, gradually became mesmerized by Kraftwerk's records. From 1969 on, Kraftwerk sought to make folk music that reflected their industrial hometown of Düsseldorf, West Germany. Their epochal 1974 track 'Autobahn', a 22-minute paean to an automobile drive on the German autobahn expressway, broke through internationally on a much larger scale than any German group had ever done before, charting high in both America and Britain. In 1982, Bambaataa and producer Arthur Baker fused the bass line from Kraftwerk's 'Numbers' with the melody from 'Trans-Europe Express', over which a vocoded Bambaataa rapped about a 'Planet Rock', emphasizing its diversity and genre-dissolving genesis. In time, it will probably be remembered as one of the most revolutionary records, alongside the early singles of the Beatles or Elvis.

Before rap, funk's intersection with technology began in the early 1970s, accelerating with Stevie Wonder's fascination with electronic synthesizers. Squirreling Moog phrases began to resound briefly throughout the nascent funk, and twenty years later would be much sampled and distorted to lay the background for California's G-Funk sound. Bernie Worrell, the conservatory-trained keyboardist for Parliament–Funkadelic also deserves much credit, developing on the work of Herbie Hancock's Headhunters and Billy Preston, banging out future funk on mini Moogs and clavinets.

It only lasted for a short while, and yet amidst the bleak recession and politically and emotionally corrupt era of Watergate, ghetto deterioration and emotional downturn, a fascination with technology became part of the music of Black America. The music of Black America always seems to delve into electronics in the face of economic stagnation, as if trying to establish a link, however tenuous, to an idealized future. Space is the ultimate utopia, in an extreme extrapolation of Marcus Garvey's visions of repatriating the New World's black masses to the mother continent. By the Seventies, George Clinton of Parliament–Funkadelic was building on space jazz bandleader Sun Ra's 'Space is the Place' to envision a Mothership taking blacks to the cosmos.

By 1982, electro emerged, characterized by its mechanical beats, at a time when society was turning to the aggressive materialism of Reaganomics in the face of economic recession. Electro was a short but very potent period of experimentation, and its influence reverberates strongly today in everything from the future funk of Beck's *Midnite Vultures* through to the edges of R&B and techno. The latter deserves special mention, because the form of mechanized, facsimile Philadelphia soul Gamble & Huff-inspired dance music pioneered in Chicago and later refined in Detroit by technologically inventive black youths, became electro's strongest progression; a point of passage to the future. In Detroit techno pioneer Derrick May's oft-cited words, techno was the sound of Kraftwerk and P–Funk in an lift. It was no coincidence that electro group Warp 9's 'Light Years Away' intones the vocoded phrase 'Space is the place for the human race' like a mantra. Hip-hop, the slick commercial R&B of black urban radio and electro have all figured significantly in Beck's sonic world. On *Midnite Vultures*, Beck uses electro as a central reference point, seeing it perhaps as the last point when technology and soul were not at odds. And also, a point in popular culture at which the colour bar and genre divisions were weakest since the beginning of rock and roll in the 1950s. In late 1999 he told the *Boston Phoenix*, 'Coming from folk music and traditional music, the song is ingrained, the idea of the American song with melody and structure. That's just part of me. But my musical taste reflects all these different sounds and ideas that I want to fit into that structure. I guess I've always liked the periods where music was getting experimental but it still was melodic, it still had a structure and was enjoyable. Like the mid-Sixties and then the early Eighties, where punk was turning into new wave and it also had elements of funk and dance music in it, and the New York bands were getting into hip-hop.'[37]

In lieu of being able to rocket into space, technology became the vessel to reach a bright new cosmos on Earth. The earliest techno artists such as Juan Atkins, May and Kevin Saunderson envisioned a technologically based escape from the bleak ghettos of Detroit. The Motor City had been laid waste, a virtual ghost town save for its forgotten black inhabitants who hadn't been able to join the flight of middle-class white workers from the inner city centre after the devastating 1967 race riots and the closure of the General Motors plant in the Seventies. They were influenced by future theorists like Marshall McLuhan and, in particular, Alvin Toffller, whose epochal 1971 book *Future Shock* spoke of 'techno-rebels' agitating for change at the edge of evolving technologies.

To the casual listener, electro, Kraftwerk and Detroit techno might all sound cold and sterile, but its creators denied this. 'Our music has to do with emotions. Technology and emotion can unite the hands,' Ralf Hutter of Kraftwerk said in 1991. Hutter and long-time collaborator Florian Schneider always stressed the notion of their music as folk music, reflecting the industrial surroundings in which they lived. Atkins spoke of techno music as 'dream music', something that would transport the listener from the gritty reality of their day-to-day lives in the freezing cold and barren wastes of urban Detroit. It comes as no surprise that Detroit techno took hold with great force in 1989–90 in places such as Manchester and Liverpool, English mirror-images of Detroit, with rusted hulks of once prosperous industries and abandoned buildings all around. In Los Angeles and Miami, electro played a key role as catalyst for N.W.A.'s insistent rhythm backings as well as Luke Skywalker's low end maximized Miami bass sound.

Minimalism was the order of the day, with sparse and cold electronic backings topped with soulful melodic washes of sound. Again, the influences ran the gamut, from Devo's mechanical 'Whip It' to reconfigured versions of Gil Scott Heron's prototype raps or Curtis Mayfield's own futuristic funk. The astonishing 'Jam On It' by Newcleus (the equal of any original by Kraftwerk in its spare and melodic, bass-heavy and rain sample-clad majesty) set the mode. The Düsseldorf influence provided the creative catalyst that helped electro's soul synthesis reach critical mass, with Kraftwerk's 'Tour De France' featured prominently in the film *Breakdance*. When Kraftwerk toured the United States, at the height of 'Tour de France''s popularity, they played an inner city club in Detroit and almost started a riot when they opened with the track because the audience was so primed for them to drop their beats.

Jamaican toasts and boasts, declaimed by DJs (who actually talked, like U-Roy) over the dub plates of MCs (who played the music and ran the sound systems) were also a key element in the evolution of rap and hip-hop. DJ Kool Herc, the legendary Bronx DJ, originally from Jamaica, was familiar with these forms. In the tradition of the dub scientists and roving sound systems, he helped fashion a new sound, one comprising the breakbeats – the rhythmic interludes in soul and funk records. Herc played the breaks over and over again, scratched from vinyl to create sequences of hard, almost static rhythm, ideal for repetitive motion and then free style dance moves under-girded by hard beats. The MCs shaped their phrasing with a similar approach, long soliloquies of rhyming words and lyrics, in mantra-like hard rhyming built to match the new sound.

In 1981, Tom Silverman of New York label Tommy Boy took Afrika Bambaataa to New York City's In The Red studio to cut a tape of his live DJ workouts. Afrika Bambaataa and Soulsonic Force debuted with 'Jazzy Sensation' in 1981 before dropping their magnum opus, 'Planet Rock' in 1982, followed soon after by 'Looking For The Perfect Beat'. To gauge the impact these records had in the summer of 1982, it's worth stating that there was nowhere in New York City where faint echoes of 'Planet Rock' could not be heard; its precise electronic bass rebounded through the streets in that hot summer. 'Planet Rock's producer was Arthur Baker, and his production style impacted heavily on latter-day acolytes such as the English band New Order.*

Bambaataa and Arthur Baker gave hip-hop one of its greatest gifts, the Roland 808 drum machine, with its sparse, almost hollowly clinical beats. Along with the Roland 909 bass line generator, the 808 became the mainstay which has survived to this day. Bambaataa would continue seeking out fusions of his eclectic influences and tastes, cutting tracks in 1984 with both soul magus James Brown and John Lydon, the front man for PiL (itself influenced heavily by dub and funk) and one-time singer and lyricist for the Sex Pistols.

Breakdancing and B-boy culture demanded strict rhythms over which to freestyle, both in their raps and in their dances. Electro became the point of departure for the early rap scene, a rapid acceleration into a future where Technics turntables, samplers, keyboards, raps and breakdancing would bring release. The skeletal music, as minimalist as Terry Riley, today sounds both somewhat quaint and compelling at the same time. 'Al Naafiysh' by Hashim is a good example, a very bare music dotted with punctuations of soul. In Los Angeles the Egyptian Lover was laying down impressive electro tracks.

In New York, there was a very unusual convergence of musical threads for a short while. Tom Tom Club (the rhythm section of Talking Heads) and white downtown New York no-wave minimal funk band Liquid Liquid, Devo and Eddy Grant, and above water some of the worst offences of all time, from Air Supply to Spandau Ballet. Great music under the surface, though, with rap and the Clash colliding; black kids danced to 'Rock The Casbah' and white kids danced to rap at the Roxy. 'There's no way you can come up with a song that's as good as 'Genius Of Love' by Tom Tom Club', Beck told *Select* in 1999. 'There's a small element of Eighties music I like, but most of it I despise. I like to take the impact of those Eighties sounds and strip them of any kind of fluff or glossiness.'[38]

From 1976 to 1987, the eclectic and inventive DJ Larry Levan at the Paradise Garage, played minimalist funk by German synth-guitar player Manuel Gottsching, Third World, Chaka Khan and Grace Jones. Herbie Hancock, one of the most experimental of all jazz greats, unleashed the mighty 'Rockit' in 1983, replete with machine rhythms banged out on a Fairlight sampler keyboard, mini Moog and vocoder, with downtown avant-garde producer Bill Laswell laying down phat bass lines. To top it off, Grandmixer DST (so called because he lived on Delaney Street in Greenwich Village) layered inspired scratches and turntable wizardry over the track. Funk magus George Clinton released 'Atomic Dog', a purely electronic funk track whose influence can be felt all over Beck's *Midnite Vultures*.

'White Lines (Don't Do It)' by Grandmaster Flash & Melle Mel was a masterpiece, a song that hasn't dated a bit, still sounding as fresh and radical as the day it was made. It took the melody from 'Caverns', a seminal track by Liquid Liquid, and turned it into a polemic on the then new cocaine epidemic. This record was followed shortly after by 'The Message', an epic decrying the

53

---

* New Order was the phoenix rising from the ashes of the great Manchester band Joy Division. Joy Division epitomized the despair of cities crushed by extreme capitalism. One reviewer aptly wrote, 'in Joy Division's music there is no warmth, only precision.'

social ills in the 1980s over a glittering wash of analogue synths and static beats. Beck, then twelve, used to ride to school on public transport: 'There'd be some kids in the back who got on way down on Vermont in South Central and they'd have their boombox blasting [Grandmaster Flash's] 'The Message.' Then, coming up through Wilshire, some white girls would get on. Then, you get up to Hollywood and some freaks would get on. and soon everybody on the bus would be singing the lines, doing the moves. It was great.'[39] The cross-pollination between black and white, between different countries, was at its peak. 'Magic's Wand' by Whodini, was co-written and produced by British synth-pop wizard Thomas Dolby. Soon New Order would be travelling to New York to get Arthur Baker to produce their million-selling 12 inch 'Blue Monday'. 'In The Bottle' by C.O.D. was an electro update on 'The Bottle' a classic track by the radical Gil Scott-Heron who, like the Last Poets, has been rapping since the late 1960s. 'The Adventures Of Grandmaster Flash On The Wheels Of Steel' by Grandmaster Flash And The Furious Five, a somewhat crude turntable cut-up of Chic, Blondie, Queen, Sugarhill Gang, Furious Five and Spoonie Gee, was like a photograph of the eclectic roots of turntablism being turned out at the moment of its genesis.

However, electro was all over by 1984. The new black urban music bifurcated radically, with two tangents that would not meet again until more recently, with the advent of a more technological hip-hop influenced by techno and jungle. Electro built the structure for techno with 'Clear' by Cybotron laying the electro-techno blueprint for all that was to come. Meanwhile, rap took a sharp turn back toward turntable beat collage over technological gadgets. By the tail end of 1984, the exhortations of the MC over the breakbeats of the DJ supplanted the cold technological, sequenced music of electro. David Toop, in his superb period piece account *Rap Attack*, remarked that rap was a direct descendant of the *griots* who still wander through the back country of Mali, Africa as they have for hundreds of years, delivering stories and folklore with their voices over minimal lute accompaniment. Ali Farka Toure is perhaps the best known musician to come from this fertile tradition, the deepest root of the blues.

The emphasis of simplicity, rolling waves of subsonic bass and ghetto rhetoric or hedonistic commentary became the pattern for rap and hip-hop. Engagingly ludicrous badinage and storytelling (witness Slick Rick's 'The Moment I Feared') became the means for the original Bronx rap to be promulgated and extrapolated from. Epic heights of braggadocio were declaimed by practitioners such as Kool Moe Dee, who bragged of wealth and sexual prowess to their disenfranchized fans, who sought escape via larger-than-life rappers and their larger-than-life claims. This wave of rap, as it became hip-hop, created characters who were supermen heroes of cartoon-like strength, in the vein of Stagger Lee, object of both fear and admiration, driven to desperate measures to achieve self-protection in a hostile environment. The boastful assertions of wealth made by most big-name rappers contrasted sharply with the reality of life for most black Americans during the Reagan years, a time when their economic power as a whole was eroded. Rap was wish fulfilment, coupled with a knowledge that the means of achieving that wish came through subverting the order of the day, hence the curious glorification/denigration of the cocaine dealer. A parallel may be found here in Jamaican popular music, where villains are ambivalently criticized and praised, one example being 'Johnny Too Bad' from the soundtrack of the 1973 Jimmy Cliff film *The Harder They Come*.

The most progressive sounds were to be constructed piecemeal in the studio, witness the revolutionary squeals and sirens layered below Public Enemy's groundshaking, bombastic raps. But technology had its place: check out the squeal that punctuates Public Enemy's 'Rebel Without a Pause' like an impending raid, with no variation in pitch and tone until it goes from being shocking to riveting. This was the sound of the black avant-garde. The sound was sampled from the opening squeal of Maceo Parker's saxophone on 'The Grunt', an instrumental by James Brown's legendary band, the J.B.s., and then compressed and manipulated. It presaged the static phrases that would proliferate in rap and ultimately render it catatonic, but when it was released on an unsuspecting public in 1989 as part of the epochal Public Enemy album *It Takes A Nation Of Millions To Hold Us Back*, it was electrifying, drawing ears both black and white to the sound of the urban underground.

Public Enemy were shocking and original, and youngsters like Beck responded to their alarming, incendiary and almost Wagnerian beats. Powered by a team of producers known as the Bomb Squad (Hank Shocklee, Keith Shocklee, Bill Stephney and Eric Sadler) as well as powerhouse DJ Terminator X, who prided himself on making very few mistakes in the tricky mechanical endeavour of turntable cut-ups, Public Enemy broke through to white as well as black youth and for a delicious moment, they were a shared secret, something revolutionary. Shocklee cited Brian Eno and David Byrne's 1981 release *My Life In The Bush Of Ghosts*, a cut-up radio and sample montage, as an inspiration. Terminator X brought a fulsome funk flavour, derived from his enthusiasm for Philadelphia DJs, to the Bomb Squad's terror dome montages.*

But what Public Enemy did was a quantum leap away from their Bronx progenitors. The pairing of Chuck D's militant hard rhyming, lightened by Flavour Flav's inspired and needlesome buffoonery as old as black history itself – serious discourse both lightened and heightened by the maniacal enthusiasm of a foil. Flav harkened back to the 'cold lampers', ne'er do wells who congregated by ghetto corner lamps to drink malt liquor and cut each other down with ever-escalating insults known as 'the dozens' (the objective being keeping one's cool until the other lost his and became furious, thus losing the contest) and be non-stop jokers, a 'sidekick and hype man' as Chuck D described it. A mythic joker, in short.

Much of Public Enemy's public face was theatre, for Flavour Flav was in fact an accomplished trumpet and piano player. Flav's alleged taste for cocaine and later the very same crack that Public Enemy had issued dire warnings against on tracks such as 'Night Of The Living Baseheads' spawned a whole host of imitators in hip-hop. Flav became a cliché, amplifying his already blown-up persona into gruesome heights of crack-fiend gurning, shockwave hair and rheumy dead-eyed madness. Regrettable also was Chuck D's slip into veiled anti-Semitism, a concession of personal defeat as his righteous rage turned to maudlin Jew-baiting.

Somewhere between N.W.A. and Public Enemy came Digital Underground, restoring the funk to hip-hop. Using P-Funk as their base board, the brilliant Shock-G invented a persona called Humpty Hump, half-Slick Rick, half-Groucho Marx, who dropped the magnificent 'Doowutchyalike' and then 'Humpty Dance' in 1990. '"The Humpty Dance" was an influential record for me,' Beck recalled some eight years later, 'probably one of the first raps that I memorized beginning to end, just an amazing record. It's really underrated. More records like that are needed in the hip-hop world.'[40] It was something of a watershed; soon N.W.A. would be no more and Dr Dre would be busting out slack West Coast jams fuelled by P-Funk and potent marijuana known as the Chronic.

As the Nineties began, though, rap and rock were increasingly polarized. Gone was the fertile crossover between new wave and early rap that had spawned electro. Gone were the contacts between downtown New York producers and Bronx rappers, between jazz greats and village scratchers. And radio's increasing shift to playlists and marketing concerns eradicated the cross pollination of genres heard on stations like WBLS. With a few sporadic exceptions, there were

55

---

* Terminator X's roots were apparent in his 1994 track 'Super Bad' which featured early pioneers such as Kool Herc, Grandmaster Flash, the Cold Crush Brothers and Fantastic MC.

now two worlds whose twain would not meet. Run DMC's collaboration with Aerosmith on 'Walk This Way', the rock-rap fusion of Holland's Urban Dance Squad, or Rick Rubin's Led Zep samples aside, black and white urban music were segregated camps. And who should walk into the desolate zone between the two but a guy with a beat up acoustic guitar.

1   McKenna, Kristine. 'Beck's First Sampling', *Los Angeles Times*, 3 May 1998

2   Rubin, Mike. 'Subterranean Homeboy Blues', *Spin*, July 1994

3   Smith, Ethan. 'Re: Fluxology – Beck And Yoko Ono Sound Off On Found Art, Family Ties, and Flying Pianos', *New York* magazine, 21 September 1998

4   Hansen, Al. *Notes On A Mini-Retrospective*, Kölnisches Stadt Museum, Köln, 1995

5   Bibbe Hansen interview with Vaginal Davis, *Index* magazine, November–December 1999

6   Tignor, Steve. 'Beck Beat', *Puncture*, Summer 1996, issue 36

7   Thomas, David. 'It's Good To Be Beck Hansen, Musical Genius', *Daily Telegraph*, 10 May 1997

8   Cohen, Scott. 'The Joy Of Beck', *Details*, August 1996

9   Norris, Chris. 'Return Of The Funk Soul Brother', *Spin*, December 1999

10 Perlich, Tim. 'Beck's Trek', *Now*, November 1996

11 Farley, Christopher John. 'Beck To The Future', *Time*, 20 January 1997

12 Thomas, David. 'It's Good To Be Beck Hansen, Musical Genius', *Daily Telegraph*, 10 May 1997

13 Rubin, Mike. 'Subterranean Homeboy Blues', *Spin*, July 1994

14 Jones, Cliff. 'Captain Sensible', *The Face*, 1996

15 Cohn, Lawrence. *Nothing But The Blues*, Abbeville Press, 1993

16 Wolfe, Charles. Liner notes, *Anchored in Love: The Carter Family*, Rounder Records, 1991

17 Sakamoto, John. 'Beck Answers His Fans', *Jam!*, 5 June 1996

18 Tosches, Nick. *Country: The Twisted Roots of Rock and Roll*, Da Capo Press, 1977

19 Loder, Kurt. 'Beck Mutates', MTV Online, 11 November 1998

20 Wild, David. 'Beck', *Rolling Stone*, 21 April 1995

21 Thomas, David. 'It's Good To Be Beck Hansen, Musical Genius', *Daily Telegraph*, 10 May 1997

22 Thomas, David. 'It's Good To Be Beck Hansen, Musical Genius', *Daily Telegraph*, 10 May 1997

23 Bream, Jon. 'Where It's At: Summer Festivals', *Minneapolis Star Tribune*, 1 August 1997

24 Babcock, Jay. 'Beck', *Huh*, July 1996

25 Babcock, Jay. 'Beck', *Huh*, July 1996

26 'Super Beck: "Loser", Artist, Rock Star, Genius.' *UHF* # 10, July–August 1996

27 Rummel, Jack and Rebennack, John 'Mac'. *Under a Hoodoo Moon : The Life of Dr John the Night Tripper*, St. Martin's Press, May 1995

28 'Cool as Fuck!' *Dazed & Confused*, May 1997

29 Jones, Cliff. 'Captain Sensible', *The Face*, 1996

30 'Super Beck: "Loser", Artist, Rock Star, Genius.' *UHF* # 10, July–August 1996

31 Ferguson, Troy. 'Beck: Where He's At', *Rip It Up*, January 1998

32 Nardwuar The Human Serviette. 'Nardwuar vs. Beck' radio interview with Beck, 18 April 1994

33 Weisbard, Eric. 'After The Goldrush', *Spin*, 1996

34 McCormick, Neil. 'Beck To The Future', *Daily Telegraph*, 6 November 1997

35 Joyce, John. 'Diary Of An LP', *Melody Maker*, 5 December 1998

36 Kemp, Mark. 'Where It's At Now', *Rolling Stone*, 17 April 1997

37 Ashare, Matt. 'Slow Jamming: Beck Reveals His Inner Soul Man', *Boston Phoenix*, 25 November–2 December 1999

38 *Select*, December 1999

39 Norris, Chris. 'Return Of The Funk Soul Brother', *Spin*, December 1999

40 *MTV*, 11 March 1998

5

RIDING THE HOG TO THE HIDDEN FORTRESS

Soon after, Beck, lacking the financial wherewithal to stay at home, started working day jobs for chump change. He moved furniture, a sweaty, thankless job that seemed like a cross between an obstacle course and the rock Sisyphus was doomed to roll up a hill only to have it roll back down. One job involved painting the inside of a lingerie store: 'I painted the whole inside of that place electric pink. We worked all night. For days all I saw was electric pink.'[1] He had fleeting jobs as a messenger, riding to work on the huffing city buses, and was also a hot dog man at children's birthday parties. Beck remembered one hot dog gig in particular: 'The party was at a rich spread in Brentwood, on a big tennis court turned into a roller skating rink. It was a lot of work carrying the hot dogs and the cart with the umbrella up the endless stairs. The girls were seven or eight years old and real snooty – too snooty to even eat hot dogs. We got stiffed on the fifteen dollar pay and stuck with two hundred hot dogs.'[2]

Later he worked as a clerk at a Video Hut, next to Pizza Hut in a strip mall. It was with considerable horror that he suddenly realized one day, 'Oh my God, everyone I'm working with is imitating a sitcom. That's why I couldn't relate to them.'[3] He also mowed lawns for Los Angeles' wealthier citizens, whose houses ascend the hills, in a vertical scale of relative earnings. Fortunately for him though, it must hardly have seemed that way at the time, his misfit presence repeatedly got in the way of holding down steady employment. He was once fired from a job as a stock boy because 'they didn't like the way I dressed. Not that I was dressing outrageously or anything. They just didn't like my style. I was just wearing jeans and a shirt from Sears. I don't know. They had high expectations for stock positions.'[4]

The one thing Beck had to cling on to during this bleak period was his burgeoning interest in music. He remained hooked on Mississippi John Hurt, and began pounding out his rudimentary blues scales and singing in the odd and compelling voice that would give his white boy blues its peculiar flavour. He started out singing high, in the keening style of Guthrie and Dylan before settling into the lower range, sounding like a cross between Fozzy Bear from the Muppets and the most weatherbeaten of Delta bluesmen, and his world shrunk to a room at home full of old LPs.

The tedious bus rides back and forth to work soon prompted Beck to take his beat-up acoustic onboard with him, playing tunes to the indifference or occasional hostility of the passengers. The route Beck rode wound down in long circles on the Vermont line, through South Central, to Hollywood, and then back again; the world of Beverly Hills and Venice Beach seemed as foreign as the moon. 'My first shows were on buses. I'd get on the bus and start playing Mississippi John Hurt with totally improvised lyrics. Some drunk would start yelling at me, calling me Axl Rose. So I'd start singing about Axl Rose and the levee and bus passes and strychnine, mixing the whole thing up.'[5] Anyone who has ever ridden those strange Los Angeles buses can testify to the hodge podge of humanity that traverse their circuitous routes through landscapes comprising barrios hemmed in by scrub land, broken-down stucco storefronts, those ubiquitous tall palms planted for the 1932 Olympics and Latinos labouring on their autos. At each stop, as the heaving, groaning buses pull to a halt, the incredibly diverse snippets of music echoing out from L.A.'s 1,001 ethnic restaurants come wafting in through the door. A rhapsody of colliding sounds: Chinese, Korean and Vietnamese music, the accordions, trumpets and guitars of Mexico, mariachi and banda music, funk, rap and the highly produced R&B singles of black urban radio and the 'classic' rock and album-oriented bland radio fare that provides a constant backdrop to all daily life. Also in amongst the mix would be faint snatches of the San Diego station 91X, the first commercial station wholly dedicated to what became known as underground or alternative music, or small soul or ranchera stations announcing advertisements for stores in a tinny, echo-laden blare. As Beck later recalled, 'Growing up in a Korean-Salvadoran neighbourhood, walking on the street and hearing hip-hop coming out of one car and ranchera music coming out of another; this intersection of culture might have a lot to do with what I'm doing.'[6]

His guitar became an ever-present accessory for Beck, though it hardly endeared him to the various ethnic neighbourhoods which he haunted any more than it would have the white middle-class suburbs: 'I used to play down at Lafayette Park, near where I used to live as a kid, and all these Salvadoran guys would be playing soccer, and I'd be practising a Leadbelly song. The Salvadoran guys would just be shaking their heads. Once in a while a ball would sail over my head.'[7] Nevertheless, the music and atmosphere of those areas stayed with Beck Hansen; just as he had felt an affinity with blues music, he gravitated naturally towards the sound and spirit of South America: 'So much of [Latin American] culture is so much healthier. It's so much more of what music is supposed to be, much less pretentious. There's something in that spirit of the music, even in the Indian music, that speaks to me. I feel closer to that than any 'alternative music.'[8] 'I love Latin music, and I'm totally obsessed by Brazilian music right now,' he told *The Face* in 1996. 'It's real true music, and the core of the human spirit is contained in those melodies.'[9]

In 1997, Beck would pay a special homage to his Latin American influences with a version of 'Jack-Ass' called 'Burro'. The song, one of Beck's most marvellous, is a traditional mariachi arrangement of the original with Beck singing in dulcet tones in well-enunciated Spanish. The mariachi band Los Camperos de Nati Cano were Beck's backing band for his richly tuneful rendition of 'Jack-Ass', arranged by bandleader Juan Morales and Beck's dad David Campbell. Moreover, Beck's thunderous low voice is laced with strong echo, making for an almost supernatural romantic machismo, which is appropriate, since even delicacy is amplified in Mexican music, as epic and bold as Diego Rivera's murals.

At sixteen, Beck, lacking the luxury of a four-track tape recorder, would record tracks on boom boxes, switch the tape into another equally shitty one and play along while recording. By the fourth time around, the hiss and distortion would saturate the tape, leaving Beck's vocal and guitar buried in the mix. He was intrigued by the sound, and up through *Mellow Gold* he would constantly screw around with this technique. Boomboxes with dwindling batteries would render his voice deep and gravely like a Delta bluesman, which naturally fascinated him. Later, on small four-track machines, Beck would record harmonies at slowed down recording speeds so they would sound higher and thinner when played at the correct speed. The effect could be irritating after a while, but it showed considerable ingenuity and self reliance. The teenage Beck gradually became fairly proficient in layering vocals recorded at different speeds. Even with his lo-fi production, his four-track work was quite skilful, and on *Stereopathetic Soul Manure* he does superb three-part harmonies – not superb in terms of being technically spotless but in terms of grasping the underlying tonalities of artists such as the Carter Family with their blended harmonies. 'When I first started recording the only thing I had available to me was a four-track and myself,' he recalled later. 'If I didn't have drums I'd play a bucket and a cardboard box. If I didn't have a bass I would just speed up the tape, play guitar and make it sound like a bass being this one man four-track band, which I'm sure a lot of musicians out there do. The way I wrote and recorded music just developed out of that. So, now I'm working in a studio and I've recorded stuff with musicians and bands, but for me the thing I've developed comes out of just being in the studio by myself coming up with stuff.'[10]

Unlike most musicians, Beck had to seek out his favourite music on his own, in corners, as opposed to the usual ways. He didn't have enough money to buy many records, but would work his way into the all-ages punk clubs to see bands from the age of twelve onwards. Other children at school would be going to KISS concerts, while the young Hansen was sneaking in to see Black Flag, who were still around at the time. 'Growing up there were never festivals. Every five years or so Rainbow or REO Speedwagon would play. That was about all.'[11] It's sometimes easy to forget how aggressively bland popular music was in the 1980s. It's still bland today, but at least there is now a veneer of diversity. Any thinking soul of that previous era was reduced to finding misplaced treasures in bargain bins at the odious commercial record store chains. If nothing was to be found there, it meant trudging for miles to tiny hip underground shops, where those with more sartorial tastes in music – punk, ska, folk, blues, reggae, English indie and other permutations thereof – were catered for. One such random rummage through a record store bin turned up a band called Pussy Galore. 'Pussy Galore was a James Bond character so I bought it,' recalled Beck. When he took it home and dropped it onto his broken-down record player, what he heard amazed him. The album, *Right Now!*, 'was so distilled and pure. It had all the elements, just turned up.'[12] Pussy Galore spun out from influences such as the Birthday Party and the Cramps, like a Cadillac Seville careening off an expressway. Their sound is unique, with harsh, brittle drums echoing in what sounds like a very tiny studio. The guitars reach almost pure saturation level, restless and itching.

Before the terms 'modern rock', 'post-modern' and finally 'alternative' were coined by marketeers to 'service product' to their outlets the post-punk on indie labels of the Eighties harboured some singular bands, notably fIREHOSE, Sonic Youth, Black Flag and X. The latter is of particular interest: hailing from Los Angeles, with poet Exene Cervenka and bassist John Doe at the core, X described a lonesome city of ruination and crushed dreams under bland surfaces. These bands were like voices in the wilderness, practising in rehearsal rooms lined with carpets, travelling and performing for little or no money and sleeping on fan's floors city to city. Henry Rollins' Black Flag journal *Get In The Van* (3.11.61 Publications) details the beatings, hunger, rip-offs and other privations these bands suffered for the express pleasure of getting up onstage and kicking out the jams for a handful of true believers. In the murky underside of the 1980s, these bands preserved the essential chaos of raw and visceral, unadorned rock when it seemed almost obsolete. Those churning waves of noise that blasted out of shredded speaker cones were elegies of angry determination. To Beck, noise became like a drug: 'Once you start doing it, you can't stop.'[13]*

Beck was coming to a turning point; it became apparent to him that emulating the Delta blues or Woody Guthrie was a cul de sac; a place of dead roads, as William Burroughs put it. That which had seemed liberating only a few years before, now seemed limited and restricting, even though it remained the core of Beck's musical world. 'Purism was a dead end,' he declared years later, 'Every few years some band comes along and connects to the primal violent energy that is the essence of

---

* Noise can become so overblown that it takes on a new face. Witness the stunning 1990 album *Loveless* by My Bloody Valentine. Guitar distortion was layered so thickly that it became like a blanket of sound, with weedy synth samples of accidental feedback melodies played over the top, and whispered echolalia voices similar to the Cocteau Twins. It is a marvellous juxtaposition of sounds, and quite unsettling at first. Designed to be played at extreme volume, My Bloody Valentine's work shows all sorts of tonal colours in the midst of great oceans of noise. Another prime example is the Boredoms' 1994 *Pop Tatari*, starting with pure shrill tones before thundering like an avalanche for the next 30 minutes. Inspired and recommended listening.

rock.'[14] Seemingly opposite trends made Beck into that rarest of all birds, an original. From raw country blues, he now started to incorporate sounds inspired by the noise-drenched independent offerings of the underground noise scene; his music became infused with the raucous element that remains one of his key stylistic reference points to this day.

Another key influence at this time was Sonic Youth, who coupled a keen sense of melody with a penchant for caterwauling guitars played with a fork, odd tunings and cheap Japanese guitars. Sonic Youth's music was unusual at the time, even when compared with contemporaries such as Hüsker Dü or fIREHOSE, in that there was a spaciousness in their music, sometimes implied, sometimes overt. Sonic Youth's guitarist Thurston Moore, bassist Kim Gordon, drummer Steve Shelley and guitarist Lee Renaldo took chances and stretched out when their alternative brethren became mired in one mode. This was due in part to Moore's tenure in avant-garde composer Glenn Branca's ear-shattering nine-guitar orchestras, part of the downtown New York avant-noise scene, as well as Moore's fondness for the soulful end of late Sixties free jazz. Sonic Youth's majestic 1990 LP *Daydream Nation* summed up everything that made them great, from *musique concrète* answering machine messages treated with echo to duelling guitar work the likes of which hadn't been heard since Television. Sonic Youth were also taste-makers, picking up on extreme free jazz and German krautrock bands like Neu! in the late Eighties, when no one else gave a shit, certainly not the writers for the indie snobzines. They also did things like appear on almost all the tribute and benefit albums they were invited to appear on, wisely tackling the high with the low and broadening their musical palette by covering everyone from KISS to the Carpenters to Brian Wilson. Noise in Beck's work is catharsis, a nod to the avant-garde it expresses frustration and motion and is rarely self-indulgent. It's a reality check, a purgative and often ends his albums. On *Stereopathetic Soul Manure*, Beck presages Japanese noise band the Boredoms' move from discordant abrasive noise to lulling trance noise. On the string-laden arrangement of 'Jack-Ass' re-titled 'Strange Invitation', Beck has discordant squalls of guitar in the far right channel, deep down in the mix and adding counterpoint.

But back in the 1980s, Beck's love of music seemed destined to remain just a hobby. Realizing that the nondescript jobs with which he filled in his time were leading him nowhere, he decided to take a chance and get at least a taste of the country outside Los Angeles – specifically, New York. 'At eighteen I was working in South Central Los Angeles in a bleak garment factory. I didn't have rich parents to support me, so I knew I was in for years of menial work. I decided I'd go and have a few years seeing what was out there before I was locked into a dead-end job. That life was on the cards for me because I had no college degree – quit school; I had nothing. At the time there was this special on the Greyhound bus: $30 ticket to take you anywhere, so I went on the great American odyssey and ended up in New York.'[15] To prepare himself for the journey, he sneaked onto Greyhound buses for short trips. Due to a strike at the time, baggage handlers had taken over from the regular drivers; poor organization and overcrowding led to somewhat lax security and Beck worked the situation to his advantage. When he made the full trip, accompanied by a girlfriend and his guitar at the age of nineteen, it proved to be a gruelling experience. The trip began inauspiciously: 'You spend about two minutes in the downtown Los Angeles Greyhound bus station and your romanticism about taking a bus trip across America will be eradicated and exterminated immediately.'[16] The long, hot journey lasted about a week, and with every mile Beck's fond illusions of being on the road in America, fostered by the Beat literature he's read as a teenager, were dashed. 'At some point in the middle of west Texas, the sun was going down, and I realized that all the straight people – all the working people – had gotten off the bus and everyone left was a drug fiend or an ex-con. I remember one of them whispering in my ear as soon as I fell asleep: he was going to slit my throat. I knew I was descending into the heart of America. I was discovering the heartland at that moment.'[17]

The bus disgorged the pair at the grimy Port Authority bus terminal on 33rd Street, a bus station of tight corridors, harried travellers who never seem to find their buses, hordes of homeless men and crack fiends harassing you to ask if they can carry your bags, sometimes tugging on them while you tug them away. 'Port Authority is the grand entry, the golden gates, the twelve gates to the city,'[18] he declared wryly, years later. In a Chaplinesque twist, he got on the wrong subway and lost his girlfriend, and he was on his own, in a strange city. She may still be down there somewhere. New York can be as foreign as Bangladesh for Americans, let alone foreigners. Beck took the subway down to the Village, looking around the streets of lore, Bleecker and MacDougal, where Dylan and his folk kin had walked around thirty years before. 'I was more interested in the folk scene in New York in the 1960s than the 1970s singer-songwriter thing in Los Angeles,' he told the *Los Angeles Times* in 1997. 'So, I came to check it out, to see what ghosts were hanging around. And, there was actually a strong scene in the Village.'[19] Dave Van Ronk, Jack Elliot, Eric Andersen, Phil Ochs, Fred Neil, Mike Millius and a host of others played at the Gaslight, Kettle of Fish and other Village folk clubs in the Sixties, all subsequently overshadowed by the emergence of Bob Dylan. Mindful of those long gone days, Beck did what seemed the obvious thing to do: he unsnapped the locks on his guitar case and sat on a corner to play. No one stopped; some people threw a quarter into his cap without pausing. He had arrived.

Shortly thereafter, while he was playing his guitar and singing in the street one day, some people approached him and told him about an open-mike at an anti-folk night in the Chameleon, a bar on 6th Street and Avenue A on the Lower East Side, recommending that he turn up. It turned out to be Beck's first gig, an event which necessitated him becoming unspeakably drunk in order to have the courage to go on. When he finally took the stage he performed 'John Hardy' with four other guys. Unlike previous depressing open mikes at coffee-houses in Los Angeles, where snooty ponytailed middle-aged folkies would play James Taylor covers, complete with thirty-six chord changes, Beck was pleased and stimulated by the atmosphere: 'This was interesting, it was just some people getting drunk.'[20] The performers at the club played hard, working away at their acoustic guitars with infectious energy. Beck was hooked.

Along with the Fort and ABC No Rio, the Chameleon open-mike nights were regular venues for punk folkers Roger Manning and John S. Hall of King Missile. Manning and Hall were misfits anywhere else, but here, banded very loosely together, they comprised a band of renegades under the rubicon of 'anti-folk'. Little understood and often overblown, anti-folk is a non-movement that neither achieved full fruition or died, being more a loose conglomeration of like-minded artists and musicians than a bona fide style. It continues today, more of an attitude than a movement. Like Fluxus, anti-folk resists definition, because definition is part of what kills magic, what kills flow and makes things static. Anti-folk thrives today, in part because it never got eaten by the media, most likely being too unpalatable and lacking a central reference point to be digested. But in rock anthology terms, its main florescence is pegged as happening ever since Lach, a downtown acoustic troubadour-musician-poet, had been hosting open mikes at the Fort, named for the Japanese film director Akira Kurosawa's *The Hidden Fortress*, since 1987.

The night Lach opened the Fort, the New York Folk Festival was being held nearby, and Lach muttered darkly to himself, 'if that's folk music, this must be anti-folk!' Folk had become a stale joke, as stale as college-trained jazzers retreading old songs rather than reinventing popular standards of the day into their own music. Folk had become mellow, safe, toothless and easily marketable. Lach reflected later, 'Folk music means the traditional music of a people, right? But for whatever reason, acoustic songwriters took on that label in the Sixties, and it stuck. I tried to

61

play in those West Village clubs, but since my stuff is as influenced by the Sex Pistols and the Clash as by Woody Guthrie, they just kept throwing me out. I was like, "What's the problem? I'm just another white guy with a guitar." That's when I knew I'd have to start my own club. Anti-folk is to folk what punk was to rock, we showed that folk was dead, that you don't need all the trappings of the industry to make your art. And real rock or folk or punk is never about rebellion, anyway – it's about telling the truth.'[21] Anti-folk is indeed like a hidden fortress, and young musicians continue to play at the Fort, now in a new place, and still run by Lach. When police closed the Fort in 1989, Lach moved a few blocks north to Sophie's, where Bob Dylan even played one night, perhaps recognizing a kinship with these upstarts.* Those who played at the Fort included Cindy Lee Berryhill, John S. Hall and King Missile, and Paleface. There were others too: Billy Syndrome, cartoonist David Chelsea. Kirk Kelly, Lach and Manning sang backup vocals on Berryhill's 1990 release *Naked Movie Star*. A number of anti-folkists turned up on various labels, some of them on major labels, but most of those contracts are void and the albums were deleted.

Anti-folk bubbled under the nose of the popular consciousness, but never broke through to the masses. It was too anarchic, disorganized, rootsy and radical to be packaged by the media. The scene was notable for its unorthodox approach in blending seemingly disparate elements, and for its non-purist attitude to delving freely into seemingly opposite genres. But the main duality that powered the loose band of renegades was between punk and folk. It was also omnivorous, assaying rock, rap and indie and whatever else was drifting around the Village. Anti-folk was as quick to reference concurrent downtown New York kindred like Sonic Youth, Pussy Galore and Kramer's Shimmydisc label, as it was to delve into Woody Guthrie or Blind Lemon Jefferson. It seems only natural in retrospect that its rag tag members, more dissimilar than similar, armed with flayed guitars and scuffed shoes, would draw Beck in, and that the anti-folk clubs should become his training ground. Taking his cues from anti-folk's simultaneous reverence for traditional folk and its desire to debase the form, Beck's vision of a new music shaped by iconoclasm and humour began to gel. 'The Lower East Side was a ghost town back then, anti-folk was all that was going on,' he reflected years later. 'It was a very cool environment. Everything you do when you're eighteen or nineteen is going to set the tone [...] It's right when you're coming of age, and you're seeing things on your own, you take a lot of that with you.'[22] Beck was to spend a couple of years in the Lower East Side, absorbing more freak out folk and noise, sleeping on couches, and not having any money. 'There's just all these people there making music and there's always a place to crash, and there's always something going on every night. I played on the streets for money. I had a few jobs. I had a job at the Y.M.C.A., taking pictures of people for their I.D.s. That lasted for about two weeks. It's really hard to find work there.'[23]

Anti-folk took traditional music and treated it irreverently, blending it with whatever was at hand. The remnants of a thousand New York scenes and moments filtered into it. Punk provided the irreverence and caustic lyric content. The Dada flame, preserved by artists, infused it with absurdity. Bluegrass, folk and blues were dredged from scratchy grooves on LPs found in bargain bins in radical book shops on the Lower East Side. Part of the impetus came from the holier-than-thou attitudes of the traditional folk scene, with its trenchant purists and their obscurist

---

* The impetus behind anti-folk reached a broad fruition with Ani DiFranco, who no matter what you make of her music, has succeeded on her own terms, without comprising one iota, and that is unique in the 1990s. She started her own label, distributes her own product, does her own bookings, and controls both the artistic and commercial sides of her career.

ways. And so a handful of misfit musicians armed with acoustic guitars set out (more or less) to deconstruct folk music, infusing it with the reality of their urban surroundings. Beck quickly absorbed his influences and refashioned them in his own image.

Roger Manning was just releasing his first album on the largely punk-hardcore label SST when Beck arrived. The scene at that time was an assemblage of late night spots, loft jams and the Lower East Side's Chameleon bar open-mike night and at casual all-night jams in Tompkins Square Park. Manning's first impression of Beck was, 'It was like seeing the ghost of Woody Guthrie.'[24] Manning's own influences ran the gamut from bluegrass legend Bill Monroe's flat picking to garden variety punk rock, and a bass style akin to Mike Watt of the Minutemen. Manning and Beck hung out, playing gigs and scrounging for enough food to buy sandwiches. Manning released several albums on SST, filled with his laconic and elliptic observations on the politics of romance, or the bitter romance of political activism. Today he continues much as he did then, touring endlessly in heaving cars from gig to gig, with a retinue of hardcore fans in every city.*

Obvious though the parallels must have seemed between Beck and the young Bob Dylan, Beck took his inspiration from earlier figures – Woody Guthrie, Leadbelly and Hurt – rather than from the artists who took their lead from those earlier folk and blues artists and became internationally known in the Sixties and Seventies. 'When I was playing in bars, I'd be doing a blues song and people would say, "Oh, a Led Zeppelin song." It would be a song Zeppelin had done, but I'd never heard their version. There are still gaping holes in my musical knowledge, stuff from the Seventies [...] With the folk stuff, I wasn't trying to do anything like what Dylan did with the original music. That was part of the anti-folk idea, to keep the basic style but not to write typical singer-songwriter songs. I was trying to keep my songs cut down, tight, not like Dylan's half-poetic style. *One Foot In The Grave* had some of those old songs on it.'[25]

The musicians and poets who performed at the open mikes would wander around the East Village and hang out in Tompkins Square Park. The band shell in Tompkins Square Park, on 7th to 10th Streets between Avenue A and B, was the scene of riotous performances of industrial, folk, hip-hop and any other style of music, played by musicians who couldn't or didn't bother to secure a permit from the park officers. Tensions between the rag tag artists, homeless people, crack heads, upscale residents of newly gentrified houses and the police ran high. Tompkins had a distinguished history of anarchy. Draft riots raged here during the Civil War era, and it was also the site of frequent union protests in the 1920s and 1930s and mass rallies during the Vietnam years. The park had been the scene of freak cop antagonism since the 1960s when police would beat hippies larking on acid in the park with batons. Like the un-gentrified edges of London's Notting Hill, the East Village was ripe for a riot, and it came in 1988. A demonstration against the proposed removal of the homeless from the park escalated out of control and became a fully fledged battle between protesters and police, landing this East Village park on the front page.

The city, then at the start of a period of government by the quasi-fascistic Mayor Rudolph Giuliani, opted to demolish the band shell, cutting the centre out of the park. The anarchic element moved elsewhere, to the squatter's communities, but the movement didn't get time to put down roots. In 1993, police illegally closed a squatter community on 13th Street, right off Tompkins, armed with machine guns and accompanied by a SWAT team. Beck, still somewhat wide-eyed and innocent about the circles in which he moved, passed through many different small subsets and scenes, such as anarchist squatter's communities. He worked at a bookstore in

---

* 'It's my tithe to the universe,' said the lady taking tickets at SXSW as she bought a very broke yours truly a ticket to see Manning. Thanks, lady, wherever you are.

the East Village, checking coats, and then after work, grabbing a quick bite to eat, would retrieve his own coat and guitar from behind the counter stacked with surplus books and head out for the night. He'd roam downtown to Lower East Side, down to the same streets which Audrey had dashed along in green hair thirty years before. 'New York's the place where if you stay in one place long enough, you end up meeting everybody,' he reflected later to *Sessions*. 'And I ran into a lot of folks, and they were real friendly, and interested in what you were doing, and there was always something going on. And you're always included in what's going on. So pretty soon, I was engulfed in this anti-folk world. It was just a very aggressive folk played with punk energy.'[26] At this time Beck was still playing Guthrie and Hurt songs, and had yet to seriously tackle songwriting himself. The shrewd Lach decided to employ some good-natured blackmail in order to encourage him to come up with some original material. When Beck showed up one night, with his acoustic guitar and harmonica in its holder, Lach informed him that he would not be able to play unless he wrote some songs. Beck was surprised at how steadfastly Lach stuck to his guns; there was no budging unless he came up with something. He got a pen and paper and 'wrote five songs about stuff like pizza or waking up after having been chain-sawed in half by a maniac.'[27] The earliest of Beck's own songs included the latter, 'Cut In Half Blues', which would show up on *Stereopathetic Soul Manure* and 'Pay No Mind', the Dylan-influenced dirge that would appear on *Mellow Gold* and speaks of Beck's almost Buddhist indifference to the squalor surrounding him. 'Pay No Mind' was as close to Sixties-style Greenwich Village protest folk as Beck would get, an inversion of a protest song, simply citing his own beatific alienation. It also conveyed the notion of Beck separating himself off from degradation in order to carry himself through; a transcendent alienation.

The pressure to write new songs was part of what kept anti-folk fresh, and it had a salutary effect on Beck's work rate. The same group of people migrated between the clubs, and once they had heard one song a couple of times, the impulse was there to come up with new material. As a result, Beck's turnover of new songs soared. Moreover, drawing on the variety of music being played around him, he also started to try out different styles quite naturally. 'Everybody was writing songs,' he recalled years later, 'everybody was influenced by each other's songs, and those people were breaking into rap stuff, and hip-hop was coming in, all kinds of things. That's where I started rapping, too, just drinking and you get on the stage, put the guitar down and start stomping your foot. There was a lot of people doing poetry, just folks speaking their minds, telling how they saw it. It was good and very liberating.'[28] This was an intensely creative period for Beck. He would take old folk songs and rework them with modern themes, mix up rap, punk and folk, and do just about anything he wanted to on stage; the atmosphere in the anti-folk clubs was non-judgemental and actively encouraged experiment. He was young, living in one of the most exhilarating cities in the world, making music, getting drunk and exchanging ideas with a group of like-minded artists and musicians; what else could a nineteen-year-old bohemian want? The lack of regular food or shelter paled in comparison to the riches on offer.

Eagerly embracing the musical freedom that the anti-folk scene thrived on, Beck began developing his own brand of surreal and impromptu lyrics. Anti-folk forced him to think for the first time about his songwriting. 'Lyrics tend to be very mundane, like shopping lists,' he once explained. 'And I try to get things that aren't really direct. It's not like a telephone booth that you look at and know it's a telephone booth. You're trying to get into the inner life of the telephone booth, all the wiring that you can't see. Music's got to work on the gut level. You don't know why or how or when, but when it hits you, it feels good. That's the first way it's got to work. But if you can figure out some way to layer it when you peel that away so that there's something else going on, it makes it all work better.'[29]

As he worked at honing his songwriting craft, Beck was influenced by poet-performer Mike Tyler, publisher of a zine called *American Idealism Rag*, or *A.I.R.*, a *Sing Out!* for the disaffected new folk mob. Mike Tyler's spoken word performances left a strong impression on Beck. Tyler in turn was impressed by Beck's range of musical knowledge and his growing abilities. 'Beck knew who Bukka White was, you know what I mean?' Tyler told *Spin* in 1994. 'Beck could get up on stage with somebody else and play the harmonica or the guitar or sing or hum or bang something and it just always seemed perfect. All the false alternative hypocrisy just seemed to fade away when I saw him.'[30]

That false alternative hypocrisy Tyler spoke of was the unfortunate fallout from the reaction against the commercial pop of the Eighties, with its stifling manufactured choruses and stale verses tailor-made for the tightly formatted U.S. radio stations. An indie aesthetic, springing from punk in the 1970s, had created a wide underground network of clubs, labels, bands and fans who effectively kept non-corporate music alive during those dark days. A nationwide chain of pamphlets, fanzines and word of mouth gave musicians and fans alike a feeling they belonged, instead of just being the outcasts in high school who were pounded on by beer-maddened jocks. All very good and well, but the indie aesthetic also gave rise to vociferous snobbery and élitism. Bands that blossomed and became better known, fed by the scene's cohesiveness and support, were subsequently reviled for their new-found fame, amidst charges that they had sold out their integrity. Signing to a major label was the ultimate grounds for the stripping away of whatever 'indie cred' a band or artist was once endowed with. The fickle tastes of the underground staple and photocopy fanzine brigade dictated credibility. In the days preceding the rise of major label albums by Jane's Addiction and, most famously, Nirvana, corporate record companies didn't give a damn about scenes like anti-folk; there was no money to be made, and there was no perceived market to buy the shit. Moreover, anti-folk was such a loose concept, hardly a movement in the accepted sense, and it remained permanently on the periphery of public consciousness, being neither mainstream nor alternative rock. In Seattle, meanwhile, hordes of bands were playing what would be tagged as 'grunge' long before the labels sniffed out its money-making potential.

Taking his cues from anti-folk's simultaneous reverence for traditional folk and its desire to debase the form, Beck's vision of a new music shaped by iconoclasm and humour began to gel. Beck quickly wrote many songs and recorded them on a boombox. Beck's first known recorded effort is known as *The Banjo Story* and is fairly readily found through, er, unofficial channels. The emphasis of some of the tracks is on juvenilia, like the balefully sophomoric 'Let's Go Moon Some Cars', as well as strongly fatalistic songs in a darker, country vein, some filled with despair. Chief among these is the startling 'Goin' Nowhere Fast', a song which Bibbe once claimed was her favourite Beck song. 'All the things they said would happen to you, don't you know they're all coming true, going nowhere fast,' laments an impossibly youthful sounding Beck, his naive vocal laced with the world weariness of street musician Ted Hawkins on his final night playing on the Venice boardwalk. Though clearly under Guthrie's spell and also owing a debt to the young Dylan, it's one of Beck's best songs, with cabbala-like lines such as 'it will tear me in three', revealing that his curious lyrical sensibility was already well formed. His guitar stumbles but it hardly matters – his vocal is so raw and wounded that it captures the listener heart and soul. The rough-shod guitar trembles throughout, Beck's hand working like an oil derrick pumping in ellipses, the strength of his statement contrasted with his hesitance. The song addresses anxiety in a particularly compelling way, the sensation of going nowhere fast a perfect metaphor for wanting to go in all directions at once and not seeing any way to go. The frustration and despair are palpable, whether the song is addressed to an acquaintance or to

Beck himself, it's a very powerful song. Tellingly, it ends on a suspended note. Perhaps surprisingly, *The Banjo Story* is one of Beck's most compelling works. 'Talkin' Demolition Blues', 'Instrumental Rag', the excellent 'You Can Be So Careless' and 'Hell' are all standouts. One track, 'Atmospheric Recordings', would turn up as the closer for Beck's 1994 K Records album *One Foot In The Grave*. The other tracks are bare bones workouts of some songs which display how well Beck was versed in folk and country.

A detour to Europe from his detour in New York would further cement his own nascent artistic aesthetic. One day, entering the smelly lobby of the awful rooming house where Beck was now living, occupied by sad old people in dirty house coats and welfare case families, he was told by the alcoholic concierge at the desk that someone was going to call him from Italy later on. When a puzzled Beck took the telephone call later, it turned out to be his grandfather. Al had somehow talked an Italian gangster who had been laundering money by purchasing art, into sending his grandson a ticket to come over. Scraping together fifteen dollars, Beck got a bus to the airport and was bound for Europe. 'I went from the dead of winter in the dregs of New York to southern Italy, having dinner with the art élite and Mafiosi of Naples.' [31]

Beck made his way with Al over to Köln, West Germany to visit his grandfather's Ultimate Akademie. Al lived above a bicycle factory, from where he co-ordinated the Akademie's various activities. A crew of young Neapolitan artists lived above one of Al's favourite bars, all not only attending his school but in a sense acting as faculty themselves, organizing and exhibiting. Hansen was like a respected older brother, always enthusiastic and pragmatic about helping others reach artistic fruition. Indeed, he was often better at motivating others than himself. Beck stayed on the floor of the Neapolitans' quarters. Days would be spent downstairs talking about plans and schemes divine and temporal, bohemian banter in three or four broken languages. 'Al was an amazing talker who could spin the most fantastic stories, and he spent most of his days in bars and cafes, surrounded by people, just holding forth,' [32] Beck recalled with affection years later. Al made regular trips down to his favourite restaurant, Chin's, owned by Hanjo Scharfenberg and Sing Ling Chin, who between them owned several of his works.

'Al really wasn't thinking about documenting his art; he was living it,' Beck told *New York* magazine in 1998. 'He was always surrounded by younger artists. It was really cool; young artists could come and put on a show within two days if they liked. Or spontaneously do performance art. If anything, Al really treated me like a contemporary. He never talked down or said, "Here's how you do it." He was like a room with open doors, and you'd just come in and be a part of it. I lived there for a while. It was very free. Somebody would get the idea after lunch to start a band, and that night we'd be performing on the radio, and there'd be a local news crew interviewing us.' [33]

Before too long, common artistic ground emerged between grandson and grandfather. Leafing through his grandfather's 'Intermedia Poems' made of newspaper, Beck would come across lines such as '*Pitfalls in the promised land–Robbers plunder the night train–English cloud received with silver lining–Cash bottlenecks pinch profits*', scattershot imagery similar to his own offbeat lyric writing. The creative atmosphere spurred Beck on to do his own art. He got hold of a sketchbook, and began pasting sundry images into it, assembling collages that used his grandfather's work as a departure point. 'I'd fooled around with collage since I was a kid, but I hadn't done anything as an adult, so the stuff I made in Köln was the first work I made.' [34] Eventually Beck would have a series of books full of collages which would be displayed in a gallery alongside the works of his misfit grandfather.

When his temporary idyll in Köln was finished, Beck had a brief sojourn through Europe, relying on the charity of those he met to see him through. 'I travelled through Europe on $150 so I was used to going somewhere with no means, not really knowing anybody, making my way through it. I was naive. I tended to trust people.'[35] He then returned to New York for his last round of singing on East Village street corners and anti-folk open-mike filibustering. Money became very tight, though, and Beck finally had to call it a day and go home. He'd even had the misfortune of being ripped off for several hundred dollars by a downtown crack addict, who tricked him with a phoney apartment deal using a thousand-word-a-minute sales pitch driven by that devil smoke. 'New York kicked me back out. I was living on the floor, I was doing that for a long time. I had a lot of bad luck. The spirits didn't want me to be out there.'[36] Cold and homeless, the romance of scuffling down the boulevards in the big city had lost its appeal. In early 1991 he called it a day and went home. The intensely creative milieu he left behind, which had helped turn him into a genuinely original musician, broke up not long after: 'I remember returning a year after I'd left New York and a lot of those people had gone.'[37]

1   Cohen, Scott. 'The Joy Of Beck', *Details*, August 1996
2   Cohen, Scott. 'The Joy Of Beck', *Details*, August 1996
3   Gilbey, Ryan. 'The Cap Doesn't Fit', *Independent*, 5 April 1996
4   Dunn, Jancee. 'Beck: Resident Alien', *Rolling Stone*, 11–25 July 1996
5   Wild, David. 'Beck', *Rolling Stone*, 21 April 1995
6   Cromelin, Richard. 'Nobody's Fool', *Los Angeles Times*, 21 July 1996
7   Dunn, Jancee. 'Beck: Resident Alien', *Rolling Stone*, 11–25 July 1996
8   Babcock, Jay. 'Beck', *Huh*, July 1996
9   Jones, Cliff. 'Captain Sensible', *The Face*, 1996
10 McMillan, Matt. 'Beck', *Exclaim*, 1996
11 *Select*, September 1996
12 Rubin, Mike. 'Subterranean Homeboy Blues', *Spin*, July 1994
13 Rubin, Mike. 'Subterranean Homeboy Blues', *Spin*, July 1994
14 Thompson, Ben. 'Reasons To Be Cheerful', *Independent on Sunday*, 15 September 1996
15 Jones, Cliff. 'Captain Sensible', *The Face*, 1996
16 Kemp, Mark. 'Where It's At Now', *Rolling Stone*, 17 April 1997
17 Kemp, Mark. 'Where It's At Now', *Rolling Stone*, 17 April 1997
18 Sessions At West 54th Street, 6 September 1997, www.sessionsatwest54th.com/
19 Hilburn, Robert. 'The Freewheelin' Beck', *Los Angeles Times*, 26 February 1997
20 BBC, November 1994
21 Bush, Melanie. 'History of the Fort', *Village Voice*, 1997
22 Sessions At West 54th Street, 6 September 1997, www.sessionsatwest54th.com/
23 Grob, Julie. 'Beck', *Thora-zine*, May 1994, www.eden.com/thora-zine
24 Rotondi, James. *Guitar Player*, September 1994
25 Tignor, Steve. 'Beck Beat', *Puncture*, Summer 1996, issue 36
26 Sessions At West 54th Street, 6 September 1997, www.sessionsatwest54th.com/
27 *Option*, May 1994
28 Sessions At West 54th Street, 6 September 1997, www.sessionsatwest54th.com/
29 Sessions At West 54th Street, 6 September 1997, www.sessionsatwest54th.com/
30 Rubin, Mike. 'Subterranean Homeboy Blues', *Spin*, July 1994
31 McKenna, Kristine. 'Beck's First Sampling', *Los Angeles Times*, 3 May 1998
32 McKenna, Kristine. 'Beck's First Sampling', *Los Angeles Times*, 3 May 1998

33 Smith, Ethan. 'Re: Fluxology – Beck And Yoko Ono Sound Off On Found Art, Family Ties, And Flying Pianos', *New York* magazine, 21 September 1998

34 McKenna, Kristine. 'Beck's First Sampling', *Los Angeles Times*, 3 May 1998

35 Kemp, Mark. 'Where It's At Now', *Rolling Stone*, 17 April 1997

36 Ginsberg, Allen. 'A Beat/Slacker Transgenerational Meeting Of Minds', *Shambhala Sun*, 27 September 1999

37 KCRW 89.9 FM, Los Angeles. 'Morning Becomes Eclectic', 19 June 1996

6

HOW TO SUCCEED DESPITE
ALL YOUR TRYING

Bibbe and Sean by now had scraped together a loan and taken out a lease on a space down on the edges of Los Angeles' Little Tokyo. Café Troy was their combined brainchild, a fondly remembered cornerstone of the emergent coffee-house scene in the early 1990s. And it was a bit different, led by a nurturing and arts-focussed philosophy that the other coffee houses were immune to. Amid the miniaturized storefronts of Little Tokyo, Café Troy was host to every polyglot multicultural permutation under the great smoggy sun of Los Angeles. It was a bohemian haunt for Chicanos, gays, blacks and Asians.

Sean Carrillo, a filmmaker and film editor, has an impressive radical pedigree, going back to the days when he was part of ASCO ('Disgust' in Spanish), an assembly of Chicano artist-activists. Open from 1990 to 1995, Troy was an island of calm and common sense in a festering sea of racial hate that was fomenting even before the infamous Rodney King incident of 3 March 1991, in which four Los Angeles Police Department officers were filmed beating the holy beejesus out of a black motorist who had disobeyed their orders to stop.

Beck returned to Los Angeles in early 1991, twenty-one years old and with no opportunities whatsoever – no rich relations, no school grants and no likelihood of escape in the near future. He was a white, lower-working-class scuffed-shoe bohemian drop-out with a guitar, some clothes and some books; and that was about it. But Beck had a natural tenacity to hang on in there, and his resistance to privation enabled him to keep plodding on. It's easy to paint this time in Beck's life as a somewhat romantic period, in the mode of a Horatio Alger story, in which eventual success vindicates the perceived weight of failure at that time. But there was nothing romantic about living in a shabby rooming house and working at demoralizing dead-end jobs, much as he had before he left Los Angeles, except now he was on his own, with no foreseeable future. The only thing that kept him in check was his music, which had progressed from pastime to livelihood, and he continued in his quixotic quest to be heard. He started making the rounds of the open-mike nights at coffee-houses and all-age punk clubs, places such as Al's Bar and Jabberjaw, the Gaslight, Raji's, the Onyx café in Los Feliz, and promoter Jac Zinder's roving club Fuzzyland. Few people took him seriously, a considerable shock after the easygoing atmosphere and encouragement of the Lower East side anti-folk scene.

He occasionally got up to do a few numbers in between the sets of other bands, some of whom would sometimes let him support them, but the audiences treated him with disinterest. Undeterred, he'd often play four or five clubs a night in this way, sandwiched between the main acts. Beck's music making was done mostly for his own amusement during this period back in L.A.; he'd bang out new tapes and give them to his friends 'I was working a $4-an-hour job trying to stay alive. I was living in a shed behind a house with a bunch of rats, next to an alley downtown. I had zero money and zero possibilities. I was working in a video store doing things like alphabetizing the pornography section for the minimum wage. I never even made flyers for my shows. I didn't know that you could get paid for playing.'[1] The video store would later be immortalized in 'MTV Makes Me Want To Smoke Crack', with the lines, 'I was working down at the video store, making some change.' A paltry $4-an-hour wage was barely enough to pay for Beck's rent at the shabby Highland Park rooming house where he'd landed on returning from New York, and his songs from this time are filled with longing references to high-protein food that he wasn't consuming. After a time, he was laid off from the Video Hut, and in the time-honoured tradition he moonlighted, signing on for unemployment benefit and playing music at night. Steve Hanft remembered him as 'living in this shed behind someone's house, recording his weird surrealist folk songs on a four-track.'[2] He would play under the solitary spotlight at Raji's, backed by only the gilded mirror that hung behind him. In the tense days preceding the Los Angeles riots, Beck made mini waves in the local circuit by doing folk raps of Ice Cube's hardcore rap songs. Afterwards he'd get a lift from friends and cruise down Hollywood Boulevard to Tang's Donut Shop, where down and outs played chess. There is something positively apocalyptic about Los Angeles deep in the night. On Highland, a huge billboard has a cryptic message, 'If it isn't perfect, bring it back!'; right under it is a strip emporium with 'LIVE GIRLS, GIRLS, GIRLS' blinking feebly in the haze. Homeless people and nighttime hustlers, hookers and drug dealers wander among the tourists, who are wondering where the Hollywood extolled in films is. 'Los Angeles is not very supportive,' Beck reflected years later. 'You'd play at a coffee house or something and people are chatting. You had to get folks' attention in Los Angeles, so I had to do things like set my guitar on fire. Just to see if people were listening. In Los Angeles people are very caught up in their lives. They don't really go out as much to hear music. It's not really a scene. There were a few of us but we were a lonesome legion.'[3]

At the far end of Sunset, where Silverlake branches off into the Spanish barrio, there is a strip mall with Soon Fah's Filipino Restaurant, Giorgio's Beauty Salon and the foot clinic, with its revolving sign featuring a cartoon of a sad foot on crutches on one side and a smiling, recuperated foot on the other. A more perfect symbol of Los Angeles' eternal seesaw between tragedy and joy, of its epic quest for self-improvement, would be hard to find. Beck lived in a prefabricated apartment with rickety stairs and concrete landings right behind the foot clinic. *Spin* magazine explained: 'Beck and his roommates would sit around at dusk, drinking beers and waiting for the sign to stop spinning. If the sign came to a halt and the happy side faced the house, they'd head out for action, but if the sad foot pointed in their direction, they'd call it a night.'[4]

However, Beck's time in New York had not been wasted, and he still persevered with the rapid turnover of songs that he had begun on the east coast. 'When I was playing around in Los Angeles, once I had played a song live, I wouldn't play it anymore. I was playing at Al's Bar on Friday, then on Tuesday at the Pik-Me-Up I'd have all new songs.'[5] He remained a small-time fixture on the scene, and something of a misfit, even among the other misfits. There was no one else strumming solo folk, and here was this guy who would shuffle into bars and sing songs to almost complete indifference. Those on the scene regarded him with some amusement, and the astute Beck took his waif-like image and parlayed it into his set. He began to reel out jokes as songs, simply out of a desire to connect with the audience in some way. 'A lot of the songs were pretty silly. A lot of the lyrics were goofy, improvised, me not taking it too seriously, which grew out of opening at Al's Bar or playing at Jabberjaw. I was trying to get people's attention because they really wouldn't give a shit if I was playing some folk dirge, which I did for years. The scene here really breeds that silliness and wackiness. A band has to dress up as legless clowns to be noticed or to cause a reaction, to provoke.'[6] Beck would often take the stage unannounced and unexpected, rapping into the microphone while twanging away. The emphasis was on spontaneity, and Beck was determined to up the ante. 'I'd be banging away on a Son House tune and the whole audience would be talking, so maybe out of desperation or boredom, or the audience's boredom, I'd make up these ridiculous songs just to see if people were listening. "Loser" was an extension of that.'[7]

Beck jettisoned his surname when he began playing around town at open-mike nights and small gigs; most people only remembered his first name when they wrote up the bill for an evening's performance anyway. A few bands took Beck under their wing. 'Nobody would take me seriously or give me shows. I would just show up and jump onstage while the other band was setting up. But Carla Bozulich of the Geraldine Fibbers and Possum Dixon were really receptive, which is really a hard thing to find in Los Angeles. Most of the time there isn't any musical community, there isn't any a connection between bands, so when I met those people it was more of a family.'[8] Beck often played at Café Troy. It was at Troy that Beck met Leigh Limon, his girlfriend from then up to the present, when she worked there. Together they would go trawl through the punk all-ages scene, taking in shows at the Highland Grounds. A striking woman, little is known about Leigh, save that she possesses a certain quiet steadfastness that matches Beck's own. She worked as a stylist before going into fashion, designing Beck's stage clothes.

Beck finally scraped up enough cash for a four-track recorder, a cheap portable machine on which he would record songs for friends. They weren't even demo tapes, because the possibility of being 'discovered' seemed as alien to Beck as making a living singing folk; it just didn't seem like one of those things that was going to happen. In some ways, liberated from the expectation of making it big, Beck's creativity surged all the more freely. In his throwaway songs he was, wittingly or not, working out his own peculiar style, shedding his influences. One such tape of these songs actually was released by Sonic Enemy in 1993 on cassette as *Golden Feelings*. The tape features Beck right in the aftermath of 'Loser''s success, working out songs he had written before the flood. He sounds so lonesome on those tracks, a troubadour on Hollywood Boulevard. The songs are raw, with all the intriguing rich melody that would characterize his later works hidden under lo-fi murmurings.

Steve Hanft, who would later direct many of Beck's videos, was one of Beck's chums during his steady rambling days in Los Angeles. They would hang out, roam the boulevards, and listen to the Melvins. Hanft was working on a self-financed, self-directed film, *Kill The Moonlight*, about a race car driver called Lance. Beck was struck by one bit from the film, in which Lance proclaimed, 'I'm a driver, I'm a winner, something's gonna change, I can feel it.' He sampled some of the film's dialogue on a hand-held tape recorder, the same one he used to keep a perpetual vocal diary, or more accurately, where he would go into inspired schpritzes, recorded at double speed, on whatever madness popped into his mind. Later, he would incorporate them as intros or segues on his early albums. As a joke, Hanft and Beck formed a heavy metal band called Loser. Later it would turn into Hanft's own band Liquor Cabinet, and then Sexy Death Soda. 'We were serious,' jokes Hanft, 'We had some lyrics in Latin, some of the songs were screaming bloody murder.'[9] Beck jammed on his first electric, a black Gibson Les Paul copy he got in return for baby-sitting some neighbour's kids.

Beck's Woody Guthrie-inspired songs, some of which ended up on *One Foot In The Grave*, weren't making him any fans. 'Playing around the Lower East Side of New York and Los Angeles, no one wanted to hear that.' His non-response forced him to change tack, and develop the humour in his music that was already so close to the surface. 'I would be in the middle of a gig there and I'd just start making up a song. I'd come up with something ludicrous, like "MTV Makes Me Want To Smoke Crack", which sounds funny when you're twenty. When I look back at music, one of the great times of music to me was the mid-Sixties, ending with seventy-three.

During that whole period of music the novelty song was really legitimate and acceptable. It seemed like all the serious artists had novelty songs at that time and were "allowed" to. The Beatles had tons of novelty songs, takes on vaudeville songs their grandparents liked. Even Dylan would have one or two songs where it's him singing, making up jokes about toilets seats and French movie stars; bad jokes. The rock world now takes itself really seriously.'[10]

In August 1991 the Sunset Junction Street Fair drew a crowd of locals and bohemians from Silverlake and beyond. Rob Schnapf, a record producer and co-owner of independent label Bong Load Custom Recordings, and his girlfriend were munching souvlaki, and taking in the sights and sounds. They paused in front of the Hully Gully stage; Beck was on-stage with his guitar, cherubic face sun-burned in the smoggy haze, singing in a voice that seemed as deep as German icon Heino's. As per usual, no one else was listening, but Beck played on, determined to the last. Crowds moved by, glancing up at the young man singing antique-sounding songs before moving on to the rickety metal rides wobbling on the pavement. Schnapf was captivated by him.

Extraordinarily, things were about to start happening for Beck. Margaret Mittleman, the West Coast's director of talent acquisitions (later Vice President) for BMG Music Publishing was at another fair he played, this time in Silverlake, and was immediately struck by his songs. She got hold of him after his performance and enthused to him about his songwriting. A wary Beck was sceptical of her praise; however, he agreed to give her a tape, which Mittleman took around to her rather less enthusiastic colleagues at BMG. Mittleman was one of the few people who saw any worth in those curious songs, fragile and crusty with weighty sentiments and scattered images. Her persistence eventually paid off and led the totally unknown Beck to sign with BMG Songs, under Cyanide Breathmint Music, named for one of the songs on the tape he'd given Margaret.

A week later fellow Bong Load co-owner Tom Rothrock was at the Jabberjaw coffee club, to see the bands Actor's Gang and Dicktit. In the break between the two sets, a fellow who had been nervously clasping a mutilated and be-stickered acoustic guitar jumped onto the stage wearing a blue beanie and shoes that appear several sizes too big for his frame. A guitar was strapped to him by means of an old rope and a harmonica was wired to his neck. Beck, for it was he, grabbed two mikes, lifted one to his mouth, positioning the other near the guitar. No one was listening as he banged out 'Cut In Half Blues', but there was something about the guy that made Rothrock walk closer to the stage. A hungry intensity and a certain rough charisma was evident here; definitely something different. The decidedly un-amused members of Dicktit motioned for Beck to get off, and Beck, still wearing the guitar, started to head out the back. On a hunch, Rothrock stopped him and asks him if he'd like to record sometime. Beck stared at Rothrock uncomprehendingly for a moment, as if he'd been asked for an enema or a gold doubloon. Then he pocketed Rothrock's hastily scribbled phone number.

Talking together later about some new talent they'd both recently seen, Schnapf and Rothrock realized they were bubbling about the same guy. They agreed that he had a unique style, but where could they record him, and who could produce him? The name of Carl Stephenson came up; the Brian Wilson of the bohemian set. Twenty-five years old at the time, Stephenson was a shy and brilliant hip-hop producer who had gotten his start producing the Geto Boys, an act on Rap-A-Lot Records. A musical prodigy who grew up in Olympia, Washington, Stephenson became a skilful violin player, and unlike most, didn't abandon it as he grew up. He also became a synth and sampler pro in time and, in the late Eighties, joined the Rap-A-Lot Records label, doing various jobs in the studio. Stephenson graduated to producer for the label's star act, the Geto Boys. Hard to think of the gentle Stephenson working with characters such as the Geto Boys, the shock rappers who unwittingly advanced the case for putting warning labels on American records.

Beck took his guitar and went down to Carl Stephenson's place. He played him some of his songs, which Stephenson liked, though he didn't care much for Beck's rapping. Then, Beck started fooling around with some slide guitar. Stephenson liked one slide lick, (which bears a resemblance to Derek and the Dominos' 'One More Chance'), and taped it on his eight-track, adding a drum track. Inspired, Beck started working on lyrics there and then. 'When he played it back, I thought, "Man, I'm the worst rapper in the world, I'm just a loser." So I started singing "I'm a loser baby, so why don't you kill me."'[11] A few hours later, 'Loser' was finished; more sessions produced 'Steal My Body Home', set to droning, de-tuned guitars which evoke essraj and tamboura, flutes and featuring grimy fatalistic lines such as 'lost my head beneath the wheel'. The two tracks did not strike either man as particularly special, just as many innovations seem ugly and failed right after they are made. All involved promptly forgot about the sessions; they were just a piece of fun, fooling around with ideas. As well as 'Loser', Stephenson co-wrote three other songs that later appeared on Beck's *Mellow Gold* album, which he co-produced; he also worked on some Beck B-sides including 'Corvette Bummer', and 'In A Cold Ass Fashion' from the Jabberjaw compilation *Good To The Last Drop*.

According to inside sources, Carl would later come to regret helping produce 'Loser', because of the apparently negative attitude towards life expressed in the lyrics, which would qualify him as the very first person to totally miss the point of the song. Beck also contributed vox and harp to several of Carl's tracks for his own project *Forest For The Trees*. His background vocals are evident on 'Jet Engine' and 'Infinite Cow', while 'Fall' has his harmonica somewhere deep in the mix. 'Carl's influence on Beck was probably more profound than Beck's influence on Carl because Beck was ostensibly a folk singer with a lot of history,' Geffen A&R man Tony Berg told the *Los Angeles Times* in 1997. 'Carl introduced him to the wedding of beats and content, and created something I don't think existed prior to "Loser".'[12] True, but this alchemical wedding of beats and folk was hardly unfamiliar to Beck, who had grown up in L.A. hearing hip-hop blasting out of car stereos and windows all over his neighbourhood. 'At the time, I was really getting into folk music, but I'd realized that a lot of what folk music is about is taking a tradition and reflecting your own time,' he reflected later. 'I knew my folk music would take off, if I put hip-hop beats behind it.'[13] In fact, he had been working towards the sound that crystallized on 'Loser' for some time. 'I had the idea in about 1988. I could play you four-track tapes from the late Eighties that I did with hip-hop beats. I don't think I would have been able to go in and do "Loser" in a six-hour shot without having been somewhat prepared. It was accidental, but it was something that I'd been working toward for a long time.'[14]

Meanwhile, a storm was about to erupt in Los Angeles which had long been brewing. L.A.-based rappers such as Ice T and Ice Cube had been warning in their raps of unrest to come for several years now, with N.W.A.'s vehement 'Fuck Tha Police' articulating the animosity many people on the street felt towards the L.A.P.D. On 29 April 1992, twelve jurors found one of the officers in the Rodney King beating incident guilty of excessive force; while the other three were cleared of all charges. As soon as the live broadcast of the verdict went out, widespread rioting broke out which lasted for the following three days. A curfew was enforced and all schools and many businesses were closed. Governor Pete Wilson dispatched 4,000 National Guard troops to patrol the streets. All told, 50 people were killed, 4,000 were injured, 12,000 people were arrested, and there was $1 billion in property damage. Across the city the riots threw up bizarre sights indeed – affluent college kids joining in the riots for fun, a white truck driver getting pulled from his truck and beaten by black toughs, only to be rescued by other blacks, Korean businesses were incinerated; Latino grandmothers looted supermarkets at an unhurried pace.

The aftermath of the riot altered the city in fundamental ways. Today Los Angeles still feels like a ghost town at night. Clubs are closed at 2 a.m. and the streets are deserted an hour later. In his superb account of Los Angeles music past and present, *Waiting For The Sun*, Barney Hoskyns noted the way people in Los Angeles band together in small groups of friends amidst the vastness of the city's urban sprawl. If anything, the period after the riots further accentuated this tendency. It was in this shell-shocked atmosphere that a curious accident occurred. In retrospect, its timing in the wake of the riots is significant; it is unlikely it would have had as strong an impact in less paranoid times.

One day Rothrock chanced across the tapes from Beck's experimental sessions at Stephenson's house. There was something in that song that a year's remove made sound altogether remarkable. Outside of the context of that casual night's doodling, the song revealed itself to be a strange fission of old and new that would henceforth strike everyone who heard it. In a racially polarized city, the song's white folk blues mixed with black rap was rather shocking. The song was comical too, with its absurdist stream-of-consciousness lyrics that seemed to address the disjointed ragtag aesthetic that characterizes Los Angeles' homes, freeways, winding hills, bodegas, barrios, buses, beaches and hundred and one racial recombinants. Sitting on a café terrace in Silverlake, you might see a green eyed Mexican-Irish-American buying croissants, a mulatto girl with light cocoa skin and long wavy hair, three Latino painters with dark eyes talking about Spengler in Spanish and a British scriptwriter who long ago left Newcastle for California, reading the paper in the corner. Somehow, 'Loser' is something that seemed part of the same melting pot world, with its jangled asides in German and Spanish, its rap closer to Son House preachin' the blues than Chuck D, its junkyard imagery and the soundbites of a fictional race car driver repeating his mantra to himself – 'Things are gonna change, I can feel it'.

The song ultimately addressed itself to those sections of society which are colloquially referred to as 'freaks', those who don't fit the demographic: outcasts, misfits; the one who never got the girl; the girl who didn't get away in time; those who were too white or too black or too loud or too quiet. The ones who laugh in the sad parts and cry in the happy ones. There is enough of a freak in everyone to ensure that 'Loser' would become larger than life, blown so far out of proportion that it could be hijacked in a dozen ways, by record companies, louts who didn't get the irony at all, Karaoke compilations and media mythologizing, used in marketing campaigns in ways that the song's singer could never have dreamt of, and wouldn't have wanted to.

'Loser' bridged two seemingly opposite genres – a stinging blues bottleneck guitar lick matched to the slack beats of hip-hop, creating a hybrid so obvious that it was remarkable no one had stumbled on it before. This was 'Loser''s brilliance: it dissolved the past into the future, working like Fluxus's cellular boundary solvents to make a wholly new sound. Its arrival in the wake of the Los Angeles riots is also significant, as it wilfully ignored categories, bridging the gap between black versus white, and old versus new. But what the novelty value of a folk and hip-hop pastiche didn't reveal was Beck's fractured poetic sensibilities, much less his black humour and irony, which flew over the heads of most casual listeners. Beck was not a clown by nature, and if he ever played that part, it was under duress. His sensibility led him to make people laugh at their own seriousness and, deeper still, to question what had made them so joyless in the first place. Therein lies a key element of Beck's joyous subversion.

Rothrock called Beck and said he was thinking of putting out a few hundred copies of 'Loser', backed with 'Steal My Body Home'. No big deal, just another indie release, mostly targeted at the friends who had loved the song when they first heard it. Beck shrugged in agreement: why not? Whatever the singer's feelings on the track, however, Rothrock sensed he was onto something special: 'Before the record even got pressed, there was all this excitement, there were bootlegs right away.'[15] Beck signed an exclusive production agreement with Bong Load on 11 January 1993, although he had mild reservations about the song's title. 'My friend Steve Hanft had a band called Loser, so the song tied in with that. It was an in-joke with friends. Then I saw someone wearing a Sub Pop T-shirt that had "Loser" on it. And I thought, "Oh, God, I hope that song never comes out. People will think I got the idea from a T-shirt." Then it eventually came out. Then Radiohead had a song called "Creep", and I thought, "They're going to think 'Loser' is from some Radiohead song.""[16]

Beck's very first recorded debut was a 7-inch single for indie label Flipside, featuring 'MTV Makes Me Want To Smoke Crack' and 'To See That Woman Of Mine', in January 1993. It wasn't even a full Beck single, but a split with the band Bean on the other side, printed on clear blue vinyl. It was included with issue 46 of Flipside, and an estimated 500 were made, making it the rarest of all Beck's releases.

His first full-length album was released the same month. The cassette-only *Golden Feelings* was a seventeen-song sampler of Beck's songs, sold for $3 at shows. From 1993 until 1995, Sonic Enemy's Peter Hughes made the tapes as people ordered them. He made about a thousand, dubbing them at home or sending them out to 52nd Street for larger batches, with a photocopied insert depicting a tableaux of stuffed animals taking tea. Lo-fi and lo-tech, the tape had white sticker labels with 'Beck' on one side and 'Golden Feelings' on the other in gold ink. The cassettes were cheap and tended to break and unravel, but the songs inside were magic. 'Special People', a stripped-down talking blues with no accompaniment, assails the idly consumerist society with scathing humour, using absurdity to lampoon 'special people' who drink 'special beer' and who are 'so sincere'. 'Super Golden Black Sunchild' features Beck slowing his vocals down on his four-track to something resembling a derelict Aaron Neville, with a rich melody and unusual chords below. The deathly decay of low-wage jobs available to underclass bohemians like Beck is illustrated time and time again on songs such as 'Soul Sucked Dry'. Here, Beck skewers his own satires and morose ruminations with slowed-down or speeded-up vocals, guitars played out of tune, abrasive noise or lo-fi hiss and hum.*

Beck's song output during the start of the year was prodigious indeed. *Fresh Meat & Old Slabs* is a tape he made for his mom's birthday on 21 January 1993. Recorded on his four-track recorder in his mother's living room, *Fresh Meat & Old Slabs*, like *The Banjo Story* before it, is a vital account of his nascent development, including skeletal early versions of 'Satan Gave Me A Taco', 'Tasergun' and 'Steve Threw Up'. One of the standout tracks was 'Fume', based on the true story of some kids the Hansens knew who pulled their van off the road one day, rolled up the windows and let off a tank of nitrous oxide they had; they all died, laughing helplessly. Beck's own attitude to drugs has always been a grey area, though in 1996 he told *Spin* magazine, 'People think that drugs are a big part of my identity, and they really aren't. I don't need drugs to be creative. That's not what my music's about. It's a creative crutch. There are aspects to the music that have something to do with disorientation, but it's more about disorientation in modern life and our culture.'[17]

On the tape, Beck quickly runs through his old open-mike standards, including 'Let's Go Moon Some Cars', a revised and doubly harrowing 'Goin' Nowhere Fast' (which opens with a sample of Woody Guthrie's 'Talking Hard Work') that is painful to listen to, so despondent and angry is this version, and even 'Cut in Half Blues'. Beck's songs of this period refer again and

75

---

* 'Golden Feelings (full-length cassette, Sonic Enemy Records, Jan 1993). The full track listing was as follows:
1 The Fucked Up Blues 2 Special People 3 Magic Station Wagon 4 No Money No Honey 5 Trouble All My Days
6 Bad Energy 7 Schmoozer 8 Heartland Feeling 9 Super Golden Black Sunchild 10 Soul Sucked Dry 11 Feelings
12 Gettin' Home 13 Will I Be Ignored By The Lord 14 Bogus Soul 15 Totally Confused 16 Mutherfukka
17 People Gettin' Busy

again to being pulled apart by predatory forces, though whether from within or without is ambiguous at best. His harmonica solo on 'Cut In Half Blues' is solid, delivered over a rolling bass line played on his guitar. The lyrics about a girlfriend who is a chainsaw murderer has a Freudian dread underpinning its silliness, with the song ending on a skid mark of a chord.

'Tasergun' is as close as Beck comes to straight, unvarnished narrative, and tells the tale of a neighbour in a shitty Hollywood rooming house. The neighbour, an old man in a bathrobe who spends his pension on porn and brings 'strange young men home', hates Beck's guitar playing and bangs on the paper thin walls with his boot. The man stares at Beck through a crack in the door until he finally loses it and busts in with a Tasergun – a charming contraption capable of delivering a 50,000-watt jolt of electricity strong enough to knock a horse unconscious. The guards along the U.S./Mexico border have used these devices indiscriminately for years on would-be migrants. Beck's deadpan delivery make the story all the more darkly comic.

'Ballad of Mexico' is an epic inversion of a 'going on the lam' tale. In the song, Beck dreams up a situation in which he is working at McDonald's only to get fired for not calling the police during a robbery. He and his friends rob the same McDonald's and split for Mexico, where Beck stays on... working at McDonald's. 'Leave Me On The Moon' would show up on the soundtrack for Steve Hanft's *Kill The Moonlight* film, while 'Satan Gave Me A Taco' was a tongue-in-cheek Greenwich Village song, written to amuse a few friends when Beck was still playing New York coffee shops and clubs.

'I like "Heartland Feeling" a lot,' Beck reflected on the radio a few years later. 'That song came out of a meeting I had with Bruce Springsteen's producer. I was still banging around in coffee-houses and I'd never really had contact with real music industry type people, especially of that calibre. So I remember him espousing the merits of the songwriter and the loss of the singer-songwriter in music and how somebody needed to go out and write about the experiences of the people in the heartland of America. But to my mind a lot of that [...] "landscape of the heartland singer-songwriter" was a cliché-ridden escape, simplistic and exploitative almost. That song was a reaction to that. So it's a fairly ironic song but it touches a certain nerve, bridges a certain intrinsic sadness in the day-to-day grind of the heartland as a wasteland, or a bland land.'[18]

'Big Stompin' Mama' is a harrowing and comical howl of a song, and fairly self-explanatory. 'Death Is Coming To Get Me' opens with a New Age incantation, with Beck delivering a pompous spiel before drifting into a furious feedback and hammering drummed tale of the Grim Reaper, who not only 'reads your diary' but gives all your household belongings away to 'people you don't even know'. 'Captain Brain' merits no mention at all. 'Go Where U Want' would surface as 'Hollow Log' on *One Foot In The Grave* and in this version is harmonically spare and lyrically rich.*

Fresh Meat & Old Slabs was leaked out to the bootleg market by a very unscrupulous 'fan' who sold copies over the internet, saying he was Bibbe and Sean, and charged exorbitantly for them. Eventually the original tape was stolen from Bibbe, who no longer even has a bad copy of the original. *Fresh Meat & Old Slabs* was a kind of dress rehearsal for Beck's first indie album, *A Western Harvest Field By Moonlight*, released on Fingerpaint Records in 1993 on 10-inch vinyl; the original pressing of 3,000 came with a finger painting made by Beck, friends and fans at a

---

* *Fresh Meat & Old Slabs.* (No label, no release, January 1993) The full track listing was as follows: 1 Let's Go Moon Some Cars 2 Goin' Nowhere Fast 3 Cut In Half Blues 4 Sucker Without A Brain 5 Tasergun 6 Grease 7 Ballad Of Mexico 8 Fume 9 Leave Me On The Moon 10 I Feel Low Down 11 Satan Gave Me A Taco 12 Heartland Feeling 13 Big Stompin' Mamma 14 Steve Threw Up 15 Say Can You See 16 I Feel Like A Piece Of Shit 17 Death Is Coming To Get You 18 Captain Brain 19 Go Where U Want 20 Totally Confused 21 Trouble All My Days 22 Kill Me

release party. Between bouts of dada noise, trashed vocals and sabotaged half-songs, Beck plays some excellent songs including 'Goin' Nowhere Fast', 'Fume' and 'Heartland Feeling'. A somewhat melancholy album, and one often derailed by Beck's more chaotic impulses, it has an ambivalence and lo-fi disdain that makes it alternately compelling and a bit of a throwaway.*

Steve Hanft was still toiling away on his film *Kill The Moonlight*, filming when he had money and raising more money when he didn't. Beck wrote three songs for the soundtrack – well, two songs and a sound collage called 'Underwater Music'. Hanft said, 'Beck was writing about ten songs a week and making a shitload of four-track tapes. Most of the stuff was weird thrasher folk songs with surreal lyrics. He wasn't getting booked to play very many shows in Los Angeles, so he would play before local bands uninvited [...] People would get into his songs because they had a lot of rhymes. Beck and his friend Martha Atwell were really into old country music. They formed Ten Ton Lid, and started playing Louvin Brothers and Carter Family songs. At one point they managed to get some shows at a bar up in the mountains of Saugus: the Big Oaks Lodge. It was a weird scene because they were playing traditional folk songs and there were old folks square dancing and college kids partying.'[19]

Bong Load presses five hundred 12-inch copies of 'Loser' in March 1993 for friends and local college radio stations to play. Backed with the mesmerizing 'Steal My Body Home', the song took off in unexpected ways. The record was duly stamped onto vinyl and sent out to various indie pluggers, including the college station at Loyola Marymount College, KXLU. No big deal, but the song was so catchy, so compelling and so radical that everyone who heard it loved it. Soon National Public Radio's Santa Monica branch KCRW 89.9 FM got hold of it. Like a mutant fungus, 'Loser' was too insistent to be ignored. It was no time at all before it crept up the leg of the radio programmers at commercial alternative station KROQ. Seattle's the END radio station began playing it in constant rotation. And then there were no more copies; all five hundred were gone. Radio jocks in New York began calling Bong Load asking for more copies; 'Loser' was the song that wouldn't quit.

Beck tried to continue as if nothing had happened, working a job during the day blowing leaves. The leaf-blowing job Beck was working at during the day was a source of delight amidst the drudgery. Like Russolo with his Futurist noise box, Beck unleashed the leaf-blower at his shows. At night he would head down to the clubs, where he was finally getting his own spots on the bill. At Raji's Beck would break out the leaf blower, blasting the stage and sending flyers, drink napkins and newspapers through the air. 'There's a leaf-blower contingent,' he joked to *Spin* in 1994. 'There's no union that I know of so far, but there's certainly a spiritual brotherhood. They are the originators of noise music. It's like a cross between a Kramer guitar and a jet-pack.'[20] 'I was doing everything I could to subvert every corner I was being painted into,' he told *Elle* magazine in late 1999. 'I'd come out onstage with a leaf blower and blow leaves at all these industry types in the audience. A lot of it was kind of Dada and free form and silly. Some of it, I think people missed the point. The corporate people thought I was a clown. They decided, "Oh, he's wacky."'[21] The leaf blower also came in handy for the record company bidding war that had just begun, a process which Beck described as, 'a neo-primitive ceremony

77

---

* *A Western Harvest Field By Moonlight* (10-inch, Finger Paint Records, January 1994). The full track listing was as follows: Bic Side (Side A) 1 Totally Confused 2 Mayonnaise Salad 3 Gettin Home 4 Blackfire Choked Our Death 5 Feel Like A Piece Of Shit (Mind Control) 6 She Is All (Gimme Something To Eat) Beck Side (Side B) 1 Pinefresh 2 Lampshade 3 Feel Like A Piece Of Shit (Crossover Potential) 4 Mango (Vader Rocks!) 5 Feel Like A Piece Of Shit (Cheetoes Time) 6 Styrofoam Chicken (Quality Time)

I never wanted to be part of.'[22] Warner, CBS and Capitol all threw million-dollar offers in his direction. One important contact came out of all the schmoozing – his future manager John Silva. Of his initial sightings of Beck, Silva recalled, 'I went to see him at Raji's maybe two or three weeks after getting a tape of "Loser", and I was so excited. I remember coming home and my wife asking what I thought. I told her, "I don't know what this guy is doing, but he's doing something important."'[23]

Steve Hanft brought down his camera and filmed Beck at Raji's. Bong Load suggested Hanft film a video for 'Loser', so he began drawing up rough storyboards based on brainstorming sessions with Beck. 'When we made the video for "Loser", we were fucking around,' Beck confessed a few years later. 'We weren't making anything slick; it was deliberately crude. It wasn't like one of these perfect new-wave colour soft-focus extravaganzas. We were just fucking around. And now they're playing it all the time. It's the same thing with the song, that song was written and recorded in six hours. No plans went into it. It's totally ridiculous.'[24]

Like many of Beck's creative endeavours, the video was a controlled accident. Steve Hanft and Beck took off around northern California, filming here and there, dropping a bit of their buddy Julien Nitzburg's unreleased film about a mountain dancer called Jesco into the visual mix. The video, made for all of $300, reflects 'Loser''s mixed-up references perfectly. It was the first visual connection most people had to the voice behind the song. And it was startling. Amidst the avalanche of by-the-numbers alt. rock videos, it was so strange and exciting to see this crude and experimental portrait of a misfit. Beck dons a three-piece white suit, topped with a ski cap and shades and busts some extremely unconvincing disco moves. Two anti-cheerleaders dance asynchronously to the song; Beck cleans a car windshield with a flaming squeegee, smiling like the Cheshire Cat. A casket propels itself around, and Beck sets his guitar on fire at Raji's, the flames licking the low ceiling.

Beck's first album with Bong Load, tentatively titled *In A Cold Ass Fashion*, was recorded during two weeks of July and August 1993 for $500; Tom's house and Carl's kitchen were the recording studios. Mike Boito played organ on 'Beercan', David Harte played drums on a handful of tracks, and Rob Zabrecky played bass on 'Blackhole', along with Petra Haden from the band called that dog on violin. During a break in the recording, Beck recorded 'Steve Threw Up ' with some help from his friends in that dog at Tom Grimley's Poop Alley studio. Rachel Haden, Petra Haden, and Anna Waronker played, drums, violin, and bass respectively. A great band, that dog started out with Anna Waronker, sister of Beck's future drummer Joey, learning to play on Joey's left-handed guitar. Anna wrote songs, hooked up with two out of three of the Haden triplets, daughters of jazz bassist Charlie Haden, and a male drummer. Together they made a pair of albums and a dash of singles on DGC (the David Geffen Company) before splitting up. They went through the same circuit as Beck, appearing at Jabberjaw and playing around Silverlake. They would later join Beck on his tour as openers, receiving a warm response from audiences.

The album was finally dubbed *Mellow Gold*, a spin on the crappy compilations put out by low-budget K-Tel Records. Beck's enduring memory of the recording procedure was of how rushed it had all been. 'When we were recording in my friend Carl's living room–kitchen area, we'd usually have about three or four hours to work before his girlfriend came home to make herself some food. So a lot of those songs, the impetus behind them, is this mad dash to finish and get all the parts down before his girlfriend came back.'[25]

Faced with a group of fans yelling for him to play 'Loser' at Jabberjaw one night, Beck asked for someone in the audience to come up and play a hip-hop beat on the drum-kit behind him. Don Burnet, known as Dallas Don, a member of 3-D and, later, Lutefisk, jumped up to oblige.

This was a departure for a Beck set, which was usually driven by the singer, his acoustic and his harmonica. Something must have clicked in his mind though, because when he ran into Burnet again at a Popdefect show in Pasadena, Beck asked him to play drums for the band he was trying to get together. Beck was going electric, unwittingly, having to meet the demand for 'Loser'. The cry 'Play "Loser"!' would follow him around the world, at every gig, in every quiet moment, in the middle of an acoustic set, as he was talking to the crowd, right up to the present. The continual demand for a song which started life as an in-joke for his friends clearly started to grate with Beck after a while, though he tried to maintain a sense of humour about the situation: 'If all this ridiculous stuff keeps on happening to me, I'm really going to have to change those lyrics. I should go, "I'm a schmoozer, baby, so why don't you rock me?"'[26]

Meanwhile, Geffen A&R man Tony Berg was one who got hold of a copy of 'Loser' and was immediately impressed with it. He rang up Chris Douridas, the host of National Public Radio's KCRW station, and raved to him about the song and the artist. Douridas in turn contacted Beck and arranged for him to come down to the radio station studio in Santa Monica and record a session for his justly acclaimed show 'Morning Becomes Eclectic', an excellent showcase for musicians of quality and distinction, largely culled from the indie/alternative axis. On 7 July 1993 Beck recorded his first session for KCRW 89.9 FM, rapping live over a backing tape of 'Loser'. He also played 'Mexico', (later released on the *Rare On Air* compilation), 'Death Is Coming To Get Me', 'Whimsical Actress', 'Pay No Mind' and 'MTV Makes Me Wanna Smoke Crack'. 'In thirteen years of radio, I've never seen anything like it,' recalled Chris Douridas, program director at Santa Monica's KCRW. 'The first time I played it ["Loser"], I got eight calls in the four minutes the song was on the air.'[27]

Beck was now beginning to get attention from all sides. He knew something was not quite right when he turned up that same night at Troy for what he presumed would be another mundane gig on the small stage. If anything, he expected to see a small crowd of fans as he walked up to the café, acoustic in hand; instead, were people lined out the door. And they all clamoured for 'Loser'. Margaret Mittleman remembered the night of his radio debut: 'I went down to see him at this coffee house that was about the size of a railroad apartment. It was totally packed,' she recalled. 'The only thing Beck had to say was, "You guys should have been here last week – there were only six people here."'[28]

When Thurston Moore of Sonic Youth saw Beck perform a few nights later at a backyard party, he was blown away. Much as Sonic Youth had championed Kurt Cobain and Nirvana, both he and Kim Gordon now began raving about Beck. Reflecting on his first view of Beck back then, Moore described Beck to *Melody Maker* as 'a zombie-fawn guided by a translucent face with sci-fi eyes.'[29] Moore was particularly impressed by the radiant, scattered imagery of Beck's songs.

In the evening of 23 July 1993, Beck opened for Lois and the Spinanes at Jabberjaw. It was his first show with a hastily assembled band, comprising mostly Silverlake stalwarts. Dave Gomez, who played hardcore punk, took over bass duties, with his Seattle buddy Chris Ballew on guitar, and old Beck pal Mike Boito on keyboards and Dallas Don on drums. 'We did a sold-out show with him and Lois, which Beck insisted on opening,' recalls Jabberjaw's Gary Dent. 'Most people walked in late, asking "So when is he coming on?" long after he'd finished. They couldn't understand why this phenomenon was opening for someone they'd never heard of.'[30] Margaret Mittleman of BMG struck up a conversation with lawyer Brian McPherson at the bar during the gig, explaining that Beck needed an attorney. She introduced them, and the three met the next day; a few days later McPherson was Beck's attorney. He would need representation, as major label A&R men began to hog the front row of each of Beck's gigs, like a bevy of potential suitors.

Beck continued playing at night, slightly dazed by the success of 'Loser', though unaware of exactly how big it would become. Bong Load didn't even promote the single; it just continued to steamroll out of view. At one point KXLU, in a fit of indie snob pique, dropped 'Loser' from their playlists as soon as commercial alternative KROQ got hold of it and began playing it every hour. Beck was so annoyed that he wrote a letter to the station to complain. 'I've been playing on KXLU for a long time. I played all their fundraisers, and listened to the station since I was fourteen years old, because the music they play is the music I'm into. As for KROQ they played my song by themselves it's not like I begged them to play it. I mean, KXLU was the first to play "Loser".'[31] The snub was corrected shortly thereafter and Beck continued his support of the station, giving them the otherwise unreleased live-in-the-studio track 'Whiskey-Faced, Radioactive, Blowdryin' Lady', recorded on 13 September 1993 for their benefit compilation album *KXLU Live Volume One*.

Billboard magazine picked up on 'Loser''s success, prematurely lumping Beck in with a scene supposedly happening in Silverlake and placing him 'at the centre of one of the most dramatic buzzes to come out of the Los Angeles music scene in nearly a decade.'[32] The rush was on, and an epic schmooze-fest, with A&R representatives from every major label turning up to woo the slightly shell-shocked singer. For a period of over nine months, Beck consistently turned them down. 'I didn't want to be in that world, you lose control. And as soon as you're on that level, it's perceived that you're asserting yourself as the greatest, a rock star.'[33]

By August 1993 Beck, Rothrock, Schnapf and Stephenson had finished up *Mellow Gold*, and Beck took off soon after up to Olympia, Washington to cut some sides for Calvin Johnson's respected indie label K Records. Johnson was amazed: 'He just made up most of the songs, eleven of them, on the spot.'[34] In October 1993, Beck recorded the first of two sessions for what would become *One Foot In The Grave*, featuring a lot of the country blues and folk influenced songs he had been carrying around since New York. Old friend Carla Bozulich of the Geraldine Fibbers called Beck up saying she had written some songs with a country flavour. Beck contributed a track of his own: 'Blue Cross', with Beck and Chris Ballew playing and singing, which Beck co-wrote and which was recorded on Beck's four track at his house, was later released on The Geraldine Fibbers' album *Get Thee Gone* on the Sympathy For The Record Industry label.

On 19 November 1993, Bong Load entered into a third party deal with Geffen, which acquired the exclusive services of Beck in the agreement. Bong Load and Beck were required to provide masters for three albums to Geffen, which had two options for the delivery of four additional albums. Beck finally signed with a major label, David Geffen's DGC Records, in December 1993. DGC A&R Representative Mark Kates said in Beck's official Geffen bio, 'We signed Beck for who he is and that includes being an artist who wants to continue to do his various independent projects. In our view, it's all just part of his creative process and it would be a waste of time to try to change him.'[35] Amazing when considering that Neil Young was once sued by Geffen for making un-commercial records. Beck singing 'Just got signed' on 'Pay No Mind' makes getting signed sound like getting shot, reflecting a healthy ambivalence and distrust of the trick cyclists in the record biz. Like the school performance of *Winnie The Pooh* all those years before, Beck felt somebody was having a laugh at his expense and maintained a deep-rooted mistrust of the music industry and its machinations. The story goes, and it is perhaps apocryphal, that Beck called a few record companies back, but only Geffen took his call. 'I remember flipping a coin. I wasn't going to do anything for a long time, but Bong Load didn't have the means to make as many copies as people wanted. Geffen were involved and they wanted to take it to more of an organized place, one with a bigger budget and better distribution.'[36]

In January 1994, DGC re-issued 'Loser', this time on CD and cassette single, and it began a rapid ascent to the Top 10 on the U.S. pop charts. Because of the terms of the contract signed with Geffen, Bong Load retained the rights to release all Beck vinyl and issued another flood of 'Loser' on vinyl. As such 'Loser' became the only song released on an indie label to reach such heady heights since the advent of FM radio. DGC signed Beck with an unusual contract which allows him to release songs on independent labels as well on their corporate one. In this he was aided by the fact that 'Loser' had kicked up a storm before any major label had become involved with it; this gave the young Beck some valuable bargaining power. 'It's part of my contract with Geffen to be able to do albums for other labels like that. I wanted the freedom. I even turned down a couple of better offers because Geffen was willing to give me that. I just want to be able to make a record without having to make concessions or feel like I'm limiting myself. Geffen has never put pressure on me to make a certain type of record. They said they would have been happy if I had done another record like *One Foot In The Grave* for them. I wouldn't know how to make a record designed for them, anyway.'[37]

One of the first non-DGC records Beck worked on was a side project called Caspar and Mollüsk, a collaboration between himself (Mollüsk) and Chris Ballew (Caspar), and recorded in bedrooms in Seattle and Los Angeles on a four-track, Beck appears on the first track 'Twig', a spoken word and noise freak-out. The collaboration was issued as a 7-inch yellow vinyl single on tiny indie Cosmic Records in 1995. Beck had met Ballew in Seattle when Ballew jumped on stage at a solo show in late 1993 sponsored by Seattle alt. rock station KNDD to provide human beatbox sounds for 'Loser'. The sold-out show at the Crocodile Café was, according to a reviewer, 'one of the most underwhelming performances ever committed on that stage. Beck dropped his harmonica and often his place and often in the same song, space and time. First-time listeners were given to comments like "Is this guy for real?", "I don't get it" and "He scares me." His invoking the name "Ozzy" over and over was likened to a mantra of madness – and indeed, more than a few left mad.'[38]

Bong Load released the 7-inch single of 'Steve Threw Up', in December 1993. The cover featured Heino, the immortal German *schlager* magus, whose rumbling low voice possesses subsonic qualities that make hausenfraue hurl their hose at him in concert. The single has no side 1, but instead sides 2 and 3, with 'Steve Threw Up' featuring that dog doing sweet harmonies. 'Steve Threw Up' is an epic tale about Steve Moramarco, of the band Bean, having a bad acid trip at a Silverlake Street Fair, during which the plethora of food he consumes there is eventually regurgitated with horrific force. The flipside is a germinal version of 'Mutherfucker' that manages to satirize both grunge and paranoia in one fell swoop. The untitled track hidden at the end of side three is known as 'Cupcake' and features Beck screaming 'What the fuck is going on?!' in what the single's sleeve dubs 'Stereo-Pathetic High Fidelity'. And that put the cap on 1993, an incredibly bizarre year for Beck. The next year he would have even more reason to ask that question.

81

1   Wild, David. 'Beck', *Rolling Stone*, 21 April 1995

2   Norris, Chris. 'Return Of The Funk Soul Brother', *Spin*, December 1999

3   Sessions At West 54th Street, 6 September 1997, www.sessionsatwest54th.com/

4   Rubin, Mike. 'Subterranean Homeboy Blues', *Spin*, July 1994

5   'Super Beck: "Loser", Artist, Rock Star, Genius. *UHF* # 10, July–August 1996

6   Babcock, Jay. 'Beck', *Huh*, July 1996

7   Browne, David. 'Beck In The High Life', *Entertainment Weekly*, 14 February 1997

8   'Super Beck: "Loser", Artist, Rock Star, Genius. *UHF* # 10, July–August 1996

9   Cummings, Sue. 'Beck: Dumpster Divin' Man', *MTV*, June 1996

10 Johnson, Calvin. 'Calvin Talks To Beck, Beck Talks Back To The Rocket', *The Rocket*, January–February 1997

11 *Option*, May 1994

12 Hilburn, Robert. 'Pop Music "Dream" Deferred No More', *Los Angeles Times*, 16 November 1997

13 Joyce, John. 'Diary Of An LP', *Melody Maker*, 5 December 1998

14 Schoemer, Karen. 'The Last Boy Wonder', *Elle* magazine, December 1999

15 Wild, David. 'Beck', *Rolling Stone*, 21 April 1995

16 Sakamoto, John. 'Beck Answers His Fans', *Jam!*, 5 June 1996

17 Strauss, Neil. 'Artist Of The Year', *Spin*, 1996

18 Boots, J., 'Interview With Beck', VPRO Radio, Netherlands, 1997. http://www.vpro.nl/3voor12

19 Hanft, Steve. *Kill The Moonlight* liner notes, Sympathy For The Record Industry, 1997

20 Rubin, Mike. 'Subterranean Homeboy Blues', *Spin*, July 1994

21 Schoemer, Karen. 'The Last Boy Wonder', *Elle* magazine, December 1999

22 Cohen, Scott. 'The Joy Of Beck', *Details*, August 1996

23 *Option*, May 1994

24 Hilburn, Robert. 'Beck's Got A Brand New Bad', *Los Angeles Times*, 14 November 1999

25 'Super Beck: "Loser", Artist, Rock Star, Genius', *UHF* # 10, July–August 1996

26 Wild, David. 'Beck', *Rolling Stone*, 21 April 1995

27 Sprague, David. 'Sudden Change Of Fortune', *Newsday*, 1994

28 Sprague, David. 'Sudden Change Of Fortune', *Newsday*, 1994

29 Joyce, John. 'Diary Of An LP', *Melody Maker*, 5 December 1998

30 Sprague, David. 'Sudden Change Of Fortune', *Newsday*, 1994

31 Nardwuar The Human Serviette. 'Nardwuar vs. Beck', radio interview with Beck, 18 April 1994

32 *Billboard*, 27 November 1993

33 Grob, Julie. 'Beck', *Thora-zine*, May 1994. www.eden.com/thora-zine

34 Sprague, David. 'Sudden Change Of Fortune', *Newsday*, 1994

35 Kates, Mark. www.geffen.com/beck/bio

36 Cummings, Sue. 'Beck: Dumpster Divin' Man', *MTV*, June 1996

37 Tignor, Steve. 'Beck Beat', *Puncture*, Summer 1996, issue 36

38 Phalen, Tom. 'Beck's Back: He's A Loser, Baby, Who Knows How To Write Songs', *The Seattle Times*, 1 July 1994

7

HIJACKED GENERATION BLUES

'Loser' was one of those curious records, a regional hit that went national, just like in the old days when vinyl ruled and FM was progressive. 'Loser' started on college stations, progressed to alt. radio, then to the commercial stations throughout Southern California and onto the next hip epicentre, Seattle. It was the Trojan Horse that broke through the industry bulwark. Like the surprise success of Nirvana's *Nevermind* album in 1990, the success of these so-called alternative albums represented a clear tide shift in record buying tastes, and one which the mainstream corporate labels were quick to jump all over. Except they didn't quite know how to capture the demographic; hence the rise of the horrid 'Generation X' cliché.

The term itself was a second-hand appropriation, taken from Douglas Coupland's book of the same name. Coupland had got the title from another book, a British paperback issued in 1964 about the mods. Coupled with Richard Linklater's 1990 film *Slacker* about bohemian kids in Austin, Texas, Generation X was supposedly a catch-all term for disaffected twentysomethings caught in the slipstream of their elders, who had come of age in the Sixties. A media classification and misnomer, Generation X was eventually shown to be more of a marketing term for a slice of the consumer pie that marketeers were having a hard time selling to, or even gauging the preferences of. One could argue that they lost interest when they realized the so-called 'Generation X' didn't have the disposable income to merit their attention. The whole notion was a scam, and much resented by the very people it was supposed to describe. The term reached critical mass in the media in the aftermath of albums by Jane's Addiction and Nirvana. Since then there has been no real underground in America, with the media jumping on every original movement and killing it with overexposure before it has time to develop into anything of interest. 'In the early Nineties, when Nirvana was about to come out, there was this consciousness just for a moment connecting everyone of my age – a consciousness of mistrusts, of the rotten fruit of the Eighties', Beck told Barney Hoskyns in 1999. 'We'd all been turned off by that point, and were searching for something genuine. And then there was a whole year where the industry tried to figure out what this was all about. And they're pretty crafty: they just went out and hired a bunch of us, and now the commercials are cooler than the videos. It's an interesting situation: who's feeding whom? Or are they like two dogs sniffing each other's behinds?'[1]

If the exposure of Milli Vanilli as frauds marked the end of the false bombast of 1980s pop music, the subsequent advent of grunge and gangster rap were necessary purgatives. In time both genres became clichés; their respective pain and rage commodified. In Britain, grunge and gangster rap made a strong but brief impact, as different trends were afoot, harking back to the heyday of Sixties guitar bands. Groups such as Oasis, Blur, Cast, Pulp, the Bluetones and others were lumped under another catch-all term – Britpop – however dissimilar they were. Oasis's Noel Gallagher wrote 'Live Forever' as a riposte to grunge's nihilism, citing Nirvana's throwaway song title 'I Hate Myself And Want To Die' as an example of the excesses of that genre that his band were out to challenge.

As 1993 ended Beck began playing warm-up gigs around town in preparation for a national tour Geffen had booked him on. 'I remember tours being booked – I just showed up. It was probably a little awkward. Being twenty-three and having a stage and a lot of speakers.'[2] Dallas Don was tied up with his other bands, so Beck recruited Joey Waronker, brother of that dog's Anna, to play drums when he went on tour in 1994. A gifted drummer, Joey had been playing in alternative band Walt Mink when he got the call from Beck. Previously he had played in a Western Swing band called Radio Ranch Straight Shooters when he was just fifteen. Coincidentally, the guitarist in that band was Smokey Hormel, who also would later play with Beck. Another recruit was Ben Cooley, road manager for Walt Mink, who came onboard to manage Beck's upcoming national tour.

Beck kicked off 1994 with a New Year's Eve gig at Al's Bar. He rang his mother to ask if her friend, the formidable Afro-American drag queen Vaginal Davis would MC. Vaginal in turn told Bibbe that she wanted to put together a band for the evening; and she wanted Bibbe to play rhythm guitar. Bibbe recruited some of the kids from the Troy and assembled an impromptu punk band. Vaginal insisted that Bibbe and Heidi, the drummer, dress up in drag of their own, with suits, ties and wigs. Shortly before they were due to take the stage, Bibbe hid behind the bar. Beck was standing with his pals in the audience, when one of them yelled out, 'Oh my God, Beck! It's your mother!' Sean Carillo turned his video camera on Beck, capturing him with mouth agape. Black Fag, the band, was born. The crowd loved them, and Bibbe, punking out in drag, was wildly applauded.

Now, with Geffen's marketing people doing the big push, 'Loser' was to go far beyond a local breakout hit spun on a few select stations across the country. For the UK edition of 'Loser' Beck did a hilarious lounge version remake of 'MTV Makes Me Want To Smoke Crack' with Mike Boito doing a very campy piano backing to Beck's vilest Sam Butera imitation. The most unlikely of hit singles, the mainstream success of 'Loser' seemed a total accident. The song arrived in a fallow landscape of grunge-by-numbers and shallow Britpop. As 'Loser' became a phenomenon, pegged as an unwitting statement for his generation, Beck was dubbed the 'slacker king' by the popular media, who had misconstrued the deliberate self-mockery implicit in the song. It was a title that would haunt him for some time, despite his exasperated protests that the song was a tongue-in-cheek throwaway, not the cry of a generation. After the surprise success of the single Beck was quickly dismissed in the popular media as a one-hit fluke, a novelty sensation. Moreover, the 'slacker' tag was one which Beck bitterly resented, and with good reason: 'Slacker my ass. I never had any slack. I was working a $4-an-hour job trying to stay alive. That slacker stuff is for people who have the time to be depressed about everything.'[3]

Such pigeon-holing rankled because it represented a restriction of what Beck felt he could be in the American public eye. 'I always felt a little distant from American culture,' he told NME in 1999, 'because, speaking in broad terms, things that truly capture the American ideal are pretty one-dimensional. I don't want to say "lowest common denominator" because I'm not snooty about it, but maybe there's not much room for ambiguity. You're really only allowed to be one thing here, so when I came out it was, "You are the slacker, that's your thing." That's great, but can't I be a couple of other things? And I think if you want to achieve true success [in the States] you have to say, "OK, that's all I am." You have to be that cartoon forever.'[4]

Looking back on the success of the song a few years down the line, Beck stated that if anything it summed up to him the difference between the Eighties and the Nineties. He cited grunge and gangster rap as covering similar territory – music made by the dispossessed of society, people who were marginalized in the money-oriented Eighties; revealingly, he once referred to it as a 'talking blues'. But he felt the song had been hijacked: 'The people who took that song to heart were the jock people, the popular people, the attractive, stronger ones. But it was really coming from someone – myself – feeling displaced from the Eighties, a time of materialism where everybody was cashing in and making money. If you went to school and you were wearing the same shoes you had a year ago, and you'd grown out of them, and your toe was coming through a hole, it was not your time. You were not accepted. The people who embraced it represented the reason the song was written.'[5]

On 22 February 1994, Flipside released a full-length Beck album, initially entitled *Telepathetic Astro Manure*, then re-named *Stereopathetic Soul Manure*, an odd job lot of tracks recorded during 1988 and 1993, mostly on four-track, some on boomboxes, and some at Wire Works and Tom Grimley's Poop Alley studios. Beck characterized the content as 'exploding noise', and while the album is often referred to as a compilation of Beck's more outré and experimental output, it fairly accurately captures all aspects of his various nascent styles, excepting hip-hop. The four-track songs are engaging lo-fi recordings of many of the songs Beck had been playing for years. Another few songs are country workouts with pedal steel, quite traditional, with 'Rowboat' echoing Jimmie Rodgers woeful and humorous love laments, complete with pedal steel guitarist Leo LeBlanc. Noise collages, spoken-word bits and metalloid Pussy Galore style freak outs like 'Pink Noise (Rock Me Amadeus)' laced with waves of distortion, are interspersed throughout. 'Folk-noise' was Beck's description of the disparity between his two albums to date, reflecting the extremes within which his music world is still held in check: Guthrie at one pole, and Pussy Galore at the other. The CD artwork for *Stereopathetic Soul Manure* features a crude map to get beer, a cover taken from the corner of the cover of a thrift-store record called *Brahms, Gigi, And All That* by the Clayton Valley Singers. Some CDs contain a twenty-fifth track, comprising an alternately ethereal and noisy sound collage, with some good old-fashioned backwards masking, and Beck muttering 'Bend over, in the clover'. This last track is a fascinating echo collage with dub-like echoes dissolving across the sonic spectrum, one of Beck's more experimental offerings and approaching *musique concrète* at times.

'Thunder Peel' is the James Bond theme song Jon Spencer never wrote, with a uniquely Beckian twist. Unusually, the guitars are tuned to A. On his cover of Jimmie Rodgers' 'Waitin' For A Train', sounding like it was recorded on a street corner, Beck harmonizes with Ken, a homeless man who used to camp out by the freeway exit near Beck's apartment. Ken sings touchingly, off-key, with a slight tinge of madness itching in his voice. Beck said, 'I haven't seen him since we recorded that,' Beck told *Jam!* a few years later. 'He used to be on the freeway off-ramp in front of my old house, but he's long since disappeared.'[6]

The techno intro to 'No Money No Honey' is taken from B12's 'Hall Of Mirrors', off the album *Electrosoma*; Beck cribbed it from a random radio trawl one night during which he heard the track on MARS, the first (and last) American all-techno station. It was a curious choice, random as it was, because B12 were one of the first techno artists to consciously try and connect back to the spirit of electro. But the rough edit right into a very raw 'No Money No Honey' is a sharp retort to the little taste of techno. Ken and Beck howl together on this, Beck's simplest of tunes, just three chords and one line, recorded on a dictaphone with the pair standing on a street corner in downtown Los Angeles.

'Total Soul Future (Eat It)' was chosen, bizarrely, for inclusion on a 1999 Rhino compilation entitled *Wire's Futurists*. A live rendition of 'One Foot In The Grave', which was to become the anchor of almost all Beck's subsequent live shows, is featured here in a recording done at a coffee house. Doing his best Sonny Terry, Beck lays down some inspired harmonica and foot stomping, augmenting the Guthrie-esque verses.

Beck once dismissed 'Today Has Been A Fucked Up Day' as 'a silly song', but it is also a terrific song, an update of the Carter Family's 'Sad And Lonesome Day', complete with banjo and Beck doing three-part harmonies, each vari-speeded to hit a different pitch. For effect, Beck does a vocal which involves him literally running around his apartment singing the verses. 'Puttin' It Down' is a straightforward staple of Beck's open-mike days. He also reprises 'Tasergun' from *Fresh Meat & Old Slabs*. 'Modesto' is a tale of being caught after dark in a 'supermarket town' of the sort that make up the bulk of California's interior, affluent towns – an environment so foreign to Beck that it feels like another country. In the song he is roundly rejected by the college girl whose dorm he passes out in; then, once out on the road, he can't get a ride. Beck's discomfort in the company of girls who won't acknowledge his presence is pained; even more so is the imagery of him warming his cold fingers on a stove. With a few stray lines Beck is able to skilfully convey the myriad tangle of a night. If poetry is basically the ability to convey the maximum depth of imagery with the fewest possible words, Beck succeeds here brilliantly.

Beck's major label debut on Geffen, *Mellow Gold*, was unleashed on 1 March 1994. The title is in sharp contrast to the sculpture on the cover of a gruesome nitrous oxide inhaler. The sculpture, reflecting the junkyard aesthetic that is never far from the album's core, is entitled 'The Last Man after the Nuclear War' and was made by Eddie Gomez from fellow Silverlake band Sukia. Under the terms of the deal with DGC, the vinyl edition was issued by Bong Load and the CD and cassette by Geffen. With production credits by Bong Load's Rothrock and Schnapf and Carl Stephenson, and recorded in sixteen days, *Mellow Gold* was a critical and popular favourite, selling over a million copies worldwide in its first year of release. The songs on the album veer from skewered folk to extreme noise freak-outs, with the more satirical narratives of 'Nitemare Hippy Girl' and 'Truckdrivin' Neighbors' showing a sharp mind under the rudimentary chords. Though Beck was dismissive of the record, saying it was a hodge podge made under pressures of time and budget, *Mellow Gold* has aged well. Compared to the grunge and rap albums released in 1994, *Mellow Gold* feels like it was made in a distant outpost, far from marketing considerations or prevalent tastes. Beck also felt in retrospect that he was a little underprepared for the expanded panorama the studio and a band offered: 'Up until that time I had played solo acoustic mostly and I didn't have much experience with drums and electric guitars and other instruments. Before I was using a pencil, and all of sudden I had all these colours to work with.'[7] The statement is a reminder of Beck's denial of all things 'slacker': if his records sounded rough and home-made, that was because he hadn't been able to afford more expensive recording technology, not because he'd deliberately aimed for a scuzzy sound. Beck had to work on boomboxes and old four-tracks, because that's all that was available to him and he was dismissive of the flood of deliberately lo-fi recordings that were issued that year: 'If I'd had access to twenty-four tracks when I made "Loser" I would have used them! I was always trying to make it sound as good as I could. I was embarrassed by a lot of my songs because of the way they sounded. I was ashamed of my music because it was so badly recorded.'[8]

In what is certainly one of the most beautiful descriptions of the creative process ever documented, Beck outlined the making of *Mellow Gold* shortly after its release to a flabbergasted reviewer from corporate music magazine *Rolling Stone*. 'The whole concept of *Mellow Gold* is that it's like a satanic K-Tel record that's been found in a trash dumpster. A few people have molested it and slept with it and half-swallowed it before spitting it out. Someone played poker with it, someone tried to smoke it. Then the record was taken to Morocco and covered with hummus and tabouli. Then it was flown back to a convention of water-skiers, who skied on it and played frisbee with it. Then the record was put on the turntable, and the original K-Tel album had reached a whole new level. I was just taking that whole *Freedom Rock* feeling, you understand.'[9]

Mellow Gold opens with 'Loser'. The UK single version of the track was released in February and quickly rose to a peak at number 15 in the charts. From the outset Beck would find a ready audience in Britain, and this at a time when most American alt.indie acts couldn't get arrested at Heathrow, let alone fill the Camden Palace. The intro to the second song, 'Pay No Mind (Snoozer)', is a fragment of Beck at double speed saying 'This is song two on the album, this here's the album,' before offering a glimpse into his own ambivalence: 'Burn the album!' 'Pay No Mind' was one of Beck's oldest songs, going right back to when Lach made him write his own songs. The melody is derivative, the lyrics a bit naive, but in twenty years' time when people talk about Beck this will be one of the songs that will still ring true. There are some vinyl copies of *Mellow Gold* rumoured to have a phantom version of 'Pay No Mind', an alternate take with a different verse called 'Got No Mind' that also shows up on the 'Beercan' CD single.

'Fuckin' With My Head (Mountain Dew Rock)' is a full grunge-Delta-blues rocker, closer in spirit to the blues records by R.L. Burnside – a very raw blues laced with a New Orleans second-line rhythm, and a jangly guitar break and huffing harmonica. Songs like these reveal that Beck had absorbed all his influences to a degree most of his peers in the alt. rock world would have had no inkling of. 'Whiskeyclone, Hotel City, 1997' is a lament of dead-end jobs and dead-end roads, with touches of boleros, Ennio Morricone, and a spoken-word bit. 'Soul Suckin' Jerk' also addresses the miseries of a dead end job, though without getting on a soapbox and decrying the injustices of class. In 'Soul-Suckin' Jerk,' Beck quits his job at a chicken stand in a mini-mall, incinerating his uniform in a vat of chicken fat.

'Truckdrivin' Neighbors Downstairs (Yellow Sweat)' opens with a fragment of a tape recording of Beck's downstairs neighbours about to begin a gruesome fight that would leave one of them with an arm hacked off with an axe. In a weird moment of synchronicity, Beck had been sitting preparing to write a four-track description of his wretched neighbours when the fight began. So unnerved was he by the swearing, screaming, and punches that he heard from downstairs, that he fled the apartment, dashing down the back stairs, getting in his beat-up pick-up and getting the hell out of there. He forgot to turn off the four-track and the entire fight was recorded. 'It was a real experience. I wouldn't have written a song like that. I was shook up, because these two fellows were very abusive and were living right below me so it impinges on your life. I could hear them all day and finally they had a huge brawl [...] I had to leave because it was too hectic. When I came back I had all this. I had the song and then after they had this argument. It's too bad I lost the tape that has the original argument because the argument went on for forty minutes. It was unbelievable [...] I was so shook up by the thing that I pulled over on the freeway and I just wrote the lyrics out and then the next day came back and sang the lyrics over the song. It was one of those experiences where life writes the songs. Which is good.'[10]

'Beercan' is an inspired production, infused with Stephenson's good-natured sonic whimsy, and sliced and diced mariachi samples. A guitar sample from the Melvins' 'Hog Leg', a Balinese gamelan break and a hilarious talking doll squeaking 'I'm sad, and unhappy!' are spliced into the mix.

Based on someone he met in the poetry scene, 'Nitemare Hippy Girl' is one of Beck's most drolly humorous songs. It is enervating to hear a song with intelligent wit buried on an album which was recorded during the dark days of grunge, a ray of light indicating that there was much more to Beck than 'Loser' might have suggested, and emphasizing once again that not only was humour a key element in his music, but it was applied with a deft and multi-layered touch.

'Mutherfucker' is a satiric poke at grunge, a straight-out Melvins-meet-Pussy Galore rocker. The final track is 'Blackhole', a song with a meditative Indian air and an epic grandeur, halfway between Appalachia and Kashmir. Celtic and Hindustani drones anchor the piece, with lovely violin by Petra Haden and Rob Zabrecky on bass. The album closes with an alt. rock cliché culled from indie rock albums, a stretch of silence and a blast of noisy experiment. Nirvana used this to good effect on *Nevermind*, for example, but Beck would continue using this device on all his subsequent albums. *Mellow Gold*'s unlisted extra track is a Moog keyboard noise smorgasbord, panning violently from left to right, like a total malfunction onboard the Battlestar Galactica.

As per his contract with DGC, Beck continued to release non-Geffen albums as a means of experimenting with different musical styles. *One Foot In The Grave*, released on 27 June 1994 was recorded for K Records in October 1993 and January 1994 at Dub Narcotic in Olympia, Washington. In contrast to *Stereopathetic Soul Manure*, Beck characterized the album as more in the vein of the old-style country blues and folk of his pre-'Loser' days. Indeed, Beck had been planning to record an album for K long before 'Loser' broke; 'K records was going to put out my record in 1992, but nobody ever got around to it. And then stuff just started happening too fast.'[11] *One Foot In The Grave* featured old songs, material that was much more in line with the kind of music that Beck had been playing up until that point than 'Loser' had been. The album featured backup vocals by Calvin Johnson of the Halo Benders and Sam Jayne, Scott Plouf of the Spinanes and later Built to Spill, James Bertram on bass (pictured on the cover with Beck), Chris Ballew on guitar and bass, Mario Prietto on bongos and Beck on vocals, guitar, drums and bass.

Beck kicked off his K set with an authoritative version of the 1931 Skip James track 'Jesus Is A Mighty Good Leader'. Recorded in a grim claptrap basement, it's no wonder those K Records sound dark – witness Elliot Smith's stuff, that grim Olympia air, rainy and wet and cold seeping into your bones, down deserted streets. Beck changes Jesus to a generic 'He', which is a neat inversion, making the song a universal backwards ode to fathers everywhere.

The raw emotion of 'Girl Dreams' marked a step forward for Beck, stripping away layers to reveal a sincere lament. Like Kurt Cobain, in Olympia Beck found an island in a sea of indie stupidity. The bubblegum twee excesses of K are well documented, but they were successful in maintaining an almost aggressively innocent pop ethos in the face of waves of sludge fest negative bands. It gave Cobain an outlet to do songs like 'About A Girl', which weren't as overtly 'grunge' as some of his other material, and the Beatlesque overtones were appreciated there. Beck said of 'Girl Dreams': 'until I came to Olympia I was never safe, I was never allowed to do that. I was really surprised when I just started playing that stuff. The only reaction that I'd ever gotten was to the obvious, novelty songs. So I had all these songs I was writing that were more personal, serious, but I just kept them to myself. It's important to have a safe space to do that.'[12]

A Hank Williams Sr. fatalism, of the sort that pervades Williams' spooky hymn 'Angel Of Death' or 'I'll Never Get Out Of This World Alive', is as strong a strain throughout Beck's work as any of his other influences, stemming from country and blues. In 'I've Seen The Land Beyond', death becomes release, in the tragic sense that emerges time and time again in the works of American writer Cormac McCarthy. The song is also a nod to the Carter Family's eerie 'Will You Miss Me When I'm Gone'.

Beck and his new band took the stage at Troy as part of their pre-tour warm-up. Beck began the show by announcing: 'This is a total harmonica freakout from 1896 called "One Foot In The Grave"', then launched into his ode to Sonny Terry. When the song finished, he surveyed the crowd and asked, 'What's with these "Loser" T-shirts? Don't you people have any self-respect?' Bye bye slacker king. The following night was the band's last one before the tour began and took place in Jac Zinder's Fuzzyland, a decrepit former bowling ally; the stage was positioned at the end of a bowling lane. After a ramshackle set, Chris Bellew told a journalist from *Spin* magazine, 'We need about two or more weeks of rehearsal.' Asked how long it was until the band went on the road, Ball replied, laughing, 'Two days [...] Well, we'll work it out on the road.'[13]

Shortly before the tour proper, Loyola Marymount University was the scene of a jam between Beck and Sonic Youth's Thurston Moore on the tiny radio station KXLU, where they performed a thirty-minute extreme noise freak-out which Moore dubbed 'Super Christ'. Beck blasted at his Moog keyboard while Ballew drummed on a metal chair and Moore unleashed foul guitar triads. Beck tweaked the ancient keyboard to sustain one note indefinitely, then raced out to do a couple of laps around the university grounds. 'Maybe he's lost?' asks one of the girls working in the studio. 'He is lost,' answers Moore. 'And sometimes he gets found. These days, he gets found a lot. It's like Hendrix, he took drugs to get straight.'[14] Beck was simply freaked out all the attention he was suddenly attracting; fame seemed like a car crash.

One unfortunate aspect of the hype that began to surround Beck was that it resulted in an effort to classify him, put him into a neat box, label him, put an expiry date on him and throw him out when his fifteen minutes were up. They say that nature abhors a vacuum; likewise; mass media hates what it cannot classify. To his credit, Beck has confounded those efforts, essentially by following his instincts. 'I don't come up with this easily digestible, what-you-see-is-what-you-get thing: "This is my hairstyle, this is my outfit," so people made up the slacker image for me. Being attached to a highly disposable segment of the popular culture – the one-hit wonders, the cartoon slackers, the video phantoms – it's a little troublesome,'[15] he told *Entertainment Weekly* in 1997, with characteristic dry humour.

A definite generation gap emerged during the coverage of his first tour, with most writers sent out to interview Beck confused by him. After all, here was someone who had come out of the dregs of the world with a song saying he was a loser. How bizarre; and how confusing. The utter lack of comprehension evinced by most of the interviewers Beck subjected himself to confirms this. In turn, the interview junkets proved to be taxing and annoying. Interviewers who had seemed sincere face to face would hustle back to their offices, and produce a catalogue of clichés in their pieces. To them, Beck was a channel-surfing Cheetos-eating slacker with thrift-store clothes and meaningless lyrics. 'It's silly,' he observed, a couple of years later. 'You spend all your time making this music and as a musician this is how you communicate, this is the way you express what you have to say to the world, and then you have to spend three times as much time as you took making it explaining the music.'[16]

His increasingly high profile alerted Beck to the fact that his appearance, as well as his music and his comments, would be commented on and dissected for meaning. 'I never thought about the way I looked,' he reflected in 1997. 'Having your picture taken a lot, and doing videos, you become a little more conscious. My main discovery, my main rule-of-thumb for fashion, is clothes that fit. Before I would just put on anything and I would never realize that something was eight sizes too big.'[17]

On 20 February 1994 Beck appeared on MTV's '120 Minutes in New York City, NY' to play 'Pay No Mind', and then jam with Mike D of the Beastie Boys and Thurston Moore, his spiritual big brothers. A solemn Beck came out with his guitar, wearing brown corduroy and a red and white sweatshirt on which was written, in magic marker, 'Tell Me I'm Ozzy Because I Am'. He wore over-sized sunglasses, and was interviewed by Thurston Moore who asked him inanities, while Beck, stony-faced, indulged in a little Dada theatre, silently picked up an old school Bell dial telephone and smashed it to bits. A commentary on communication, mayhaps? He also performed 'Heartland Feeling' on HBO's *The Larry Sanders Show*, and reappeared on KCRW on 1 March to play 'Bogusflow', 'Dead Man With No Heart', 'Hard To Compete' and a demo tape of his side project with Chris Ballew, called 'Howling Wolves'. Beck also played 'It's All In Your Mind' and two songs dating back to the days of *Fresh Meat & Old Slabs*: 'Totally Confused' and 'It's All Going To Come To Be'.

After a 2 March *bon voyage* gig at Aaron's Records in Los Angeles, Beck set out on his tour supporting *Mellow Gold*, but was adamant about what he would and wouldn't do. 'I figured if people wanted me to come and play my songs for them, I'd come and play them. But they have to know that it's not all going to be like "Loser".'[18] Beck began his tour supporting *Mellow Gold* at SXSW, the epic schmooze fest in the so-called 'Music Capital of the World' in Austin, Texas. Beck was immensely relieved to see that Roger Manning, his anti-folk crony, was somewhere on the bill of 130 names stretched over five days. He jumped up to play a few jigs and reels with Manning before his own slot later that night. Manning was glad to see him, and was astonished to hear Beck had hit the pop charts. 'I was blown away,' recalled Manning. 'Here's this timid little guy on the edge of the scene – he's the last person we would have guessed to succeed.'[19]

Beck's own show was an unmitigated disaster. Maybe nerves got the better of him, but his performance came across as unintentional Dada theatre. Beck recalled, 'I was playing to a tape machine and the band started doing free-jazz shit over it. I was screaming into this cheap mike, and I broke a lot of stuff and started humping the bass player and knocked my mike over and hit this poor girl in the head. I remember watching the room just clear out.'[20] The beauty of it all was the shocked expressions on the faces of the hopefuls who play this charade of a music fest hoping to get signed by a major. Later on, Beck ran into a hirsute giant of a man on 6th street, who told him that his gig was the best performance he'd ever seen and gave him a medallion as a gift. An inscription on it read: 'God grant me the courage to change what I can, the serenity to accept what I cannot change, and the wisdom to know the difference.' It was only later that Beck realized he'd been talking to Gibby Haynes of the Butthole Surfers, the Austin-based band that had truly embodied an alternative to the mainstream and made *SXSW* seem flaccid by comparison.

His uncertainty about which way to go meant that Beck's stage shows were evolving as the band went along, throwing anything and everything into the mix to see what happened. 'We started doing very confrontational, completely experimental shows that left everyone confused,' Beck later told the *Los Angeles Times*. 'We'd start a song, then go into some fusion, then into these free-form odysseys. I didn't know what else to do because I didn't know about myself and my future. I was just having fun. People hated us or thought we were saying "Fuck you".'[21]

In the frantic first days of the tour, more and more of what Beck saw seemed appalling. Before performing in New Orleans in late March, he walked down Bourbon Street and passed one of the garish margarita bars catering to drunken college students in a post-Mardi Gras bacchanal. Inside there was a karaoke machine with, as Beck recalled it, 'five fraternity boys onstage, beer mugs in hand, trying to do "Loser" and not knowing what the hell the words were. They did this mumbling and head butting. Finally they just faded it out. Someone showed me a grunge karaoke tape and "Loser" was actually on it. If you make the karaoke scene, you have really arrived.'[22]

On a cold Tuesday, Beck, the band and his friends from that dog, the openers for this leg of the tour, rolled into New York. They took off down to St. Mark's Place, kicked around Beck's old haunts, ate falafel on their daily retainer, and skimmed the record bins in second-storey walk-up record stores in old brownstone buildings. Beck spotted a handheld karaoke machine down at the crazed stores on 14th Street that hawk everything from mung beans to stereos and bought it on the spot. That night the two bands played the fabled avant-noise club the Knitting Factory, at 47 E. Houston Street, right on the border where the East Village dissolves into uptown's monolithic glass ruins-to-be. Despite the cold outside, the Knitting Factory was sweltering hot with the perspiration of hundreds of teens, who started moshing insanely from the first note of that dog's set. By the time Beck came on, the audience was howling with abandon. Joey

Waronker egged them on by paying tribute to his elders, the Butthole Surfers, duplicating their famous lighter fluid on the cymbals and a match display of pyrotechnics. As flames licked the low ceiling, guitarist Ballew shouted 'Spam Rock!' and Beck and the band paid reverse homage to John Zorn's skronk with their lounge core version of 'MTV Makes Me Want to Smoke Crack'. A song more apt than ever because MTV was buzz binning the 'Loser' video into hype rotation. Beck did an acoustic 'Nightmare Hippy Girl' and caterwauled through 'One Foot In The Grave', cracking the boards under his boot heel and dropping a few asides at Pearl Jam's expense. Breaking out the karaoke machine Beck attacked 'Fuckin' With My Head' and 'Soul Suckin' Jerk.' For 'Blackhole,' that dog's Petra Haden jumped onstage with violin in hand for a hypnotic folk dirge that sent a shiver through the Factory. [23]

Three days later Beck opened for no less than Evel Knievel, the motorcycle daredevil who awed every teenage boy in the 1970s by jumping his motorcycle over thirty buses, missing and breaking every single bone in his body (and who said the Seventies sucked?).

With a gig nearly every other night, Beck was now on the same circuit that broke Jeff Buckley's health. In a non-stop road fest, the band took in Philadelphia, Toronto, Detroit, Columbus, St. Louis, Kansas City, Boulder, Salt Lake City, San Francisco, Memphis, Los Angeles, Lake City, Denver, Dallas, Cincinnati, Indianapolis, Pontiac and Chicago. It was the alternative equivalent to the old chitlin circuit that took black R&B and soul acts through an exhausting string of one-nighters and endless travelling between towns, not sure where you are, what time it is or where the next meal is coming from. 'You find yourself somewhere in the middle of New England, where the only place left open is some sports bar where all they have are potatoes because everything closes at six. It's completely hunter-gatherer,'[24] Beck later told *Papermag*.

As the tour progressed, Beck became the recipient of hostility from both mainstream media and the old indie network, which he had nominally appeared to be part of. When both sides work against the middle, perhaps it's a sign of progress, but this was little comfort to Beck. It was a confusing time. 'I remember being really shocked after *Mellow Gold* came out and going on tour, and all these kids were there. It totally disturbed me. Who are all these young people? I'd been playing Mississippi John Hurt covers in coffee shops to a bunch of thirty-, forty-, fifty-year-olds. Then all of a sudden there were these teenagers. It was very surreal.'[25]

On 18 April, before Beck played a gig at Slim's in San Francisco, Canadian radio personality and self-billed prank artiste Nardwuar The Human Serviette called him at his hotel, having finagled an interview. A tired but game Beck played along as Nardwuar ran through his tired schtick of baiting his interviewee-victims until they explode. Beck, known for his patience and grace, finally took the bait. 'Why should we care about you Beck?' demanded a shrill Nardwuar, egging him on, 'Is it because of your hair?' Beck, incredulous, laughed, 'I don't give a shit about my hair.' 'C'mon Beck, speak up, voice of a generation!' shrieked Nardwuar, before finally, in exasperation, Beck cut the prank interview short with: 'why don't you just fuck off?' and hung up. Beck told the *Toronto Sun*, 'He was totally freaking me out, he was on a mission to destroy Beck, and I was like "Be my guest." It got really vicious, something like all these commercial radio stations were playing me before the college radio stations got a chance was all my fault.'[26] Geffen promptly made the paper puff gesture of banning Nardwuar from interviewing all Geffen artistes.

91

1 Hoskyns, Barney, *World Art Magazine*, issue 19, Autumn 1999

2 *Rolling Stone*, 30 September 1999

3 Wild, David. 'Beck'. *Rolling Stone*, 21 April 1995

4 *NME*, 16 October 1999

5 Thomas, David. 'It's Good To Be Beck Hansen, Musical Genius', *Daily Telegraph*, 10 May 1997

6 Sakamoto, John. 'Beck Answers His Fans', *Jam!*, 5 June 1996

7 Saunders, Michael. '"Loser" No More: Beck', *Boston Globe*, 23 August 1996

8 Jones, Cliff. 'Captain Sensible', *The Face*, 1996

9 Wild, David. 'Beck'. *Rolling Stone*, 21 April 1995

10 Boots, J., Interview with Beck, VPRO Radio, Netherlands, 1997. http://www.vpro.nl/3voor12

11 Nardwuar The Human Serviette. 'Nardwuar vs. Beck' radio interview with Beck, 18 April 1994

12 Johnson, Calvin. 'Calvin Talks To Beck, Beck Talks Back To The Rocket', *The Rocket*, January–February 1997

13 Rubin, Mike. 'Subterranean Homeboy Blues', *Spin*, July 1994

14 Rubin, Mike. 'Subterranean Homeboy Blues', *Spin*, July 1994

15 Browne, David. 'Beck In The High Life', *Entertainment Weekly*, 14 February 1997

16 McMillan, Matt. 'Beck', *Exclaim*, 1996

17 Thomas, David. 'It's Good To Be Beck Hansen, Musical Genius', *Daily Telegraph*, 10 May 1997

18 *Option*, May 1994

19 Browne, David. 'Beck In The High Life', *Entertainment Weekly*, 14 February 1997

20 Norris, Chris. 'Moonwalking In L.A.', *Spin*, December 1999

21 Cromelin, Richard. 'Loser Gets Amnesia and Thicker Skin', *Los Angeles Times*, 30 April 1995

22 Rogers, Ray. 'Loser?' *Interview*, August 1996

23 Robbins, Ira. 'No "Loser", But A Winning Night With Beck', *Newsday*, 25 March 1994

24 'The Evolution Of Golden Boy Beck', *Paper* magazine, July–August 1996, www.papermag.com/magazine/beck

25 Kemp, Mark. 'Where It's At Now', *Rolling Stone*, 17 April 1997

26 *Toronto Sun*, April 1994

8

DON'T YOU MIND PEOPLE GRINNIN' IN YOUR FACE?

Beck was famous now, though there were those who were only too ready to inform him that his proverbial fifteen minutes of fame were nearing their end. But for every naysayer, there were two who loved what Beck was doing; particularly other musicians, who were quick to rally to his side. Jimmy Page, the famed Led Zeppelin guitarist, in an online AOL chat in 1999 commented, 'Beck is doing some very interesting work. His first album was amazing. He hasn't stopped titillating the imagination ever since.'

In May Beck booked time at the legendary Sun Studio in Memphis, the same simple room where Elvis Presley, Johnny Cash, Roy Orbison and Carl Perkins had fashioned blues and country into rockabilly and then rock and roll. Beck cut a great version of Skip James' 1931 blues tune 'Devil Got My Woman', his Martin guitar resonating richly in the room's hallowed acoustics, all twangs and slides.

A few weeks later, Beck found himself sandwiched in the middle of a seven-band mega-alternative show in Detroit along with Volvo, Sprawl, Superbunk, and Spooge – humourless alt. rock groups every one. Rising to the challenge, Beck strapped on his guitar and harmonica and gave the audience something unexpected – an all-acoustic set that killed the mosh pit dead. He changed the chorus of 'Pay No Mind' to 'I've got no mind' and gave them a super-slow version of 'Loser', changing the lyrics to 'I'm a softie, baby, so why don't you squeeze me?' All was confusion in the crowd; then Beck finished, the Afghan Whigs came on, and it was business as usual.

At the Rave in Milwaukee, Wisconsin, in front of a crowd of a couple hundred 'hippies and grungers', Karp opened with a blasting smorgasbord of sound, only to vacate the stage as quickly as they came. The teenyboppers hid in fright until Beck loped onstage, and announced himself and his band with the crashing, cutting chords of 'Mutherfucker', raw and loud. A cursory 'Fume' and 'Whiskeyclone' set the stage for the acoustic set, like a parting of the clouds, with 'Alcohol' and an extended 'Bogusflow'. The crowd surged forward with the first chords of 'Loser' and began stagediving en masse like lemmings. A sensational 'Blackhole' followed. The crowd were won over and stayed that way right up until the end, which came with a dynamic version of 'Beercan'.

By the time the band hit Minneapolis's 1st Avenue Club, where Prince cut most of *Purple Rain* 'One Foot In The Grave' had become the centrepiece in the acoustic section, the anchor of the show and as naked and raw as Beck got, with just harmonica and a stamping foot. The song serves as a grounding point, a reaffirmation of the country blues core holding Beck's musical world in place. For his opening act, Beck tracked down locals Dave Ray and Tony Glover – two-thirds of his favourite Sixties folk-punkers Koerner, Ray and Glover. It was a great chance to play with some of his youthful inspirations, connecting to their spirit of raucous folk. For his acoustic set Beck played 'Bogusflow', the otherwise-unreleased 'From My Brain' and a reeling 'One Foot In The Grave' before bringing Ray and Glover back onstage to join him in a folk *ménage à trois*. Together they performed the Carter Family's 'John Hardy' and Mississippi John Hurt's 'Ballad Of Stagolee', as well as Beck's own 'Alcohol'. 'We were doing that totally off the cuff,' Beck recalled later. 'That's the nature of that music. That's where I come from. The music isn't really a set thing, it's not quantified and scheduled. It comes from the musicians, and when other musicians come together, it turns into something else.'[1] When Ray and Glover left the stage, the band went into 'Loser', Beck pumping his fist in the air. He jumped, landed off-balance and fell flat on his ass; as he got up he was laughing fit to bust.

On 3 July Beck played an all-ager show at the Oz in Seattle, with Geraldine Fibbers and Karp opening. He strummed through a solo acoustic set of 'Fume' and 'Mexico'. Afterwards, Beck returned to indie pop haven Olympia for the first annual Yoyo A Go Go Festival, organized by Yo-Yo Recordings, joining unknown bands and perennial indie faves such as Jad Fair, Yo La Tengo, Codeine, Versus, Built to Spill and Calvin Johnson's Halo Benders. On 16 July Beck closed the day's show, preceded by onetime Boston subway busker Mary Lou Lord and Team Dresch; he sang some country songs before marching in the Lakefair Parade. Beck later contributed 'The World May Loose Its Motion' to Yo-Yo's *Periscope: Another Yo-Yo Compilation*.

After his intense period of live work, Beck was eager to get back to Dub Narcotic and record a proposed follow-up to K Record's *One Foot In The Grave*. He recorded about fifteen songs in July, returning in June 1996 to record a second batch, but the album remains unreleased. If anything, the songs weren't fully marinated, instead being spun off from scattered songbooks he carried around with him but had a propensity for losing. By 1997, Beck was also expressing doubt about the material, feeling that it was outdated. 'I actually recorded a bunch of stuff about two years ago, but I haven't had the chance to get back up there and work on it. I have a lot of stuff sitting around. I don't know if any of it's worthy to inflict on the world. There's certain songs that I did so long ago and I'd have to contend with different people in the audience wanting to hear those songs and I'm just not going to play them. There are some songs that I was playing when I was nineteen. I just don't play 'Satan Gave Me A Taco' anymore.'[2]

Soon after, Beck was trundled off on a plane from Los Angeles for the gruelling flight to Australia, for a winter time tour of the Antipodes. Australia has a strong indie circuit, and Beck played nine gigs in two weeks, through Brisbane, Sydney, Perth, Adelaide, Melbourne, Canberra and Newcastle. He recorded a radio session for Sydney's commercial alternative station Triple J on 22 August. Opening with 'Beercan', Beck then tried out some new stuff and rarities he was road testing, including 'Color Co-ordinated', a demo of 'Minus', which would appear on *Odelay*, the unreleased 'Scavenger' and *Stereopathetic Soul Manure*'s 'Thunderpeel'. 'Hard To Compete', never officially released, is a superb commentary on being an average Joe in a world of perceived giants. In tracks like these Beck's humanity and empathy reflect Guthrie's and, in common with Guthrie's songs, Beck's pieces are not products of sympathy for the downtrodden, but are coming from one who has been down in the dregs too. It is startling and comforting to hear someone voice songs like these, particularly when indie stars who graduated to the majors generally became as distant as Van Halen had seemed a decade before. Beck played 'It's All In Your Mind', a personal song of which he commented, 'I do have songs that are ironic and don't wear their heart on their sleeves. we don't really live in times that accept that. A lot of those songs were written by a teenager, you feel a little vulnerable at that age about exposing yourself. If you listen to "It's All In Your Mind", I have newer songs that wear their emotion more on the sleeve. I can look at those things a little more; it's not as painful.'[3]

94

Beck closed with another rarity, 'Grizzly', and then he was off on a brief pit stop in Auckland, New Zealand where my man Nick Beaumont witnessed him paying homage to the indie-jangle-noise Flying Nun scene. Flying Nun is host to a stable of curious and often excellent bands that absorb the best and worst of American and British indie rock and transmute it into something unequivocally their own, reflecting all those empty beautiful vistas. And then another long flight to Asia. Less than one year after jumping on between bands setting up, selling tapes at his shows and living in a rooming house with weirdoes peeking in at him in the bathroom down the hall, Beck took the stage in a space age disco called Neptune II in China. Two gigs in China's booming coastal cities of Wanchai and Makati followed; the trip was getting stranger by the day.

A tour of Japan followed, with gigs in Kawasaki, Nagoya, and Osaka, fascinating and puzzling at the same time. All this new scenery and so little time to absorb it in. The 'Loser' craze had peaked; maybe Beck thought he was just coasting through the dregs of a one-hit wonder tour. The song 'Cancelled Check' had its origins on those blustery Japanese autumn days, staring out the windows of sterile concrete hotels. 'I wrote "Cancelled Check" back in 1994,' Beck told National Public Radio in 1998. 'I was on tour and I was in a hotel room in Tokyo, jet-lagged, and they had some American programming on. They had some infomercial with Tony Robbins, the motivational guy, motivating. There was one thing he said; "The past is a cancelled check, your maximum point of power is now!" And my life felt like a cancelled check, so the image of that turned into the song that night.'[4] In fact, it wasn't Tony Robbins, whose shellacked hair and toothsome grin reflect his message, promulgated on late-night television and in bookstores across America. Beck had actually tuned into another motivational merchant, Ed Vanton. Vanton, owner of a level of self-belief bordering on the maniacal, parlayed his sales pitch into a multi-million dollar late-night infomercial business. These are the prophets of America's bizarre sales cults, which like New Age hypes like *The Celestine Prophecy* offer easy answers to people with no hope. A certain spiritual vacuity in modern American culture has led people to be able to be suckered into almost anything, whether it be imminent alien contact or $59.95 video tape series on making money in the cut-throat ultra-capitalism of today. Sadly, this is one of America's prime exports, and as people become more estranged from family, neighbours, traditional religions and ultimately themselves they become susceptible to anything that seems to have a strong centre of gravity, no matter how ludicrous.

Beck played two gigs at Tokyo's Liquid Room and a one-off in Honolulu, Hawaii before returning home for a much-needed rest. Shortly thereafter he had an unexpected encounter with Jon Spencer of the Jon Spencer Blues Explosion, and formerly of Pussy Galore, who kept reading in the indie press that Beck was citing Pussy Galore as an influence. Unaware of the hoopla surrounding 'Loser', Spencer met up with Beck in Los Angeles and talked at length about the blues. While the Explosion were recording their exquisite 1994 caterwaul of an album *Orange*, Spencer phoned Beck up and asked him to do vocals for a track called 'Flavor.' Beck not only agreed, but also appears in the video for the song. Four minutes, thirty-three seconds into 'Flavor' Beck drops in with a scat sung vocal literally phoned in. 'It took a long time to do because we did it over the phone and had a lot of technical problems,' Spencer recalled. 'I really like what he did. It's funny because it's obvious some people aren't into it being on the record just because the guy had a hit song. I mean, what the fuck?'[5]

After a mere six weeks off, Beck was back on the road on another North American tour. On 21 October he played Toronto and did an acoustic set comprising unreleased rarities 'Scavenger', 'Beginner's Luck' and a very haunting germinal version of 'Brother', a heartfelt song that would later surface on the 'Jack-Ass' EP. At the Middle East Café in Cambridge, Massachusetts, Beck played a ninety-minute set captured on the *I'm A Schmoozer, Baby* bootleg. Before playing

'Loser', Beck announced, 'We change the name of this song every night, any suggestions?' He substituted, 'Pronto Questo, I love you Al Vega' for the chorus. He tried out a tentative 'Cancelled Check', apologizing for it sounded 'a bit like the Grateful Dead', and relating the story of its hotel infomercial origins. On a skeletal version of 'Static' (same title, different song from the one on *Mutations*), Beck played some lovely Nick Drake-style finger picking, with declensions and a hushed beauty all its own. He fumbled slightly and eventually abandoned it, in the light of the Bostonian students refusal to stop talking through his set. But he seemed relaxed and chatted freely with the crowd as they thinned out and disappeared, perversely amused by the absurdity of the whole night.

Beck then took off to Europe for a gruelling string of gigs at small clubs. But he refused to skimp on his set lists despite the size of the venues, and performed eighty-minute sets on average throughout France, Spain, Italy, Denmark and Germany. In Madrid, at the Revolver, he whipped out an acoustic medley comprising 'Puttin' It Down', 'Cyanide Breathmint', 'Nitemare Hippy Girl', 'I Get Lonesome', and 'Alcohol'. The tour progressed against a background of bleak weather and small venues, and big pots of burbling food on the back ovens of club kitchens, all through the Netherlands, Sweden and Norway. In England, he recorded a Radio 1 Evening Session on 11 November, performing 'Static' before heading out to Manchester and up to Scotland in freezing weather for a one-night stand at King Tut's in Glasgow.

After a standout ninety-minute show on 28 November at London's Astoria, Beck appeared on *Top Of The Pops* to perform 'Loser' with a one-off backing band specifically recruited for the show. 'It was a group of eighty-year-old men playing; some were dapper, sprightly elderly gentlemen who still had hair. There was a portly guy with a Friar Tuck playing guitar. Then we had a hunched, slightly demonic old man, and he was playing drums. There's a genius part where the camera cuts to him like there's a break on drums, and he does the slowest drumstick spin ever executed in the history of rock drumming. It was really beautiful.'[6] By now Beck was obsessed with reconfiguring 'Loser' to show off its farcical nature. He would improvise lyrics, do a sickly version with wah-wah and a drum machine, have members of the audience sing it, do beat box versions of it, or play it as a lounge track.*

Beck took on Belgium, France and the Netherlands before returning home for gigs in California, including one at the last Fuzzyland gig, the roaming club where he used to scam his way onto the stage. Jac Zinder, the promoter for Fuzzyland, as well as the first music critic to write about Beck, had recently died in a car crash. Like Al Hansen, Zinder was one of those catalysts who energize other people, and was justly mourned.** Death was nipping at the edges of Beck's world, reinforcing that fatalism that runs like a dark streak through his songs. Zinder's death was just the first of many people in Beck's circle. When Johnny Cash asked Beck to open for him, Beck rang up Leo LeBlanc, the pedal steel player who had laid down such spare and elegant pedal steel guitar lines on songs such as 'Rowboat' and 'Modesto'. Leo told Beck that he was about to have an operation and couldn't play pedal steel, although he would be able to play lap steel. The performance was fine, though Beck noticed immediately

---

* Kurt Cobain of Nirvana likewise made fun of 'Smells Like Teen Spirit''s throwaway lyrics by savaging it with a mock-Gregorian vocal on *Top Of The Pops*. Former Dream Syndicate and Velvet Underground alumni John Cale caught Beck's *Top Of The Pops* appearance at home in Wales on television. Cale was knocked sideways: 'The beauty of it hit me right between the eyes. The energy gained from seeing Beck sustained me until I could start working on my own material.' (*Mojo*, March 1997)

** Jac Zinder was a musician too. His *Chairs I Have Known* was released posthumously on the Catasonic label and included a great rendition of Brian Wilson's instrumental 'Pet Sounds'.

how tired and gaunt Leo was and how he struggled slightly with some of the notes. He died of cancer two weeks later.

Johnny Cash had extended the invitation after his producer Rick Rubin had played him some of Beck's country songs. Cash would eventually do an excellent cover of Beck's 'Rowboat', and would comment: 'Beck's got that mountain music in his blood'.[7] Cash's dark country, streaked with fatalism and a certain dread, had retained all its cachet for a new generation of listeners. The man in black was and is timeless; songs like 'Ring Of Fire' and 'Folsom Prison Blues' connect back to original country music, those strange tunes of child murderers, Biblical plagues and outlaws with ambivalent aims. It was an honour for Beck to open for the man, as Cash not only possessed impeccable authenticity, but was also married to, and performed with, June Carter, part of the Carter Family clan. Opening for Cash was a tie with the past in an era where so much of the past is disposed.

In early October, during a break between tours, Beck began laying down demos on his four-track for his second major label album. After a month-long North American and European tour ending at an 18 December gig at Los Angeles' famed Troubadour, Beck started working with the Bong Load squad of Rothrock and Schnapf at the helm again. He ploughed through a huge trove of mostly piano- and guitar-driven songs, many of which he had been working out on-stage for the past months. The trio went down to Sunset Sound Studio in January and together plodded through dozens of songs, but only one track ended up on the finished album – 'Ramshackle'. The only two other tracks ever to see the light of day were 'Feather In Your Cap' and 'Brother'.

In brief, Beck quickly recorded an entire album but swiftly became dissatisfied with the songs. 'Feather In Your Cap', while a great song, neatly points out what was wrong with Beck's approach to his music at the time. The melody strays too close to James Taylor, the lyrics seem tentative and unsure, and an angular piano solo closes out the song, either strained or brilliantly oblique, or both. It ends on an uncertain note and the effect is of Beck trying to link the disparate dots of his new direction. The song grows on the listener after repeated plays, but overall it feels hesitant, as if its author is uncertainly reaching for something else. This was Beck's second go round with the song; it had just appeared on a K Records 7-inch, sandwiched between 'It's All In Your Mind' and 'Whiskey Can Can'. In that version the song is even more tentative, ending very abruptly. It seems Beck had been thinking a great deal about where next to go with his music. It was fitting that the second version of 'Feather In Your Cap' formed part of the soundtrack for the Richard Linklater film *Suburbia*, with its plot of restless teens orbiting around a suburban convenience store, always thinking of ways to escape.

'Brother' is a haunting song, one of Beck's most emotional and bare, which ended up on the masterful 'Jack-Ass' U.K. EP Beck played all the instruments on the track – piano, bass and guitar. 'Brother' came from the original sessions when I was starting the *Odelay* album,' he later revealed. 'The album was going to be more like that, folky and dark. But I just wanted to do something a little more lively. The thing with *Mellow Gold* was the songs were so slow. I wanted to have an album where the songs were a little more dynamic for playing live.'[8]

On 16 January Beck laid down his third radio session for long-time supporters KCRW 89.9 FM's 'Morning Becomes Eclectic', with Chris Douridas presiding. That Beck was in a transitional phase was emphasized by the fact that he chose to delve back into the blues, performing Skip James' 'Devil Got My Woman', 'Feel The Strain Of Sorrow Never Ceasing', the tragicomic 'Cancelled Check', 'Curses' and two Son House songs, 'John The Revelator' and '(Don't You Mind People) Grinnin' In Your Face'. The blues seemed perfect for this uncertain time, with Leo and Jac's death, and Beck perhaps feeling he was on a musical track about to splinter and send him derailing. Following his instincts, he took a sharp left turn and tracked down the Dust Brothers, the production duo of John King and Mike Simpson who had produced the Beastie Boys' *Paul's Boutique* as well as a whole host of rap acts on Los Angeles' Delicious Vinyl label. It was a connection he had been trying to make for a while, largely because the pair had their own studio in Silverlake, and he liked their collage production style. Wanting to work more hip-hop into his music, he made a decision to abandon the songs he'd written and try an experiment.

Beck talked to Mitchell Frank, owner of Silverlake nightclub, Spaceland, host to many of Beck's early gigs, and good friend of the Dust Brothers, about the possibility of getting in touch with the duo. The Dust Brothers, in turn, had first heard of Beck through Frank. In 1992 Frank had invited Simpson to lunch and raved about Beck, whose 'Loser' was at the time unreleased, a hip secret between producers and scene cognoscenti. 'Have you heard of this guy Beck?' Frank asked the pair. Of course Simpson had heard of *Jeff* Beck, he said, referring to the masterful ex-Yardbirds guitarist. Frank said, 'No, no, not Jeff Beck. It's this local kid. He recorded this song "Loser" that's like a rap song with folk guitar. It's going to be a huge hit.' Bong Load was just about to press the initial five hundred copies and send them the first of them out to KXLU.

After 'Loser' became a smash, Mitchell Frank would sit at the bar in the back of Spaceland with the Dust Brothers and regularly nag them about the fact that Beck wanted to meet them. Finally, after two years of chasing the duo, Beck finally arranged to come by the Brothers' home studio, the PCP Lab, and try a track or two as an experiment. 'I wanted to work with the Dust Brothers because I really wanted to get more into the hip-hop and working with beats,' he told *Huh* in 1996. 'They had this mystique about them. I was actually scared of them, I thought they would kick my ass, but they're cuddly, they're computer freaks.'[9]

Beck set a date and one night in February walked the couple of blocks from his house in Los Feliz to the Brothers' Silverlake house-cum-studio. The Dust Brothers operate in an aerie above Silverlake, their famed PCP Lab, where they live and work. Outside are trees and cicadas and dusty red sunsets. Inside are Macintoshes with enormous monitors, a mile of cables and a twenty-four-track Neve mixing board, with Yamaha NS-10 studio monitors. The Brothers work using OpCode's SoundVision and keep their music stored on hard drives. Two turntables with spiral mats spin all the time, and records are taken from the Brothers' 10,000-plus collection of vinyl. There isn't much space to operate, and the room with the recording equipment resembles nothing so much as a hive. They work here until well after midnight, powered by bong hits, take-out food and their own inspiration. They are always busy and always creating.

Partners John King and Mike Simpson have produced everyone from the Rolling Stones, Hanson (the Dust-produced 'MmmBop' was a U.K. chart topper) and Vince Neil of Mötley Crüe to Beck. They keep one foot in straight commerce, dealing with major label acts who need their hipness quotient and line up at the door for the privilege of working with them, while keeping the other in the down and dirty world of space-age underground funk, with the likes of Sukia and their own Nickelbag Records.

The two albums the Brothers are best known for are Beck's 1996 *Odelay* and the Beastie Boys' 1989 *Paul's Boutique*, considered their masterpiece, and certainly the highest apogee of the art of sampling. It is not mere hyperbole to say that *Paul's Boutique* had over 250 unlicensed samples, in those halcyon days when samples needed no clearance and were a needle drop away from the creative process. The Brothers sampled everything from the Beatles to Funky 4+1 in a collage that astounded those in hip-hop but fell flat on public ears unprepared for such a change from the multi-platinum and somewhat moronic debut from the Beasties, 1986's *Licensed To Ill*.

Mike Simpson and John King were two middle-class white university students when they met; both were DJs at colleges in Claremont, California – two white guys in the middle of the Eighties trying to get rap through to their contemporaries. 'Rap was constantly, amazingly innovative and cool,' King told the online zine *Addicted To Noise* in 1996. 'Every time a new rap record would come, it would just be a major event for us. We would be so excited and go back to our little DJ studio that we had and start just scratching the records, and mixing them up, and play them on our show. We'd get immediate feedback, the phone would never stop ringing.'[10] King came from punk, skateboards and dope and was studying computers and economics, while Simpson leaned toward rap and philosophy. Since no one else around them played rap, their common ground quickly bridged a friendship between the two and they eventually formed a tight, acerbic team, one balancing out the excesses or weaknesses of the other. King talks half as much as Simpson, but his ingenious stoner logic is often right on target, like a Zen archer, working intuitively. King is the anarchic conscience, the ghost in the machine. Simpson is the linear thinker with calm and measured solutions. A perfect left brain-right brain pairing, one abstract, the other grounded in logic. Their mixes confirm this; no matter how outrageous the tampered samples are, there is a unique spaciousness and solid engineering behind their productions.

The Brothers were unusually sonically inventive, straying far from one branch of rap that was beginning to use static rhythm as its source of transcendence. In rap this was best epitomized by Too-Short's 'Cuss Words' in which the young rapper throws down twelve-minute proto-gangster raps over one never-ending and never changing beat. The Brothers were pulling the other way, paralleling sonic experimentalists like Prince Paul of Stetsasonic and later De La Soul and DJ Premiere of Gang Starr, layering sounds until the source samples were transubstantiated into something entirely novel. The Brothers, likewise, would throw in everything they could find into their radio shows, using records of speeches, birdcalls and especially sound effects albums. The Brothers were particularly galvanized by Public Enemy and the Bomb Squad.

Fate intervened one day in the form of Orlando, a rep from Delicious Vinyl, a Los Angeles hip-hop label. West Coast rap at the time commanded absolutely no respect, so when he came into their studio at the Pomona college radio station, with a 12-inch of 'Cheeba Cheeba' by an unknown named Tone-Loc, the Brothers were sceptical. The Brothers played it and were blown away and began heavy rotating the single on their show. Soon after, Orlando brought Tone-Loc down for an interview. Tone-Loc walked in with a joint behind his ear, which was duly smoked. The Brothers, in herbalized comfort, played a few of the four-track collages they had made for their radio spots. It was Tone's turn to be blown away, he immediately expressed a desire to rap over the tracks. Orlando made a phone call to Matt Dyke and Mike Ross, the joint heads of Delicious Vinyl, and in a matter of days the Brothers became the label's in-house producers.

By 1988, they had moved to Los Angeles and their productions of rappers Tone-Loc, Def Jef and Young MC were multi-platinum sellers, with Tone-Loc's Dust-produced 'Wild Thing' going to number 2 on the pop charts in 1989. 'The current in hip-hop was very sparse,' Simpson observed, 'and we were using all these textures, sampling and just layering odd sounds. People described it as being very "dusted", these multi-layered soundscapes, so we called ourselves the Dust Brothers.'[11]

Simpson and King, being middle class and white, had a different cultural subset than their black peers, and looked back to a childhood and adolescence of very horrific MOR light rock. They would shamelessly use samples from Loggins & Messina, the Eagles, ZZ Top, the Beatles, Steve Miller Band, Sweet, Mountain, Pink Floyd and Deep Purple in their aural collages, cut and pasted alongside the more familiar Cameo, Funkadelic, Commodores, Sly and the Family Stone,

Funky 4+1, Trouble Funk and the Sugarhill Gang. There was something about this miscegenetic splicing that was beguiling to the ear, as if two Seventies radio stations, one funk and one AOR rock, were constantly cutting into each other's air space. This is a prime example of what writer Matt Ashare cites as the Dust Brothers retro-futurism',[12] again, the envisioning of an archaic future, a perfect past. 'Rap music is all about the beat and the low end, and we just stuck that onto rock music, and it seemed to work.'[13]

It was, ironically, their production of the Beastie Boys' *Paul's Boutique* that nearly buried the Brothers just as they were out of the gates. The Beastie Boys had fled Brooklyn for the West Coast, shell shocked by their sudden fame and looking for a new direction. There were only so many cans of beer you could spray at the audience, only so many haggard go-go girls in a cage, only so many hotels rooms to destroy, only so much PCP any human can smoke. As the sons of Jewish intellectuals, and former punk rock and downtown New York art/noise-niks, the Beasties took a trek across country to find new sounds, maybe to find an escape hatch. They met the Dust Brothers, who invited them back to their studio to hear some of their stuff. Simpson said. 'They were like, "Wow, this stuff's incredible, can we buy these songs from you?"'[14] Simpson later recalled. Instead of selling them the tracks, the Brothers signed on as producers and worked feverishly on a new album with the Beasties.

Although now considered a classic, *Paul's Boutique* was derided by the press and was an unmitigated commercial bomb. The public seemed dumbfounded too, not knowing quite what to make of the seven-panel foldout LP cover which, if wrapped around the head, gave a panoramic view of a Brooklyn Street. The effect on the listener was similar: the sounds seem to have an extra dimension, a 3-D barrage in a world of flat beats. 'It was ahead of its time,' King stated in 1996. 'Back then other producers and engineers would just look at us like, "What the fuck are you doing?"'[15]

Rappers such as Chuck D from Public Enemy were prepared to diss and denounce the Beasties in light of their joke debut (which was, most ironically, the first rap album to reach number one), but were quietly impressed by the depth of funk and early hip-hop knowledge displayed on *Paul's Boutique*. Simpson reflects, '*Paul's Boutique* made it okay for people to start doing a lot of fucked-up shit on their records. And it was so well received in the artistic community that it didn't matter quite so much how it did commercially.'[16] The pop culture references beloved on hip-hop are scattered across the grooves like seeds, and there are wonderful couplets approaching pure poetry by the Beastie Boys on the album. Toward the end of the record, the Brothers sample George Carlin, the white comedian who use to brag about coming from 'White Harlem', shouting *'Goddamn!'* A fitting statement for this fine work.

By 1990 the first golden era of rap was over, as the ground rules concerning the samples that were its bread and butter were changed. In 1989, when the Sixties pop combo the Turtles sued De La Soul for supposedly 'butchering' their frothy hit 'Daydream' for use on De La Soul's masterful *Three Feet High And Rising* album, publishing companies smelled blood and closed in for the kill. Now every grunt of James Brown on any rap record would have to be licensed from the publishers and paid for. While not affecting the DJs, who played live and could drop whatever they felt into the mix, producers went through a brief panic. But the Dust Brothers were already using samplers and computers to sample, chop up the beats, re-arrange them end-to-end, distort them, reverse them, drown them in echo or reverb or add metallic noise. Also, the hunt for ever-greater obscurities that would evade sample clearance began, accelerating a process of historical re-investigation of older and obscure music that had been part of hip-hop's ethos since Kool Herc. Instead of being a hindrance to creativity, the tighter rules on sampling acted as a spur to creativity. Technical difficulty can as often as not act as a spur to creativity; though overrated, the Beatles'

1967 LP *Sgt. Pepper's Lonely Hearts Club Band* is a notable testament to pushing four-track tape recorders to their maximum utility.

In 1990, after recording *Paul's Boutique*, the Dust Brothers bought big Macintosh computers, and outfitted them with OpCode's Studio Vision. A supremely adaptable piece of software that Simpson likened to a canvas with an infinite palette, Studio Vision enabled the Brothers to record on their own time, at home. Simpson explains, 'Sampling and sequencing was very new, and we used those machines in ways that nobody had ever used them before. We'd load it with a sample, loop the sample, and keep doing that until we had twenty-four tracks filled with these loops that ran the entire length of the song. Then we'd sit down at the mixing board and arrange the song using the mute buttons on each track. If you turned on all the tracks and listened back to the tape, all you'd hear was a total mess.'[17]

The Dust Brothers seldom produce a song in the classic sense, but have struck out boldly on a deconstructionist tangent, rearranging the elements of a song and adding their own fabled dust until it resembles a whole new beast. The Brothers as often as not depend on the original artist to come in and fill in new instrumental breaks, and then re-mix and tweak the sound to their exacting specifications. 'Our best work comes through on the material that we've co-written, rather than on the things where we just produce,' Simpson explained to the *Boston Phoenix* in late 1996.[18]

As sample licensing became prohibitively expensive, the search for the perfect break began to include found sound, wildlife records, sex instruction records from the Sixties, comedy tracks, industrial noise and, in time, original sounds played on instruments and given a new texture with effects. Samples also became dirtier, influenced by people like the Dust Brothers; the static of scratched records on Dee-Lite's 'Groove Is In The Heart' was something of a watershed: it celebrated the physical artefacts of this emerging art-form, the actual worn vinyl carted around by DJs.

The cultural worth of rap was hotly debated, often along racial lines. Many white people were vehemently turned off by rap's bombast, and it was as alienating to many as bebop had been in its day. But although countless scores of shitty rap records were churned out as the genre became a moneymaking proposition, the artistry of cut-up turntable collage, with two Technics turntables on a flat heavy board, supported by stacked milk crates, was as revolutionary as punk, enabling young non-musicians to create something out of nothing.

By 1992 musicians were an integral part of rap production, with guitarists, drummer and bassists layering over samples to create a thicker brew. Squalls of funk guitar or ruthlessly distorted organ could be heard in records by Ice Cube or the earliest Wu-Tang Clan productions. The cost of sampling that had seemed a curse was a blessing in disguise, spurring on hip-hop producers to create their own sounds from scratch.

In an era where sameness is omnipotent, where tracks seldom venture past one key change, and predictable formulas are flogged to death, the Brothers sought the controlled chaos at the roots of hip-hop, when Herc would take only the choicest breakbeats and collage them together. The Dust Brothers' influence extended far beyond rap as they branched into rock, their reputation for good engineering and efficient, low-cost computer recording creating a resumé thick as a brick. What had begun as a lark in college radio stations, throwing on random records into the mix, now served them well. Their tastes remained diverse and experimental; they had brought in dub reggae and Israeli singer Ofra Haza into the mix back in 1989. They produced incredible albums for old skool rap auteur Biz Markie and Los Angeles space-funk band Sukia, as well as remixes for everyone from Korn to Motörhead and Ice-T. The Dust Brothers had kindred spirits across the pond in James Lavelle's often brilliant Mo'Wax label, itself a product of largely white infatuation with black hip-hop. The emergence of DJ Shadow and the U.N.K.L.E. project (recorded in Los Angeles mostly) seemed to indicate a new globality for hip-hop, tying in with and inspired by the underground scene documented on such albums as *Lyricist's Lounge* or the new hip-hop artists from Tokyo to Paris, working out their craft far from the absurd New York vs. Los Angeles divide.

The remarkable thing about Dust productions is how deceptively loose they sound; their structure only becomes apparent with repeated listening. The Brothers aim to inject a little air into the mix, whereas the common tendency, particularly with samples and sequencers, is to saturate the hard disk with sound. This, intentionally or not, harks back to the bare production of the Fifties and Sixties, when an omni-directional microphone would be placed in a room and recorded straight to two-track, as in the Chess label blues recordings done in Chicago in the Fifties. 'We could make very precise records,' explains Simpson, 'but that would defeat the purpose. The looseness makes it more digestible. It's not as intimidating that way. A big problem in music is that a lot of bands have this attitude like "Behold our music". They alienate the listener by being so tight. Then you get a band that's being loose and having fun, and it allows the audience to have fun too.'[19]

In essence, the Dust Brothers' production method shatters the linear notion of recording verse-chorus-verse songs. 'When we're working with an artist, after the first couple of days when they start to get a sense of what we can do with the computer,' Simpson told *ATN* in 1996. 'They realize they don't have to play their part exactly right in every part of the song; it totally frees up the artist's creativity. They just get more of a free-expression thing; especially when you're working with somebody like Beck, who is so creative. He immediately got it and realized, "Hey, I'm going to come in here, and I'm going to have fun." Once they're done with their part, we'll go in and do the work.'[20]

Working on *Odelay* proved to be a rewarding experience for all parties concerned. The Brothers would line up some beats or pull out a record from their voluminous collection, or one of Beck's eclectic LPs, and Beck would become fired up, scribbling down lyrics, and coming up with melodies and music at a rate that amazed the producers. The duo would then take his ideas and build samples and beats around them; the songwriting became a truly collaborative effort. The Brothers cut beats from soul and jazz drummer Bernard 'Pretty' Purdie's albums, looped them on their Macintoshes, and had Beck record random bass, guitar or organ over it, looking for tasty bits that they would further cut and loop, narrowing down to riffs or phrases which could form the basis of a song. Simpson called it 'research', saying 'We worked in two phases, the pre-Lollapalooza [tour] phase and the post-Lollapalooza phase. The pre-Lollapalooza phase was basically Beck just trying to get ideas out of his system.'[21] 'New Pollution' and 'Devil's Haircut' were written and recorded on the same day. Rather than come in with more or less finished songs which he had worked out at home on an acoustic, Beck was trying to abandon the script before walking into the studio, breaking with the way he was used to working in an attempt to inject freshness into the process of writing and recording. 'I don't want to know what it's going to sound like before I go into the studio,' he stated in 1997. 'I want to be surprised. I want to feel some sense of surrender and helplessness. I want to be entertained while I'm writing the songs, to be excited and turned-on.'[22]

By taking away the safety net of producing cut-and-dried songs before entering the studio, Beck was opening the music-making process up to the vagaries of chance, accident and the unexpected. In an interview with Neil Strauss of *Spin* magazine, Beck talked about his new approach in terms which strongly echoed the performance art of Al Hansen and his Fluxus contemporaries. 'People say that what I'm doing is like switching channels on the TV. But I don't really look at it like that: I look at it like it's integrating the flux and the chaos and making something substantial from it. It's not about randomness, but taking that randomness and giving it some body. It's not really channel surfing. It's more letting a batch of weeds just grow, as if nature is just organizing, shaping, and moulding this thing.'[23] King and Simpson emphasized that *Odelay* is very definitely Beck's record, although the credits on almost all the songs are split three ways. *Odelay* is not only multi-layered but surprisingly porous, in part because of the Dust Brothers' 'multi-track and mute' sampling technique, though also because gaps were left when samples couldn't be cleared. In addition, the combination of samples and Beck's own playing created unexpected tonalities. '*Odelay* is me getting down to business,' he stated in 1996. 'I probably feel it's a stronger and more representative album. It definitely embraces the hip-hop element a lot more, the energy of it. I come from the blues and folk and the rhythms of that music that correspond to hip-hop.'[24] Despite having played folk music since he was a teenager, Beck's affection and interest in hip-hop was long-standing; Schooly D, Kool Moe Dee and N.W.A. all made a big impression on him. He recognized an innate kinship between hip-hop and folk, both being forms of 'music that comes from non-professional areas. With hip-hop, you don't need a studio, you just need some turntables and some recording thing. You could do it in your living room. That's the spirit of hip-hop. And folk wasn't about recording studios. They're both non-elitist forms of music.'[25] In a sense, Beck was trying to beat the beast by becoming the beast; if you're afraid of computers, immerse yourself in creating things on them. If you fear the corporate beast, find out how the corporate beast works. His spin out into hip-hop took a similar trajectory: 'I found myself rejecting so much new music, everything that is part of our culture. Then I just spun all around and decided to embrace it all; the machines, the rap, the loud guitars, every emotional level. And just go with it all; an experiment.'[26] It had been two years since Beck had recorded *Mellow Gold*, and he was now brimming over with ideas for his music. Inspired by working with the Dust Brothers, he now wanted to deconstruct, cut and paste and fully exploit the possibilities that their studio and expertise offered. Initially, much of *Odelay* sounded like the chaotic 'High 5 (Rock The Catskills)', major freak-outs, the sound of Beck letting off steam and getting ideas out of his system.

The Brothers were struck from the start by Beck's enthusiasm, drive and willingness to collaborate with them. In an era where the producer and artist relationship is most often one conducted on an unequal playing field, and is subject to great incomprehension as well as marketing and record company nagging, Beck and the Brothers were redefining the parameters. They were taking a cue from hip-hop, where this breakdown of the divisions between artists and techies had already begun. With people like Staten Island's Wu-Tang Clan, producers, rappers, DJs and instrumentalists were bound together like King Arthur's Knights of the Round Table, often doubling up on different tasks.

One day Beck brought in an album by Mike Millius, a Seventies country performer who had recorded for Columbia Records. Millius was a small fixture on the Greenwich Village folk scene in the Sixties, hanging and playing at the Kettle of Fish. The Brothers were appalled and fascinated by what they heard. Simpson said, 'Millius's songs were really corny, and he had an awful voice, but there was something about it, the vibe of it was so cool. "Sissyneck" was inspired by this band Country Funk,' said Simpson, 'that funk element with a really good backbeat, and then country guitars, and country melodies.'[27]

One track from this first recording tourney, and which remains unreleased even though it was initially slotted to be on Beck's 1999 album *Midnite Vultures* was 'Inferno'. Beck characterized the track as 'a freak-out, just eight minutes of chaos, a testament to taking it all the way.'[28] The track was an aggressive, upbeat sample fest – in fact, there were so many samples contained within the song that the task of licensing it proved too formidable to attempt. 'We hooked up an 808 beat with a loop from the Frogs, and then we had Bunny and Tigra (from L'trimm) on top. I doubt it will ever see the light of day because it costs too much money to clear a sample these days.'[29]

Beck spoke often at the time of his frustrations at the way the music industry forced the artist to limit output to only one album every two or three years, and to tour each album, rather than allowing the artist to release material as it evolved. Clearly, such an approach, designed to maximize sales, has a limiting effect on a creative mind; in this attitude Beck has much in common with the Artist Formerly Known as Prince, who also derided the record industry's emphasis on one record, released once a year. Originally planned for the fall of 1995, *Odelay* was delayed because Beck had to tour with Lollapalooza for five months. To *UHF* magazine in mid-1996, Beck mourned the loss of the artistic freedom that prevailed in the music industry of the 1960s: 'That era of putting out two albums a year, which is really healthy musically, is long gone. It would be better if you didn't need to sell a million records, if you just sold a handful, then put out another record in six months and sold another handful.'[30]

'Diskobox' was one *Odelay* track that would only find release on international versions of the album, including the U.K. one. A masterful funk groove, 'Diskobox' is held together with piano and a stinging drum sample from Carlos 'Sherlock' Holmes' track 'Black Flag', sabotaged by Beck, Jon Spencer and Judah Bauer of Jon Spencer Blues Explosion, with Beck producing a vocoder-driven vocal that sounds halfway between Sly Stone at his PCP-bent worst and Pussy Galore's extemporaneous noise making. 'The best music looks easy,' Beck commented in 1998, 'but once you try to get into the mind of it, you realize how tough it is. I've recorded with Jon Spencer, we got together in the studio for a week or so, and I saw how hard he works, tapping into that primal blues thing they do in their live shows. We have a similar studio ethic, fairly all-consuming and dictatorial, but at the same time letting chaos reign [...] It's a weird dynamic necessary to make it work, capturing the spirit of the music but pretending like you're not catching it.'[31] 'Everyone was real excited about "Diskobox",' Spencer observed. 'They called the A&R guy from Geffen down to the studio and he's saying, "Oh, this has to be the single!" And then, nothing.'[32]

The 1995 Jon Spencer Blues Explosion *Experimental Remixes* EP features a two-part remix of 'Flavor' by Beck, Mike D of the Beasties, and Mario Caldato Jr. This second version of 'Flavor' is significant as stylistically it foreshadows the electro-funk Beck would delve deep into on *Midnite Vultures*.

April found Beck in the Netherlands for the Fast Forward II festival. John Darnielle of the Mountain Goats spent the better part of an hour sitting on the steps of the town of Doornroosje with him. Beck was quite ill and the two men spent some time bitching about how just being around people can tire you out. Beck wound up cancelling the tour, which was supposed to have followed the festival, and returned home. He took stock of what had been happening up until then while he was recovering from exhaustion and illness. He would take off into the hills above Silverlake, and walk along through the dust and sparse foliage that points up the fact that Los Angeles is an artificial garden made to bloom in the middle of desert scrubland. His enforced time off gave him time to reflect and plan before reapplying himself to the album that was to cement his reputation as pop music's most dazzlingly eclectic star of the decade.

1   Bream, Jon. 'Where It's At: Summer Festivals', *Minneapolis Star Tribune*, 1 August 1997

2   Bornemann, Tim. 'Beck Meets Squeegee', 2 April 1997. Slo-Jam website. squeegee@frontier.wilpaterson.edu

3   Boots, J. 'Interview with Beck', VPRO Radio, Netherlands, 1997. http://www.vpro.nl/3voor12

4   Siegel, Robert and Wertheimer, Linda. 'All Things Considered', National Public Radio, 1998

5   Interview with Jon Spencer. *Magnet*, issue 29, November 1994

6   Dunn, Jancee. 'Beck: Resident Alien', *Rolling Stone*, 11–25 July 1996

7   Joyce, John. 'Diary Of An LP', *Melody Maker*, 5 December 1998

8   Bornemann, Tim. 'Beck Meets Squeegee', 2 April 1997. Slo-Jam website. squeegee@frontier.wilpaterson.edu

9   Babcock, Jay. 'Beck', *Huh*, July 1996

10 Scoppa, Bud. 'Dust Brothers Are Where It's At', *Addicted To Noise*, 1996

11 Cromelin, Richard. 'Nobody's Fool', *Los Angeles Times*, 21 July 1996

12 Ashare, Matt. 'Eat Their Dust: Meet The Men Behind Beck And The Beasties',
    Boston Phoenix, 28 November-5 December 1996

13 Browne, David. 'Beck In The High Life', Entertainment Weekly, 14 February 1997

14 Cromelin, Richard. 'Nobody's Fool', *Los Angeles Times*, 21 July 1996

15 Ashare, Matt. 'Eat Their Dust: Meet The Men Behind Beck And The Beasties',
    Boston Phoenix, 28 November-5 December 1996

16 Ashare, Matt. 'Eat Their Dust: Meet The Men Behind Beck And The Beasties',
    Boston Phoenix, 28 November-5 December 1996

17 Ashare, Matt. 'Eat Their Dust: Meet The Men Behind Beck And The Beasties',
    Boston Phoenix, 28 November-5 December 1996

18 Ashare, Matt. 'Eat Their Dust: Meet The Men Behind Beck And The Beasties',
    Boston Phoenix, 28 November-5 December 1996

19 Ashare, Matt. 'Eat Their Dust: Meet The Men Behind Beck And The Beasties',
    Boston Phoenix, 28 November-5 December 1996

20 Scoppa, Bud. 'Dust Brothers Are Where It's At', *Addicted To Noise*, 1996

21 Cummings, Sue. 'Beck: Dumpster Divin' Man', MTV, June 1996

22 Mehle, Michael. 'Beck's Progressive Risks Pay Off', *Denver Rocky Mountain News*, 18 May 1997

23 Strauss, Neil. 'Artist Of The Year', *Spin*, 1996

24 Saunders, Michael. '"Loser" No More: Beck', *Boston Globe*, 23 August 1996

25 Rogers, Ray. 'Loser?' *Interview*, August 1996

26 Ginsberg, Allen. 'A Beat/Slacker Transgenerational Meeting Of Minds', *Shambhala Sun*, 27 September 1999

27 Scoppa, Bud. 'Dust Brothers Are Where It's At', *Addicted To Noise*, 1996

28 Weisbard, Eric. 'After The Goldrush', *Spin*, 1996

29 'I Love The Smell Of Methane And Bananas In The Morning', *Mean* magazine, December 1999

30 'Super Beck: "Loser", Artist, Rock Star, Genius', *UHF*# 10, July–August 1996

31 Ferguson, Troy. 'Beck: Where He's At', *Rip It Up*, January 1998

32 Interview with Jon Spencer. *Magnet*, issue 29, November 1994

9

SILVERLAKE BABY-G SYMPHONIES

Beck's days were spent at the Dust Brothers' PCP Lab, labouring intensively on the tracks for the new album. At night he would relax with friends, play tunes for his own enjoyment and occasionally hit the town. He was dismayed to find that the blues he had loved was slowly but surely being turned into a joke, a soundtrack for beer ads. Investors had opened up the House of Blues, done up like a faux tar paper and tin shack in the South. All that fauxness proved very expensive, of course. 'I went to the House of Blues to see Ali Farka Toure, and the audience was eating and talking and answering their cell phones. Ali Farka Toure was just shaking his head. It left a bad taste in my mouth.'[1] But when the Bong Load cats invited him down to Fat Possum, blues artist Junior Kimbrough's place, Beck got a chance to watch R.L. Burnside record in 'a shed-juke joint on the side of the road. It was a fluorescent light affair.'[2] Beck laughed at the contrast between the functional shed and the House of Blues' artificial conflation of it. 'There's some good blues still happening, like Cedell Davis and Junior Kimbrough and other artists on the Fat Possum record label that hasn't been slicked up and turned into a Levi's commercial.'[3]

By 20 June Beck was sufficiently recovered to do a series of five gigs in small clubs up and down California in preparation for his participation in the Lollapalooza Festival. He had assembled a new band including Joey on drums, Mike on keys, Lance Hahn on guitar and Abby Travis on bass. Hahn, and later on, Sunny Reinhardt, were drafted in to replace Chris Ballew, who had gone off to find success with his own band, The Presidents Of The United States Of America, whose song 'Peaches' echoed out of bars from Paris to Melbourne.

Donna Dedman, editor of *Gellow Molde*, the first Beck fanzine, was at the 21 June show at San Jose's Cactus Club and was surprised to see Beck dressed in full cowboy garb with 'a huge cowboy hat almost larger than his body. The opening band was Steve Hanft's band, Liquor Cabinet, the outgrowth of Loser, the heavy metal experimental band with Beck on guitar. With a backdrop of *Star Wars* playing on screens around the small club Beck came and watched Liquor Cabinet before getting up on stage and rocking the Cabinet. Afterward Lutefisk, Dallas Don's band, came on while Beck took a breather and 'Beck then came on again and rocked. It was a really fun show.'[4]

That same day, Al Hansen died. A maverick to the end, he'd still been hitchhiking around Europe and sleeping on people's floors well into his sixties. In the end art won out, just as he'd said it would, in the guise of his grandson, who would embark on cultural sabotage, the operator inside the Trojan Horse, infiltrating the mainstream. It was ironic and sad that the elder Hansen died just a few days before Beck embarked on Lollapalooza, where he was to enact an unintentional Fluxus piece of his own, a string of chaotic gigs with a loose script and an uncertain outcome. He would perform his ragtag set to bewildered young Americans expecting him to come out and do 'Loser' and be done with it.

Beck finished three gigs in Southern California before taking off to New York for Al's memorial service, where he performed 'Lord Only Knows' and 'Ramshackle'. 'Al was really the glue for this whole social fabric,' Beck told Barney Hoskyns in 1999. 'What amazed me was going to his memorial, and watching all these artists and actors he'd known come out and tell stories about him for hours and hours. If he hadn't been there, so many paths wouldn't have crossed.'[5] The memorial service culminated, appropriately, in a happening with performances by Al's Fluxus friends and cronies, reflecting his artistic ethos of spontaneity. 'It involved a gay wedding, a projection of 16-millimetre film, the throwing of toilet paper around, it created a toilet paper tent, a mini-amphitheatre of toilet paper, and people walking around with toy guns,' Beck told *Spin* in 1996. 'It was all choreographed, but there was a certain element of chance, and the two who were getting married were tied up and they had to saw a chair in half. I remember being so overwhelmed with this spirit of […] I don't know what, some other force overtaking me. More than anything it made me want to make music that was more celebratory.'[6] As a direct result of the anarchic service, Beck begins to infuse the album he was working on with joy, enthusiasm and commitment, paralleling Al's own, in contrast to the prevailing angst-rock of the day, as well as incorporating Al's 'trash as treasure' aspirations. The slight deadlock Beck had been experiencing was resolved and he left the service invigorated. 'I was so exhausted after touring with *Mellow Gold* and the whole overload of the "Loser" thing that I probably should have taken six months off. But I had all this stuff I needed to get out and I wanted to push myself. I was afraid that otherwise I might just settle like a stone at the bottom of the ocean and just stay submerged forever.'[7]

On 4 July, American Independence Day, Lollapalooza kicked off at the Gorge in George, Washington. Beck would perform a set on the main stage after Jesus Lizard, the Mighty Mighty Bosstones and Elastica had pumped up the daytime crowd, and before Cypress Hill, Hole, and Sonic Youth closed the evening. Big venues were still new to Beck, and his performance reflected the fact that he would have to work to become accustomed to all that extra space. Beck stepped out in a shirt he picked up from someone's floor he crashed on for a night, thinking it was his. His shoes stank because they were the same ones that he walked on New York streets looking for a job and not having a clue who to ask. All he had was some change in his pocket, and a couple of guitar picks and some snot-dried tissues because he had a cold for a while. It took forever to get here, thousands of nights of scuffling to the stage at some café with a low ceiling and strange lighting that glares off every table top at him ('What the fuck is this... an art gallery?'). Now there he was, with 40,000 suburban kids out there waiting to see what he'd do.

So Beck and his old jerky boy and girl crew from Silverlake took the stage, clutching instruments like power drills. Beck stepped up to the mike, every millisecond before he arrived there a lifetime. 'Alright, this next song is...' And then he invented some bullshit, because how many of these people knew anything about him besides a song they heard on the radio? Beck yowled into the mike and jumped like a freak whose mom didn't give him his Ritalin. He did every move he ever wanted or didn't want to do. He jumped up on the speakers, jammed on the guitar like the skinny white kid he was. And he got zero reaction. 'It's funny,' he told *The Times* a couple of years later, 'we were playing all the songs and the kids who were there couldn't give a fuck. They didn't even clap for me.'[8] Doing double duty alternative penance, he also performed on the second stage where he played a mostly acoustic set. If anything, Beck seemed more at home there, with lesser known bands, playing for more diverse and appreciative audiences. Beck found a particular kinship with Doo Rag and Cypress Hill. Courtney Love, too, warmed to Beck, commenting that Kurt Cobain would have loved him. Beck had to share dressing rooms at some venues, once with the Cypress Hill guys. They talked for a bit and realized that they had grown up a mile apart. When he said he was from Pico Hill, they were shocked; they'd thought he was from England.

On 7 July, Beck spent a burning hot day trawling around suburban Denver, eating at a Steak House and taking a forty-minute cab ride to get essentials at an enormous Target Market. Back at the hotel, the Sports Bar was crowded with the cream of the alternative universe, scaring the beejesus out of tourist families. Outside Beck vaguely noticed three Denver cop cars pull up with a screech. Marching in, the cops scanned the room through their stern shades and found what they were looking for. Marching up to Beck, 'they told me to stand still, took my license and held me for half-hour. They were looking for a sex offender, and told me somebody was using my name and birth date and had warrants in Pennsylvania.' Realizing Beck was not their man, they let him go wearily up to his hotel room with a broken air-conditioner. Collapsing on the bed in the 102-degree heat, Beck listened to the kids of the alternative nation© 'combing hallways and lobby looking for action.'[9] 'Blue plastic seats,' was how Beck recalled the concerts. 'Empty, very empty, and it's 105 degrees, and there's a small cluster of youngsters who are displaying their energetic support, but they're about a mile and a half away, and there's ten security guys closing in on them. At that point there was a lot more happening at the falafel booth than where I was standing. It was a good experience because the other bands were really bored, too. We played a lot of ping pong.'[10] Days off from the tour were spent combing bookstores and watching films. Beck took in a lot of cinema, a comfort amid all the shallowness of the Lollapalooza spectacle.

On 23 July in Toronto, after performing 'Novacane' during his all-electric main stage set, Beck ambled off to the second stage where he did an acoustic set comprising everything from 'John Hardy' to 'It's All In Your Mind' before an impromptu rag'n'reel improvisation, and a specially amended version of 'Nightmare Hippy Eurochick'. Kind of bewildered and maybe bored, Beck closed out with a supreme encore medley: 'Ozzy'-'Asshole'-'I Get Lonesome'-'Satan Gave Me Some Vitamins'-'Mexico'-'Totally Confused'-'Rowboat'. At other times he closed with something called 'Aroma Of Gina Arnold', a riposte to the writer who had called him 'man-child'.

At New York City's Randall's Island the stages were a mile apart, and rains had turned the playing ground into a swamp. Beck was ferreted on a golf-cart flying through the mud. He later told *Huh* magazine, 'It was one of those situations which call upon your character to rise above and maintain yourself and to keep plodding ahead, whilst being pummelled by sods of horrid, wretched Randall's Island muck. I remember opening my mouth to sing the first word of the day and a huge clump of mud went in my mouth. Nailed me. You try to carry on. I always find comedy in those kinds of performance mishaps. I always think that adds a dimension to the show you never could create on your own.'[11] The founders of Fluxus would have been proud.

If nothing else, Lollapalooza gave Beck a chance to see what was happening all over the country, and to discover something of the weird, discarded nature of the alternative nation. It's not too hard to imagine what he thought of all the subtle corporate inroads at the events, amidst all the political sign-up gloss. Nestled next to Greenpeace and voter registration booths, stalls selling rancid hippie oils and incense and overpriced shirts, there were tents of Sega game machines. Lollapalooza itself was straying far from originator Perry Farrell's vision of a touring platform for genuinely alternative artists; soon it would be a memory; yet another casualty of the tawdry media myth of an alternative nation. If anything, the festival was exceedingly conservative despite its surface accoutrements of piercings and tattoos, supposed emblems of individuality... just like everyone else.

The final Lollapalooza gig was on 18 August at Mountain View, California's Shoreline Amphitheatre, where Beck broke out a handful of the tracks from the new album that he'd been playing intermittently, including 'Novacane', 'Where It's At' and 'High 5 (Rock The Catskills)'. Bored with playing 'Loser', he would continue to get audience members to do beatbox versions with him, trying to reconnect with that old school hip-hop participatory spirit. But the punters didn't quite know what to make of it, and were by and large confused by his new direction, standing and watching him with the numb stasis of indie cynicism.

On 25 August Beck performed at the Reading Festival in England, where he was gaining a rabid following. He played 'Pay No Mind', a stinging 'Loser', 'Asshole' and a reeling 'Beercan'. Stopping in for an evening session at Radio 1, he recorded 'Cyanide Breathmint', 'Jack-Ass', 'Static' and Son House's '(Don't You Mind People) Grinnin' in your Face?'. While in London, Beck was invited to lunch with American rock anti-icon Neil Young, who asked him to play at his annual show benefiting the Bridge, the charity for multiple sclerosis. Young was the only Sixties musician who commanded solid respect from the youth of the Nineties, mainly for sticking to his guns and pursuing his single note guitar lines with admirable tenacity. They had an immediate rapport, with Beck responding to Young's characteristic warmth and interest in the true spirits who had been lumped in under the alt. rock label. After Young had played in Buffalo Springfield and, intermittently, with Crosby, Stills and Nash, he went solo and recorded a string of classic albums that cast a slightly sour eye on the excesses of the Sixties and the wreckage that decade had left behind. Young, like Beck, fixed a sometimes bleak eye on what surrounded him, but never pandered to cheap cynicism or despair. If anything Young is as close a venerated elder as Beck has.

Shortly thereafter, Beck rode the Chunnel train to play the Bataclan in Paris, where during 'Truckdrivin' Neighbors Downstairs' he got the audience to do call and response yodels of 'O-de-lay!' Later, requests were sent from the stage for human beatbox volunteers, for a positively speed-driven version of 'Loser', which, writer Peter Michel noted, '[left] both him and his foil, not to mention the rest of us, breathless.'[12] Beck's performances continued to alternately thrill or confuse the audiences, but evidence of his cross-cultural impact was confirmed by the strong audience reactions in the U.K. and continental Europe. At a festival in Switzerland sponsored by the makers of a sports drink bolstered with extracts from bull's testicles, Beck and the band met some unexpected critics. 'So we have several thousand disgruntled strapping brutes of snowboarders tanked up to the max. We were giving it our all. There was a forty-foot gap between them and the stage, and they were still able to nail us all pretty directly with empty cans. After a few songs I was using my guitar to bat cans from disgruntled sports enthusiasts back into the audience. It felt like we were A Flock of Seagulls opening up for Napalm Death.'[13]

After a long tour, extending out into Japan, Beck returned to the U.S. on 19 September to continue working on his new album, but the all-consuming studio insanity that had powered the first part of the sessions was over. Beck now told the Dust Brothers that he wanted to spend no longer than a day laying down new songs. First off were 'The New Pollution' and 'Devil's Haircut', both largely written and recorded in the same day-long sessions, followed soon after by 'Sissyneck'.

On 28 October Beck took a day off to play Neil Young's annual Bridge Benefit, where he played an all-acoustic solo set, comprising 'Pay No Mind', 'Sleeping Bag', 'John Hardy', 'Hollow Log', 'One Foot In The Grave', 'Rowboat', 'Asshole' and 'It's All In Your Mind'. Beck often chose to close with the latter, which began as an outtake at the 1993 sessions for *One Foot In The Grave*. A simple lament, lyrically and musically a dirge, conveys Beck's sadness at not being able to connect with a friend, who had perhaps taken offence when none was meant, and who is surrounded by a horde of people who sour the individual with their own 'scared and stiff' dissension and fears. The theme is universal but perhaps is particularly relevant to people of Beck's age, who have such trouble communicating, as their interactions are based around feelings they lack the words to articulate, and who so often make do with petty sarcasm instead.

At a glorious hometown show, on 11 November at Club Spaceland in Silverlake, Los Angeles, Beck debuted what would become his massive slow-jam 'Debra'. What began as a joke would actually build a bridge to Beck's future excursions. Beck and the Brothers had cut the track as a soul interlude amidst all the pile-driving songs for the new album, a spoof on soppy R&B bands who were dominating the charts at the time. With Beck's drive to get to the heart of every monster, 'Debra' slowly blossomed into a brilliant admixture of prime Prince, Warren G, Los Angeles radio station Power 106 slow-jam and, even further back, Teddy Pendergrass and Curtis Mayfield Seventies' soul workouts. The pastiche developed slowly into a show-stopping set piece that was reconfigured with every performance, gaining horns, backup vocals, extended interludes and Beck schpritzing about Jenny and her sister Debra until the song began propelling him rather than the other way round. Power 106 is part of Los Angeles' radio landscape, a seamless stream of R&B and hip-hop mixes, dashed with the cool patter of a gravelly voiced DJ. 'Living in Los Angeles there's a lot of driving involved,' Beck told *Buzzine* in 1997, 'and once you hit Power 106 on the radio, there's no deeper bass. It's a wonderful genre of music. It's so passionate and committed to itself.'[14]

'I was really drawn into the whole slo-jam thing for a couple of years, to a point of obsession,' Beck explained to *Sessions*. 'And I just started writing these things, because a lot of the lyrics are really Los Angeles. And if you listen to R. Kelly's "I Like The Crotch On You", he's really talking about his sexuality and he's heartfelt. So "Debra" is really drawing from that world. I didn't want it to be seen as a parody, because it's coming from me.'[15] 'I just hated all the contemporary R&B stuff', Beck explained to the *Boston Phoenix* in late 1999. 'So I really had to challenge myself and ask myself why I was reacting so strongly against this stuff. Why do I hate Boys II Men? So I started buying the records and listening to them. I grew to have an appreciation for it. I started getting into R. Kelly and Silk and Jodeci, and something that struck me was that the soul thing was there, the gospel element is there, the emotional intensity is there. And also there's humour and sleaze and lecherousness and so many elements to it beyond the one-dimensional image of the soul man breaking it all down. If you listen to these R. Kelly songs, they're fucking hilarious. At the same time, he's deeply sincere, and there's real deep emotion and poignancy there. And then the chorus of the song is "I like the crotch on you." Now is he being funny? Or am I laughing because I don't get it? That's the fine line that I love.'[16]

At a benefit gig at Silverlake's Spaceland, in its earliest, rawest incarnation, 'Debra' was a bizarre falsetto croon over nothing more than a metallic hambone drum machine beat. It's rawness was reminiscent of Suicide, the unique duo who would trawl the No-Wave clubs of New York, crooning ten-minute mantras about 'Frankie Teardrops' over primitive-in-the-extreme electronic backings. Lyrically the song's basic structure was already complete; every version after this would be an extrapolation. Beck apologized at the end: 'All right, sorry, I've been listening to Power 106 a little too much. Men II Boyz', to which an audience member, drunk on Spaceland's huge tankards of beer, shouted out 'Go on and play me some hip-hop!' Soon 'Debra' would progress to an echo-drenched falsetto extravaganza that would have put the famed 17th-century castrato Farinelli to shame, laced with delicious Hammond organ in the Jimmy Smith mode, some jazzy guitar fugues, tight drums and two slides down the bass, old skool soul style. Beck's vocal would reach glorious dub reggae-like distortions of taped sections and falsetto shrieking counterpoints – imagine Ennio Morricone scoring strings for Teddy Pendergrass at his panty-moistening best. The whole thing is wrapped up in a lovely Prince-at-Paisley Park ambience circa 'Money Don't Matter Tonight'. The whiff of pastiche remains with some of the high notes agonizingly reminiscent of Take That. Ramsey Lewis' 'My Love For You' off his 1973 classic jazz-funk slab *Funky Serenity* provides the looping wah-wah sample.

Within a year or two Beck would take his falsettos into the stratosphere and get into some real Marvin Gaye-style emoting. In a neat inversion, it seemed as though Beck's pastiches were capable of taking on a life of their own, becoming infused not with the irony he was so often accused of, but with real feeling; what began as a joke became a masterpiece. There are glorious moments in the multiple live (and bootlegged) versions of 'Debra' when Beck achieves that most remarkable thing, pure soulful expression. As he hits a falsetto, he sounds like Jackie Wilson, absolutely inside the sentiment. He achieves the soul dream of intimacy with his audience, and the number of white performers who can do that can be counted on one hand, as so few are willing to take the risk to court their audience, involve them, in that way. Beck skewered machismo with his eunuch falsetto, emoting masculinity in a neutered disguise. The lyrical content of the song reinforced the point, with Beck as a working-class lothario, seducing a J.C. Penney employee named Jenny with ludicrous gifts of chewing gum, Zankou chicken and the promise of a real good dinner that he would even (gasp) pay for himself. The punch line was that he wanted to get with Jenny, and her sister Debra as well, in white working-class inversion of the slo-jam ethos.*

Having dropped the first of his prototype future-funk bombs, Beck took a bleary-eyed flight halfway around the world, to Australia and New Zealand. It was the end of one stretch of the road for Beck, as he abandoned his unsteady, sporadically brilliant *Mellow Gold* period, for something new. The decision to change direction came partly as a result of the fallout surrounding the sudden success of 'Loser' and Beck's inability to handle it. 'After "Loser" came out our shows became confrontational. That song drew in a certain type of audience, but at that point, I was still basically playing folk gigs. The "Loser" thing was really a side project from my folk stuff. So there were a couple of awkward years where I was trying to figure out exactly what I wanted to do. Did I want to do something that was confrontational and explosive, or do something that was more country and folk-based, or did I want to create a whole different thing that I'd never really imagined before? I opted for the last one.'[17] Beck had come to the fork in the road, and it's safe to say a certain maturity and perspective on his own life, music and direction were pointing the way forward.

On 29 December, in the middle of the Australian summer, Beck hit Freemantle to guest at Summersault 1996, very appropriately as a segue between Sonic Youth and the Beastie Boys. Under the blessed Freemantle sky, site of so many great gigs, Sonic Youth's 'Diamond Sea' evaporated over the course of fifteen minutes into blissful waves of feedback and harmonies. Beck stepped to the mike and dropped in with harmonica, joining right into the outro of the Sonic Youth song, before playing an all-acoustic set solo, featuring a foot-stomping 'One Foot In The Grave'. It was a grand return to his early folk days after his recent sonic experimentation in the studio and full-band tours, and both performer and crowd responded warmly to the simplicity of one man, guitar and harmonica. Continuing the theme of continuous motion, a perfect prelude for the death of alternative rock and the spawning of the New Thing, three imps known as Mike D, MCA and Ad-Rock of the Beastie Boys then leapt onstage to body rock and beat box along with Beck, before segueing into their own set. Feedback mantras, folk and hip-hop, in a triune union.

By the time the Beat poet Allen Ginsberg declared Beck 'the best voice of his generation', Beck's lyrics were already the source of much musing and analysis, in much the same way that Bob Dylan's often obtuse lyrics and liner notes in the Sixties were scrutinized. 'The words are the most important part to me, because if the words suck, then I can't listen to something,' Beck told

---

* A classic Beck gig, the 11 November 1995 Spaceland show in Silverlake, California, was later committed to CD-R bootleg. Dubbed *Hi-Fi Pollution*, it featured a set list of 'Puttin' It Down', 'Sticks And Stones', 'Painted Eyelids', 'Pay No Mind', 'Alcohol', 'Debra', 'Dead Melodies' and 'One Foot In The Grave'.

Thora-zine in 1994. 'I never had money to buy equipment and have a band with a big sound. All I had was an acoustic guitar, you can only go so far, so I had to make up for everything else with having words that would interest people.'[18] Of course, that didn't necessarily mean that the words Beck came up with were the words his audience heard. 'I remember talking to some journalist in Hong Kong,' he recalled in 1996. 'And he read me out lyrics to one of my songs that weren't anything close to the ones I wrote. They were so much better. I've been kicking myself ever since that I didn't write down what he thought they were.'[19]

Beck's deep love of language powered his craze for slang and regional and cultural twists on the Queen's English. In the neighbourhood where he grew up, it was Spanish, not English, that was spoken most often, and he grew up with a passion for dialect and, in particular, outmoded colloquialisms: 'There are a lot of those in traditional and folk songs: certain turns of phrases that have been lost from modern-day discourse.'[20] In turn, these added an exotic quality to Beck's lyric-writing, an intriguing ambiguity, working by hints and suggestions rather than straightforward statements.

It is precisely Beck's ambiguity, both in his lyrics and in the way he collages his music together, that makes it so hard for the American media and even many of his fans to feel comfortable with him. This leads to the accusation that his eclecticism is just another form of self-protective irony, a claim that Beck roundly rejects: 'That sounds like you're just trying on a bunch of different hats; like now I'm going to do a punk song, and now I'm going to do a hip-hop song. It's more trying to have a musical language, like a toolbox. A whole lot of different stuff [...] Whatever comes out, comes out. I don't really filter it.'[21] Beck repeatedly stated his desire to avoid the cult of personality in his music – in which the voice of the songwriter takes over from the song he or she is writing – and his belief in the tradition of songwriting. 'A lot of people write songs for their own image, for their own purposes [...] I really look back to a time when there were songwriters, and it was a craft. The song could be sung by a lot of different performers, it wasn't just associated with just one person. That's a really healthy thing. It takes the ego out of it, a little bit.'[22] Taken in such a context, the avoidance of too many autobiographical touches, for example, in Beck's songs could be interpreted as an attempt to just let the song speak for itself.

As late as the mid-Seventies, songwriters would have their songs performed by a host of performers. Songwriters like Fred Neil were largely unknown except by other songwriters or singers, who made monstrous hits of his compositions; these included Nilsson's 'Everybody's Talkin'' and 'Dolphins', which every folkie who could twang an open D, from Tim Buckley to Beth Orton, has assailed. Songs were freely covered by others, and often reconfigured so broadly that they improved on the original; the Byrds' take on Bob Dylan's 'Mr. Tambourine Man' took the original places it would never have gone. That cross-pollination between artists rarely occurs today, and its absence is particularly conspicuous in popular music. Not coincidentally, Beck is one of the few modern pop musicians to be covered by unexpected others, witness Johnny Cash's superb take on 'Rowboat' and Tom Petty's version of 'Asshole', though as he admits himself, 'Now what I'm doing is more experimental, I don't think you could necessarily take many of the songs off *Odelay* and do a cover of them.'[23] The absence of good cover versions is a notable, and regrettable, feature of contemporary music. Perhaps the explanation for it is tied to the fact that many modern artists are belaboured by the notion that their opinions, as expressed in their lyrics, are the *sine qua non* of everything. Stepping into someone else's song and singing or playing it is a powerful thing indeed, and a great interpreter such as Frank Sinatra or Elvis Presley can awaken aspects of the song that its composer may not even have been aware of.

The false sincerity of Nineties music is as repugnant as the vacuous power pop of the Eighties that it sought to supplant. Drawing perhaps on the inspiration of Fluxus, and the experience he'd

'I'd like to think that no matter what style I'm delving into,
my personality and artistic integrity reveal themselves.'

'My whole
generation's mission
is to kill the cliché.'

11

On the Lollapalooza Tour,
1995: 'It's funny, we were
playing all the songs and
the kids who were there
couldn't give a fuck. They
didn't even clap for me.'

Beck plays live with his unvarnished half-incinerated plywood, no-name acoustic guitar of lore. Speaking in 1994: 'It's a guitar I bought for 60 bucks through the paper. I wouldn't sell it. It's not worth more than 60 bucks. It's withstood a lot, though. I used to set it on fire at the end of every show.'

111

At the Phoenix Festival, 1996: 'I can understand that you might be tempted to make commercial shit and compromise to do it. I try not to compromise on anything. We associate becoming an adult with compromise.'

IV

The Country Blues: 'This was the real stuff. I stopped everything for six months and was in my room finger-picking until I got it right.'

Back in New York City: 'New York's the place where if you stay in one place long enough, you end up meeting everybody... So pretty soon, I was engulfed in this anti-folk world. It was just a very aggressive folk played with punk energy.'

2 March 1997, Kilburn National, London: 'Damn, y'all are too fast! Y'all been listenin' to too much Jungle! A man cannot play the blues that fast!'

VI

'Los Angeles is a desert, in more ways than one. So the idea is it's all makeshift. That goes into a lot of my songs, but I love it here. It's such a blank slate, a generic city; you can make it whatever you want.'

10 May 1997, Brixton Academy, London: 'People come to try and bum rush my show. Bring me bicycle helmets and Brussels sprouts. That is so dope!'

VII

'The people who took 'Loser' to heart were the popular people, the attractive, stronger ones. But it was really coming from someone – myself – feeling displaced from the Eighties…If you went to school and you were wearing the same shoes you had a year ago…you were not accepted. The people who embraced it represented the reason the song was written.'

VIII

'I believe in the philosophy of flux. There are so many elements flying in so many different directions that you really have to go with what feels right instinctively. The nature of the universe is fairly whimsical and nonsensical. In the most sombre, beatific peacefulness there's complete chaos and maniacal laughter. Music that doesn't reflect that is boring.'

had of his own grandfather's modus operandi, Beck's advice to new songwriters was to emphasize absurdity and spontaneity, jettisoning the knotted brow school of 'nightmare bogus poetry'. Of course, he didn't say it as straight as that: 'It's not such a holy thing eat a burrito, write a song. Set your guitars and banjos on fire, and before you write a song, smoke a pack of whiskey and it'll take care of itself. I just let whatever comes out come out without thinking about it much [...] Everybody's got their own songs. There should be so many songs out there that it all turns into one big sound and we can put the whole thing into a pickup truck and let it roll off the edge of the Grand Canyon.'[24] Elsewhere, in an interview in *Bam* magazine, he described his songwriting technique as follows: 'I open up a big cabinet, and I have a collection of helmets. I put on the different helmets, and I take three bottles of Robitussin and drink them really quickly. Then I set my hand on fire. I have to write down whatever comes to mind pretty fast, before my hands burn off.'[25] Beck's tongue-in-cheek analysis of his songwriting here involves fire, what Freud would call sublimated sexuality of some sort. Both Beck and Al Hansen were obsessed with the notion of fire, extinguished matches, impotency and potency. The crippled egos behind body builders, pop singers and bikers and biker chicks; the sacred music of the Muses, a sly seduction, stealing fire from Zeus.

'You could look at some of my lyrics and think it's a bunch of random gibberish that I made up off the top of my head,' he told *Spin* in 1996, 'But it really isn't at all. I couldn't sing it if it didn't mean something to me, if it didn't relate to some experience or some running joke I have with a friend. Even if other people don't really get them, still there's this sense that it's real.'[26]

Generally mischievous in interviews with American music journalists, Beck would often open up more to foreign journalists, as often times they didn't have such a godawful hankering for the obvious. In a 1998 interview with Brazilian journalist Pedro Gonçalves, he revealed his songwriting method: 'I need to be alone. If there are people near, they end up talking to me and the talking disturbs me. But I don't isolate myself; songwriting isn't a prison. The writing is a veranda with a beautiful view, a view that is mutable. It's a view over all humanity, the songwriter's view is the most beautiful in the world.' [27]

Beck's love of samples has notable antecedents, such as Brion Gysin and William Burroughs' cut-up experiments with speech recorded on old reel to reels. John Lennon and Yoko Ono made an album in 1968 for which they manipulated the tuning knob of a radio to make instant collages. A very early and crude sampling was the tape loop, a small segment of tape that could be layered, dubbed and redubbed to form collage soundscapes. The use of tape loops by avant-garde composers such as Karlheinz Stockhausen, whose 1965 composition *Hymnen* is a collage of 132 national anthems, can be oddly moving. When something is taken out of its context, a new context is formed, even if the rearrangement is accidental or a chance operation. Terry Riley's 1965 'It's Gonna Rain' used the sound of a minister in multiple tape loops which, when played for a while, tends to make the listener forget not only the original minister, but also what he is saying and where it originated from. Sampling, as practised by everyone from Kool DJ Herc in parks in Brooklyn in 1978 to the Dust Brothers in their sci-fi studio, is the logical outgrowth of the collage. It is important to make this connection back to the roots of modernism, to Picasso and Braque's Cubism, to Schwitters' *merzbow*. 'I love the sound of cut-up music,' Beck once revealed. 'It really speaks of our time and how we're conditioned to hear things and the way we receive information from TV and magazines. Just bits and pieces piling up. I liked the idea of using the hip-hop technique of samples but approaching it from folk and talking blues.'[28]

Latter-day critics have frequently levelled the complaint that Beck is a consummate chameleon, changing to fit his environment. But in many ways the inverse is true: it is Beck's inability or unwillingness to blend in that marks him out an original. 'To me, a chameleon is someone really dilettante-ish or contrived. No matter what Bowie or David Byrne or the Beatles or anybody did, their personalities were always there underpinning the music. I'd like to think that no matter what style I'm delving into, my personality and artistic integrity reveal themselves.'[29]

Just as samples are a highly appropriate reflection of the diverse and high-speed streams of information that assail us today, Beck's conscious eclecticism seems only a fitting approach for an experimental pop artist to take. One criticism of Beck that never seems to die is that he is an impersonal, ironic deconstructionist. A cynical postmodernist merely commenting on commentary. Articles and interviews deride him as a channel surfer, a musician akin to a bored slacker skimming through television channels. It's an accusation that he vehemently denies: 'There's an implied impatience to channel surfing. I'm not bored with anything I'm doing. I'm not impatient, either. The public consciousness is moving to a point where we can assimilate two or three things at the same time.'[30] 'I feel like the music that we make is very much a product of growing up with TV and media,' agrees John King. 'Very fast, fast switching edits on TV, attention spans getting shorter and shorter. I've definitely grown up in it, and Beck's even younger, so he's probably grown up with more diversity and quicker switching between different things. Maybe it's thinking faster. Not a shorter attention span but just thinking faster.'[31]

One writer compared Beck's stylistic morphing, brilliantly, to using the Web rather than channel surfing, with each window opening out onto another. The Web has revolutionized the way we process information; it is a lot closer to an abstract, tangential flow of thought rather than the old linear modes of going from point to point in a linear way. It is almost a graft of the neuronal byways of thought onto the sterile circuits of computers. This is bound to find reflection in music and the arts more and more, particularly as these forms are so often the first line in making sense of new technology. The inverse of that is one can roam the Web or chat with creative people for hours and hours and hours and not really achieve any momentum. For the Web is also the first medium to perpetuate stasis as much as flux. Likewise, samplers and computerized audio editing tools can lead one down byways with diminishing creative returns, as the ever-increasing number of producers and musicians who get locked into constantly remixing and editing their work can ably attest.

One person who has suffered immensely from this stasis masquerading as flux is Carl Stephenson. During the period when Beck and the Dust Brothers were working on the album that would become *Odelay*, he was on his 113th remix of 'Dream', a song that had been basically complete when 'Loser' came out. Stephenson's *Forest For The Trees* album is so saturated with music you have it slice it sideways to avoid having it all fall apart. A beautiful treat, and a musical smorgasbord, but it is an album that almost never was: at one point, following endless hours of fine tweaking and mixing, Stephenson felt the music was getting the better of him and threw some of the mixes into the ocean. 'We began getting phone calls from Carl around the time of "Loser", and he was expressing all these fears,' his mother, Mary Stephenson said. 'Carl would pick up on all kinds of things that you or I would never even notice, and he'd make them his reality. With "Loser," for instance, he was scared to death that Beck was going to get killed by somebody because of the line in the song.'[32]

Perhaps recognizing a streak of obsessiveness inside himself, Beck chose to let his muse have its way with him, instead of fighting it. 'A lot of what I'm trying to do is intuitive, surrendering to some other logic, so it doesn't become forced,' he told the *Los Angeles Times* in 1996. 'I tend to do better when I just let the album take on a life of its own. It usually has its own plan somehow. Almost as if you're the transmitter, the facilitator of this whole thing. When you're in the studio sixteen hours for the twentieth day in a row, it's so unconscious at some point, you don't know what the hell's going on. The real music starts to happen when you get to that point where you're just letting go and you're creating some monster.'[33]

'I'm always recording,' Beck once told MTV, 'so when it's time to put out a record I just take from the stuff I have and put it out. It's all simultaneous, all happening at the same time. The records from 2000, they've already been recorded. So in the year 2000, I'll re-record *Mellow Gold*, so they'll all be inverted. But it's all happening at the same time.'[34] This somewhat cryptic comment is reinforced by the scattered wrong dates in Beck's album and single credits, with songs on 1994's *Stereopathetic Soul Manure* credited as being written in 1996, or *Golden Feelings* tracks used as B-sides in 1993 listed as being 'evacuated onto four-track in 1998'. Like Hansen's happenings, Beck's songs were treated as fissures in day-to-day reality, coming from somewhere unfathomable.

In interviews at the time when he was making *Odelay*, Beck sometimes spoke of the notion of 'inverted funk': 'Some of the songs on *Odelay* are a little bit too loose. We had to pull in the reins, make it a little tighter. An inverted funk,'[35] he told *Huh* in July 1996. Tighten up; inverse funk. It's another element in Beck's offbeat cosmology, paralleling the notion that his albums are a timeless thread looping back on itself, a commentary on the idea that the past creates a vision of the future, and back again. It's less new-age than it sounds, and is the signifier of a good musician who realizes the timeless nature of inspirational music, and is still in touch with the blues in hip-hop. It also acknowledges that funk embraces awkwardness, something very useful for white people, strained as they are by logic and lack of intuitive reasoning. Ever watch a chicken strut? There you have a root for funk dancing. All ritual dances hark back to nature and rituals for controlling the uncontrollable by utilizing motion. Watching movies from Hong Kong, as well as Mexican and Arabic television variety shows, Beck had unlocked one of the secrets of funk: how to dance funky. 'You've got to do it real jerky,' he told *Spin*'s Neil Strauss. 'That's the thing people don't know: The stiffer and more awkward you are, the funkier you are. It's this weird inverse-funk thing. If you look at the funkiest dancers, their upper bodies are totally stiff while another part of their body is doing something else. People usually think they're just supposed to relax and feel the beat. But that's not funky at all. Tightening up your body, and being real jerky, that's the funkiest.'[36] White people are at their funkiest when they take their stereotypic up-tightness and rigidity and blow it out of all proportion. In that way, Kraftwerk, David Byrne and Devo are the essence of white funkiness. David Bowie singing 'Foot Stomping' on *Soul Train* in 1975 is white funk par excellence.

Inversion is a theme that crops up often in Beck's interviews; inverted funk or the notion of soulfulness as inverted awkwardness. 'My whole generation's mission is to kill the cliché,' he told *Rolling Stone* in 1997. 'I don't know whether it's conscious all the time, but it's one of the reasons a lot of my generation is always on the fence about things. They're afraid to commit to anything for fear of seeming like a cliché. They're afraid to commit to their lives because they see so much of the world as a cliché. So I'm trying to embrace the world and all this stuff in a way that doesn't seem cliché. I'm creating the new cliché.'[37] If, as Beck said, our generation's mission is to kill the cliché, he is working toward that by inverting clichés. Instead of simple parody, pastiche or irony, this inversion echoes Brazilian concrete poet Osvald de Andrade's ethos of cultural anthrophagy – eating all cultures and digesting them into something unique – that reflects its host as much as its origins. Beck is far from a culture vulture or the lame postmodernist his detractors bill him as; his strength lies in his willingness to embrace what he doesn't understand, or what appals him.

This is the antithesis of retro, with its cloying kitsch and inflated symbols taken out of context. There is deep pathos in Gainsbourg, there is haunting weight in Bacharach and David, there are grimy Soho streets in John Barry that transcend the irony with which enthusiasts of retro-kitsch approach these artists. The lounge culture epitomized by Fifties and Sixties arranger-composers Esquivel, Martin Denny and Henry Mancini were something Beck wove into his music, along with the Brazilian stylings of bossa nova and samba. But the appreciation seemed to be sincere, something those immersed in the retro-kitsch scene that sprang up in the Nineties were immune to.

This immunity to sincerity marked the high water mark of irony. Taking the perceived excesses of the past and lauding them satirically, taking on the accoutrements and icons and fashions, the Los Angeles Retro Fitters saw fit to indulge in crass kitsch whilst reviling it, turning themselves into reflections of their own disdain. At its best, the lounge core movement was perhaps a commentary on irony, and if so, was sporadically brilliant. What its constituents, in polyester suits and wigs, often missed was the beauty and real brilliance in things such as the music of Burt Bacharach. This lounge core set hovered around places like Los Angeles' Dresden Rooms, camping it up on the red leather sofas. Obviously, there were those who really loved the things they'd found, and some were attracted by the ebullience of the excesses of the past, an implied freedom so lacking in the sterile Nineties. Others drifted in and found there really was treasure among all the trash.

Amid the excesses of the lounge revival, back-handed compliments became sincere. The retro East Hollywood scene was something Beck 'observed affectionately from the fringes without really getting involved. But I have great admiration for the hardcore enthusiasts.'[38] He cited the Royal Crown Review, playing Forties swing music, in vintage zoot suits and swinging chains, buffed brogues and flash hats. The very best of these enthusiasts of the past are true archivists in a way, historians who preserve the past by documenting it, by copying. And preserving its excesses or a perceived inflated view coloured by nostalgia, in some ways preserves a dead scene better than anything else could. At its most basic, the lounge revival was a rejection of the wearying nihilism of the Nineties alternative scene, as expounded by bands such as Biohazard, Stone Temple Pilots, Pearl Jam and Rage Against the Machine; and that was something Beck could definitely relate to. 'Odelay was really a reaction to the whole grunge thing,' he told The Times in 1997. 'By the end of 1994, I was sick of hearing another band moping. I was sick of the pain and the agony. There was no commitment. I hated going to the show and the band was standing there going through the motions. The whole grunge thing became an excuse to not perform. You'd be watching these bands that weren't sure if they wanted to be there, so why do I want to be here? The prevalent attitude of people my age at the time was they didn't want to commit to anything, a job, a girlfriend, or even an idea.'[39] Angst seems to be one of the concomitants or by-products of technology, rapid growth, industrialization and migration; being displaced by motion rather than propelled forward by it, like trains leading nowhere. And the proponents of that music frequently stemmed from the white middle-classes – the very comfort that suburban life offered lead to frustration; what was there left to rebel against if you had a comfortable family life, a full belly and a warm bed? Steve Hanft called it 'Al-tern-it-off'.

In an interview with the Los Angeles Times in 1996, Beck expanded on the theme. 'I look at all the music I love: country music, blues, samba, hip-hop, Moroccan, whatever. There's that element of celebration in the music that is so sorely missing. I'm not saying that angst and irony aren't valid. They're so much a part of our time. But the musicians I admire: Willie Nelson, Chico Hamilton, Hank Williams, Maybelle Carter, Ella Fitzgerald, there's dozens – there's something that reaches me in that music that has this real multi-level range to it that a lot of the music I hear now doesn't.'[40]

Boil it all down, and you get the Beck of *Odelay*, making a stand for polymorphic music-making and, ultimately, getting back to sheer entertainment. You get a live act with traces of theatre, slapstick and melodrama, music that draws on myriad influences, the sheer dynamism of which puts most of Beck's contemporaries to shame. It's a music of possibilities, unrestricted by issues of genre. 'I met Snoop Doggy Dog a couple of months ago on tour in Europe,' Beck told *The Rocket* in 1997. 'He came up and said, "I love your stuff. I love what you're doing with hip-hop." I didn't think that exchange was possible, but the more I meet people in that world, they're totally listening to what's going on in the alternative world, they're really open. The opportunities are there.'[41] At the heart of it was Beck's determination to keep his music fresh by leaving it open to chance and accidents: 'I'm not really a perfectionist, because I keep recording something until I get a mistake. As a musician, my first instinct is to play it good, and that always comes off stiff. Then when it loosens up, the mistakes start happening. That's when it starts working out. Mistakes lead you to where you're supposed to go.'[42]

'He's a sponge for ideas,' Simpson told *Entertainment Weekly*. 'I've never encountered anybody like him that can play with so much soul. While all this stuff just seems to flow out of him so effortlessly and seemingly at random, he does have a very strong vision, so it's an odd balance of focus and completely unbridled enthusiasm.'[43] No wonder he was so enthusiastic; Beck was finally getting to make the album he'd always wanted to make.

1   Dunn, Jancee. 'Beck: Resident Alien', *Rolling Stone*, 11–25 July 1996

2   Dunn, Jancee. 'Beck: Resident Alien', *Rolling Stone*, 11–25 July 1996

3   Babcock, Jay. 'Beck', *Huh*, July 1996

4   *Gellow Molde* fanzine, September 1995

5   Hoskyns, Barney. *World Art Magazine*, issue 19, Autumn 1999

6   Weisbard, Eric. 'After The Goldrush', *Spin*, 1996

7   Hoskyns, Barney. 'The Mix It Up Kid', *Mojo* magazine, March 1997

8   Porter, Charlie. 'Beck To The Future', *The Times*, 25–31 October 1997

9   *Online Diaries: The Lollapalooza '95 Tour Journals*, Soft Skull Press, January 1998

10 Dunn, Jancee. 'Beck: Resident Alien', *Rolling Stone*, 11–25 July 1996

11 Babcock, Jay. 'Beck', *Huh*, July 1996

12 Michel, Peter. 'Summersault '96', *Blah Blah Blah* fanzine. December 1995–January 1996.

13 Dunn, Jancee. 'Beck: Resident Alien', *Rolling Stone*, 11–25 July 1996

14 Parker, Aaron. *Buzzine*, 1997

15 Sessions At West 54th Street, 6 September 1997, www.sessionsatwest54th.com/

16 Ashare, Matt. 'Slow Jamming: Beck Reveals His Inner Soul Man', *Boston Phoenix*, 25 November–2 December 1999

17 Wiederhorn, Jon. 'The Many Faces of Beck', *Guitar*, January 1999

18 Grob, Julie. 'Beck', *Thora-zine*, May 1994, www.eden.com/thora-zine

19 Dunn, Jancee. 'Beck: Resident Alien', *Rolling Stone*, 11–25 July 1996

20 Strauss, Neil. 'Artist Of The Year', *Spin*, 1996

21 Exan. 'Beck And Me', MTV, May 1996

22 Burnett, Erich. 'Losing The "Loser" Mentality', *Scene*, August 1996

23 Burnett, Erich. 'Losing The "Loser" Mentality', *Scene*, August 1996

24 Rotondi, James. *Guitar Player*, September 1994

25 *Bam*, July 1996

26 Strauss, Neil. 'Artist Of The Year', *Spin*, 1996

27 Gonçalves, Pedro. *Blitz*, 3 November 1998

28 Gundersen, Edna. 'Beck In The Saddle Again', Microsoft Music Central, November 1998

29 Wiederhorn, Jon. 'The Many Faces Of Beck', *Guitar*, January 1999

30 Foege, Alec. Reader's Poll 1997, *Rolling Stone*, 23 January 1997

31 Cromelin, Richard. 'Nobody's Fool', *Los Angeles Times*, 21 July 1996

32 Hilburn, Robert. 'Pop Music "Dream" Deferred No More', *Los Angeles Times*, 16 November 1997

33 Cromelin, Richard. 'Nobody's Fool', *Los Angeles Times*, 21 July 1996

34 Exan. 'Beck And Me', MTV, May 1996

35 Babcock, Jay. 'Beck', *Huh*, July 1996

36 Strauss, Neil. 'Artist Of The Year', *Spin*, 1996

37 Kemp, Mark. 'Where It's At Now', *Rolling Stone*, 17 April 1997

38 Cigarettes, Johnny. 'Gouda Vibrations', *Vox*, March 1997

39 Porter, Charlie. 'Beck To The Future', *The Times*, 25–31 October 1997

40 Cromelin, Richard. 'Nobody's Fool', *Los Angeles Times*, 21 July 1996

41 Johnson, Calvin. 'Calvin Talks To Beck, Beck Talks Back To The Rocket', *The Rocket*, January–February 1997

42 'Super Beck: "Loser", Artist, Rock Star, Genius', *UHF* # 10, July–August 1996

43 Browne, David. 'Beck In The High Life', *Entertainment Weekly*, 14 February 1997

10

UDON NOODLE SHEEPDOGS
& THE NEW THING

Beck and the Brothers did touch ups at Conway Studios, Hollywood Studios, Hollywood; the mixing for *Odelay* was finished in December, the week before Beck's Australian tour. Twelve tracks were selected from the forty songs which had been recorded. According to Beck, the title was at one point going to be *Robot Jazz*, suggesting the idea of spontaneity in machines. He also joked to *Blah Blah Blah* fanzine that he was thinking of calling it *Le Tough*: 'it's toughness embodied and dismembered, with that little touch of class. When you put "Le" in front of a word it makes it a little classier. I want everyone to know this is a classy operation and no expense has been spared to bring the most luxurious sounds to this project.'[1] The choice of image for the cover was somewhat whimsical. With the deadline a day away, Beck chanced across the perfect image. Opting against putting his face on the cover, he chose instead a stock shot of a Komondor sheep dog jumping over a hurdle, taken from *The Complete Dog Book*, published by the American Kennel Club. 'I came to a picture of the most extreme dog. He looked like a bundle of flying udon noodles attempting to leap over a hurdle. I couldn't stop laughing for about twenty minutes.'[2]

As a taster for the upcoming *Odelay* world tour, Beck took off to Noorderlicht, Tilburg in the Netherlands for a show on 18 March, solo and acoustic, opening for Sonic Youth. After trying to engage the audience and pretty much failing, Beck split up 'Mexico' into four parts, an approach reminiscent of old-time medicine shows. With typical perversity, the only song he played off the forthcoming album was the closer, 'Lord Only Knows'. Steve Shelley, drummer for Sonic Youth, recalled that 'Every night after the show we'd climb on the bus and have these wine-and-cheese parties and all watch fucking pretentious Gainsbourg videos.'[3] Beck credits Shelley with introducing him to the late, great Serge Gainsbourg, the French singer whose albums were epics of omnivorous cultural consumption, taking in reggae, funk, disco and whatever else was on the plate in the Sixties and Seventies. Gainsbourg's career was all the more notable because he began as a fairly standard interpreter of French *chanson*, with early Sixties tracks such as 'La Javanaise'. Unattractive physically though endowed with great charisma, Gainsbourg charmed a number of beautiful women into both his studio and his boudoir. His collaborations with Brigitte Bardot and Jane Birkin were masterful, erotic and overblown in a way that is quite alien to Anglo-American popular music. The risqué content of his songs, his passion and his unmitigated decadence – pure rock and roll – endeared him to Beck, not to mention his humour. 'Beauty is found at the bottom of the garbage can, and Gainsbourg looked for it mightily. My favourite album is the *Melody Nelson* record from '70 or '71. It's the greatest marriage of the rock band with the orchestra that I've ever heard.'[4]

On 31 March Beck parachuted into England, to play another solo acoustic set, this time splitting up 'Heartland Feeling' into two sections and closing, oddly, with 'One Foot In The

Grave'. On 5 June Beck played solo and acoustic at Toronto, Canada's Regency Room, taking the tiny stage with his guitar and mike through possibly the oldest public address system known to man. During the performance he alluded to the secret past of the room: 'I understand this is the first show here in the upper chambers of the Masonic Temple. Some trap door is probably going to open up and someone is going to have to rescue me from some Masonic dungeon. There will probably be a flogging party going on.'[5] Again, Beck only played 'Lord Only Knows' off the new album, as 450 hardcore Beck freaks sat on the floor like an old skool hootenanny and called out requests. During a loose and informal set, which included a lot of bantering with the audience, Beck played 'Asshole' and 'Nitemare Hippy Girl'. Taking a break, he rigged up a crusty old Roland 808 drum machine, letting static beats rip through the old room, invoking 33rd degree Mason science. A posse of three audience members acted as improvised beatboxes, while Beck rapped and did the splits, stage front; unfortunately, the effect proved less than dazzling. This was a raw laboratory test for the outstanding shows to come, and Beck was testing out the various elements he would stir to combustion.

After a release party and in-store performance at Tower Records on the Sunset Strip in Los Angeles, *Odelay* was released on 17 June 1996 in the U.K. and a day later in America. A melding of all of Beck's influences, the album stunned critics and a large segment of the record buying public. *Odelay* debuted at number 16, selling 181,000 copies in three weeks. For a time it seemed that it had peaked, but sales picked up as Beck continued touring and people got used to the strange combination of sounds on the album, and soon the album went gold.

Sales suggested that *Odelay* crossed all demographic lines, becoming a soundtrack for a dozen disparate musical tribes. The slow but steady success of the album was an indication of both the new plurality in Nineties music and also the revolt against Eighties production values and approaches to songwriting, all clean edits and linear chord progressions. Beck achieved widespread accolades from critics, many of whom hailed *Odelay* as the best album of 1996, and received awards in both the U.S.A. and the U.K.. Country, hip-hop, exotica and strains of Indian film music, were all combined to produce an album that by the end of the year was hailed as the best of the year by mainstream music publications *Spin* and *Rolling Stone* in the United States and *Mojo*, *NME* and *Melody Maker* in the U.K.. Beck had not only vindicated himself, but astonished everyone.

Odelay was shocking at first, sounding polished and ragged at the same time. The album opened with the mighty 'Devil's Haircut', a monumental track. 'Devil's Haircut' immediately assayed the diverse sources Beck was exercising his alchemy on – Dick Hyman's Moogs, the drums of jazz/soul legend Bernard 'Pretty' Purdie, death metal and lounge core for starters. It took Beck years into the future and crystallized what *Odelay* was about – reconfiguring the past into something wholly new, killing the static of nostalgia by using the past to create the future. Whether or not the future was to be 'a golden land of opportunity' remained to be seen, but with songs like this there was a sense of inexorable forward motion. At maximum volume, 'Devil's Haircut' makes one's pulse start racing. The lounge horns, the skipping beat, the thundercrack Pretty Purdie rim shots, and finally the Pussy Galore overdose of ultra-distorted guitar accompanied by Beck screaming bloody murder at the end was almost too good to bear. It was danceable, it was bold, it was sharp and it was deadly cool. It compressed everything that was right on about Beck into three minutes; a perfect single.

'Electric Music And The Summer People' was the original title for 'Devil's Haircut'. 'I thought, what if Stagger Lee showed up now?,' Beck told *The Face* in 1996. 'The song had this Sixties grooviness, and I thought of using him as a Rumplestiltskin figure, this Lazarus figure to comment on where we've ended up as people. What would he make of materialism and greed and ideals of beauty and perfection? His reaction would be, "This is disturbing shit!" I can understand that you might be tempted to make commercial shit and compromise to do it. I try not to compromise on anything. We associate becoming an adult with compromise.'[6] Whereas in most versions of the song Stagger Lee is either praised or feared, Beck tried to step into his shoes, seeing the world through his eyes.

'Devil's Haircut' made inspired use of a sample from 'Outta Sight' by Sixties Belfast soul-rockers Them, featuring a raw, snarling Van Morrison vocal. The track was a cover of the 1964 song of the name by James Brown. When the Dust Brothers contacted James Brown's publishers for sample clearance, they insisted on 50 per cent of 'Devil's Haircut' publishing for themselves, even though Brown and his band played nothing on the Them song.

In the early years of hip-hop, you'd be hard pressed to find a song that didn't have a sample of either James Brown himself yelping, shouting or exclaiming 'Good God, I want to step back and kiss myself', or a stinging guitar by Jimmy Nolan or hard rhythmic bite from Bootsy and Catfish Collins. Brown earned nothing from these early samples, leaving him determined to get payback as samples began to have to be cleared. Only through intensive negotiations was the Them sample cleared for inclusion on 'Devil's Haircut'. Simpson said, 'I'm totally scared of sampling now. I will probably not do much sampling in the future, just because the Beck thing was such a nightmare. As a songwriter, I have no problem paying people their fair share. But the publishers feel like they have you by the balls, and they really flex on you and leave you no alternative but to pay them.'[7]

The second track on *Odelay*, 'Hotwax', Beck characterized as a West Coast travelling song, with a little bit of Spanish in the chorus. Indeed, the song is perfect for driving a low rider down Sunset, and is pervaded with the same laid-back air as War's classic 'Low Rider'. It's West Coast funk; Silverlake Baby-G Jeep Beat symphonies, evoking the car washes that dot the Los Angeles landscape advertising 'HOT WAX' for automobiles. Beck pal Ross Harris from the band Sukia makes an appearance on 'Hotwax'. 'Who are you?' asks a little girl, to which the Wizard (Ross Harris) replies, 'I'm the enchanting wizard of rhythm.' Beck insisted tracks such as 'Hotwax' were meant to be totally unironic. Hotwax's pulse draws on samples from 'Song For Aretha' by Pretty Purdie, plus a fragment from 'Up On The Hill' by obscurities Monk Higgins & The Specialities.

'Lord Only Knows' was, in Beck's words, 'A fare-thee-well tune, my closing-time song, a last salute, and the last hurrah. Another mis-spent evening.'[8] As a last hurrah, it was a perfect song to sing at Al Hansen's last happening, his memorial service. 'Lord Only Knows' features Beck breaking down with one of those clichéd Eighties heavy metal fingertap scales and zippy playing that expressed nothing except technical over-reaching, and which were about as creative as painting by numbers. How many Britney Foxx guitar solos were perpetrated during the dark ages of the 1980s? Oh, the horror! The Dust Brothers shattered 'Lookout For Lucy' by Mike Millius, and threw it into the mix.

The original title for 'Lord Only Knows' was the Chicano slang greeting 'Orale!', meaning 'go on!' or 'way to go!', which greeted the opening of every can of beer during the sessions for the album. However, the engineer mistakenly wrote down the song's title down as 'Odelay'. Observing Brian Eno's famed dictum 'Acknowledge your error as a hidden intention', the error was considered fortuitous and eventually gave the album its name. The seizing of a mistake in this way epitomizes the free appropriation of chance ideas inherent in the genesis of *Odelay*. Coincidentally, the word also referred back to Jimmie Rodgers' legendary yodels, where he would intone 'Yo-de-lay-hee, yo-de-lay-hee-hoo!', or even 'O-delay'©, some glorious 1970s tube echo pedal that was produced for about five seconds in Taiwan before being discontinued.

It's also a call and response, echoing the MCs and the hip-hop crowds at block parties of old. Showing his enthusiasm for mutated language, Beck noted, 'It's a word you grow up with, you know what it means, but you never knew literally what it means. It's a word that I associate with being among friends and enjoying myself.'⁹

And therein lies the gestalt at the core of the album: a joyful exclamation rather than an angst-ridden dirge. That said, there is an undertow of darkness on the album, as there is on all of Beck's work. The drones that Beck is fond of anchor the more heady up-tempo party tunes to the ground. 'There's some dark stuff on *Odelay*,' he told *Rolling Stone* in 1997. 'But I wanted it to feel good, too, in the way that any life-affirming music does. Like Brazilian music, because that's one of the main kinds of music that I listen to for my own pleasure. You've got a country there that's so riddled with poverty, and then there's this music that's so full of spirit. But it isn't just phoney happy music; it's genuine. That's often the case in struggling cultures or among struggling people: The music does just the opposite. If you have time to make really dark music, then it's a privilege. I've always felt that way.'¹⁰

A potent satire of America's conspicuous consumption and craving for novelty and sensation, 'The New Pollution' is all the more biting for being coupled with such an upbeat melody and tempo. 'The New Pollution' samples a rollicking sax solo from 'Venus' by Joe Thomas, treated with echo. The 'doo-doo-doo' intro, layered over a flute loop, Beck referred to as 'inverted funk'. Moreover, the title hinted at Beck's love of marrying opposites, escaping the restraints of conventional rock lyrics to create an image both inviting and repellent.

Dipping into the drone bag that Beck carries like a mojo sack, to dispense a little magic and a respite from the fireworks, out came 'Derelict'. The song is pervaded by a strong wind from the East, with hints of gamelan metalophones in the background, and laced with essraj and harmonium. Beck, like Jeff Buckley, came from a New York underground obsessed with Indian ragas and Sufi devotionals by the likes of the remarkable Nusrat Fateh Ali Khan and Ali Akbar Khan. The song evokes an industrialized Bollywood soundtrack, the film *Metropolis* if it had been shot in Bombay. When the tabla and tamboura come in, they lend the track a magisterial gravitas, not so much sonic tourism as sonic adventurism. Indeed, *Odelay*'s 'samples' are often not samples at all. Simpson: 'Beck would play for a while and we'd take the best pieces and make a sample out of that, and then he'd put stuff on top of that, and sometimes we'd sample again. So a lot of the things on the record that sound like samples are actually Beck playing. He can play every instrument. He played 95 per cent of the instruments on the album.'¹¹ Sonic experimentalism prevailed, fuelled by Beck's enthusiasm and the Dust Brothers' capacity for enabling him to actualize it. Beck noted: 'I spent a lot of time trying to get a sound that's not so fresh-sounding, make it sound old and crusty by miking weird shit, putting the guitar amp in the fridge. We'd take sounds and I'd play them on a keyboard and just fuck them up with delay, or I'd put it through an amp in the bathroom and re-record it on another tape. We'd be in the studio sixteen hours a day just doing silly stuff with that.'¹²

Beck's love of the sitar is well documented but, wary of merely sampling the sound and using it straight, on 'Derelict' he took that sound and warped it. His inspiration came from jazz guitarist Gabor Szabo: 'Gabor Szabo's a freaky jazz-guitar guy from the 1960s. One album called *Jazz Raga* is corny psychedelic. Basically, he cut a record, then the next day he was in a shop and he bought a sitar. So he got all excited and just went and played sitar over everything. And he didn't know how to play the sitar. The song starts out, doo-doo-doo-diddle jazzy guitar stuff, but then all of a sudden the sitar goes wah wah! It just sounds so fucked-up and good.'¹³ Gabor Szabo's guitar style mixed his native Hungarian folk music heritage with jazz and a lovely gift for branching out into exotic sounds. He was an important influence on guitarists like Carlos

Santana, who covered his 'Gypsy Queen'. Szabo also played in Chico Hamilton's quintet along with Charles Lloyd and in 1965 he played with Charles Lloyd's quartet with ubiquitous bassist Ron Carter and teenage master drummer Tony Williams. By the time Szabo went solo and started cutting his jazz exotica guitar odysseys, he had hooked up with Bernard 'Pretty' Purdie. Purdie's drumming is so hardcore that it defies the imagination, rim shots with slamming Gene Krupa precision, and snare hits with Max Roach bebop wrist rolls. Purdie has anchored the backbeat for everyone from Aretha Franklin and Miles Davis to Donny Hathaway. His soul jazz styling is often imitated but never equalled, a drummer par excellence with such precision that it defines funkiness.

Beck, taking five from recording *Odelay*, was skimming through the junkman's blue book, the *Recycler* and saw that a guy in Santa Monica was selling a sitar and tamboura. He immediately hopped in his Chevy and blasted down the Boulevard to the guy's house. Returning to the PCP Lab, Beck told an amused Simpson: 'the guy tuned it up for me and taught me how. Let's record something.'[14] In fact, that may not be a tamboura at all on 'Derelict', but a Caribbean rhythm box fitted with an echoing mike. A Univox drum machine, a temperamental piece of hardware, under-girds the rhythm. Beck's friend Paolo the Skateboarder plays the essraj, an Indian violin. The sonorities of the brittle essraj, super-resined bow being drawn across the strings, give the song a poignant delicacy. The harmonium is haunting and the song's odd tempo trebles the effect. Beck plays a Moroccan thumb piano he had lying around the house, analogue synth twitter across the stereo spectrum, and what sounds like an old style Nikon camera flash warming up laces the whole track like a sibilant snake. 'Lay my soul in the fallow field' intones a muted Beck, dredging his country-tinged fatalism onto deserted shores. In an otherwise rather damning review of *Odelay*, *Melody Maker* reviewer David Stubbs accurately captured the feel of 'Derelict' as 'broken down and windswept with a recurring guitar like a panhandler's jingle.'[15] A precursor for 'Derelict' could be Tom Waits' 'Clap Hands' off 1987's majestic *Raindogs*, with its junkyard gamelan clanking away in random pentatonic notes.

The song 'Novacane' was inspired by the ultra-macho testosterone film epics such as 'Convoy'; as Beck noted, 'the last convoy, a convoy with no destination, fully powered, unlimited supply of diesel. The convoy is continually growing. A concatenation of brakeless trucks speeding towards an invisible doom.'[16] The Dust Brothers gave Beck some walkie-talkies for the track, which he used to literally radio in his vocals.

'Jack-Ass' riffs off a beautiful loop from *Astral Weeks* by Van Morrison, and 'It's All Over Now Baby Blue' by Them. *Odelay* samples artists who themselves have reinterpreted other people's songs, with Them covering both Bob Dylan and James Brown. This furthers the notion of what Howard Gissage, quoted in Marshall McLuhan's *From Cliché To Archetype* (Pocket Books, 1970), refers to in the lines, 'Today's archetype was yesterday's art form, day before yesterday's cliché, and the day before that it was the last word.' Furthering the obsession with rescued clichés, the original title of the song was 'Millius'. A mike used to record drum cymbals was used for much of Beck's vocal on the track.

For 'Where It's At', the centrepiece of the album, a snippet of 'Needle To The Groove' by electro-rappers Mantronix peppers the mix. Beck brought in a favourite record by his beloved art-terrorists the Frogs and slipped in the phrase 'That Was A Good Drum Break' from 'I Don't Care If You Disrespect Me (Just So You Love Me)'. The Dust Brothers took a horrid Sixties sex education album used in classrooms called *Sex For Teens – Where It's At!* for the 'What about people who swing both ways, you know AC/DCs?' sample.

Continuing the trend of using unusual recording techniques for his vocals, Beck sings through a vocoder on the track, echoing electro's robotic soul. Again visions of an archaic future,

123

a gleaming past. The presence of Money Mark is auspicious, considering that Mark Nishita-Ramos is an archetype for the polyglot cosmopolitan of the future, as he is of mixed Mexican and Japanese heritage, is involved in redefining the parameters of music, and laces his albums with extreme soul. Both Money Mark and Beck's pal Mike Boito laid down Hammond keyboards like Jimmy Smith playing out in the chicken shack, Beck overdubbed bass, then layered a rap over the top. David Brown blew a hot muted trumpet lick. 'Where's It's At' was, according to Beck, 'something I wanted to say about hip-hop, a tribute to where it all started.'[17] The song goes back to the block parties of yore, when the MC held the street block in thrall, and deliberately uses out-of-date old skool hip-hop references. 'The old B-boy terms are really good: We had one of those 'how to breakdance' posters, and it had a glossary section with definitions of all the B-boy terms. There were some amazing ones that I hadn't heard in fifteen years. I like older slang and outmoded colloquialisms. I always try to stick a few in.'[18] The crux of *Odelay* was one of encouraging participation between performer and listener, and in that sense, it achieves a certain flux-ness, echoing the Fluxus crew's desire to break down barriers between audience and performer.

Beck called 'Minus' 'a rebuttal'.[19] The track is something of an anomaly on the album, recorded at G-Son studios with Beastie Boys' producer Mario Caldato Jr. and Brian Paulson. "Sissyneck' is the morning after a full night of line dancing and cocaine. It's the achy-breaky heart after the triple bypass. It's a get-together at the recreation centre Ping Pong tournament,' Beck told *Interview*, helpfully.[20] Elsewhere, he mentioned the song in connection with a reference to David Alan Coe getting a perm. The reference to country wild-man Coe, who penned such indomitable classics as 'Drink Canada Dry' and 'Take This Job And Shove It' is an apt one. Coe is the black sheep in the country corral, dabbling across the board in both blues and southern-fried rock. Like Beck he refuses to stay put in a genre where marketers can sell him to the public, and in the early Nineties Coe was labelled 'alt.country' by his label, out of lack of anywhere else to put him.

Beck was intrigued when he found a talking Barbie doll complete with a cell phone that chirped 'Let's get some pizza!' and promptly dropped it right into 'Sissyneck'. Mattel©, the doll's manufacturer, dug in its heels and refused to grant clearance, though. Beck commented, 'Mattel made us take it off the record. They said if we tried to approximate it in any form, we would be ruined. We thought we may be able to get away with it, but we played it for an eight-year-old, and she immediately shrieked with recognition, screaming, "Cell Phone Barbie! Cell Phone Barbie!"'[21] On live performances of 'Sissyneck', however, DJ Swamp played merry hell with the sample, making an icon of vacuous consumption stutter.

'Sissyneck''s electric, eclectic country funk flavour was inspired by a combination of the band named Country Funk, and Dick Hyman's 'The Moog And Me' off the album *Moog: The Electric Eclectics Of Dick Hyman*. I tried to keep the Moog sound to a minimum on the album,' Beck explained. 'It's such a trendy instrument now and can easily be overused. I used the Moog mostly for textures and kept it low in the mix rather than push it up front like, "Hey everyone, look at me, I'm playing a Moog!" That kitsch aspect of the Moog is very repulsive. I was going for a more human feel, so I would try to process it to get different sounds, maybe like a screaming bat.'[22] Mike Boito plays carnival organ doubling up with a sample stripped off Sly Stone's 'Life', and skewered by guitarist Gregory Leisz, who wheels in his huge pedal steel guitar rack and lets loose with some inspired, fluid country flavours.

'Readymade', contains a small slice of bossa nova guitar work from Brazilian master Laurindo Almeida. Brazilian music had long been favoured listening for Beck. The title of the song makes a sly reference to French dada artist Marcel Duchamp's 'ready-mades', where he would take things such as a urinal from a men's room and hang it on the wall of a gallery. Some critics argued that *Odelay*'s eclecticism worked against it, that it suggested diversity for its own sake and had no unifying factor guiding its use. 'I wanted some balance,' acknowledged Beck, 'or else it wasn't going to be effective, a bunch of chaos thrown at you. So something like "Readymade" is super-simple, almost like a folk song, except it's got a beat under it.'[23]

One of the 'deconstructed noise freak outs' from the first phase of the album's recording, 'High 5 (Rock The Catskills)', is perhaps the core of the album. The song contains a sample from 'Mr Cool' by the motorcycling musician, Willis Vincent, performed by Rasputin's Stash. 'We went crazy on "High 5 (Rock the Catskills)",' Beck told *Huh*. 'It's a chaotic cut-up flying-everywhere-at-once song, with the Dick Hyman bump'n'grind. We spent weeks on that one. That's what I go for a lot, putting three or four songs into one.'[24] Mike Boito plays organ, David Brown plays saxophone. Beck's vocals were recorded on a five-dollar plastic microphone purchased at electronics chain store Radio Shack. The song features an interlude of seven seconds of Franz Schubert's 'Unfinished Symphony No.9 in B Minor'. As so often occurred in the making of *Odelay*, chance played a part in its inclusion: 'When you're sampling, you just pick out a record and pull the needle down,' Beck explained. 'It's a chance operation in that way, a John Cage thing. You place your faith in a higher guiding force, the Eternal DJ. Oh Eternal, Mighty Turntable of the Cosmos.'[25]

For the track, Beck and the Dust Brothers sampled an ancient block party rap from the early 1980s, when designer blue jeans were a much-coveted symbol of status, wealth and style. Much has been made about young Beck freaks chanting the Sassoon raps in concert without quite knowing what Sassoon jeans are. For Beck, they are reliving those days in the early 1980s when designer jeans were the *sine qua non* of cool, but to a thirteen-year-old, what does it mean?

'High 5 (Rock The Catskills)' aroused further accusations that Beck was deliberately writing nonsense lyrics, a claim that he repeatedly denied. 'I couldn't sing my songs every night if I thought, "Oh, I just scribbled this down; it doesn't really mean anything.,"' he told *Playback*. 'It's got to have some connection to me [...] I've written hundreds of songs, and I got bored of saying things the same way. I wanted to use the language differently [...] The words have got to feel good, and they have to sound good; they have to fit the rhythm. That's the hardest thing. You got a melody, you got this thing that's musical, and you want to stick words on it. Words can really weigh something down. And if you put in the wrong words, I'm telling you, it'll ruin the music; it'll ruin the melody.'[26] On another occasion, he told *Details* magazine, 'My songs don't have images – captions, maybe. It's more like the police report of what happened; the shoe size, not the shoe.'[27]

'Ramshackle' was produced with Tom Rothrock and Rob Schnapf of Bong Load Records and the sole remnant from the pre-Lollapalooza, pre-Dust Brothers sessions to make the final album. Charlie Haden, jazz bassist and father of that dog's Haden sisters, plays on the track. "Ramshackle' is just south-western, San Fernando Valley, San Gabriel, the ranch houses, like cardboard cut-outs. Brown atmosphere,'[28] Beck told *Jam!* 'There's nothing else like "Ramshackle" on *Odelay* because I was recording at the Dust Brothers' house and there's tons of people hanging out, a party atmosphere. Not an atmosphere conducive to introspection.'[29]

The album ends with a snippet of found noise; one night there was a freeze-up on the Dust Brothers' computer as they tweaked with a song. A tiny snippet of the song kept playing over and over, blasting out of the studio monitors. 'We just taped it,' Beck said later. 'That was the machine's two cents, its attempt to contribute to the album in some way.'[30]

Beck has been quoted as saying that the sequencing of the songs on *Odelay* was done in a definite order. A fan once posted a hilarious interpretation of *Odelay* as a perfectly sequenced album for sex. That interpretation is suspect at best, but the album has a flow to it that is as organic as pesticide-free peaches. The only time *Odelay* seems claustrophobic is when the density of ideas defeats the implied spaciousness of composition and mix, a problem partially solved when some samples had to be removed for legal reasons later on.

Right after the release party Beck departed for more sessions at Dub Narcotic in Olympia, Washington, this time for a proposed, but as-yet unreleased second K Records album. 'I really want to put that out because playing 'Asshole' and 'Sleeping Bag', it's the equivalent of still playing *Mellow Gold*, that side of my music. I've written so many songs in that vein that aren't represented on *Odelay*.'[31]

On 16 June Beck played at the Beastie Boys' Tibetan Freedom Concert in San Francisco, California with the Beasties, Sonic Youth, Foo Fighters, Pavement, Smashing Pumpkins, Sean Lennon and Fluxus and 'Hollow Log'. Three days later he was at KCRW 89.9 FM to do another 'Morning Becomes Eclectic' session with the ever affable and soft-spoken Chris Douridas presiding. Beck did a very rough but by no means unwelcome set comprising 'Regular Song', 'Jack-Ass' and, at Douridas' urging, Jimmie Rodgers' 'Waitin' For A Train' complete with impressive yodelling. Beck closed with 'It Ain't Your Time'.

As Beck geared up for touring *Odelay* he found his old band splintered; Mike Boito played organ on *Odelay* but had begun cobbling together the band Brazzaville with David Brown, another Beck friend and *Odelay* sideman. Beck lamented, 'My last bass player joined Elastica, my last guitar player joined Porno for Pyros, the axeman before him is in Presidents Of The United States Of America. My band's like a quarantine farm team, we spay and neuter people to go on to other bands.'[32] It was time to recruit some new faces. Keyboardist and tabla player Theo Mondle, guitarist Smokey Hormel (a.k.a. Smokestack) and bassist Justin Meldal-Johnsen, joined Beck and Joey. Justin Meldal-Johnsen played bass with Medicine until the end of 1995; he was also a studio production co-ordinator and a session man for the likes of Tori Amos. Smokey, a journeyman musician in the best sense, up for the get go, had played in the legendary band the Blasters.

In 1985 Smokey was in the Radio Ranch Straight Shooters with a fifteen-year-old Joey Waronker, and later toured with Joey as part of the touring band of X's John Doe. 'It's a funny twist that I'm playing with Joey now in Beck's band,' Smokey observed. 'Radio Ranch Straight Shooters was Joey's first band and he was just incredible. He was a neighbour of my parents and I became his friend. He was so young that we couldn't play clubs with him [...] Joey left with Beck in 1994. I auditioned for Beck in 1995 for Lollapalooza, but I was booked for a Bruce Willis tour of Planet Hollywoods. Beck couldn't make up his mind in time so I just left with Bruce Willis.' Smokey was especially revealing about Beck's attitude to other musicians, and his lack of confidence in his own abilities during the awkward transition from solo acoustic guitar player to band leader. 'Beck wasn't able to take his music serious yet. Good musicians intimidated him [...] Beck is surprisingly traditional in his musical mind. He comes from a country blues background. When he was a kid he taught himself to play like Mississippi John Hurt. He listened to a lot of Jimmie Rogers so we have that in common. I wasn't very familiar with the experimental guitar players like Sonic Youth, which Beck was into, but I learned what to play by copying it off the record. Beck likes things a little off and sloppy. On some songs, I'll even de-tune the guitar to get that vibe, approaching it like a non-player.'[33]

With a new band and a new sound, Beck was finally ready to take the sonic chemistry set he'd created with *Odelay* on the road.

1 Michel, Peter. 'Summersault '96', *Blah Blah Blah* fanzine. December 1995–January 1996

2 Dunn, Jancee. 'Beck: Resident Alien', *Rolling Stone*, 11–25 July 1996

3 Powell, Alison. 'The Urge For Serge', *Interview*, April 1997

4 Powell, Alison. 'The Urge For Serge', *Interview*, April 1997

5 Stevenson, Jane. 'Nice Try, Beck, But You Can't Hide Talent', *Toronto Sun*, 6 June 1996

6 Jones, Cliff. 'Captain Sensible', *The Face*, 1996

7 Cummings, Sue. 'Beck: Dumpster Divin' Man', MTV, June 1996

8 Sakamoto, John. 'Beck Answers His Fans', *Jam!*, 5 June 1996

9 Doss, Yvette C. 'The Chicano Jew Chats About His Life', *Frontera* #4, 1996

10 Kemp, Mark. 'Where It's At Now', *Rolling Stone*, 17 April 1997

11 Babcock, Jay. 'Beck', *Huh*, July 1996

12 Babcock, Jay. 'Beck', *Huh*, July 1996

13 Wiesbard, Eric. 'After The Goldrush', *Spin*, 1996

14 Wiesbard, Eric. 'After The Goldrush', *Spin*, 1996

15 Bennun, David. 'Beck To The Future', *Melody Maker*, 16 November 1996

16 Sakamoto, John. 'Beck Answers His Fans' *Jam!*, 5 June 1996

17 Johnson, Calvin. 'Calvin Talks To Beck, Beck Talks Back To The Rocket', *The Rocket*, January–February 1997

18 Strauss, Neil. 'Artist Of The Year', *Spin*, 1996

19 Sakamoto, John. 'Beck Answers His Fans' *Jam!*, 5 June 1996

20 Rogers, Ray. 'Loser?' *Interview*, August 1996

21 Dunn, Jancee. Beck: 'Resident Alien', *Rolling Stone*, 11–25 July 1996

22 Perlich, Tim. 'Beck's Trek', *Now*, November 1996

23 Babcock, Jay. 'Beck', *Huh*, July 1996

24 Babcock, Jay. 'Beck', *Huh*, July 1996

25 Babcock, Jay. 'Beck', *Huh*, July 1996

26 Philbrook, Erik. 'Beck: The New Solution', *Playback*, 1997

27 Cohen, Scott. 'The Joy Of Beck', *Details*, August 1996

28 Sakamoto, John. 'Beck Answers His Fans', *Jam!*, 5 June 1996

29 Johnson, Calvin. 'Calvin Talks To Beck, Beck Talks Back To The Rocket', *The Rocket*, January–February 1997

30 Sakamoto, John. 'Beck Answers His Fans', *Jam!*, 5 June 1996

31 Bornemann, Tim. 'Beck Meets Squeegee', 2 April 1997. Slo-Jam website. squeegee@frontier.wilpaterson.edu

32 Perlich, Tim. 'Beck's Trek', *Now*, November 1996

33 Davis, Billy. 'Interview with Smokestack', *American Music* zine, 6 August 1998

11

LOSE CONTROL FOR FIFTEEN MINUTES (INVERTED FUNK)

Beck departed for his grand *Odelay* tour, with a more specific stage show in mind than on his previous tour. The idea had been germinating in his mind for some time: he wanted to take his performances further, to entertain and engage the crowd, paying homage to James Brown's legendary road shows of the Sixties, when the Godfather would excite his audiences to hysteria. Smokey Hormel brought in videos of Jackie Wilson and James Brown on the Sixties television show *Shindig*, and together they would study them. They began to work out co-ordinated dance steps; 'We would work on that,' Smokey acknowledged. 'Beck's a good dancer and he seems to be getting ready to push that further. What he lacks in technique he makes up for in fearlessness and willingness to go for it.'[1]

In late 1998, Beck told *Melody Maker*, 'We take inspiration from old soul performers and R&B music, trying to capture that sense of spontaneous musical expression that seems to be erased from most alternative music. People just don't release themselves and go with the music. They're afraid to dance. They're afraid to look foolish. It is foolish, but you can't think that way, or it's not going to come off. It's about not being afraid, bringing the music to the people so they feel it, so that it's OK for them to let go.'[2] Taking his beloved hip-hop back to its roots, Beck hit upon Sixties R&B, just as he had looked back from Dylan to Woody Guthrie and Leadbelly earlier in his career, going back to the source every time, and taking his lead from that.

This time around Geffen bestowed the tour with a perk – lighting director Susanne Sasic, who had worked with both Nirvana and Sonic Youth. Despite a very limited budget Sasic, together with Beck, worked out a lighting scheme that wasn't static, allowing for improvisation from both band and lighting crew. She installed foot-boxes onstage that would trigger the Diskoboxes, two boxes filled with fifteen 100-watt reflector floodlights and fronted by multicoloured panels, custom built for Beck. The Diskoboxes create random patterns on the boxes triggered by the music. Beck put them facing out into the audience, echoing avant-gardist Tony Conrad's flicker films as well as the dance floor where Travolta busted his disco moves in *Saturday Night Fever*. 'I do wish, for the acoustic numbers when he's out there by himself, that he would remember to turn them off, which he doesn't always remember to do,' Sasic reflected. 'That's when I wish I had an override switch. But he gets such pleasure out of turning them on and looking over and seeing that they're working, that I would never want to take that away from him [...] Beck puts on a real show in the traditional sense,' she added, 'he's got a follow spot on him because he runs around so much, something most bands I work for don't do.'[3]

On 27 June in Santa Ana, California, Beck and his new band began what would become something of a tradition, a warm-up for his upcoming tour with a show at the 550-seat Galaxy Theatre. The following night he played a two-hour show at The Glass House in Pomona. It was a long way from the first gig he had ever played with a full band, next door at a coffee house in 1993.

Beck flew into Kristiansand, Norway on 3 July for the first date of what would be dubbed the 'European Decadence Tour'. The first show was at something called the Quart Festival. Visions of Vikings drowning in vats of beer come to mind, but more significantly, it was Beck's chance to visit the land of his mythic great-grandfather and raise a tankard in his honour. 'There's a Viking element to our lineage, a lot of genetic idiosyncrasies that probably go back to some fjord in Norway. Al was big on Norwegian mythology.'4

A gastronomic tour ensued as the lads took the good ship *Odelay* on a rampage across Europe. Feasts of *fromage* in France, *linzer torte* and cripplingly strong Turkish coffee in Austria, tankards of beer in Germany and many, many more tankards of beer at the Feile Festival in Thurles, Eire. Body popping, breakdancing and moonwalking were all brazenly committed as the tour bus rolled through the continent. So, in addition to a new stage set and songs, Beck and the band were refining their instincts with Europe's fine gastronomic treats. At the Dour Music Festival in Belgium, the promoter had thoughtfully provided Beck's band with a highly memorable cheese plate. 'If you put your nose above the middle of the plate, you would inhale the most monstrous malaise of smell that has ever been conceived in the history of cheese,'5 Beck remembered.

At Scotland's T-In-The-Park festival, down to go on second last, Beck rocked a huge tent. Alistair Anderson, a Beck fan since his younger sister told him to listen to *Mellow Gold*, wrote 'When it was time for Beck to come on the whole place was totally packed out, dripping with sweat and very mental. Beck took the stage with the words, 'What the fuck is this pole?' and right from the start the band went for the kill. "Loser" was hammered out half-way through' with the introduction 'This one's for all those who didn't buy the album.' *Odelay* had just been released and the new songs sounded even better than *Mellow Gold*. The show climaxed with a chaotic and full-steam ahead version of 'High 5' and I left the show with every nerve in my body alive.'6

In Cesena, Italy, Leigh flew in to join Beck, who got rapturously drunk and breakdanced, quite perilously, on stage. At one point he asked the audience, 'Do you all like techno? Like to freak out to that shit? Like to freak out, period? Alright, well, we got you covered!' before unleashing a monstrosity known in Beck-lore as 'Freakout Eurobeat', a response to the horrid ear-splitting Euro-techno that could be heard everywhere in European cafés, bars and discos. With 'DJ Stagecoach', a.k.a. Joey, pressing the button on a pre-programmed drum machine, Beck bellowed the charming lyrics: 'She fucked me up the ass, and she looked just like (tour manager) Ben Cooley, when she fucked me up the ass!' Mercifully, the song never saw release. Later, Beck tackled 'Debra' with an explanation; 'Back in the early days, back in Bakersfield, we were really influenced by Take That and the Backstreet Boys, so we just wanna take it back to our roots. Back when we were really into, uh, colon cleansing. Our colons got so clean, we wrote a few tunes like this one.' To think of Bakersfield, that dry, dusty inland Californian town, hometown of country legend Buck Owens producing anything like 'Debra' is like thinking of tuva singers rocking straight out of Slough.

On 19 July, with *Odelay* already out a month in the U.K., Beck and the Crew descended on Shakespeare's hometown of Stratford-upon-Avon, ready to roll the juggernaut at the Phoenix Festival. As Beck toured Britain's plentiful summer festivals, he commented in awe, 'It's so hot here I'm feeling like I'm at Lollapalooza again, but I would say the crowd here are a little more initiated. They know what to expect, to come here to camp out and freak out, and surrender to some pagan rock thing. Maybe Americans want more of a shopping-mall experience, with everything in neater packages. It's a very medieval scene here. Bodies passed out and refuse and debris all about – people sweating and wearing strange clothing in various degrees of inebriation and hallucination. Human specimens of all sizes and forms, really just an orgy of activity. I can't imagine after four days of this what the derangement of consciousness will be.'7

Beck's Wrecking Crew pulled into Nederland on 21 July to play at the legendary stoner emporia the Paradiso, in Amsterdam, where everyone from Joy Division to Deep Purple has been bootlegged with commendable attention to sonic quality. In this dank pit of rank smells and spilled lager and hash sweat, Beck and co. slammed out a 90-minute set. For all the festivals the tour took in, Beck was aware that the music they were making worked best in an indoor environment. 'I'd say probably the clubs are better for us, because what I'm doing has experimental edges to it. It's not like bring-down-the-house-type songs. Some of it gets a bit random. It's not always a solid groove you can just lock into. It's got more of a performance aspect to it.'[8] Moreover, at indoor venues he was invariably playing to punters who had paid to see him, as opposed to a more general crowd.

The performance planned at the Mount Fuji Festival on July 26 and 27, with the likes of Red Hot Chili Peppers, Green Day and Rage Against the Machine, was cancelled due to typhoons. On a perfectly hot day in Los Angeles, the entire Silverlake contingent descended on the Santa Fe Loading Docks to play a benefit for Beck's godson, Banjo Sky Harris, the autistic son of Ross Harris from Sukia. The Dust Brother's Nickelbag label represented, with 10 Cent and Sukia on the bill. The intriguingly named Marty's Sexual Organs, Joe Baiza's Mecolodiacs and Ozomatli roamed about in advance of their sets, eating delicious tacos. Nearby were Boston busker Mary Lou Lord, Beck's old drummer Dallas Don from Popdefect, and Beastie Boys sideman Mark Nishita-Ramos, a.k.a. Money Mark. The Dust Brothers DJ'd, playing early Kool and the Gang, Frank Sinatra and Jorge Ben records. By 8 p.m. when Beck took the stage in his captain's uniform, the crowd was hyped. Beck introduced the band, who came on dressed in suits, brogues and ties; they were, to quote Miles Davis, 'clean as a broke dick dog'. During the gig that followed, Beck intermittently howled the non-sequiturs that would punctuate every performance from now on, exclamations off the top of his head, tapping deep into whatever he was feeling at that moment. 'I got some soy sauce here!' he shouted, before breaking down some super 'Hotwax'. At midpoint, Beck got out his famed Jazzercise plywood acoustic, singed to crisp perfection. 'Readymade' was dedicated to his Steve Hanft, while Joey Waronker got a drumming solo spot; Sukia's Eddie Gomez came on stage for a spot of chanting and extreme dancing.

After saluting the Silverlake Posse, Beck and his new band kicked off the first official date of what would prove to be a long, long, long *Odelay* tour with a show at Minneapolis' First Avenue. His opening band was the similarly sonically adventuresome Cibo Matto, two Japanese girls and Smilin' Sean Lennon on bass. Beck and the band were a little tentative and Beck started off monotone, as disco lights flashed and he bodypopped. The acoustic set proved a welcome respite, as Beck stepped up with confident folk and country blues under hot lights, joking with the crowd. Clearly, he was more at ease here than he had been at his Lollapalooza dates. Something had happened, as if all surrender to chance operation had loosened him. He seemed bent on getting through to the crowd. The rhythm section of Waronker and Meldal-Johnsen broke it down on 'Beercan' before segueing into 'Debra' as Beck swigged from a bottle of wine with abandon. Alcohol to fortify the nerves, eh, old boy?

In Buffalo, after a standout performance by Cibo Matto, Sean Lennon obliging on bass, Beck and his band delivered a masterful set at the sold-out show, Beck bedecked in striped shirt , beige slacks and a scarf. Earlier in the day they had appeared on Toronto's Much Music TV Special going through an all electric set before finishing with their fare-thee-well rendition of 'Ramshackle'. That night, with public television filming Beck for a tour documentary, the audience at the show squirmed in the rather sterile atmosphere of having all the house lights on. All 1,500 fans were wildly enthusiastic, and young. Beck and the band, all in suits, dropped into 'Devil's Haircut', by now the standard opener for the shows. It was a cool, enervating choice, defying concert wisdom by playing one of the best barnstorming songs first, getting the crowd on their feet. 'My brain is melting,' joked Beck, as he blinked at the lights, 'It's the truck headlights of doom.' The band piledrive with confidence through 'Lord Only Knows', 'Where It's At' and 'Sissyneck', balancing their live bit with MIDI triggered samples. Beck's acoustic section featured a singalong 'Truck Drivin' Neighbors Downstairs', and a resounding 'One Foot In The Grave'.

At Boston's Avalon, the show had its own peculiar dynamics, speeding and slowing, pacing itself. With Money Mark playing koto scales with his right hand and Latin-tinged funk with the left, as the crowd pogoed like Sid Vicious' ghost. With 'Thunderpeel' Beck cited the questionable inspiration of pop vocalists Color Me Badd, before breaking out three-pickup Jerry Jones Neptune, tuned to open E. Beck said, 'I get this one out of the way early' before kicking into 'Loser'. The band was tight, the banter inspired.

On 1 September at Hoboken's NJ Maxwell's, Beck did a smashing 70-minute all-acoustic show, even doing a totally left field cover of the mouldy Kansas Seventies smash 'Dust In The Wind', which was justly saluted with hundreds of raised Bic lighters. A colossal medley of 'I Get Lonesome'-'Truckdrivin' Neighbors Downstairs'-'Alcohol'-'Modesto'-'Cyanide Breathmint'-'Painted Eyelids'-'Fuckin' With My Head' ensued before a powerful rendition of 'Heartland Feeling'.

In St. Louis, Australian punk fiddlers Dirty Three opened, surely the only band of fiddle players to have moshers. Beck and the band were now in suits, ties and cowboy hats. 'A clothing company sent me two free suits. And they felt good – ceremonious.' However, Beck had the misfortune of receiving the devil's own haircut from some very mean-spirited scissors in Cleveland: 'I looked like I was twelve. It was pretty funny when I put the suit on.'[9] St. Louis writer Randall Roberts got it right away, one of the few writers from the big papers to do so. Roberts wrote, 'Beck sermonized, sampled, pogoed, pleaded, testified, and breakdanced. Not an ounce of slack was to be had. Since the last time Beck was here in 1994, he's figured a few things out about live performance.'[10] Roberts noted, correctly, that most so-called alternative rock bands don't give a shit about their audiences, hiding behind a heroin-soaked 'cool' and their own apathy. Beck seemed engaged, wanting to communicate. Like all good things, it took a while before Beck connected, rather atypically, with a mesmerizing rendition of 'Derelict'. Beck had achieved what he had set out to do on this tour: engage the audience in celebration rather than angst. Later that year, at a show at Bataclan in Paris on 29 November, 'the whole crowd broke into this soccer chant for some reason, so I just changed the music I was playing to fit the chanting. Audience participation is very important to me. I don't believe in the generic rock show structure, which is, by nature, bland and non-inclusive. There shouldn't be a barrier between the crowd and the performer, someone standing around with a guitar so they can be adored.'[11]

It seemed Beck himself was struggling with irony. Being a white funkster was irony enough, but where did the sincerity creep in? Was he serving up genuine appreciation, or peddling facsimile soul? En route to Dallas on the tour bus, *Spin* writer Neil Strauss asked Beck whether a soul revue with a full horn section was on the cards. Beck, still mulling in his mind over the line separating parody from tribute, replied, 'I'd be afraid of it becoming too much of a parody. I'm sure there's some people who think that already. But to me it's not at all, it's pretty sincere. There's a sense of humour to it, any good music has humour in it. That's just my instinct: to get away from the cliché. Or to take the cliché and exploit it and blow it up as intensely as possible. But that can get you into the territory of parody or kitsch. It's really easy to do that. To do something that has some personality, some modesty to it – to do something sincere and direct, not cloying or phoney, that's the challenge.'[12] Kitsch: sentimental, pretentious, popular low-brow trashy bad taste, or as Czech writer Milan Kundera once expounded on the subject, going back to the roots of the word, 'the avoidance of shit', the doily on top of grandma's pink toilet taking your attention away from the shitter itself.

'So much of this age group or generation, and even I've been guilty of this in the past, takes something that's 1970s and twists it around, either making fun of it or embracing it,' Beck told Strauss. 'There's not a lot of direct, inspired stuff. Sure, music always feeds off itself and its past, but there's not a lot of commitment. There's always this snatch of, 'We're just kidding, we don't really mean this.' It's this continual need to goof on something our parents did or that we did ten years ago. That's something I would really like to move away from. That's why I was initially attracted to folk music, and ultimately hip-hop. It's so potent. It has possibilities.'[13]

But if country, folk and blues were where Beck had come from, he had long been wary of remaining trapped by their restrictions, just as he would always baulk at limiting himself to any one musical form. One thing music can never be is static, and purists miss the point by trying to preserve the past at the expense of the future. It's self-defeating and ridiculous. The folk song gathers its fine patina by continual reinterpretation, as the Greenwich Village folkies sought to do in the Sixties. A song like 'Stagger Lee' went through 150 mutations before resurfacing in 'Devil's Haircut', and the song's Lloyd Price sample does more to connect it to that tradition of reinterpretation than any direct reading. 'I played folk music for so many years when I was getting started that it got a little boring, to be honest. There's something that I'll always love about the honesty and the directness of acoustic music. But I wanted something that was a little more stimulating and challenging to me personally.'[14]

Beck and the band came out each night, determined to play rather than go through the motions. And reflecting Beck's growing interest in things like Brazilian music, they displayed a desire to invite the audience in rather than push them away. Because of his well thought out aesthetic, Beck had a game plan for the shows. Like Al's happenings, the structure would be there, to allow something to happen. It's a misnomer to think of happenings as just chaos. Al would have a rough script written out, which in itself, could lend a hand to chaos. Contradictory for sure, and giving the happening its friction.

At Dallas' Bronco Bowl, (and if anyone can enliven the Bronco Bowl they're doing something right) Beck, probably remembering when he was a small guy at punk all-ages shows, stepped up to lecture the mosh pit: 'The laws of physics dictate that if you're twice as big as the person you're crowd surfing on top of, *you're probably fucking up their situation*.' Beck put his all into the show that night, mimicking Elvis's karate moves, breakdancing and pulling off James Brown-style grunts. Ninety minutes later he gasped, 'Dallas, I funked too hard tonight,' before collapsing. The band looked confused, before apparently deciding to escort him offstage. Even a booking agent raced backstage in panic at Beck's predicament. Of course, the whole thing was a tribute to James Brown's wonderfully choreographed collapses onstage in the Sixties, when he would be mock-ushered offstage by a band member, a cloak wrapped around his shoulders, only to throw it off and come back to the mic for another song. Sure enough, Beck re-emerged, propped up by members of the band, towel around him, for an encore – a superlative 'Debra'.

The theatrics were growing exponentially; each show would have a different twist. Cowboy boots and suits would give way to sparkling satin and pearled snap Nudie suits, just like the ones wildcat George Jones once wore. A huge mirror ball was suspended from the ceiling with two coloured gels shining on them, sparkling light over the auditoriums. This echoed a certain romanticism in Beck's music, definitely one of his major driving forces, as surely as he can be sullen, boastful, humble, lucid, and elusive. When Joey Waronker cites Beck as 'the most complex person I know', it's hardly hyperbole. 'I've always loved the Nudie suit,' Beck told *Rolling Stone*, 'I've always thought of it as one of the greatest clothing styles in any music.'[15] As Nudie suits could cost up to $20,000, Beck would hire them at $100 a time, from Paramount Studios. 'The suit makes me feel feminine, weird. It's shining and silly and I enjoy it. I always fantasized about having one when I was younger. I was very much enamoured of Fifties country and western, Hank Snow, Hank Williams, they had amazing suits.'[16]

Beck expressed frustration that by appearing on stage in a rhinestone suit he would instantly be presumed to be referencing Elvis; he'd been thinking country rather than King of Rock'n'Roll, and stopped wearing the suits after a while as a result of the misinterpretation. In our culturally impoverished lives, clichés and short sound bites are substituted for knowledge. Even pop culture, *especially* pop culture, is broken down into byte-sized bits and simplified for easy filing. It's one of the by-products of the information age, where the vast sums of input must be processed quickly and stored or be lost. In the rush to process the onslaught of information, snap judgements are made to gauge worth, and are often absurd. Hence knowing who Elvis is requires less processing than knowing who George Jones is, simply by virtue of Elvis' ubiquity in our culture. And what's weird is both Beck and Elvis were looking back to the same cultural reference point, that of the Fifties country star, with his larger-than-life glitter, a country boy made good.

By the time the band rolled back into Santa Monica, they were primed like a two-dollar wino. On an 11 October dream bill with Sukia and Ween, the Beck crew unfurled a huge backdrop of the Los Angeles Airport control tower, with its space age Jetsons legs, the pink and purple lights glittering off the mirror ball, evoking a Texas town country ballroom in the Thirties. 'Truckdrivin' Neighbors' and a rendition of 'Asshole' called 'Man-child', was introduced as a 'Tom Petty cover, in a roundabout way'. The title was a jab at one of the writers at an indie rag who called him 'man child'; the comment was surely not made out of malicious intent, but it was insensitive none the less to dote over Beck's cuteness at the expense of his music. Beck was increasingly sensitive to the fact that he was twenty-six and a full-grown man now. Gone was the thrift-store chic of Lollapalooza, replaced with a sharp-as-tacks suit. Leigh Limon was a strong positive fashion influence, using her own fine taste in apparel to suggest ideas to Beck. Electric blue shirts and satin ties, ascots round the neck, cut, tailored and fitted to size, were the order of the day. The gig culminated in Beck attempting a bizarre Russian Cossack dance, prompting another mock-collapse and retirement, which sent the audience bananas. Five minutes later he was back, in a white sequined jump suit and blue ascot, for 'Debra'. At the culmination of the song, he appeared to break down in tears, inconsolably shuffling between the different members of his band for sympathetic hugs. A rousing 'High 5 (Rock The Catskills)' finished the job.

Oakland Tribune reporter William Friar saw the show and his subsequent piece raised familiar questions about Beck's originality: "Lord Only Knows' is a nice little jam, with Beck doing mid-air splits and slamming out power chords on his guitar, Pete Townshend-style. Here's where the problems started. Beck played at being a guitar hero on that song, just as elsewhere he played at being a folk singer or a country blues harpist.' Oops, Beck must have pushed the wrong button, because guitar heroes are one of the sacred cows of the age. Friar lauds Beck's 'amazing facility with musical pastiche, but he treats his borrowings with ironic detachment, which brings out that feeling in his listeners as well. A lousy singer and an adequate but hardly inspired guitarist. Live, without much of the sampling and sound effects found on his albums, his music was revealed as pretty simple stuff, often little more than three chords played over a heavy bass beat. Still,' he wound up, 'Beck is an original talent. You can't take him completely seriously. And, no matter how intense his playing or physical his stage presence, you suspect he doesn't want you to.'[17]

Now compare this to what Tom Waits, the junkyard magician and nighthawk maestro, watching the same show, opined: 'I love Beck. And the show was terrific, it was just wild. I've never seen anything like it, he wore a white suit, and he did a thing with his guitar, spinning the guitar around his body like a ring. Unbelievable, he has some great moves. A lot of variety, it really knocked me out. He's not afraid to let the needle go over into the red. I knew I wanted to listen to more of it, because you feel something familiar, recognize something you feel in common, a love of some of the same things that you are bringing out into your own music.'[18]

A few days out (see a pattern beginning to form here?) and Beck was off to Japan for a gruelling ten-date Japanese trip through Osaka, Nagoya, Kyoto and Tokyo in twelve days. Beck spent his days sleeping off fever and exhaustion, still making time to learn a few words of Japanese, scan the Shibuya in dazed amazement, with its million-and-one neon lights laid out in vertical strips undulating in flashes that make your eyes sting. Breathing in blasts of perfumed air from fashionable blokes on the platform of the Ginza line on the subway system, navigating the ultra-crowded trains by himself; sitting and watching, seated next to a sleeping mother and daughter. Going to a store called AIRS with bootleg videos from every single nook and cranny of the musical earth. Eating meals in sushi bars with swinging lanterns and foul gutters outside, and 200-dollar glasses of brandy. And skimming through the incredible Shibuya record store selections of Jorge Ben albums unavailable even in Brazil.

Somewhere along the line, Beck managed to step in and huff a great harp solo on Kahimi Karie's track 'Lolita Dollhouse'. Karie is a fascinating member of the new international pop jet set. Her hard stare is hardly innocent and her music is effervescent and laced with breathy vocals, but there is an omnivorous cultural perspective to her work; she scrutinizes things. Her music takes in everything from a cover of Jorge Ben's 'Take It Easy My Brother Charles', another of Serge Gainsbourg's '*Dis Moi Quelque Chose Avant Dormir*' and several collaborations with pop auteur/defect Momus, as well as namechecking el Records' Mike Alway in French. Karie and Cornelius, her then-boyfriend, were lumped in along with bands such as Pizzicato Five, as part of the vanguard of a scene centred on discos, record stores and cafes in Shibuya, Tokyo. Media invention or not, it was an interesting parallel world when the rest of the world was listening to Oasis and Stone Temple Pilots. The *shibuya-kei* was galvanized by the obscure, élitist and avant-Edwardian pop confections of the late, lamented el Records. Home of Momus and others, el tried to preserve gentility and a perverse English grace in the face of laddishness, succeeding in their own modest way, namely by being reviled by everyone except the Japanese.

Swinging in a changing world, Kahimi Karie broke out of the *shibuya-kei* ghetto to make her own identity, something that parallels movements in contemporary (youthful) Japanese society. Even ten years ago, Japanese youth still fitted the reserved image that stereotyped them. But increasingly there is a greater distance than ever between them and their elders. Part of the thrust is economic, the security that ensured a smooth progression through life has broken down a bit. Japanese youth are more outward looking than ever and this time around they are looking around at each other and outside their country as well.

Karie split for Montmarte, Paris, chasing the vibe of Françoise Hardy and Serge Gainsbourg that had blown her mind ten years before in Tokyo. In common with other artists she used the forgotten styles of the past as a spur to her own music. These new transcendent inversionists, or transcendental ironists, are an international vanguard. Their ranks include Pulp, Portishead, Stereolab, Tindersticks, Tortoise, Archer Prewitt, Beck, Momus, Cornelius, Kahimi Karie and a dozen others that escape notice. All are bands with a pulse, delving into krautrock, dub, lounge, Brazilian music, Gainsbourg and other weirder things like American composer Harry Partch or film composer John Barry. From the Sixties, the Beach Boys' *Pet Sounds* is a touchstone, as are the Zombies and the Pretty Things. Curtis Mayfield, Jorge Ben and Gal Costa. Ennio Morricone, the Kinks, David Bowie on *Hunky Dory*. The Wu-Tang Clan and Burt Bacharach, Erik Satie, Neu! and Kraftwerk are key references. Tricky, Goldie and Björk are part of this too. They pick the best of everything, transcending the limitations of all their various genres. People will look back at now and think that this was one of the most explosively creative times ever. Are we blind to it?

Musicians on a tangent similar to Beck's, including New York hip-hoppers the Beastie Boys, France's Air, England's Stereolab, Japan's aforementioned Cornelius and Boston's Jon Spencer Blues Explosion are key figures in the emergence of an intelligent late Nineties pop music. All fully utilize recent advances in inexpensive studio production software to manufacture music that acts a instant commentary on the mind state of youth globally. They are part of the first truly global pop music movement, facilitated by technology and (ir)reverence to neglected music of the past.

Momus, the Scottish exile pop savant, who pointedly states, 'I'm into flux and uncertainty and paradox and inauthenticity', met Beck in London in December 1996. Momus asked Beck if his music was consciously pastiching black music. Beck replied that it wasn't and that a lot of black people came to his shows. Momus told him about French playwright-ex-thief Jean Genet's play *The Blacks*, which insists that if there is a single black person in the audience, that person should be placed in the front row and have a spotlight shone on him throughout the performance. 'Western culture has been changed utterly by black energy,'[19] he noted.

Beck was once the only white kid on the block. 'I'm not involved in the hip-hop community,' he told *UHF* in 1996. 'In some ways I'd rather be a part of that world because it seems more fun. When people are singing, they're actually singing. You turn on this alternative music station and you can't hear what the hell these bands are saying. There's no character. The voice is the character of the song. Maybe an R&B song is cheesy and slicked up, but at least you can hear the voice and there's some emotion in it. Somebody's committing themselves to it.'[20] R&B was an enduring influence on Beck, witness the sharp suits and snappy full-band choreography of his stage show. 'I look at the Stones, all the great music of the Sixties, it was inspired by R&B, and that's really lost now. What we now call alternative is white suburban and has nothing to do with hip-hop. You've got these bands coming out now that like hip-hop, but the only way they can react to it is to make fun of it. I spent the last few years trying to tune into what's happening in R&B and hip-hop. I find a lot more of it inspiring.'[21]

As Lux Interior of the Cramps once noted in *Re:Search*, much of indie angst rock has to do with imploding emotions, is self-centred and solipsistic, whereas much of gangster rap deals with external events, like appraising a woman, drinking, smoking, plotting revenge, driving, motion, making money, securing status and position. Both aim to be 'real', both end up sounding farcical. The white indie rock expression of 'soul' is one of intense self-examination, with cathartic truths gathered at great personal expense. It can also be very fucking tedious to listen to. 'Gangster rap is just as bad as angst-rock,' Beck told *Huh*, 'It's all put-on. I don't know why it's so scary for people to just come out and do what they do and say what they actually think. Maybe they don't know what to think so they think what everybody else is thinking. They think that they're thinking but they don't know what to think.'[22]

On 1988's 'Bring the Noise' when Public Enemy's Chuck D rapped 'Can I tell 'em that I never really had a gun?' it was a riveting inversion of the empty supremacy disseminated in many rap lyrics. Uniting this mind/body schism is what causes the friction that makes music dangerous. The few attempts to combine the two worlds have been absorbing to behold, even if they fail. The 1993 soundtrack to the film *Judgement Night* paired a dozen rap/hip-hop artists with a dozen alt. rock bands, and there were revelatory moments, such as the Cypress Hill and Sonic Youth collaboration 'I Love You Mary Jane'. But on other tracks the estrangement was all too obvious. 'The interchange between black and white music doesn't seem to have continued,' Beck observed in 1997. 'For alternative bands there doesn't seem to be much of an understanding left.'[23] Not reviving the past but integrating it into the present takes patience and dedication, and putting things in quotations is the laziest way to address the past. With *Odelay* and its subsequent tour, Beck was actively involved in mixing and matching from the history of popular music, aiming to make a inclusive, celebratory music that was, as far as possible, atemporal. 'I want to avoid sounding contemporary because then it's already dated. I'm trying to get to this place where you can stand outside the parameters of what's possible. If you can get outside the designated standards, then you'll preserve yourself [...] Music's all about a release. It's about letting go of the hand of our day-to-day existence.'[24]

1 Davis, Billy. 'Interview with Smokestack', *American Music* zine, 6 August 1998

2 Joyce, John. 'Diary Of An LP', *Melody Maker*, 5 December 1998

3 Johnson, David. 'Beck And Call: Lighting Design For Beck's Rock Music Concerts', *TCI* magazine, April 1997

4 McCormick, Carlo. 'Interview With Beck Hansen', *Playing With Matches*. Smart Art Press/Plug In Editions, 1998

5 Cigarettes, Johnny. 'Gouda Vibrations', *Vox*, March 1997

6 Alt.Music.Beck Internet Newsgroup

7 *Select*, September 1996

8 Burnett, Erich. 'Losing The "Loser" Mentality', *Scene*, August 1996

9 *Rolling Stone*, 30 September 1999

10 Roberts, Randall. 'Chameleon Of Creativity', *St. Louis Post-Dispatch*, 4 October 1996

11 Perlich, Tim. 'Beck's Trek', *Now*, November 1996

12 Strauss, Neil. 'Artist Of The Year', *Spin*, 1996

13 Strauss, Neil. 'Artist Of The Year', *Spin*, 1996

14 Hilburn, Robert. 'The Freewheelin' Beck', *Los Angeles Times*, 26 February 1997

15 Kemp, Mark. 'Where It's At Now', *Rolling Stone*, 17 April 1997

16 Slo-Jam Central website. http://earth.vol.com/~debber/beck/mainpg2.html

17 Friar, William. 'Beck's Live Show Defies Judgement, But It's Some Fun', *Oakland Tribune*, 12 October 1996

18 KCRW 89.9 FM, Los Angeles. *Morning Becomes Eclectic*, 19 June 1996

19 Momus, London, March 1997. momus@world-net.sct.fr

20 'Super Beck: "Loser", Artist, Rock Star, Genius', *UHF* # 10, July-August 1996

21 Johnson, Calvin. 'Calvin Talks To Beck, Beck Talks Back To The Rocket', *The Rocket*, January–February 1997

22 Babcock, Jay. 'Beck', *Huh*, July 1996

23 'Cool As Fuck!' *Dazed & Confused*, May 1997

24 'Cool As Fuck!' *Dazed & Confused*, May 1997

12

COULD YOU PLEASE
VALIDATE MY PARKING?

By the time Beck and the band hit Stuttgart and Stockholm and Paris, their self-dubbed 'European Decadence Tour' was well under way. By now Beck was ending the shows with full backwards falls, being carted out on stretchers and returning with not only a Nudie suit, but a jackass head mask, made of papier-mâché. The jackass was another of Beck's personas, the joker who is man enough to laugh at himself, always braying when things get pretentious or stuffy.

Beck played in Manchester, London and Dublin and before returning home for a triumphant 14 December show as part of commercial alt. rock station KROQ's 'Almost Acoustic Christmas Show', at the Universal Amphitheatre. The first week of the new year found him in New York City for an appearance on radio shock-jock Howard Stern's show. Hoping to wrongfoot his pop star guest, Stern asked, 'You're not like a rock star type, you don't even have groupies. You don't have any women backstage or anything like that. Is that true?' To which Beck replied, 'We have a 400-person boys' choir. They just hang out and sing', rendering Stern momentarily speechless – definitely a first.

Talk show host and comedienne Rosie O'Donnell got a craving for Beck. She invited him on to her demurely named *The Rosie O'Donnell Show* after brandishing a copy of *Odelay* one day on-air and saying, 'Who the hell is Beck?' When guest Tracey Ullman informed her of the dynamic pop icon, schooling her in all things Beck, O'Donnell was intrigued enough to subsequently bring a small boombox on air and say, 'Here's this new song "Loser" off *Odelay*.' Beck was amused by the incident, saying, 'That really puts it in perspective with how most people out there perceive you. Musicians think everyone's aware of what they're doing. And the truth is people have no idea. You could be on MTV thirty times a day, and people still don't know.'[1] One day he ran down from the audience and plopped himself on O'Donnell's couch, to her astonishment. He was perfectly charming and gracious, a gentleman in fact, telling her how to drop phrases like 'funk legit'.

After an appearance on television's *Saturday Night Live*, on 11 January 1997, Beck and the band played New York City's Roseland Ballroom. Beck's all-ages show began at 5 p.m., in order to let all the youngsters attend. He was working out a new thing with his lighting people, Intellabeams glittered on a mirror ball. As lo-fi originators Yo La Tengo ended their set, Beck took the stage announcing, 'Moshing has been dead since 1992, now in 1997, we got the "Tighten Up"!', before doing a smashing version of the 1968 Archie Bell and the Drells' song, throwing the splits and the boogaloo in for good measure. Continuing his programme of indulging his awkwardness to achieve funkiness, Beck was echoing a period in the early 1960s where being 'uptight' had a positive ring to it, meaning to be alert, focused and on it (check out 'Uptight', Little Stevie Wonder's 1966 hit and Gerard Malanga's definition in *Uptight: The Velvet Underground*). The antithesis of slack, Beck, through sheer force of will, was trying to achieve an exegesis.

On 20 January 1997 Beck did an impromptu performance for Radio Free Los Angeles. RFLA, a pirate station, was broadcasting one step out of the clutches of the despotic FCC (Federal Communications Commission). With severe prohibitions on unlicensed radio broadcasters empowering them, the FCC have been known to disassemble pirate stations with sledge hammers and harass and threaten operators with jail terms and quarter-million-dollar fines. The similar upsurge of pirate stations that powered the rise of jungle in the U.K. met with similarly Draconian repression. Free communication and free assembly are at the centre of every bohemian underground movement's contention with government. Beck performed fittingly morose renditions of an old Baptist hymn that had been popularized by both the Carter Family and Woody Guthrie, 'I Ain't Got No Home In This World Anymore' and Son House's 'Don't You Mind People Grinnin' In Your Face', closing with 'Pay No Mind'.

Beck took on the Salem Armoury, Oregon, in his 8 February show. The venue – a high-school gym with weapons stored in the basement – immediately sent out a bad vibe to many of the faithful gathered therein, and bestowed a rather downbeat air on proceedings. After a disappointing performance by Athens art-space-avant rockers Olivia Tremor Control, DJ Swamp, in his first appearance with the band, spun the Doug E. Fresh old skool classic 'The Show'. DJ Swamp, an Ohio DJ and the Merlin of the Technics, beat out scores of turntablists to become DMC victor in 1996. He approached tour manager Cooley after a show in Cleveland and handed Cooley a videotape of himself mixing and scratching tracks from *Odelay*. Beck and the band watched the tape in delight. Within weeks, Beck called Swamp and invited him to tour with them. It solved a nettlesome problem, namely that of synching the tapes of samples and extraneous Dust magic that couldn't be replicated into the live show. Swamp had vinyl discs of the samples cut to wax and began working out with the band.

Swamp spun an intro fanfare, and Beck ran out onto the stage in his powder blue Italian suit, flashing his red plaid silk lining. With difficulty, Beck managed to shake the crowd out of their torpor (many were more than a little stoned) and got them onto their feet. Alizarine Jemiah, a fan present that night, noted, 'I finally understand why Beck plays against a playback, in a live setting, the playback just becomes another instrument. Samples here, beats here, and the band know what they want to play and what they don't. The playback just makes the whole sound more thick and strange. They played the album version of "Where It's At" and then segued into the extra-funky deep house remix.'[2] After a ten-minute mind-blowing experience with DJ Swamp, who from now on would play a set between the set and the encore, Beck returned in the rhinestone Nudie suit and rocked the Catskills a little more, whipping the crowd into chanting 'Ooo la la Sassoon', 'Sergio Valente', and 'Jordache turn it out!' At the end, Beck exclaimed, 'You guys are the shit!' to the revived punters. Al Hansen once made an astute notation of the fact that, at happenings, 'The people who had been holding back the most, once they became involved enjoyed it very, very much.'[3]

Beck paid special attention to the sequencing of the show this time around, careful to start the audience up with an expressway-to-your-skull opener like 'Devil's Haircut' or, on occasion, 'Loser', then working through 'Novacane', 'Lord Only Knows', 'Minus', or 'Sissyneck', 'The New Pollution' and 'Hotwax', sustaining energy at high clip before taking it down for the acoustic solo spot, where a revolving number of songs dating as far back as *The Banjo Story* would be played before the ultra call and response *tour de force* that was 'One Foot In The Grave'. Then with the band back on, they would start to pick up again slowly with dirge and drone songs like 'Derelict' before dropping funk bombs like 'Where It's At' on the assembled masses. 'Where It's At' would slowly be lengthened into an extended hip-hop symphony, using the remixed versions drawn out vamps to lay the groundwork for Beck to exhort the crowd with catch phrases such as

'6.4 equals make out', where he would get the audience to shout out 'Where It's At' when he dropped his arm, again and again until they reached that much vaunted 6.4. Rockers like 'Thunderpeel' and 'Mutherfucker', would lead into Smokey doing awe-inspiring slide solos on 'Jack-Ass'. Then DJ Swamp would begin his solo spot, building riffs out of scratches, using hip-hop vinyl to work in the clichéd solos from Deep Purple's 'Smoke On The Water' and other classic rock chestnuts. For an encore the band would return with a fiery 'High 5', with Theo Mondle laying down fat Hammond organ and samples and Beck at the edge of the stage getting the crowd to go nuts with call and response cries.

On 18 February 300 American critics voted *Odelay* best album of 1996 in New York's *Village Voice* annual 'Pazz And Jop' poll with twice the votes of The Fugees' *The Score*. After the release of the album, and healthy sales, some industry pundits posited that the album had peaked, but the fawning attention of critics and Beck's relentless touring kept extending the life of the album on the U.S. charts, where it stayed for 55 weeks. By now every publication worth its salt was declaring *Odelay* 'Album of the Year'.

When Beck and the band got to Las Vegas, that monument to American aspirations, Beck was horrified to find out that a bogus guitar claiming to be his was hanging on the wall of the Las Vegas Hard Rock Café, next to Eddie Van Halen's striped Stratocaster and Billy Squier's Cubist Kramer. 'That's a lie, they can't possibly have a guitar of mine, because I've never given away any of my guitars,' he complained to *Jam!* 'I wouldn't get rid of that guitar. I was at a guitar store a while back and some dealer said he would pay me two grand for it. It's a guitar I bought for like sixty bucks through the paper. I wouldn't sell it. It's not worth more than sixty bucks. It's withstood a lot, though. I used to set it on fire at the end of every show.'[4] This was the guitar he'd used on *Odelay*, and Beck was hanging on to it for sentimental reasons.

In the U.K., to coincide with a brief British television and concert mini-tour, DGC released the third single from *Odelay*, 'The New Pollution', on 24 February. The seven-inch single featured the previously unreleased track 'Electric Music And The Summer People'. The first CD featured 'Electric Music', and an Aphex Twin remix of 'Devil's Haircut', called 'Richard's Hairpiece', and the second CD features new track 'Lemonade', and a Mario C and Mickey P remix of 'The New Pollution'.

'Electric Music And The Summer People' was the original title for 'Devil's Haircut'. The phrase was one that fascinated Beck, and he would later write a B-side with the same title, trying to bottle the cavalier ebullience of summer, and echoing Blur's 'Girls And Boys' in doing so. The track pumps along with a New Wave fuzz guitar, campy harmonies and hand claps. He would later amp it up and re-cut it.

Richard D. James, the Cornwall electronics nut and master of ambience contributed a fascinating remix of 'The New Pollution' with his trademark frenzy and languor knocking boots in an analogue synth lab. Beck's vocal is sped up into a squirrelly refrain, while James' filters and circuits run circles around the melody.

'Lemonade' starts with a thrash techno, like Aphex Twin's more horrific work, what one writer in *Select* once memorably dubbed 'the sound of a cat being fed through a fax machine', before it breaks into a rolling fingerpick-led chorus with lulling harmonies with Beck pal Rebecca Gates of the Spinanes. One of the most beautiful moments in Beck's work, it's an echolalia hum of words that delves deep into a place usually only found in Syd Barrett's more private musings; no other song by Beck better captures the kinetic push and pull between traditional folk and explosive noise. The fiery extroversion of the clipped, distorted verses are matched with the folk introspection that reveals Beck's emotions. A more complete snapshot of the dualities powering Beck's music would be hard to find, even if the song feels almost like a throwaway.

The video for 'The New Pollution' was released on 18 December. Beck had decided to direct the video for the song himself, though he referred to the making of it as 'my own private *Apocalypse Now*'. He cut together a fantastic collage of pulsating low-grade kinetic art visuals with a sampling of some of his inspirations. Beck had watched the Mötley Crüe *Livewire* video in fascinated horror, and wove a parody of himself and the band into the video, resplendent in spandex, mesh shirts, fright wigs and Crüe tribal marks, with Joey banging a drum kit outfitted with an upside down pentagram. Nods to the Beatles' derided classic *Magical Mystery Tour*, Kraftwerk, and Serge Gainsbourg swirl in juxtaposition to the song. Homages to Sixties music show *Hullabaloo* float in and out of the mix, along with horrid Eighties video effects. A bevy of pony-tailed girls surround Beck as he does a theatrical *Lawrence Welk Show* schtick. The video closes with a panoply of visions in a crystal ball with photos of a young Beck and Hank Williams. Commenting on his videos, Beck said: 'It's sort of absurdist, but it's also about this completely selfish desire to step into that fantasy, to see what it feels like to be behind that mask and enter into that madness.'[5]

Continuing the cavalcade of kudos, Beck received three Grammy Award nominations, though he didn't hear about them for some time – 'Nobody called, because everyone assumed I knew.' He eventually found out from a fellow shopper at the supermarket in Los Feliz. 'Next year, I'm going to try to get a nomination for "books on tape",' he told *Entertainment Weekly*, 'That's the Grammy to get. It was a little surreal, but it feels good to be validated, to be acknowledged. For a while, I was one of the scapegoats for the whole slacker–Generation X thing. Somehow the perception changed, and I'm grateful.'[6] 'I do think they're opening the umbrella a little bit to include stuff that isn't standard Grammy fare,' he conceded to *Rolling Stone*, adding, 'I'm somewhat of a traditionalist, maybe someone who came up on folk rock or singer-songwriter stuff can relate [to that]. Maybe that's it, maybe not. Because other things that I do are just pure deconstruction, just dismantling the whole notion of songwriting. It's exciting for me. It means more possibilities, and I have a lot of ideas.'[7]

Beck and his band performed live at the Grammy award show in New York City's Madison Square Garden, Beck looking dashing in a black suit that had been custom fitted for him, with a black shirt and blue tie. This time there was a new addition to the growing mojo sack of treats in the shape of a three-piece horn section comprising old Beck buddy David Brown on alto saxophone, David Ralickie on baritone saxophone and trombone, and Jon Birdsong on trumpet. Ralickie, a friend of Mike Boito, Beck's old keyboardist, also used to play with Joey Waronker. He also moonlights in Brown's superb band Brazzaville. Their super seductive blend of Afro percussion, Brazilian melodies and Chinese opera makes Brazzaville one of the Silverlake bands that majors should be throwing buckets of cash at. The horn section, dubbed the Brass Menagerie, join Beck and the other lads for a smoking version of 'Where It's At' that had the famous people in the audience in the crowd jangling their 'ice' and shouting 'Where it's at!' in the call and response chorus.

Beck won Best Male Rock Vocal Performance for the single 'Where It's At', (a hilarious result for a song sung through a five-dollar plastic mike and vocoded) and Best Alternative Performance, presumably for his commendable efforts to introduce Fluxus, Dada, hip-hop and vaudeville into a very sterile alternative world, though they neglected to mention this in the program for the Awards. 'What can you really do in the mainstream to shake things up except just be yourself and be genuine and let that come across?' Beck commented afterwards. 'Face it, most of the stuff is pretty watered down and schlocky and glossy. And to get up there and let it go and be rocking between Whitney Houston and Sting and sing "hirsutes with the parachute fruits" is pretty good. There's something perverse about it, but that's the way it should be.'[8]

Hobnobbing with the likes of the cuckolded Presidential wife Hillary Clinton and Celine Dion (whose LP, voted Album Of The Year, outsold *Odelay* by seven to one).

After the surreal Grammies experience, Beck was off on Concorde to London, and appeared on both *Top Of The Pops* and *TFI Friday* to perform 'The New Pollution'. On 2 March Beck took the stage at the Kilburn National. DJ Swamp, outfitted in a cowboy hat and bandanna wrapped round his face like an Old West bandido, sliced and diced a post-techno fanfare with a vinyl voice hyping the crowd with 'Lon -Lon -London'. A magisterial voice came over the public address system: 'Ladies and gentlemen, let's have a big welcome for the Best International Male!'

Flashing a 'V' for victory sign, Beck took the stage and the band broke straight into the instrumental 'Unit Is In Effect'; a knife-sharp switch and they were into a thrashing 'Devil's Haircut' known as 'American Wasteland': 'Beck is sliding across the stage, the first person in a decade to attempt robotic dancing; for a few bars he is holding his guitar over his head, while his bassist and guitarist stand frozen on either side of him. Beck finishes "Devil's Haircut" by roaring the title with the force of a furnace blast.'[9]

Indulging in ultimate theatrics for the crowd, he extracted a pair of binoculars 'to check out how mah freaks are doing.' The London hipsters tittered when he exclaimed, "We're going to setcha up, because y'all are way too sexy for your outfit.' Steamrollering through 'Novacane', 'Lord Only Knows', 'Thunderpeel', 'Sissyneck' and 'Hotwax', the band took an unusual, unseasonable detour into Beck's electro Hanukkah track 'Little Drum Machine Boy'. This segues, even more bizarrely, into Beck's lovely East 17/Take That parody, 'Freakout Eurobeat', with Beck clambering to the top of a stack of speakers to holler, 'You're all fucking me up the ass!'[10] For 'One Foot In The Grave' Beck regulated with impressive fluency, getting the audience so hyped that they started clapping double time. Out of breath, he petulantly stopped in mid-song to protest, 'Damn, y'all are too fast! Y'all been listenin' to too much jungle! A man cannot play the blues that fast!'

Back in the States, Beck donated a tune enigmatically titled '?' to Los Angeles college radio station KXLU-FM's benefit compilation *Demolisten: Vol. 2.* on No Life Records. For the show on 19 March, in Fort Lauderdale, Florida Beck had recruited two new opening bands, an inspired choice of Berlin's sonic terrorists Atari Teenage Riot followed by Sweden's Cardigans, fronted by chanteuse Nina Persson. The combination was somewhat akin to a firm spank followed by a rub to take off the sting. Part of Atari Teenage Riot's approach is to severely boost the mid-frequencies in their mix, giving an edgy adrenaline, fight or flight urgency to their music. ATR's Alec Empire saw this as a way to shock their audiences awake, the very antithesis of hip-hop or techno's lulling big bass, which he believes simulates the bass frequencies one hears in the womb. Their all-out aural assault accompanied by vicious strobe lighting made more than a few audience members ill. When it came to Beck's set, he paid tribute to T-Bone Walker by playing his guitar over his head for 'Devil's Haircut' and then shaking it for that added vibrato. For 'Novacane' the crowd went nuts moshing, with 250 gorilla men doing their age-old schtick of pushing people out of the way to get to the front, a pointless display of drunken power mongering. The only thing that scared them off was Beck brandishing an acoustic guitar, at which all the meatheads fled for the bar. On an extended 'Hotwax', incorporating 'Little Drum Machine Boy' Smokey and Justin doing beatbox rhythms and co-ordinated steps in tandem with Beck. 'On 'Derelict' Smokestack harmonized on the choruses with a handheld Vocoder. Then came 'Loser' with Beck rapping out the verses in the new staccato rap MC'ing style, with pauses and concentrated bursts of rhyme. For "One Foot In The Grave", Beck unequivocally notified the crowd, "I don't need no cocaine, none of that shit. You now what time it is? IT'S TIME TO R-E-G-U-L-A-T-E!". 'Beercan', was riotous, with DJ Swamp spinning out the breaks, scratching backwards, flipping the vinyl into the air and slapping it back down just in time for the next cue, as Smokey jammed right into "High 5" [...] Some kids were yelling at him "Beck, you are America's last hope!"'[11]

On 30 March Beck appeared at the Spectrum in Philly to drop science on his biggest sell-out audience ever. Atari Teenage Riot alienated and the Cardigans lulled in their now standard punch-'em-and-lay-out-a-pillow-to-sit-on tag team opener. Nearly 8,500 people showed up to hear Beck dance, rap, joke and preach. After a blazing opener of 'Devil's Haircut' Beck stepped to the mike and said, 'Never before in the entire history of the entire planet have so many people shouted out "Where It's At" at one time!' Later on, he lauded 'this fine facility where so many impressive athletic endeavours have been perpetrated.' Smokestack was praised by Beck for 'keepin'' it lonesome' and the Brass Menagerie, now fully integrated into the band, broke wind on 'Hotwax' as Beck dropped in vocal tastes of Colour Me Badd's 'I Wanna Sex You Up' and 'Little Drum Machine Boy'. The crowded stomped and chanted for 15 minutes for an encore, shouting 'We want Beck.'[12]

In Toronto, brilliant hip-hop experimentalists the Roots and Atari Teenage Riot opened. With Swamp warming up the crowd, Beck appeared on the stage of Toronto's Varsity Arena wearing his navy blue suit and baby blue shirt and tie. A notable feature of many Beck gigs was the way he made efforts to ensure no one in the crowd was getting a raw deal. 'A lot of times kids will come out and they will have a very raw expression, "I can't communicate or articulate how I'm feeling or what I'm going through, so I'm going to kick this guy in the face,"' he told *Sessions*. 'It's very common, so we try to pass out etiquette books in a way. Telepathic etiquette books. Go to page 268, paragraph 7, it says "do not kick that fourteen-year-old girl in the face. It's not a hip thing to do."'[13]

From the first chords of 'Devil's Haircut', through an eighteen-song, ninety-minute set culminating in a fifteen-minute encore of 'High 5', audience involvement was near total. A disco ball refracted coloured light down on the 4,500-strong crowd. Chris Wahl wrote in the *Toronto Sun*: 'When he wasn't robotically breakdancing, Beck was jumping around the stage, chucking microphones around like hand grenades and throwing his guitar in a 360-degree spin around his body, especially on the grinding funk and hard guitar of "Novacane". He treads a razor-thin line between cool and camp.'[14]

Two days later Beck and company rode into Akron, Ohio for yet another sell-out show. At 9:30 the arena went dark and DJ Swamp entered wearing cowboy hat and bandanna. He scratched as the band took the stage, jamming on 'Unit' with the Brass Menagerie laying down long, loping brass phrases over scratches, basses, guitars and drums. Under a huge geometric backdrop Beck took the stage in white pants and a red and white striped shirt. Rough and shaggy, he took his trusty Silvertone and jammed right into 'Devil's Haircut'. At the start of the acoustic part of the set, he announced to the crowd that Allen Ginsberg had died that morning, adding that four other people he knew had also died that week. Clearly emotional, he proceeded to play 'Pay No Mind' for them. Ginsberg had planned an MTV 'Unplugged' show with Paul McCartney, Bob Dylan, and Beck doing spoken word and music performance shortly before his death.

Beck returned for a hometown gig on 25 April at L.A.'s Universal Amphitheatre, before a much needed few days of rest and decompression. Meanwhile, elsewhere in Beckian circles came the sad news that 'Loser' producer Carl Stephenson's demons had gotten the better of him and he was committed to the UCLA Neuropsychiatric Institute and Hospital. It would be a two-month stay. For the record, he emerged a happier man.

Beck dropped in on London, England on 6 May for an appearance on Jools Holland's *Later* where he performed a short televised set of 'Devil's Haircut', 'Sissyneck' and 'Jack-Ass'. Taking in Manchester, Birmingham, and a smashing show on 10 May at London's Brixton Academy, Beck took England by surprise with a tremendous show during which, for some reason, a cadre of fans threw heaps of Brussels sprouts onstage. 'People come to try and bum rush my show. Bring me bicycle helmets and Brussels sprouts. That is so dope!' Beck exclaimed from the stage. *NME*'s John Mulvey paid tribute to the frenetic pace of the set: 'My God, he works it. Starting the gig in an outfit that suggests tight, pinstripe, double-breasted blazers will be *de rigeur* for homeboys in 1997, he leads his band through a series of frozen, faux-machismo poses that make them look like Burton's mannequins from the 1970s, the decade taste should've forgot. He kung-fu kicks, Cossack dances, pogos like a bastard, moonwalks and just about pulls off a back flip before being carried offstage. During calmer moments, he threatens the sprout-chuckers, drinks a toast to the audience and delivers a brief but informed lecture on the genius of harmonica-toting bluesman Sonny Terry.'[15] Collapsing theatrically at the end of the show, Beck was taken away on a stretcher by two St John's Ambulancemen before returning, despite their protests, in a rhinestone Nudie suit.

Then it was on to Germany and the Pink Pop Festival in Holland where thousands of stoned freaks wandered on a Hieronymus Bosch landscape as Beck and his cronies kicked 'Where It's At' into the setting sun. Back in the States, Beck toured some distinctly odd places, such as St. Louis' Pointfest 8, a horrid festival in a mosquito-ridden field with an alternative line-up but even less of the fun of Lollapalooza. Beck was sandwiched somewhere between Echo and the Bunnymen, the Rollins Band, and Better Than Ezra. Beck took the stage with the band, all in suits, flash and sharp amidst all the false histrionics and posing that had preceded them. A wave of relief swept the crowd, and despite sputtering mikes Beck kicked, danced and whipped his way through a high voltage set. He announced 'Loser' with 'Let's take it back to 1993!' and everyone went back, parched and wobbling to their cars parked in $10 spots.

Dr Octagon, brainchild of the twisted and brilliant minds of legendary rapper Kool Keith, DJ Q-Bert, the 'Charlie Parker of the turntables' and tech-spert Dan 'the Automator' Nakamura, debuted as the opener for Beck's Detroit show. They dropped their Dr Octagonecologyst set on unsuspecting heads. Between them the trio account for some of the most innovative minds in hip-hop, if not the most innovative, with the Automator on the drum machine, DJ Q-Bert on the turntables, and Kool Keith on the mike, along with their crew of Sir Menelik, as 'hype man,' and Prince Paul as MC. This was a road test for Dr Octagon's Lollapalooza jaunt that never happened, as the ever-unpredictable Keith got sidetracked with his rhymes from the year 3000.

Beck took the stage for a sold-out show (6,200 punters) at Boston's Brandeis University in his trademark powder-blue suit, swinging a cane like a cross between Big Daddy Kane and a 19th-century dandy. 'I am the artist currently known as Beck and you are all my folks!' he announced into the mike. Searchlights glittered on the mirror ball, sending the room into a dizzying spin, and hyping the general admission crowd to manic heights. Despite the lousy acoustics in the cavernous gym, which drenched the mix with a long pealing echo, Beck persevered with a singularly lunatic crowd. After 'Novacane', a series of sneakers started sailing onto the stage. Beck admonished the audience with urbane wit and charm: 'Before you throw that next item of clothing, that next shoe, let me just ask you to think twice about it and maybe donate that to a homeless shelter in your area. As you can see, we're well taken care of in the clothing and shoe department and don't need any more, especially when it's thrown in our faces.' The rowdy crowd pushed forward, squeezing sorority sisters against the railings, leading the gentlemanly Beck to cut 'Hotwax' dead in the middle, and ask 'Gentlemen, please be careful of these ladies down in front.'

Jon Garelick, writing in the *Boston Phoenix*, commented, 'It was Ellington addressing the mosh pit. But then, swallowing the mike like Ad-Rock, Beck added, "In other words, BACK THE FUCK UP!" To cool the crowd out a little, he did a smooth monologue intro for "Debra", for which he informed the crowd, "I'm a full-fledged man, and I'm not afraid to cry." These extemporaneous phrases Beck would try out on the crowd, and if the reaction was positive, he would file them away for use in his future songs. It was as if he was trying to expand the creative song writing process to include the audience. The aforementioned phrase would reappear in slightly altered form as one of the spoken asides in future single 'Sexx Laws'.[16] The encore was a fifteen-minute 'High 5', which Beck performed resplendent in a black satin and rhinestone Nudie suit, topped off with a cowboy hat.

On 12 June in Los Angeles Steve Hanft staged a premiere at Laemmle's Sunset 5 Theatre for his film *Kill The Moonlight*, which had finally been released. Six years in the making, predating and inspiring some of 'Loser', *Kill the Moonlight*'s day in the life of mythic race car driver Chance, played by Thomas Hendrix, had provided 'Loser' with the famous sample, 'I'm a driver, I'm a winner. Things are going to change, I can feel it.' Beck did a seven-song acoustic mini-concert at the theatre for the premiere, starting with a country flavoured intro. He played 'Leave Me On The Moon', an ancient song dating back from the days of *Fresh Meat & Old Slabs*, and featured on the film's soundtrack. Taking time out to remember Ken with 'No Money No Honey', Beck then yodelled through Jimmie Rodgers' 'Waitin' For A Train', 'Rowboat', a freeform 'Sunset 5 jam' and a country cover of the Doors' 'Light My Fire'. Beck contributed three previously unreleased tracks – 'Leave Me On The Moon', 'Underwater Music', and 'Last Night I Traded My Soul's Innermost For Some Pickled Fish', for the soundtrack, which was released on the Sympathy For The Record Industry label.

Hanft and Beck also announced a concert film of Beck's *Odelay* tour by Steve Hanft, featuring unreleased videos from Beck, as well as performance art and comedic sketches. The tentative title for the film was *Computer Chips And Salsa*. Beck also published a book of photographs from the tour; the bulk were by his new designated photographer Charlie Gross, though material by girlfriend Leigh Limon, and pal Autumn DeWilde were also included.

'There's a lot of chaos in Beck's music,'[17] Steve Hanft once commented. Often as not, the chaos in the videos was more muted and had a different pacing than the song's dynamic tempo. Taking the hoary old country cliché of 'Workin' In A Coal Mine' Willie Nelson made a cameo as a wizard for the Hanft-directed 'Jack-Ass' video, with Nelson sprinkling handfuls of gold pixie dust on belaboured miners. The video debuted on 27 July.

In the summer, Beck and band flew to the Continent to do a tour through the festivals, sweeping through Glastonbury in England, (where he was sandwiched incongruously between Massive Attack and Phish) followed by Switzerland and Denmark, Portugal and Belgium. *Odelay* was becoming a never-ending tour, a mission to spread the word, with Beck as the foot-stomping, body-popping, wise-cracking preacher testifying to an ever-growing flock of converts.

1   Browne, David. 'Beck In The High Life', *Entertainment Weekly*, 14 February 1997

2   www.beck.com

3   Hansen, Al. *A Primer Of Happenings And Time/Space Art*, Something Else Press, 1965

4   Sakamoto, John. 'Beck Answers His Fans', *Jam!*, 5 June 1996

5   Hoskyns, Barney. *World Art Magazine*, issue 19, Autumn 1999

6   Browne, David. 'Beck In The High Life', *Entertainment Weekly*, 14 February 1997

7   Kemp, Mark. 'Where It's At Now', *Rolling Stone*, 17 April 1997

8   'Beck's Progressive Risks Pay Off', *Denver Rocky Mountain News*, 18 May 1997

9   Gilbey, Ryan. 'The Cap Doesn't Fit', *Independent*, 5 April 1996

10 Williams, Simon. Live: London Kilburn National Ballroom, *NME*, 15 March 1996

11 Giffoni, Carlos. http://www.geocities.com/sunsetstrip/3226/putt.htm

12 DeLuca, Dan. 'Now A Real Showman, Beck Holds Big Audience In Thrall', *Philadelphia Inquirer*, 1 April 1997

13 Sessions At West 54th Street, 6 September 1997, www.sessionsatwest54th.com/

14 Wahl, Chris. 'Beck Blows Roof Off Varsity Arena', *Toronto Sun*, 3 April 1997

15 Mulvey, John. London Brixton Academy review, *NME*, 4 January 1997

16 Garelick, Jon. 'Beck Is Better Than The Real Thing', *Boston Phoenix*, 5–12 June 1997

17 Violanti, Anthony. The *Buffalo News*, 21 August 1996

13

THE RED BALL SPECIAL

After the Mount Fuji Festival in Japan, Beck headed home to start an American festival tour with the unlikely HORDE Festival crew, a multi-band tour with Neil Young as headliner. HORDE featured Neil Young and Crazy Horse, Beck, Morphine, Primus, Kula Shaker, Ben Folds Five, Toad the Wet Sprocket, Leftover Salmon and Medeski, Martin and Wood. Eight shows, seven cities – Wisconsin to New York. On 1 August, HORDE opened in Sommerset, Wisconsin. Beck joked that he wished he had been invited on the oestrogen-blessed Lillith Fair: 'I wish, man. I definitely need more yin/yang balance. These festivals tend to be pretty masculine.'[1] In ninety-degree heat, Beck rocked the swampland, strutting like Mick Jagger in his Nudie.

With the full time addition of the Brass Menagerie and two backup vocalists, Beck felt he had the perfect set up: 'This is definitely the band. This is the fourth one I've played with and this is the thing that works, so you'll be seeing us taking it to other places in the future. It keeps getting bigger. It's up to nine people now. We were watching The 'History of Funk' the other night [...] and it's so funny how it can escalate. That whole period in the 1970s, where everyone was outdoing each other and P-Funk ended up with like forty people onstage. All the other bands had to stop. Kool and the Gang was like, "What are we going to do, get sixty people?"'[2]

On 8 August HORDE dropped in on Great Woods in Massachusetts. Beck stood in the wings watching Soul Coughing, prepping himself for his appearance. DJ Swamp kicked it off with spun wax asking 'Are you ready? Are you ready?' The band emerged one by one, dressed formally in black, followed by Beck in a white suit and cowboy hat... and a white feather fan. 'This show is so hot,' he told the assembled throng,' I got to get my fan out and cool myself off.'

With an ever more inventive and theatrical stage show, including a huge backdrop like a cross between a Twister board and Damien Hirst's 1994 painting 'Agramine', an unusually whimsical ode to Pop Art, Beck took to shedding jackets and shirts like a butterfly in chrysalis. Beneath every layer was another layer. No wonder he'd needed the fan. 'DJ Swamp was mixing up the Chemical Brothers' "Block Rockin' Beats" like you wouldn't believe. Then he started picking up the records, throwing them up and catching them, passing them behind his back, spinning around, and rotating them between his two turntables; all while still playing the sample!'[3]

Not all were days of wine and roses, though. At Leeds, for the V97 Festival, lost in the shuffle of forty bands, all Blurry Shakers, Dodgy Bluetones and Ashy Reefers, Beck met an uncomprehending drunken wavering laddish mass of an audience who heckled and shouted abuse. The tinny sound and the all-ages crowd, who hadn't just come to see Beck, resulted in a poorly received set.

On 31 August at Vancouver, B.C.'s Pacific Coliseum, Beck and the band ended their massive fifteen-month *Odelay* world with a two-hour show for 4,000 screaming Beck maniacs. Being filmed by Steve Hanft for the proposed tour documentary *Computer Chips And Salsa*, the band planned an extra special encore of 'Motherfucker', for which they dressed up in Spinal Tap leather, chains and giant wigs. Beck was resplendent in shiny tight leather pants, boots and an enormous black wig.

At the MTV Video Music Awards on 4 September, Beck received so many awards that he could barely carry them away. He used the occasion to indulge in a gleeful piece of Dada theatre with MTV's John Norris:

Norris: We are here with Beck who, um, we are still working this out. Is it five awards or four that you won tonight?

Beck: We don't know our mathematics but we do know that 6.4 equals make out.

Norris: Right [...] So which of these awards meant the most to you? 'Best Direction' must be cool.

Beck: (Grabbing the mic) That was cool, actually, I'm glad you brought that up, because as you might not know I got put in a headlock as I was trying to say my acceptance speech earlier in the evening, so I'd like to take this opportunity to properly say a few words. First, I'd like to say that I'm gonna lose control for about fifteen minutes tonight, then I'm gonna be real cool tonight, blow it up again tomorrow. I would like to say that it was an incredibly fun video to make. I wanted to thank my band, my crew, for help on the video and everyone who worked on it. So it was really great and I appreciate everyone's hard work on that. I just had to get it out of the way.

Norris: (Wrestling the mic back) You can hold it if you want [...]

Beck: We can hold it together (taking the mic back again).

Norris: (Grabbing the mic to himself) [...] the man has won 'Best Male' two years in a row, a testament to your virility.

Beck: Virility, yeah, I've been doing a lot of men's circles in the last year. It started off with the award last year; I felt I had to measure up to the masculinity inherent in such an award in that category. I didn't think I could possibly beat R. Kelly twice. By the way, I wanna give props to R. Kelly, I'm totally down with him. I will try to bear that burden with cheerful pride and strong, virile sensitivity.

Norris: Hopefully, we'll see him back here sometime very soon with more videos from *Odelay* and whatever you're up to next.

Beck: Actually we're done with the thing for awhile. We did that last little hurrah with Willie Nelson for 'Jack-Ass'. We are satiated for the moment.[4]

As an encore, like bringing a speeding train to a halt, Beck and his Crew appeared on public television's *Sessions At West 54th* on 6 September, filmed at Sony Music Studios in Manhattan. 'It's the last hurrah,' Beck told the crowd. 'It's been a long tour, so we've been out for about eighteen months. We're going home tomorrow, this is the last gig, so you're getting us when we're all used up.'[5] Beck emerged looking sharp – short hair, white shirt, blue shirt and tie – and let the audience have it for ninety minutes. The set featured the by now familiar 'freeze frame'

147

poses, a tearjerking 'Debra' ending with Beck seeking consolatory hugs from the band. During 'The New Pollution', Beck, now wearing a dark blue suit, even got down and did the funky worm. During 'Ramshackle', he commented, 'We don't normally do this one because the kids who come to our shows, it's a little too slow for them, but y'all look like a real slow livin' crowd to me.' 'One Foot In The Grave' was particularly frenetic, Beck slapping a tin percussion box as an accompaniment to his wailing harmonica. For the encore – a resounding 'High 5' – the band re-emerged in costume, three of them all in white, with jackass heads.

On 29 September, Beck and American country music legend Willie Nelson dueted on the Jimmie Rodgers tune 'Peach Pickin' Time In Georgia' on the *Jay Leno Show*. Continuing their friendly contacts since the days when Nelson appeared in the 'Jack-Ass' video as the enchanting wizard, Beck played for Farm Aid in Illinois on 13 October, opening with a duet with Willie on the same song. On 19 November, at the 900-capacity El Rey Theatre in Los Angeles Beck did a special country show. 'Beck Acoustic With Friends' featured nineteen-year-old fiddler Gabe Witcher, Little Feat keyboardist Billy Payne, pedal steel guitarist Jay Dee Maness, and Smokestack, Showboat and Stagecoach. 'We did a gig that was inspired by the Farm Aid show we did with Willie Nelson, a proper gig in Los Angeles with the band,' Beck told *Rip It Up*. 'I had a lot of material already fitting that vein, and we just did the songs and they were a little more filled out, with a violin player, pedal steel, and a piano player. It was nice.'[6]

After openers Whisky Biscuit had strummed through their low key set, Beck's band opened with 'The Red Ball Special' an Opry-style instrumental, echoing the days of the Health & Happiness shows, Beck hollered 'Y'all going to light my fire!' before launching into his country version of the Doors' 'Light My Fire'. Relaxed in jeans, satin Gene Autry shirt and boots, Beck premiered two tracks from his future album *Mutations*, 'Cold Brains' and 'Dead Melodies' (which dated back to 1995) out for a test spin. For 'No Money No Honey', everyone sang along lustily, moving Beck to comment, 'I don't know how many times I played that at coffee shops trying to get people to sing along!' He delved deep into his roots, with a cover of 'John Hardy' telling the crowd, 'This was one of the first songs I ever learned to play' and a terrific version of Skip James' 'Jesus Is A Mighty Good Leader' with Smokey playing stunning slide riffs. Elsewhere he and the band refitted Odelay tracks with full country pedal steel, fiddle and organ vigour. 'The Red Ball Special' was played as interlude and hype several times, keeping the pulse going between slower songs like 'Ramshackle' and 'Sissyneck'.

On 16 December Beck was back at the El Rey Theatre opening for none other than old Bob Dylan. Beck dug deep into his back catalogue for the all-acoustic solo set. Opening with Jimmie Rodgers' 'Waiting For A Train', followed by a rare rendition of 'Lampshade', Beck played 'Cold Brains', 'Sing It Again', 'Dead Melodies' and 'Nobody's Fault But My Own', which would later emerge on *Mutations*. He also threw in some Skip James material before closing with 'I Get Lonesome'. Possibly recognizing a kindred spirit, Dylan thanked Beck for playing afterwards, and predicted a bright future for him. Beck was thrilled with the experience. 'I'd never felt that energy from an audience ever,' he enthused. 'It was just great, and very positive. Strange, very fanatical and respectful. I'm just used to a bunch of people being rowdy and talking and jumping around. And he definitely has some freaks. It was so quiet. I'm not used to that attentiveness. It was a microscope zooming above. Usually I'm used to banging away in a void.' Beck met afterward with Dylan, 'Dylan was great, very warm and normal, which was a surprise. And he was into it, having a good time. We played a very small club, about 500 people, so he was enjoying himself.'[7]

In December 1997 Beck was named the most important person in the world (check it out!) in a poll of musicians and critics conducted by London's *Select* music magazine, beating both Noel Gallagher from Oasis and Liam Howlett from the Prodigy. *Select* editor John Harris:

'Beck's the best lyricist in pop music, an American poet. English people live vicariously through him.'[8] It was refreshing to see America sending out something into the cultural atmosphere other than rancid hamburgers and identikit grunge bands.

In his interviews of the time, Beck repeatedly accentuated the notion that he was a conductor, orchestrating an event, much in the same guise as Al Hansen doing his happenings. The score had room for chaos written into it; scripted chaos. 'It's the way I approach everything. It's the only thing that makes sense to me, because no matter how much you plan or try to work things out ahead of time, or try to guess how it's going to go, it's going to go whichever way it wants. I'm just following a natural, intuitive logic and I usually find I get to the same place via a different route. You just got to let it take you there. That's if you haven't pulled your hair out before then, which believe me I do all of the time.'[9]

At the heart of Beck's approach was an attempt to get back in touch with the primal power of music to move people. That necessitated a rejection of the conventional image of a rock star, with all its inherently egotistic baggage, to let the music speak for itself. 'To me, rock star conjures up something like a mystic,' Beck told *Rolling Stone* in 1997, 'someone who sees himself as above other people, someone who has the key to the secret that people want to know [...] there's something élitist about it. I never related to that. I'm an entertainer; you're performing for people. It's not a self-glorification thing.'[10] Hence the appeal of the areas that his own grandfather had worked in: by allowing chance in, you restrict the influence of your own conscious mind, and then all sorts of interesting things can happen. 'I definitely want to experiment with John Cage's chance operation,' Beck told *Spin*, 'taking away your own instincts and letting the music just be a true expression, not coloured by personality. I wouldn't do anything like that for the sake of doing it; it would have to have some flavour to it. You can have a system or a plan, but ultimately the thing that's going to be interesting is the unintended, where all the machines break down, the mistakes.'[11]

Very Zen; making perfect mistakes, action paintings with one brushstroke. But it requires clarity of mind, and a thorough understanding of form, before form can ultimately be dispensed with. This is where all the years Beck spent learning to play country blues and folk, picking out patterns, paid off. Not in technique, but in the realization that he could break down barriers without killing the whole song in the drive to experiment. 'Starting out as a folk singer, I have a very strong sense of form,' he explained in 1997. 'If I were a painter, it's like I'd spent the first ten years with a piece of paper and a pencil. Now I'm using any colour at my disposal. So there's something in my background where I'm not completely lost in all of it. I have that form; it's instinctive in what I do. I've been a student of songs for so long. You recognize when a song is working and how a song should go. In a way, you're a storyteller with sound. You know that at this point something should happen in the plot, or you should get rid of this character.'[12]

When Beck was elected *Spin* magazine's artist of the year, he allowed himself a rare moment of boasting: 'I don't mean to sound rude, but to be honest, there wasn't much competition.'[13] The *Spin* cover was truly bizarre, with Beck's face reconfigured by computer to make him look like an anaemic elf, complete with black hair, make-up and eyeliner. No one at the magazine would own up to having manipulated the image; they even said it was a printer's error. Beck was clearly angry at the cover: 'If you don't fit into someone's mission of what a musical personality should be in 1997, then they'll just make you into it [...] They even changed the structure of my face! That's weird. It's fucked up. The bottom line is, they made me look like a junkie. But I'm not a junkie. I'm not self-destructive.'[14]

Perhaps the most shocking thing about Beck was how simple and unpretentious he was in his day to day affairs, when not touring. Without a heroin habit, a motorcycle or any of the accoutrements of fame, he maintained links with his family and friends in Silverlake, despite living in Pasadena. In May he bought a Pasadena home for just under $1.3 million, a 5,200-square-foot place on an acre of land, far from Silverlake, Los Feliz or Pico Hill. Built in the Fifties, the post-and-beam house is in a wooded area with rolling hills. Silverlake is Los Angeles' bohemian heartland, and it is where the Hansen clan have all made their homes at one time or another. Channing moved there after completing his studies at San Francisco's Art Institute. Bibbe and Sean live here also and so did Beck before he packed up for Pasadena. 'When we're looking at Silverlake, we're looking beyond the obvious, tasteful, white, West Hollywood, resting on your Laurel Canyon,' said Bibbe. 'We put the fun in dysfunctional.'[15] Peter McQuaid interviewed several Silverlake residents for a spread in the *New York Times*, comparing Silverlake to the East Village before gentrification decimated its hodge-podge charm and shabby chic. Silverlake has a distinguished liberal history, being a seat for leftists in the Thirties and gay activists in the Fifties. Nearby is Los Feliz, where Beck lived in the aftermath of *Mellow Gold*, and has since become a trendy, if a bit more upscale neighbourhood than Silverlake. At night he would dine with Leigh, his family or close friends at Sansui, a Japanese restaurant in Los Feliz.

At home, Beck would listen intently to albums of music by Moroccan Gnawa musicians; trance music predating organized religion, pagan incantations that address the soul of humanity in the rawest manner. He would dig into contemporary blues, such as CeDell Davis and R.L. Burnside. Stereolab and Apples in Stereo would be a modern kick, both bands taking a disparate range of influences from kitsch lounge to motorik Krautrock epics to John Cage, Mick Ronson, King Tubby, Pharoah Sanders, Captain Beefheart, the Rolling Stones, Eddy Grant, even bloody Sebadoh. Jorge Ben, hip-hop slo-jams and old-time country and blues would complete his listening palette. In an interview with *Jam!*, Beck ran down his perennial choices as 'Sly & The Family Stone's *Stand!* Woody Guthrie's *Dustbowl Ballads*. Leonard Cohen's *Songs From A Room*. I go through a lot of music. I don't really have any favourites. I have songs I like, or part of a song I like from one album. It's rare that you find an album where every part of the album is great. I listened to side two of *Abbey Road* recently, and I thought that was pretty amazing. I hadn't listened to it since I was a kid, and I never noticed how all of the songs go into each other continuously. That's really interesting.'[16]

But if there was one style of music that Beck returned to time and time again, it was the music of Latin America that he'd heard in his neighbourhood when he was growing up. The influence of Brazilian music on Beck's music first became apparent with the recording of 'Deadweight'. Written after some gigs in Portugal, the track shows Beck developing into a full-fledged pop auteur, using his multi-instrumentalist skills to their full potential. One of Beck's best tracks, 'Deadweight' is delivered in a cracked voice, the lyrics featuring scattered images of beer patios and elliptical conversations; Beck sounds as though he is articulating the ennui of aimless conversations to a backdrop of bland music in the background. An accomplished production with bongos, organ, harmonies intertwining expertly, 'Deadweight' descends into a break with spiralling synths and fleeting scratches, like sounds scavenged off distant radios. The lead off track on the 1998 soundtrack to the Cameron Diaz–Ewan McGregor film *A Life Less Ordinary*, 'Deadweight' is a song as addictive as sin, with a chorus cribbed from an old Gerry and the Pacemakers album; 'Don't let the sun catch you crying' perfectly capturing the late afternoon tropical idyll in all its idle lacklustre.

'I met with the filmmakers of *A Life Less Ordinary*, and they talked about the movie and the scene that it was going to be for,' Beck told *The Times* in late 1997. 'I knew they were capable, and I also knew what they were into aesthetically, so I would do something in their vein, which is also my vein. When I was home I had two days, so I created it, and there are no samples on that song, which I'm really glad about. On a lot of soundtracks, bands give their throwaway songs. But if I'm going to commit to something, it's got to be quality.'[17] Touring and record-making commitments meant that Beck passed on further tantalizing offers for film music, including a possible collaboration with John Waters. He was even offered the part of Jimmie Rodgers in one film, but turned it down: 'I don't want to inflict my acting on anybody. I already inflict my dancing abilities.'[18]

Beck closed out the year with a special summertime New Year's show at Australia's Bondi Pavilion in Sydney. After the show, he stood at the balcony of his hotel overlooking the beautiful beaches of Sydney, watching a young girl seeing in the new year by vomiting violently. Rather a sobering way to start the new year.

In Melbourne, Beck and the band gave the opening 'Unit Is In Effect' a touch of bossa nova. Beck cracked a whip on stage, crying 'I'm a gonna make some ass move', resplendent in his pinstripe suit. The live show was now smooth as clockwork, as tight as a Busby Berkeley dance sequence. Smokestack and Showboat showed off their co-ordinated dance steps in 'The New Pollution'; Beck left the stage during a reprise of 'Unit Is In Effect', to return in an all-white leather creation and a white sailor's cap. 'Where It's At' saw him pull off leg splits, body-pop and drop his knees to the stage à la James Brown, as befitted the *new* hardest working man in showbusiness. But for all the seemingly limitless energy which he put into his shows, Beck was beginning to grow weary of performing the same songs. 'After this run in Australia and New Zealand, I'm gonna start recording, he told *Rip It Up* in early 1998. 'We were gonna do Asia too, but I want to get back and get to work on some new material – it's been over two years, so it's long overdue. I started recording *Odelay* in October 1994 and finished it nine months before it came out, so it's a long way back for me. It's beyond being tired of the songs. They become so much a part of who you are after a while, part of your vocabulary and part of your mannerisms. We've lived these songs inside and out.'[19]

'I got back from the *Odelay* tour and I probably should have just taken some time off,' Beck told *Rolling Stone*. 'But aside from "Deadweight", it had been a few years since I'd been in the studio, so I was insanely anxious to do something creative with the band; go in and just do some stuff real quick. So I scared up a bunch of songs I had sitting around. These songs go back four years. I had a lot of songs that were a little more contemplative, quiet and folky. Some of them I tried to record for *Odelay*, and they just didn't pan out.'[20]

Roger Joseph Manning Jr. – no relation to Roger Manning of anti-folk fame – replaced Theo Mondle on keyboards for the recordings which would make up *Mutations*. A multi-instrumentalist, highly proficient on drums and guitar, Manning arrived from tenure with bands such as Jellyfish and Imperial Drag, cult bands both. Manning and his cohort Brian Kehew form the duo the Moog Cookbook, who did two great albums of vintage analogue synthesizer covers of alternative and classic rock anthems, attacking them with pompous arpeggios and great blasting Moog fanfares. Moog Cookbook also did a fantastic remix of 'Kelly Watch the Stars' by French synth-popsters Air; Manning and Beck's bass player Justin Meldal-Johnsen also toured with Air in late 1998. Manning is quick to cite music others would revile, including Rick Wakeman's work with Yes and Chick Corea's syrupy fusion work. His taste for prog rock and jazz-fusion notwithstanding, Manning is an exceptional player with a wide-ranging ear and sensitivity to ambience that adds much to Beck's more recent work.

Having finished touring in January, Beck called his manager, John Silva, after only a week or so to express his interest in getting back into the studio. As luck would have it, Silva had recently met producer Nigel Godrich in town at an Oasis gig; he was winding up some recording work

151

with Los Angeles singer-songwriter Jason Falkner. Beck called him up and before long Godrich had agreed to produce his new record. 'He's very quiet and studied and obviously very intelligent,' said Godrich in recalling his first impressions of Beck. 'I thought he'd be a bit more aggressive and loud. All the kind of rap stuff on *Odelay* is pretty aggressive, but he's quite cerebral. My exposure to him previous to that had only been the singles off *Odelay*. So I went away and listened to the whole of *Odelay* and sat there and thought, "Bloody hell, what does he want me to do?"'[21] They had two weeks before Godrich, whose previous credits include Radiohead's masterful *OK Computer*, was due to fly back to England, and work started immediately. From the off, the working relationships between all concerned were gratifyingly smooth: 'It was very serendipitous. Everybody fell in love with each other. It was all meant to be. Nigel completely clicked in, and he totally got it. He has impeccable taste, but he's also really adventurous. He's got mad skills, as they say, but he's not too precious about it. When I say two weeks, it was two weeks STRAIGHT, locked in a room, so it was pretty intense, It was coming, whether we liked it or not.'[22]

Beck and Godrich were faced with the difficult task of booking studio time at short notice. By chance, the only spot that was available and suited their needs was studio A at Ocean Way Studios in Los Angeles. Ocean Way is a studio of long standing repute. It's the place where Ray Charles recorded 'I Can't Stop Loving You', where Brian Wilson performed infinitesimal tweaks on 'Good Vibrations', and everyone from Frank Sinatra to Duke Ellington has held sessions. On *Mutations*, the wide separation of the mix into distinct left and right channels echoes the recording of those earlier records, made at a time when stereo was a novelty exploited to its fullest. 'That board is analogue,' Beck observed of Ocean Way's mixing desk, 'and has only a left or a right button. There's no panning knob, so it's either left, right, or middle. The board was from the Sixties, and a lot of the stuff we used was pretty old. I've been using Pro Tools and a hard disk recording since 1992, and I'm a real believer in that technology. You can do a lot with it without spending a lot of money. But I was anxious to try something that was more linear. With computers there are so many things you can do, you can really get bogged down. There's something beautiful about just going for a moment and then capturing it on tape with whatever you have to work with.'[23]

Between 21 and 22 February, Godrich and the band tested the waters by recording and mixing 'Cold Brains' and 'Electric Music And The Summer People'. Godrich was blown away by Ocean Way – by his own admission the best studio he'd ever worked in. The console in studio A was a gold antique called a Delcon and featured humming analogue tube amplification. The studio had a huge room where everyone except Joey sat together. Godrich was much taken with the band members and people and musicians, calling Joey 'one of the best drummers I've ever recorded' and Justin a 'brilliant bass-player.'[24] The band had prepped with a few days' rehearsal at Beck's house, where he showed them how the tunes went. The night before the first session, Beck had stayed up into the wee hours at home, working out some new songs in addition to the ones that had been marinating over the past four years. 'Static' and 'Cold Brains' dated from sessions for *One Foot In The Grave*, if only in skeletal form. 'Sing It Again' and 'Dead Melodies' dated from 1994–95, written for Johnny Cash, and songs which Beck thought half cooked at the time.

'Cold Brains' and 'Electric Music And The Summer People' were complicated songs in Godrich's estimation, yet, in testament to the road-warmed musicians, 'Cold Brains' was finished in a day. 'Electric Music And The Summer People' now featured a sitar solo, timpani and four keyboard solos. Cut once before as a B-side, the track had now been radically reconfigured, with Beach Boys harmonies that would have Brian Wilson cranking up his car stereo on Santa Monica Boulevard and snapping his fingers in time. Also witness the glorious Szabo sitars twanging in the extreme left side of the stereo mix. The result was a consummate Sixties tune – all the atmosphere of a *Hullabaloo* episode in amped-up Technicolor, but with a thoroughly modern sensibility, never pandering to retro fixations. It was the Banana Splits versus Peter Sellers in *The Party*.

With the sessions having gone so smoothly, all concerned were eager to press on and get a whole album down. Godrich was scheduled to take a holiday, but called Beck to tell him that he'd be happy to put off his vacation to finish the record. Beck was delighted, and recording recommenced on 19 March, lasting until 3 April. The two agreed that they would record and mix one song per day, and would abide by the end results. Beck would run through the song that they would be tackling that day for about half an hour, then they would set about recording it. Once the basic tracks were done, the band would listen to the playback and work out where the overdubs would go, with Manning tinkering out a keyboard riff or Smokey laying down one of his lonesome solos. By the time the first song, 'Static', was cut, Beck was already coaching the band through 'O Maria'. 'O Maria' begins with a Neville Brothers soundalike tack piano, with the bass played loose behind the beat, and a muted trumpet. The barrelhouse piano was tweaked slightly with effects because the studio only had a huge ornate grand piano. The Brass Menagerie rolled in and David Ralickie laid down his superlative trombone solo while Manning played Hammond organ. Radiohead visited Godrich in the studio, and were amazed at both the quality of the songs and how quick the recording process was. Beck was unstinting in his praise of Godrich: 'Some producers play around and twiddle with knobs forever, and you're there for five hours and they're still getting the snare drum set up. That can definitely squelch any creative energy happening in the studio. Nigel was great, he'd have the microphones up in fifteen minutes, and by that time everybody had learned their part, we'd play it two or three times and then that'd be it. So after about seven or eight days it was almost a whole album done. You just saw this album being born. We almost felt guilty, it was too easy.'[25]

'Sing It Again' was cut totally live except for a snippet where Smokey dropped in. Beck sang the vocal live, and they went through it four times, Godrich performing an inspired, George Martin-like, rapid-fire edit between the four takes, complete with mix downs; this was where his technical mastery really began to come into its own. 'Sing It Again' was originally written for Johnny Cash, a lovely waltz for the end of the night, with a Willie Nelson Tex-Mex flavour. Acoustic nylon guitar reminiscent of classic Mexican interpreters of *boleros* Los Panchos, with piano and steel guitar, sets the mood, while the heartfelt harmonica solo ranks among one of Beck's best. The *bolero* is a melancholy rumination of the Latin soul, with an instantly identifiable feel. The first *bolero* was 'Tristezas' (Sadnesses), written in Cuba in 1910 by Jose Pepe Sanchez. Mexico's Los Panchos (1944–1983) were one of the primary practitioners of the form, with Alfredo Gil playing the *requinto*, a small nylon-stringed Spanish guitar that helped give the music its distinctive feel. The slightly melancholy air of the *bolero* is evident in Beck songs throughout his career, going as far back as 'Whiskeyclone', and shows how well schooled he is in what writer Nick Tosches called 'the gnarled roots of rock'.

Perhaps the key track on what would become *Mutations* is 'Tropicalia'. The song takes its name from Brazil's late 1960s arts movement, a feverish attempt to merge high- and low-brow taste, folk music and city sophistication with avant-garde string arrangements atop complex African rhythm patterns. The movement drew its name from the works of artist Hélio Oiticica, a Bahian artist, and maker of installations. In April 1967 he installed his piece 'Tropicalia' inside the august surroundings of the Museum of Modern Art in Rio. The installation illustrated the crash collision of old and new, of a Brazil rapidly modernizing into cities of chrome and glass while every hillside was ringed with the favelas, the tin shacks of the urban poor. Oiticica invited the viewer to step inside, take off their shoes, and walk around. There were lush tropical weeds underfoot, gravel, tin roofs, bland pre-fab constructed walls, and in the back, a dark room where one walked in only to find a television blaring. After that, the exit.

Tropicalia emerged in Brazil in 1967. Since a military coup by conservative officers in 1964, freedom in the country was being eroded as the generals sought to quash dissent. But as the military tightened its grip on freedom, the youth rebelled. The repressive regime of General Artur de Costa e Silva had sparked off student protests. Another form of rebellion was expressed in music. Tropicalia was one of those spontaneous movements so typical of the Sixties. Its two leading figures were Gilberto Gil and Caetano Veloso. 'Tropicalia was a bit shocking,' Veloso recalled, 'we came up with new things that involved electric guitars, violent poetry, bad taste, traditional Brazilian music mass, low-class successful music, kitsch, tango, Caribbean things, rock and roll and also our avant-garde, so-called serious music.'[26] Tropicalia also made great use of Brazilian modernist *concrète* poetry, particularly that of Brazilian poet, Oswald de Andrade (1890–1954). Andrade was a guru for the movement, conspicuous by his physical absence but omnipresent in his influence. Andrade's 1924 manifesto 'Pau Brasil' called for Brazilians to become cannibals of culture, To eat the West and the East and expel them both as something wholly Brazilian.

For music that sought to incorporate chaos, much of Tropicalia was well structured and thought out according to dictates of *concrète* poetry, the rigour of the avant-garde and magnificent orchestrations. The Veloso-Gil song 'Bat Macumba' strung together words in joyous abandon around a tight structure, each verse dropping words until the middle word was 'bat' and then rebuilt word by word to the end, making an bold, emblematic 'K' when written on paper. The thin flat guitar that laced even the most romantic ballad with harsh and astringent tones pervades Tropicalia music. Gil's interest in the Beatles and folkloric Brazilian rhythms rubbed shoulders with Veloso's twin strains of romanticism and insurrection, contemplation and calls to action.

Like Fluxus, Beck's track 'Tropicalia' slots in perfectly with his quest to make treasure out of trash, using the discarded elements of pop and traditional culture to fashion something relevant and modern. Beck consciously refrained from stepping into the 'exotica' trap and making a pastiche of hot tropical beats or some other Latin cliché. The song makes his love of Brazilian music explicit, and illustrates a fascinating new twist in his music. The lyrics are remarkable, the first full fruition of a more adult Beck, with each line leading into the next like pieces of a masterly puzzle. An extraordinary song in every sense, 'Tropicalia' takes elements from Tropicalia itself – the *cuica* sound heard on Jorge Ben Jor's 'Charles, Anjo 45' (a Brazilian percussion instrument that one writer aptly referred to as 'sickly' with its wet bowed chirps and squawks), and bossa nova's off-key guitar strums. This electronic samba was to be the lead single off the album. The parallels between Tropicalia's reinvention of the musical alphabet in Brazil and Beck and his fellow travellers in the pop internationale mixing high and low, old and new and influences across the cultural and colour spectra are striking.

'I grew up in a Latin district, with Salvadorians, Mexicans, and all of the music that I heard has an African rhythm,' Beck told *Blitz* in 1998. 'This is fusion music par excellence. Brazilian music is simultaneously Western and African. In Tropicalismo, all the sounds from West to East converge. This music is extremely contagious, it has enormous happiness, and it's genuine and human. We're not allowed to broach similar happiness in rock, to us it isn't allowed. It's why I play this music, that I write songs like this, since emotions can be expressed, emotions that it's not possible to express by others' music. This music implies love for life, unconcern, sexuality and intelligence. To me, my heart beats with the sound of this rhythm.'[27] Rita Lee, one-time vocalist with radical Brazilian Tropicalia group Os Mutantes, credits the current resurgence of interest in Tropicalia to the times we're living in: 'It must have something to do with the turn of the millennium, the rising curiosity and re-reading the best of what the 20th century has produced, art wise, all over the world. When I first heard Beck I really felt a musical familiarity with what Os Mutantes used to do twenty-five years ago, I'm sure he hasn't listened to us before, so there's really something in the air making what was a flash future music into a new/old awakening.'[28] And of course, destroying the boundaries between new and old was exactly Beck's line of work. Clearly Brazilian music got under Beck's skin from an early age and stayed there. 'One of my best friends, David Brown, who plays in my band as well, went to Brazil and came back six months later fluent in Portuguese, and with a sack full of cassettes of early Seventies' Jorge Ben, Caetano Veloso', he told *Ray Gun* magazine in early 1999. 'It was just one of those things where you hear it and it instantly attacks your immune system until you are completely at its mercy. For years, it was pretty much the only thing I would listen to. It seemed like it had all the elements – the groove, the beats, and an insane melodic flair. And when I could get people to translate lyrics, the lyrics had a humour and soulfulness. The music in general had an incredible uplifting effect without being cloying or too sentimental. The music is incredibly simple on one level, but so much of it embraces complexity and is harmonically ambitious, but at the same time is really basic. It's also music that was created under incredible oppression and poverty. it's transcendent music.'[29]

For 'Cancelled Check' Beck and the band detuned the grand piano and stuck paper clips on the hammers to accentuate the barrelhouse piano sound they got on 'O Maria'. At the end of the track, the musicians headed off into a funk jam; pedal steel player Greg Leisz dropped in and added to the country funk flavour by joining right in. The musicians were so good, that the decision was made to make them wear paper bags over their heads at one point during the recording, to increase the chances of them playing a wrong note and make the whole thing sound looser. 'Tropicalia' was done in a day, Justin playing upright bass, Smokey playing the *cuica*, and everyone grabbing shakers for the percussion work. 'Cancelled Check' embraces pathos and is self-referential with the braying jackass in the background. 'I immediately need to dismantle anything too sharp and coordinated', Beck revealed in 1998. In a tone which suggested that Fluxus blood flowed strongly in his veins, he continued, 'Is it a desire to disrupt the clichés? […] I would like to let the art stand still and let the viewer/listener do the subverting.'[30]

With an avant-jazz outro that would have brought tears of joy to Sun Ra's eyes, the recording of 'Cancelled Check' ran deep into the night. As 3 a.m. rolled around at Ocean Way, studio fever began to set in. Godrich and Beck sat at the mixing board, puzzled as to how to end the song with some finality. The band had rented heaps of percussion instruments for the album, much of which had gone unused, and it was cluttering up an entire corner of the studio. 'All kinds of crazy Brazilian stuff, weird, stuff that looked like medical tools and handmade African stuff and timpani drums,' recalled Beck. With bills for the rentals adding up, Beck had a flash of 'inspired idiocy' and had the engineer turn on the microphones. Rousing the band from the rest and recreation room, where they were watching videos, Beck led them into the studio for a spontaneous percussion happening. A therapeutic freak-out ensued as everyone began banging and crashing on the instruments. 'We had people flying through the air, people were bleeding actually,'[31] Beck told National Public Radio. That may not be so far from the truth: on the recorded version you can hear someone shout 'oww!' amidst the cacophony of randomly banged congas, timpani and cymbals. Beck and Godrich tagged an excerpt of the outburst as a coda to the song and that was that.*

The song had progressed significantly from its origins as doleful dirge in a Tokyo hotel room in 1994. Even the live readings of the song performed at places like Boston's Middle East soon after sounded tentative, definitely a song in progress. Four years later it was fully marinated, and sounded like something Roy Rogers could have sung had he ridden off into a polluted Shibuya nightfall rather than a Western horizon.

On the elegant ballad 'We Live Again', a very French harpsichord carries the sub-melody in circles. David Campbell did a beautiful string arrangement for the track, to a backing track of harpsichord, upright bass and acoustic guitar. Godrich mixed it with the stellar arrangements by Reg Scott on those fantastic Scott Walker solo albums in mind, using one of the classic Ocean Way reverb plates to drench the mix in luscious reverb. On 'Dead Melodies' Joey made a percussion set out of an upside-down gasoline can and a steel ashtray, which Godrich duly miked and Beck and Smokey played acoustic guitar over. The song was over and done with in three hours total.

For 'Nobody's Fault But My Own', a song written in a basement in Olympia on a rainy day, Beck wanted to infuse the track with a taste of India. He got two acquaintances, Anthony Saffrey and Fred Sesliano, to play sitar and essraj respectively. Again, David Campbell wrote an impressive string arrangement for the track. Beck played guitar and some sitar, with overdubs by Saffrey and Sesliano. Beck's fondness for the sitar is well documented; indeed, he's used it on virtually every record he's made. 'You can look at it from the viewpoint that a sitar is retro, that it conjures up psychedelic albums from the Sixties,' he acknowledged to *Rolling Stone* in 1998. 'But it's also an ancient instrument. It's a beautiful sound in any time, any place. When I was younger, one of my favourite sounds was the Delta blues slide guitar, which also has that richness and groaning quality that is, to me, the most primal musical sound. We made an effort to use it with some taste. We laid it back in the mix so it was just part of the texture.'[32]

"Diamond Bollocks" was one of the most accomplished bits of recording really,' said Godrich. 'Beck had an idea that he wanted to do a bit of a rock opus. We did four different sections of music with the intention of splicing them together. One of them turned out really cool, so we ended up making it longer and turning it into the verse. I spliced it and copied it and copied it and then copied it again, so it's almost like a loop, but not quite. The beginning section is like a pastiche French thing with a harpsichord and then the second section was like a spy thing and then there was the acid rock section. Then he just wrote a melody over it. But that one took nearly three days because essentially it was written in the studio.'[33] Unlike its stylistic antecedent 'High 5', which took weeks of work to edit into a seamless groove, 'Diamond Bollocks' was the result of recording different styles and editing them into place almost by chance operation, making actual tape edits. Engineers just don't dare make cuts into actual tape anymore; it's a risky operation, but it can create sublime accidents. The title of the song itself draws on Beck's love of colloquialisms, in this case the Cockney phrase 'diamond geezer' as well as the English slang for testicles, that he'd picked up on tour. 'Diamond Bollocks' is a three-tiered melange of Gainsbourg, crisp and dry drums, Mancini harpsichord, Beach Boys chorale, Pussy Galore power chords on phaser, Rush-like arpeggios, grunge bass and Nirvana pacing, sound effects and clanging percussion. 'Looking back at some dead world that looks so new' is pure Tropicalia, Beck at his acerbic best, and a fitting commentary on our disposable culture. With a mellotron

---

* For Beck's interview on National Public Radio, the harried transcriber wrote down one of the song's lyrics as 'I don't want to bathe' instead of 'I don't want to beg'.

swell at the end strongly reminiscent of Manning's early Pink Floyd and Yes leanings, the coda shows the brilliant sense of melody that has made all of Manning's work, from Jellyfish to Imperial Drag to *Moog Cookbook*, noteworthy. On National Public Radio, interviewer Karl Wertheimer, noted the way in which several of the songs on *Mutations* married delicate arrangements to brutal lyrics. 'I like the spicy and the sweet,' Beck acknowledged, '[they cause] friction, and also [balance] each other out. I came up in music scenes where people were playing very aggressive hard music, loud, a lot of noise. And I always played acoustic guitar and didn't have a band and couldn't make a whole lot of noise. So I developed all the noise and feedback and that energy in the lyrics. The lyrics were like my distortion pedal.'[34]

'Bottle Of Blues', a swing blues, took half a day and features blues harmonica chugging like a train over synth blasts, another fine example of the fusion of old and new endemic to Beck's work. Old synths and old harmonica licks are merged into something utterly original, without any readily identifiable stylistic reference. The origins of the track can be traced back as far as November 1994, when Beck, in a piece in *Sassy* magazine, commented: 'Like the song said, "Hard, ain't it hard, to love the one who doesn't love you." Hard it is, but nothing's easier than dwelling on it.'[35]

'Lazy Flies' was begun the night before Godrich was scheduled to go home. They worked until 5 a.m., laying down double-tracked acoustic guitar to the accompaniment of Joey working a shaker. By the time they finished, everyone was totally beat, and Beck's voice acquired that lethargy that only comes after staying up all night to finish something. 'Lazy Flies'' guitar work references both the lush arrangements on Serge Gainsbourg's *Melody Nelson* album as well as some Django Reinhardt flavour courtesy of Smokey Hormel.

'Runners Dial Zero' was a bonus track on non-American editions of the album, and was inspired by the call which came over the PA when the girl at the reception needed a runner. 'You'd just hear "Runners Dial Zero" all the time,' recalled Godrich, 'and [Beck] didn't have a title for this last song, so that became it. It's a beautiful track, and basically we just got a fucked-up vocal sound and a fucked-up piano sound. I actually left before that was mixed, my cab turned up to take me to the airport. I was really, really exhausted and really sick on the plane on the way back. When we landed at Heathrow I thought I was going to faint.'[36]

'Runners Dial Zero' is simply extraordinary. Somewhere between John Lennon's cathartic 1970 album *Plastic Ono Band* and Alex Chilton's 'Kangaroo', the song is guided along by nothing more than a very haunting piano reminiscent of French classical/modernist composers Erik Satie or Maurice Ravel. Though the sonic picture would suggest the hand of Nigel Godrich – the track sounds closer to Radiohead's *OK Computer* than anything else on *Mutations* – he was bound for England when the track was mixed. Assistant engineer John Sorensen stepped up to the board, along with Meldal-Johnsen. There is nothing else quite so haunting in Beck's catalogue; the track is pervaded by a lonely feeling, like being lost on emotional moors or stranded in a room full of mirrors. If 'One Of These Days' is a Brian Wilson-influenced song, then 'Runners' is equivalent to brother Dennis Wilson's unreleased (though bootlegged) 'Carry Me Home' a devastating song of being emotionally adrift, or Brian Wilson's own ''Til I Die'.

There is a hint of emotional trauma in these songs; they contain some of Beck's most corrosive imagery. This is balanced by an unabashed romanticism tinged with regret, a romantic corrosion. Rupert Goodwins, a British Beck fan with a knack for solid analysis, opines 'The structure is more akin to a hymn than a pop song, you can hear echoes of say, Johan Sebastian Bach's "Air On A G String". Some of those modulations are very Bachenalian, a good deal more complex than it appears. There's frequent use of synth effects (including that omnipresent crackling and an intermittent rumble) and a slow underpinning walking bass that complements the piano perfectly. The vocals are also heavily treated, slowed down by 20 to 30 per cent, but at one point there's one slowed-down vocal in harmony with a full-speed vocal. The production sounds sparse and spacious.'[37] *Mutations* is an album of muted sonorities, but with a thousand influences compressed into the grooves; many of the tracks are linked by a romantic escapism, mirrored in the sonic adventurism of the Indian sitar and essraj in 'Nobody's Fault But My Own', the Brazilian excursion of 'Tropicalia' and the space folk exile of 'Runners Dial Zero'.

Beck picked eleven songs and that was it, the whole album over and done with in less than two weeks. One complaint about Nigel Godrich's production by fans was that it severed Beck from his folk roots, but in reality severing the moorings of Beck's country blues and folk and sending it into space does much to give the album its unique flavour. Uncomprehending reviewers sought to tag *Mutations'* as a retro nod to 1960s and 1970s California singer-songwriter albums, but it was so much more than that. Beck succeeded with his basic criteria to make timeless songs, not addressing one period or epoch, and transcending nostalgia or a false image of the past. If anything, *Mutations*, lyrical themes viewed the past with regret.

158

Mutations was something Beck clearly had to get out of his system; he referred to it in the press at the time as a contemplative album, and a record that he'd done for himself. 'I just want to hook up people who want to hear what we did and leave it at that. I got sick of all this drum'n'bass stuff. I like it, I got my club on, but I felt like it was becoming a little gratuitous [...] I started out playing folk songs, songs written by thousands of people over hundreds of years, and I still believe in the tradition. Songs are vehicles for personalities at this point, which is definitely interesting. But sometimes the song means something greater, and should be a vehicle for anyone who wants to sing it.'[38] Having produced an album of quietly dazzling diversity in record time, Beck now set about making the 'official' follow-up to *Odelay*.

1   Bream, Jon. 'Where It's At: Summer Festivals', *Minneapolis Star Tribune*, 1 August 1997

2   Martin, Richard. 'Beck Hansen May Be The Hardest-Working Man In Show Business'. www.wweek.com, 1996

3   Dupont, Marissa. www.beck.com

4   MTV Video Music Awards, 4 September 1997

5   Sessions At West 54th Street, 6 September 1997, www.sessionsatwest54th.com/

6   Ferguson, Troy. 'Beck: Where He's At', *Rip It Up*, January 1998

7   Boots, J. Interview with Beck. VPRO Radio, Netherlands, 1997. http://www.vpro.nl/3voor12

8   Ferman, Dave. 'Beck To The Future', *Fort Worth Star-Telegram*, 3 November 1998

9   Margetts, Jayne. 'Je Suis Un Revolutionaire', *Reverberation*, 1996. www.thei.aust.com-isite-beck.html

10 Kemp, Mark. 'Where It's At Now', *Rolling Stone*, 17 April 1997

11 Strauss, Neil. 'Artist Of The Year', *Spin*, 1996

12 Hughley, Mark. 'Beyond The Boundaries', The *Oregonian*, 28 August 1997

13 Strauss, Neil. 'Artist Of The Year', *Spin*, 1996

14 Kemp, Mark. 'Where It's At Now', *Rolling Stone*, 17 April 1997

15 *New York Times* magazine, 22 August 1999

16 Sakamoto, John. 'Beck Answers His Fans', *Jam!*, 5 June 1996

17 *The Times*, 25–31 October 1997

18 Dark, Jane. 'The Best Albums Of The 90s', *Spin*, November1998

19 Ferguson, Troy. 'Beck: Where He's At', *Rip It Up*, January 1998

20 Decurtis, Anthony. 'Beck: Q&A', *Rolling Stone*, 26 November 1998

21 Joyce, John. 'Diary Of An LP', *Melody Maker*, 28 November 1998

22 Sakamoto, John. 'Music Oddball Beck Gets Mutated', *Jam!*, 8 October 1998

23 Wiederhorn, Jon. 'The Many Faces Of Beck', *Guitar*, January 1999

24 Joyce, John. 'Diary Of An LP', *Melody Maker*, 28 November 1998

25 Colliton, Carrie. 'Can A One Man Band Go Solo?', *Music Monitor*, November 1998

26 Adams, Scott. 'Cry of Conscience', *Arete*, 1990

27 Gonçalves, Pedro. *Blitz*, 3 November 1998

28 Nielsen, Jeff. 'Viva Tropicalia', *Ray Gun* magazine, January 1999

29 Gladstone, Eric. 'Musical Mutations', *Ray Gun* magazine, January 1999

30 Breslauer, Jan. 'Conversation With Beck', *Playing With Matches*, February 1998

31 Siegel, Robert and Wertheimer, Linda. 'All Things Considered', National Public Radio, 1998

32 Decurtis, Anthony. 'Beck: Q&A', *Rolling Stone*, 26 November 1998

33 Joyce, John. 'Diary Of An LP', *Melody Maker*, 28 November 1998

34 Siegel, Robert and Wertheimer, Linda. 'All Things Considered', National Public Radio, 1998

35 Hansen, Beck. 'Tiny Beck: Your Personal Advice Columnist', *Sassy*, November 1994

36 Joyce, John. 'Diary Of An LP', *Melody Maker*, 28 November 1998

37 Godwins, Rupert. 'Analysis of "Runners Dial Zero"', Alt.music.beck, 1999

38 *Mutant Machine*, unknown source, 1998

159

14

VESUVIUS JACUZZI

With the recording of *Mutations* now behind him, Beck had some spare time to indulge in several collaborations and remixes. Along with Willie Nelson he recorded a cover of the Floyd Tillman country classic 'Drivin' Nails In My Coffin' for inclusion in the soundtrack to *Hi-Lo Country*. Beck sounds positively delighted on this track, with an infectious joy and a slightly different voice that led some fans to wonder whether it was really him singing.

Beck also recorded a duet with country singer Emmylou Harris for a tribute to Gram Parsons, the pioneering country rocker who famously envisioned a new 'cosmic American music', something which Beck could justifiably claim to be making. The pair covered 'Sin City', from *The Gilded Palace Of Sin*, recorded by Parsons during his spell with the Flying Burrito Brothers. 'I like singing with people, and I learn a lot every time I do it,' Beck revealed. 'Collaborations aren't done enough, but that's what made Ella Fitzgerald, that's what made Johnny Cash – connections to a musical community and being able to learn and develop out of that. It doesn't happen any more, and it seems like a lot of bands are cul-de-sacs that don't connect to any other streets, but I'm all for dialogue and participation.'[1] Emmylou Harris told *CDNow*, 'It was pretty straight ahead. Beck had his country band that he had just done some shows with at the El Rey. He was actually hoping to do 'Sleepless Nights', and he found out that Elvis Costello had already done it, so he decided on 'Sin City'. Beck sang it in a more traditional way than even Gram did. Beck understands that there are all kinds of ways to push the envelope: You can go back, you can go forward, and you can go from side to side.'[2]

Beck also remixed French electronic duo Air's 'Sexy Boy'. Beck's 'Sex Kino' remix is extraordinary, with its spare electro flavour and slightly vocoded vocals. It presents a weird, neutered idea of sexy, a eunuch synth baroque extravaganza. Beck drops in some vocal asides, in a sped up funny voice – a nod to a nod, Beck echoing Prince echoing George Clinton. The remix is both erotic and anti-erotic, and therein displaying an ambiguity that would resurface full force on *Midnite Vultures*. Beck was also slated to do a remix for exuberant Japanese kitsch'n'cut-up pop band Pizzicato 5, but he was just too busy. One track he did complete was 'I'm So Green', a cover from superlative German experimental rock band Can's classic *Ege Bamyasi* album, which featured wild man vocalist Damo Suzuki. The track was made for the Dust Brothers' Can tribute album, which has yet to see the light of day. Beck's version of 'I'm So Green' is superb, and reveals how skilled he was becoming at uncovering fragments of buried melody and extrapolating from them. The track marks a sort of midpoint between *Odelay's* intrepid 'deconstructionist noise freak-outs' and *Midnite Vultures'* stealth funk.

A loose band of shadowy art-renegades known as ®™ark (or 'art mark') – media terrorists specializing in absurdity and confronting the corporate ogre through, as they put it, 'the subversion of restrictive copyright laws' – put out a thirteen-track CD called *Deconstructing Beck* in February 1998. Philo T. Farnsworth, the pseudonym for their anonymous spokesman, told the *NME* that they chose to issue the CD, filled chock-full with slice and dice cut-ups of Beck's music, 'because Beck's good, but still a product. I don't even have to buy a Beck record to hear him. We're bombarded by images and sound more and more every year. It makes sense to me to take all this stuff that's pushed at us and do something with it.'[3] Brian McPherson, Beck's attorney, said 'Bragging about copyright infringement is incredibly stupid. You will be hearing from me, Universal Music Group, BMG Music Publishing and Geffen Records very shortly.'[4] Some of the pieces were just noxious avant-garde exercises, but Jane Dowe managed something unique with 'Puzzels & Pagans' taking the first 2 minutes and 26 seconds of 'Jack-Ass' and cutting it up into 2,500 pieces, reshuffled using probability functions. The CD was meant to point up the fact that works which used samples extensively to build new works cannot in turn be sampled without clearance. 'While Beck may be a superb artist,' said Farnsworth, 'his lucrative persona remains just another product that others get rich from, and one that we need to subvert.' Perhaps wary of the negative publicity Geffen's lawyers sent cease-and-desist letters, but did not follow up with legal action. Asked what Beck's response to the CD was, his publicist, Dennis 'No Comment' Denehy said, 'none at all; Beck has a copy, but he's not really commenting one way or the other. I don't even know if he's had a chance to listen to it.'[5]

On 7 May at the Santa Monica Museum of Arts the 'Beck & Al Hansen: Playing With Matches' show opened. In the works for a long time, the exhibition was the result of efforts by curator Wayne Baerwaldt. Baerwaldt had assembled a sizable trove of the elder Hansen's collage work, and amongst the folios had found several of the collages Beck had made when he was visiting his grandfather in Köln in 1990. Though initially reluctant, Beck warmed to overtures from Baerwaldt about doing a joint exhibition of both Hansens' work. Beck was motivated largely by the desire to see his grandfather get his due as an artist outside the realm of ephemeral and now long-vanished happenings. Beck said of his own collages, 'It's a bunch of biker/body-builder/computer collages I did when I was nineteen, but the show will mostly feature his works. We're going to re-create the famous Yoko Ono piano drop,' he added. 'You got to watch out for those Fluxus types; they have fast hands and lead boots.'[6]

Al's own collages are laden with big bosomed women rendered in washed-out Technicolor, lazing by pools, on fur rugs with a feather up their ass or pinching each other's nipples. Bikers and biker chicks are scattered throughout his work, riding roughshod. The suppressed Freudian fire is symbolically extinguished in Al's art; burnt out matches and singed cigarette papers and cigarettes gathered from gutters are assembled into fertility dolls. Beck's collages, in a similar vein, assay muscle men with ridiculous conflation of pectorals and biceps, as impotent in their own way as Al's bosom biker women, put upon and paraded around. Despite their physical attributes, they seem victims of forces they don't fully understand; they seem to have bought into systems that oppress them with double-edged rewards. Al's matchstick ziggurats, like phallic totems, are burned out at the tip of each match.

Beck's collages contain images of static travel, frozen aeroplanes in quadruple postcards, computers and archaic electrical diagrams, and a repeating motif of identity photos with burned edges. In Europe, where identity photos can be found discarded in subway passages and on streets, those blank eyes stare out like the china dolls behind glass. Who are those people? It's like finding photos of phantoms, lonely souls roaming the subways and preserving their non-images at photo kiosks for an identity that will never be realized.

Delving into the grimy roots of modernism, when Braque and Picasso were creating their first Cubist collages, art historians have affixed two perhaps arbitrary labels to Cubism's development. They signify the beginning stages as Analytical Cubism, geometrical forms in dull greys, like a Paris morning in February seen through a broken prism. Synthetic Cubism is categorized as Cubism's realization of what it had stumbled onto – namely being able to, as

161

Norman Mailer put it, approximate four dimensions into one. Using all sorts of shapes, stencilled lettering, collage paste-ups, and flash colours, it was the first step in the rapid acceleration of modern art, reflecting changes in society, industry and communications. But an attendant angst, fear and uncertainty nipped at the edges of the new art movement, a reflection of the impending war and catastrophe to come. It was no accident that when Picasso and Braque began to do their primeval cut-ups, they were peppered with shreds of newspaper streaming bits of static information into their paintings. One of Beck's collages is called *Vesuvius Jacuzzi* and is arranged radially around a burned photo, like the caldera of Vesuvius itself. Shredded poetry, bus tickets and crumpled postcards radiate outward, like an overhead view of the volcano.

For the Santa Monica opening of 'Playing With Matches', Beck worked out a loose programme for the exhibition together with his family, and chose to launch it with a bang. Beck's brother, Channing Hansen, a third-generation Fluxus artist, performed one of Al's most poignant pieces, 'Elegy for the Fluxus Dead'. 'The original performance consisted of reading a list of the Fluxus dead, then wrapping one's head in masking tape to the tune of "I Can't Help Falling In Love With You",' Channing explained. 'In my version I performed and recited the Elegy in a duet with a videotape of my grandfather in his last performance of it. To my grandfather's list I added his name.'[7] Channing's almost solemn and ritualistic elegy touched some and confused others, as was the intention. It was typical of Fluxus to commemorate while skewering the formality of commemoration.

For the opening of 'Playing With Matches' Beck and his bandmates chose to do a bit of their own performance art, and a piece that makes the best of Beck's essential humanity and humour. In their alter ego of the Dream Weavers, they had prepared a horrific inversion of every New Age cliché, entitled 'New Age Evisceration 1'. It was, according to Beck, 'a combination of Yanni and Tony Robbins, the longest twenty minutes of your life.'[8] With the audience seated in one of the Bergamot's galleries, the speakers rumbled with teeth-chatteringly low bass hum, escalating to the point of pain. The audience faced a mock-up of a garage complete with a basketball hoop. The garage door slowly began to open, revealing Beck and Roger Manning. Beck emerged in a George Clinton freak-out blonde wig, bellbottoms, a fake mustachio, and a hideous shirt. Roger Manning, dressed as a guru, played pompous arpeggios on the cursed Yamaha DX-7, tool of the most devilishly soulless licks ever perpetrated. Beck stepped up to a keyboard of his own and accompanied Manning with horrid synth trills. Between them stood a ten-foot-tall computer screen made of cardboard, with an algebraic equation daubed on it.

Beck and Manning continued playing super-sustained notes as the audience squirmed in discomfort; then, Justin stepped in tight velvet pants, a fake beard, and an Afro wig, playing bass. Beck was mumbling incantations through a vocoder: 'This is the eruption of your inner teenager'. Smokey and Joey came out playing bongos. Following that, Swamp and an unidentified miscreant emerged in horse masks, and began kicking the computer around. All of which was a prelude to the man in a dolphin costume with a giant penis strapped around his waist. Beck's voice rose in mock hysteria, as if the thirteenth prophecy of the Celestine Prophecy was imminent: 'Imagine naked dolphins... imagine dolphins, naked, fucking a computer!' And, indeed, the dolphin man proceeded to screw the computer with great solemnity. The New Age soul enema continued apace until Beck whipped out a chainsaw, which erupted in a thunderous coughing fit before roaring to life. He brought it down onto the synthesizer, echoing Nam June Paik's 'One For Violin', where he came out with a violin only to smash it to smithereens. Beck destroyed the synth, sending it shooting off its stand. Beck told *Village Voice* 'One of this year's personal high points was the debut of my band Dreamcatcher [aka Dream Weavers] at the opening of 'Playing With Matches'. I've been working on it for years. It's a motivational New

Age musical and visual experience. I prepared by meditating twenty-nine hours a day at least three days beforehand, and I shed my skin about five times to prepare myself to give the gift of wisdom. We had a dolphin healing ceremony, a six-foot dolphin come out with a four-foot penis, and after that I chainsawed a DX7 keyboard. I look at it as trying to get into the mind of the monster.'[9]

Next up was Channing Hansen gleefully overseeing the recreation of Al Hansen's famed 'Yoko Ono Piano Drop'. One can only wonder what the curators of the museum were thinking as a piano was hauled to the edge of the building and thrown off. Beck was awed at both the event and the reaction of the people present: 'I was really taken aback at how moving it was. First, there was this huge sound of the piano hitting the ground. There were four hundred people there, and as soon as the piano hit the ground they were swarming around it, ripping it apart, giving pieces to Channing to sign. And there were all these sounds of the hammers and the strings and the keys being ripped out of the piano. I wasn't expecting that at all. There was this sound of a piano being ripped apart and torn to shreds. It was like the piano shipwreck, and the audience became the wave pounding it onto the beach.'[10]

Yoko Ono said of Fluxus, 'I should point out that we never did anything that would have hurt someone. We didn't kill animals. With Fluxus, there might have been a hint of danger, but Al made sure no one was ever standing underneath the piano.' Beck agreed, 'That whole shock-value thing came later, in the Eighties.'[11] Which is why Fluxus still not only has relevance today but is probably more needed now than ever. It would be interesting to see new artists cast off the shackles of useless theorizing taught by embittered and jaded instructors and strike out on their own, using absurdity to level the playing ground between audience and artist. In so many ways, the audience is the performer, and the artist is a sideshow.

The last seditionary act in pop is to engage the audience to act or, even more revolutionary still, to create. When Jim Morrison of the Doors saw a performance of the Living Theatre in 1969, he was much taken by the way the performers shouted 'Why is it illegal for me to take off my clothes?' as they disrobed, got off the stage and into the crowd, shouting and baiting the audience to act and to think. His drunken approximation of that performance a few weeks later in Miami got him arrested, ostensibly for lewd behaviour, though taped performances of the show reveal Morrison's true motivation: 'How long are you going to let people tell you what to do?' he shouts. 'What are you going to do about it? WHAT ARE YOU GOING TO DO ABOUT IT?'

Too often artists insulate themselves in a cabal bound by incomprehensible codes which are designed to exclude, and which foster an air of cool ironic detachment. In music, the avant-garde's great failure is its inability to embrace rhythm. The works of Greek composer Yannis Xenakis are all very good and well, but without a pulse there is little on which to anchor any of his more arcane theorizing. If the avant-garde does not engage the hips, it becomes purely intellectual and thus will fail to engage the mind. Cynical artists tend to mesmerize with disgust, reflecting society or their patrons' own excesses. Is the artist a mirror, a refractor or a black hole? Or a locus for the audience's energy?

In ancient cultures, the shaman was proxy to the gods for the village – a channel, a refractor. Musicians or artists who merely produce for riches or amusement are upsetting a very empty apple cart. Art has now become self-serving and self-referential to the point where it cannot progress in leaps and bounds anymore; it has become as static as the bulk of popular culture, a mirror of the larger culture's dread and alienation.

If one of Fluxus's goals was to democratize art, then technology provided the means to realize the goal. Indeed, it is often the most alienating aspects of new technology that can spawn artistic innovations. Romanticism came about as a reaction to industrialization. The Internet, in turn, will spawn new motion – the accessibility of tools to the ordinary man will hasten motion, democratize it. This is the essence of Fluxus, not an $80 coffee table book commemorating things that took place in a gallery in Wiesbaden thirty-five years ago. If all art is destined for a coffee table, then God help us all. In a Fluxus broadside manifesto of 1965, George Maciunas wrote: 'Art-amusement must be simple, amusing, unpretentious, concerned with insignificances […] have no commodity or institutional value. The value of art-amusement must be lowered by making it unlimited, mass produced, obtainable by all and eventually produced by all.'

Every technological advance has spawned a subsequent revolution in art, whether it is the printing press spawning the Renaissance or the telephone and light bulb spawning modern art. The bomb, it could be argued, helped foster the impetus for Abstract Expressionism, an explosive rupture borne out of uncertainty. Is it safe to say modern art was a side effect of migration, war, technology, industrialization and, most importantly, communications? There are great parallels with Cubism today in schemes such as object-oriented programming for computers, building programmes with pre-arranged blocks, and the fuzzy logic of artificial intelligence, which seeks to accommodate the unexpected. Today the advent of digital video cameras, computer editing and music recording software is threatening to put the entire spectrum of art where it belongs, in the artist's hands. Artists can gain enough savvy to create, package, present and sell their own art, become their own distribution network, be their own gallery, become their own production company and record label. As these last twenty years of wealth polarization have taught us, the yuppie is often the middleman, one who sometimes possesses no creativity other than profiting from the ideas of others.

Artists have rarely been able to use commerce for their own ends; it has been their great failing. Indeed, they have often been unwilling to, but essentially that line of thought is a cop out. If there is to be any bohemian revolution it will have to be profitable, for its creators. Happenings are still valid, events that work as magnetic attractors for potentially creative people frozen in the guise of spectators. Al Hansen believed that right until the end, involving rather repelling people. That art historians find Hansen's happenings so hard to codify they'd rather bypass them entirely points up the fact he was working in a fertile area that defied conventional analysis. Too often analysis ends in paralysis; if ideas are not translated into action, they often remain static and never achieve flux. The best 20th-century art is a hymn to motion, to the clack of wheels on the rails, to aeroplanes, to the Internet. Funny that such hymns are often best sung on an old acoustic guitars and with rusty voices.

If anyone is Fluxus in the present tense it is Beck.

In the preface to his 1997 Tour Travelogue *Beck! 1997 Travels*, Beck writes: 'We vibrate, we reverberate, and we are Beck. We are not a club, a committee or a subsidiary. We are a miasmic enterprise; a time zone synchronized with dead oceans. Upon entering our area, you are no longer a visitor, nor a spectator. You are a participant in a crude experiment. Once fulfilled, this experiment cancels itself out, the only vestige left – these photographs. Let them warm you like the embers from a once noxious conflagration.'[12]

'Loser' was an instant classic because it fused the future with the past to create the present, unbeknownst to any of its creators. It remains undated when so much of the music of that era is already forgotten because it dwells in that high-friction zone between genres, between eras, races and generations but, much more importantly, because it is fantastic at parties because it brings the freaks out of the woodwork to dance.

Beck's collages, with their bright colours, relative lack of clutter and a certain evocation of Pop Art's ebullience, seem to parallel the works of graphic designers who have emerged in the late Nineties. Mike Mills, designer of superb album covers for Jon Spencer Blues Explosion, Air and Beck himself amongst others, uses sharp, bold pop colours, whimsical lettering and paper cut outs to fashion an aesthetic that perfectly parallels the music inside. And that aesthetic is oceans apart from the dismal static formalism of most of the Britpop crop's LP sleeves, or the opiated distance of grunge album covers. The only other artists who seem to offer album sleeve designs that conjure some excitement, some flash and edgy sharpness are the Japanese. Special note should be made here of the design on albums such as Cornelius' *Fantasma*, which evoke an era when covers were as sharp and bold as the music inside. Thurston Moore once commented on first getting the Beach Boys' 1966 *Pet Sounds* album and being struck by how weird and cool the cover was, only to find the music inside doubly cool and weird.

The album artwork favoured by contemporary bands such as Suede reflect a lazy aesthetic, with images of lissom wasted couples lolling absently on a bed – the outgrowth of the ethos of *The Face* magazine, with its monotonous revisionism of aesthetics, and of what ugliness is. For fifteen years these magazines have embraced ugliness, lauded it, slapped price tags on it, lauded it in the shape of junkie models or amateur wastrel clubbers – but they cannot transcend it, they cannot make it interesting or eye-catching. Such imagery aspires to be grim, urban and of the street but you would never see the B-boys in Ladbroke Grove embracing it. It smacks of middle class-vicarious thrills and infects everything from fashion to fine arts to graphic design.

Two bands whose sleeves have consistently attempted to break out of this malignant ugliness are Pulp and Beck, which take bad taste and fine art and mix them together seeking, perhaps, some transcendence from either. Tomato, the graphic designers behind album covers such as Underworld's *Second Toughest In The Infants*, have also begun working toward this new transcendentalist aesthetic, referencing Abstract Expressionism with Mark Rothko-esque or Franz Kline-like stark, bold slashes of paint, achieving a sharp and striking imagery, and one that is dynamic rather than oppressive. Tomato's book of images has a parallel with the photos collected in Beck's 1997 tour travelogue. Put together by Beck and Mark Leroy of Mark Designs, with Matthew Fontaine assisting, the 58-page book consists largely of designated Beck photographer Charlie Gross' images of flux. Beck with Willie Nelson down the coal chute on the 'Jack-Ass' video shoot; Beck and the band in Shakespearean gear at Stratford-Upon-Avon; Leigh Limon's shot of a monochromatic Beck amidst the explosive cartoon effigies in Tokyo's Ginza, and dozens of dynamic live shots of Beck's band cast in blurred hues of blue, pink, yellow. Images of hotels, taxis, cars, dressing rooms intimating the curious sensation of standing still in the middle of a tour's constant motion. Pictures of Beck, sniffling in damp Ginza rain, under neon lights that bleed red and blue. But Beck's face isn't a mask of dejection of blank dispiritedness, rather he gapes in numb wonderment, staring squarely at the viewer.

Pulp and Beck lead the pack, with the sleeves for 1998's *This Is Hardcore* and the 1999 'Sexx Laws' single respectively, this time tackling the tawdry world of sex, taking cues from the garish Seventies porn films that provides the *beau monde* with questionable soundtracks. And splattered hues of half-discarded clothing, synthetic and garish, but not desiccated in the way that the same reference points would be assayed in, say, *I-D* magazine. Both the 'Sexx Laws' single and the cover of *Midnite Vultures* are designed by Yamataka eYe of the Japanese band the Boredoms. EYe takes computer technology and abuses them skilfully to highlight their synthetic filters and tools, using them crudely to splash violent neon purple, green, reds and yellows that would have made the editors of 'street' pop culture/fashion mags in New York or London run retching to the lav. But the overall effect is playful, self-deprecating and again, parallels the shocking dynamism of the music contained within.

Beck has consistently worked with fringe artists, often musicians moonlighting as graphic designers, far outside of the corporate graphic design structure to get a loose continuity of album covers that reflect the transcendent collages contained inside. Eddie from the Silverlake band Sukia is the artist behind *Mellow Gold*'s nitrous inhaler, set against apocalyptic red skies by Robert Fisher, with photographs by fellow Sukian Ross Harris. *Mutations'* artwork was originally slated to be designed by Mike Mills but Beck and Fisher instead compiled a sequence of photos of artist Tim Hawkinson's work. A latex inflated man, Pneuman, floats on a string in the corner of a grey gallery, fading into a Balloon Self-Portrait. Inside, a severed fingertip pulsing with pencils for veins, and the pink tendrils and folds of the ambitiously titled Wall Chart of World History from Earliest Times to the Present.

Illustrator Jason Mason, from band Silverlake band Wisky Biscuit, made the drawing on the inside cover of the Australian 'Cold Brains' EP. It depicts two anonymous figures shaking hands tentatively, with thought bubbles over their heads reading 'I think what you think'. Significantly, they have no mouths with which to voice this sentiment, only eyes. This ties in what Beck has said about the unheard young, who haven't the words to express what they feel, the self-professed freaks whose ability to communicate with each other has been severely corroded by alienating drugs, saturation with media and endemic violence in societal and personal relationships. But the drawing ties in with an unspoken subtext in Beck's work, that amidst the current of joyfully perverse auto-eroticism and 'mourning of dead relationships' of *Mutations* is a new understanding that needn't shout to make itself understood. This is a thread that winds in a loop throughout Beck's work; it came through strongest on 'Pay No Mind', which never seemed like a defeatist's anthem, but rather represented a turning away from the clot of horror inflicted on one day by day, weakening the spirit, and casting one's eyes off to the horizon. Therein lies a certain romanticism in Beck's work, more elegiac than escapist. Another illustration on a *Midnite Vultures* 2000 Tour t-shirt has a group of people all jumping to their feet yelling, 'We are all individuals!', echoing the line from Monty Python's *Life of Brian*.

Beck is hardly the sum of his references or his influences, which is why he so loathe to state what they are. He denies the validity of electing 'favourites' on a hierarchical plane of importance, instead linking them to emotions or moments. Every moment predicates a favourite song. Every moment elicits a different feeling, a shifting point of perspective.

Beck's strength lies in his willingness to embrace what he doesn't understand, or what appals him. Whereas the Smashing Pumpkins donning Goth clobber or U2 awkwardly parodying European tourists gone to Miami seems contrived, Beck doesn't seem to be wearing a costume. The division between public persona and real life dissolves. That's Fluxus. This new dandyism where Beck inverts notions of tastefulness, stepping up in vinyl and corduroy, is an accompaniment to a corresponding surge in musical or artistic creativity. Inevitably, it reaches an extreme, often self-indulgent and a retreat to simplicity is warranted. In Beck's case his solid grounding in the simplicity of the folk blues gives him an ironclad point of reference, a base, like an old and familiar pair of jeans.

On 17 May Beck kicked off the first date of his latest tour with a by now traditional first show at the Galaxy Theatre in Santa Ana. Beck announced from the stage that the Galaxy was his 'favourite dinner theatre on the west coast'. Dim lights and the 550-person capacity made for the ideal setting for a Beck concert, intimate and electric. Beck ambled out in tight black pants and red shirt, with shaggy locks, as the band played 'Unit Is In Effect'. This was Roger Manning's first gig with the band, and he looked perfectly comfortable as Beck and the band debuted 'Tropicalia', 'Cold Brains' and 'Hotwax', with Smokey playing a *cavaquinho* guitar.

On 24 May, Beck and his crew were at Wigan in England to play at Haigh Hall with John

Martyn, DJ Shadow and the Verve. As the sun set over Haigh Hall, thousands of lager maddened lads descended to the edge of the stage, obnoxious and slurring hoarse terrace chants for their own amusement. So tightly packed to the front were they that people started fainting and had to be passed hand over hand out of the pit; a recipe for disaster. Master folkie John Martyn ambled out with an acoustic guitar and a percussionist, to be greeted with cries of 'YOU FAT BASTARD' and 'YOU'RE NOT SINGING NO MORE'. From the side of the stage Beck, with his wire rim glasses and pea coat, stood with Nick McCabe of the Verve, watching John Martyn struggle valiantly with sound problems and the hecklers, cheering him on. After Martyn vacated the stage, the set-up for Beck commenced, and the band, with new keyboardist Roger Manning took the stage, with the lilting chords of 'Unit Is In Effect' ringing across the field. A chic Beck in black PVC trousers, a black military-style jacket and tousled hair appeared to rousing cheers from the field. Beck pulled out all the stops, doing the splits over camera and microphone cables and body-popping like a loon during 'Novocane'. The crowd were going crazy and the paramedics and security men down the front had no respite.

Beck, sensing the havoc, stopped to talk to the audience, saying 'a few weeks back we found ourselves gigless, so we thank the Verve and we're very glad to be here'. As the audience finally calmed down Beck greeted Wigan and told the audience to 'cast their minds back to 1994' for 'Loser' in an Indian raga style, with ripples of feedback, followed by a superb 'Debra' on which he held the falsettos long and true. He laid 'Deadweight' and 'Diamond Bollocks' on the crowd, making special mention of Nigel Godrich when introducing the latter. Beck repeatedly pleaded with the crowd to back off so that the people at the front could avoid being crushed, receiving warm applause from those affected. An extra-long 'The New Pollution' brought proceedings to an end, with Beck brandishing a white plumed fan and a whip and apparently elated that, against unpromising odds, the music his band made and his own personality had pulled the crowd round. *NME* opined: 'it's not quite right that this glossy United States hipster should be in a field, for a start, and every old cultural stereotype is undermined when you realize that it's the American on speaking terms with irony and the British contingent who are utterly serious [...] Maybe it's the way his falsetto and feather fan dance send out signals that have even the butchest Gallagheralikes blushing and shivering. Tonight, everyone is Beck's special lady. And the strange thing is, no-one even thought he was their date.'[13]

After a spin through Spain and Portugal, summer brought Beck to Cleveland, Ohio, for the next leg of his tour, with openers Sean Lennon and Ben Folds Five. Justin was by now sporting green hair and Smokey looking like he'd stepped out of a James Elroy novel. At the beginning of the show, an enormous painted backdrop of the Grand Ole Opry's white plume feathers unfurled, and for the encore a backdrop of the Los Angeles airport tower was revealed. Beck sported his powder blue suit, accompanied by bright orange New Wave glasses. Ever a man to give his sartorial tastes full rein, he returned for the encore in a sleeveless zebra print T-shirt, exclaiming: 'Nobody gets out of here alive, 'cause tonight were going to party like its 1983, y'all!' Not that the other members of the band were backward in referencing that most bombastic of decades. For his solo spot, DJ Swamp riffed on Survivor's horrid bombastic 'Eye Of The Tiger', alongside the Troggs' 'Wild Thing', painstakingly but fluidly building a collage out of scratches and cross fader.

Live performance clearly lit a spark in Beck Hansen. He bounded onstage at Clarkston wearing a white suit, plaid striped shirt and white trousers. Brimming over with energy, he took out his binoculars and looked at the crowd through them: 'I'm seein' y'all, y'all me freaks! Thanks for coming out everybody, this is the biggest crowd we have ever played in front of, doin' it for 14,000 Detroit FREAKS!' 'Debra' featured more skyscraping falsettos; in fact, Beck managed to work them into virtually every song he played. For each successive performance of the song, Beck's histrionics would treble. He would teeter at the edge of the stage, crying his heart out over Jenny and Debra, throwing microphones and towels down like a Sloane Square debutante. He would storm offstage, heartbroken, drag himself back to sing a stanza or two, weep on Smokey's shoulder, and collapse on a speaker cabinet. The Brass Menagerie would play baleful trombone slides and trumpet as Beck hit piercing falsetto notes. At the end, Beck would croak into the microphone like Teddy Pendergrass, 'Don't worry about me, I'll be all right.' Come the encore, he was still giving it 100 per cent, telling the audience 'I'm about to kick some beats, which have never been kicked before, and drop some style that hasn't ever been dropped before. I wanna hear the biggest "Where It's At" in the annals of history, it's going to rock the nappies off babies and the humps off camels!' At the finale, Manning was delivering some truly epic Sun Ra riffs and Joey was raised up on a cord.

By June Beck was opening for the Dave Matthews Band in Toronto, Canada. As a new addition to the stage set, a two-tiered stage was erected complete with slides for boogaloo moves from one level to the next, which worked to full effect during 'The New Pollution', standing at the precipice, cracking his whip with abandon, fanning himself with a fan and then sliding down and doing the 'tighten up' during 'Where It's At'. Smokey and Showboat also would use the slide to slip down at the beginning of 'The New Pollution' and waxing the stage for Beck's famous 'tighten up' in 'Where It's At'. As had become his wont, Beck informed the crowd that if they could get up to 6.4 out of 10 in terms of total involvement, they had hit make out city.

After the 7 June show at New Jersey's Giant Stadium, hip-hop performer/producer Sean 'Puffy' Combs (a.k.a. Puff Daddy) appeared backstage and badgered Beck into honouring some half-promised offer to collaborate on a track. Beck, Puff Daddy and DJ Swamp drove into New York City, where they spent an entire night working on an impromptu track at a studio. It will most likely never be released, which is a shame because it would have been an interesting bridge between musical worlds, and more importantly, because it features classic Beck lines such as 'I'm gonna go insane for fifteen minutes, then I'm gonna be cool for the rest of the night' and the immortal, 'Like a fake I.D., I'm stepping like Chico DeBarge giving you a vocal lesson.' By Beck's account, a drum loop was made, tracked and rolled, and everyone was head nodding and Beck stepped up to the mike whereupon he laid down an impromptu soul stirrer about the ever-increasing price of his hormone injections. 'It wasn't even a song, it was a failed experiment,' he later revealed to *NME*. 'I was singing about how expensive my hormones were, and I just got the blankest look from him. In a diplomatic way, we were shown the door.'[14] The look of abject horror on Puff Daddy's face indicated that perhaps this wasn't to be a collaboration of historical note. By daybreak Beck was convinced the track was finished, and all Puff Daddy had to do was lay down his own vocal, but Puff decided not to. 'It didn't really work out, so it ended up on the Mary J. Blige record, and he took my vocals off.'[15]

At the Starlake Amphitheatre in Pittsburgh, the black curtain dropped, the band came out, with Showboat and Stagecoach coming down the ramps. Beck's acoustic section was almost always unscripted, with Beck playing whatever struck him as appropriate and meaningful for the moment. On the set-lists taped to the stage there were no songs written in for the acoustic slot. The electric sections were subject to whimsical change, and the band was getting tight enough so that they could cue each other into different songs. They had worked out the structure to the point where experimentation was fluid. Moving around 'Jack-Ass' and cutting 'Minus' on a whim. Beck snapped his whip during 'The New Pollution' like Jagger's 'scarred old slaver', a maniacal gleam in his eye. He did the New Jack swing thing on 'Debra' with an extended smooth talk about rainbow pasta. A certain licentiousness was creeping into the mix, with Beck humping speakers and things, only partly in parody. Beck's falsetto was rousing the crowd to screaming fits. Beck did cartwheels and splits, an intensely physical show. Khakis, a button-down shirt, and a navy blue jacket, later, a matching plaid three-piece suit. A short and perfunctory 'Thunderpeel' and 'Sissyneck' featured stinging harp playing amidst Kraftwerk jerky funkbot moves. Breaking into tears only to storm offstage and re-emerge on stage left to placate the crowd: 'it's all right. I'm going to be all right.' Before getting everyone to lose their collective nut over 'Where It's At', 'Loser' was given the full Brass Menagerie treatment, with Brown and Ralickie turning into a J.B.'s soul punctuation. 'Lord Only Knows' segued sharply into 'Sissyneck', which was given the Pussy Galore makeover. As soon as Beck began to hit falsetto heaven with 'Debra', a good deal of the rockers in the crowd turned on their heel and left, shaking their heads.

After Beck's Tibet 1998 appearance was cut short by bad weather, he took off for Mt. Fuji, Japan for the Fuji Fest. Returning home on 7 July, Beck went straight into recording his new album at his house in Pasadena. 'I tend to record in houses and do it cheaply, and don't owe anybody anything, so I don't have to make it sound like this or like that to make people happy,' he told *Rip It Up*. 'And I'm pretty possessive over the way it all sounds and comes out.'[16] Beck had outfitted two rooms with a modest but powerful arsenal of recording equipment, and with the help of various helpers, and with the Dust Brothers on site, he was ready to begin.

Meanwhile questions regarding the release of *Mutations* began to arise. In late 1997 Beck was stating in the press that the album would be released on Bong Load. Originally set for release on 9 September, the album was then pushed back first to 20 October, because of artwork changes and sundry tweaking. That was the official story; many suspected that it was a case of backroom wrangling. As late as August, both Tom Rothrock and Shauna O'Brien, who works with Beck's management team at Gold Mountain, were saying that *Mutations* would be released on Bong Load. Yet shortly thereafter, machinations of unknown sorts moved it over to DGC; Rothrock had admitted that on hearing that early mixes of the album, he realized that the quality of the music would tempt DGC to acquire the record for themselves. Beck dourly noted, 'Originally *Mutations* was just going to materialize. It was going to come out on Bong Load, and then come out on three hundred labels at a time because we anticipated the demand would be so large that we would need every record label in North America to put it out.'[17] On 3 November *Mutations* was finally released, on DGC. Bong Load retained its customary rights to the vinyl edition, but they appeared to have lost. Press releases stated that this was not the 'official' successor to *Odelay* but an interim project. To an outsider it might have seemed someone in the DGC marketing department got cold feet when they realized *Mutations* would not sell as well as *Odelay*. No publicity, tours or videos were planned.

169

1   Ferguson, Troy. 'Beck: Where He's At', *Rip It Up*, January 1998

2   *CDNow*, November 1998

3   *NME*, 27 February 1998

4   www.lawgirl.com

5   Goldberg, Michelle. 'Beck The Untouchable', Metro Active Music magazine, 1988

6   Dark, Jane. 'The Best Albums Of The 90s', *Spin*, November 1998

7   Mirkin, Steve. 'Old Pollution: Where It's Art Exhibit Shows That Beck's Love Of Pop Garbage Runs In The Family', *Rolling Stone*, 11 May 1988

8   Mirkin, Steve. 'Old Pollution: Where It's Art Exhibit Shows That Beck's Love Of Pop Garbage Runs In The Family', *Rolling Stone*, 11 May 1988

9 Morales, Ed. 'Looking Beckward', *Village Voice*, 15 September 1998

10 Morales, Ed. 'Looking Beckward', *Village Voice*, 15 September 1998

11 Smith, Ethan. 'Re: Fluxology – Beck And Yoko Ono Sound Off On Found Art, Family Ties, and Flying Pianos',
    New York magazine, 21 September 1998

12 *Beck! 1997 Travels*

13 *NME*, 26 May 1998

14 *NME*, 16 October 1999

15 'I Love The Smell Of Methane And Bananas In The Morning', *Mean* magazine, December 1999

16 Ferguson, Troy. 'Beck: Where He's At', *Rip It Up*, January 1998

17 *Mutant Machine*, unknown source, 1998

15

HANSEN: FINE ARTS & TOILETRIES

Before setting up an East Coast debut for the 'Playing With Matches' exhibition, Beck left for a family vacation in the Adirondacks with his mother and brother Channing. Beck had contacted Sonic Youth's Thurston Moore with the idea of playing at a happening to follow the exhibit opening at the Thread Waxing Space on 15 September, with a companion happening to be held at the Roxy that night in downtown New York City. Moore quickly made some calls and gathered Don Fleming of Dinosaur Jr. and Gumball, and Jim Dunbar, who had gotten together a similarly impromptu band for the *Velvet Goldmine* soundtrack.*

The happening was to have a different flavour than its West Coast predecessor, with Beck's brother Channing explaining the more open-ended structure of the event. 'If you ever really knew what was going to happen, it wouldn't be experimental theatre,' Channing said. 'I supply a skeleton structure for the piece, and it's the artists and other performers who have the instructions and put the meat on.' Beck concurred, 'In art, the mistakes, the accident is always much more of a turn-on. In life nothing ever turns out how you plan it.'[1]

The happening, 'directed' by Channing, was to feature Beck, his mother Bibbe, singer Marianne Faithful, Thurston Moore's one-off band and original Fluxartist Larry Miller and performance artist/musician Rebecca Moore, among others. Beck, along with his brother Channing and mother, attended a charity preview of the exhibit at the gallery, with the hipsters and downtown demimonde set straggling in their finery, all having paid $150 for the honour of attending the opening. Perhaps that was the most Fluxus aspect of the evening. The schmoozing and voracious consumption of hors d'oeuvres began, as the media jockeyed with each other to swarm on the golden boy. Beck, sounding hoarse and a bit tired, wearing skin-tight black and white, mingled and roamed like a mother hen, gamely answering the insistent newsmen's questions.

Beck paid tribute to Al, telling the press: 'Al really made beautiful things, out of things you wouldn't ordinarily think of as artistically valid, and he would infuse them with something beyond their limited possibility. Al validated experimenting with your environment, experimenting with sound, experimenting with an idea.'[2] Al was never as widely known in his native country as he had been in Europe; moreover, those who had heard of him frequently associated him with performances rather than with visual art. The exhibition was therefore

---

* *Velvet Goldmine*'s attempt to capture glam's synthetic camp failed on all counts save for its colourful visuals. An inversion of an inversion, the movie was hollow and dull, and a joke to anyone at all familiar with glam's electric subversions. In revisionism, it is easy to lose sight of the elements that fired the moment in the first place – the Piccadilly palare, the melding of Chuck Berry and Syd Barrett, Berlin cabaret, the midnight hustlers and Soho trade, the low-rent glitter queens trying to inject colourless lives with glamour, silver guitars and short, sharp licks. What David Bowie called 'Woolworth's trying to be Jean Genet.' All of which the film missed, choosing instead to focus on the most banal and sterile clichés, all done in that humourlessness so typical of the Nineties.

partly an attempt to redress the balance. Beck also mused on how his involvement in both music and art was an exception to the case: 'It's rare, and it shouldn't be. If we were all coming out of Italy, making both music and art wouldn't be strange, it would be very normal.'[3] America is oftentimes a culture of specialists, so much so that an American engineer can spend a lifetime without hearing an opera. Thinking across these divisions is almost anathema to American pursuits of wealth. It seems that the country's cultural impoverishment leads us to consume disposable products in lieu of anything that might confuse us or be ambiguous.

Beck's presence ensured the preview was a media event, and photographers and TV crews trolled around looking for sensation. Certainly none was to be found in the art, which many people regarded with fake curiosity. However, a collective gasp did go up as Gwyneth Paltrow, Liv Tyler, and Kate Moss emerged from the bathroom together, flashes twinkling on their sparkling faces as photographers crawled over each other to snap pics.

Adam Flaherty, a long-time Beck fan, was on hand as the day's events got underway: 'Thread Waxing Space was not what I expected, a huge stuffy room. The walls were covered in the fantastic art of Beck and Al, sculptures of the human body made out of cigarette butts, pictures of people and guns made out of Hershey's candy wrappers, amazing artwork. We [...] caught a glimpse of Vaginal Davis, a 250-pound black man with a wig on preaching about how (s)he loves everyone, and talking about penises [...] Beck [was] wearing a skin-tight blue-black-grey camouflage style shirt, [...] teeny little black tight pants, and grey high-top Vans [...] We walked by Bibbe who was doing an interview and went into the back part of the room where it was dark and they were showing a video compilation of the making of [the] "The New Pollution", "Jack-Ass", "Where It's At", and "Loser" videos and incorporating videos of Al playing an interesting game of checkers with a friend and Beck when he was about six years old [...] I walked around after and found a roll of wrapped-up toilet paper on the floor that Beck had because someone gave it to him during an interview as a joke. The sticker on it said: *HANSEN specializing in 20th century fine arts and toiletries*. Bibbe walked by me. I told her that I thought her show at the Roxy was going to be awesome. She said thanks, and joked that now it would probably suck because I told her that.

'We caught a cab over to the Roxy where there were lots of tables and all the tablecloths were Twister boards [...] people were passing around Fluxus-type cards that said to do things like "pass the card on to the person next to you and shake the hand of the person who gave this card to you" and "fold this card up as little as possible and hand it to the person next to you". There was this stoned guy fighting with a plant. He was hitting it and knocking it over and picking it up and punching it and turning it upside-down so all the dirt would fall out. It was funny. There was another guy walking around with a little plastic tape recorder whistling into it. When Vaginal Davis finally told everyone to take their seats – she was backstage and there was music playing – she started singing "I'm cuckoo for Caucasian cock" over and over.

'Vaginal Davis came out in a dress claiming she was from Germany-Africa, a new country, and she had a few volunteers who were from there as well. These were two seventeen-year-old guys and she got them up on stage and took their shoes off. She called their bare feet their shrimp and she poured maple syrup and maraschino cherries and whipped cream all over them and sucked it off their feet, it was weird. Then she sung a song called "Cherries in the Wind"'.

Moore's impromptu band Foot-in-Fluxus took the stage and opened with a caterwaul of stark noise, with Moore sliding his guitar strings against the amplifiers, while Don Fleming and Jim Dunbar accompanied on bass and drums and a male go-go performed valiantly in the face of its erratic rhythms.

Fluxartist Larry Miller brought out a ladder, climbed up and touched the ceiling and then came down and left the stage. For the next segment, J. Mascis of Dinosaur Jr. pulled out a chair and sat on it stage centre. Larry Miller walked from side to side telling Mascis what to say in small segments and Mascis would yell the segments at the top of his lungs. The crowd giggled. 'When Vaginal introduced Beck,' Flaherty noted, 'she said "This is my beautiful godson Beck Hansen, who has the longest white penis I have ever seen!" Beck thanked people for coming to his grandfather's tribute and talked for a minute about his grandfather and some weird video he made.' Beck's short impressionistic film, what he piquantly termed 'an electronic hard-on that we made today called *Over The Hill*', was projected across the ceiling as the guests moved in. Beck introduced Marianne Faithfull as 'one of my favourite voices', and she sang three songs in her unique voice, so ravaged by hard living it has acquired a patina of luminescence, not unlike Lotte Lenya's riveting performances in her husband Kurt Weill's *Threepenny Opera*.

Channing Hansen reprised Al's Elegy For The Fluxus Dead then everyone left the stage and people started leaving, except for Marilyn Manson's band showing up. Flaherty recalled, 'When the place was almost empty except for fifteen people, all the performers came out again and sprayed silly string everywhere and broke wine bottles into a little pile of shattered glass, they turned on these weird little plastic toys. Beck was under the keyboard with a microphone and a little plastic tape recorder laying on the stage on his back talking into it. Beck, looking a little partied-out, and now rocking a shiny red jacket and clutching at a bottle of champagne, screamed, "You'll learn to love me!", a very obscure quote from "Twig", a song on his Caspar and Mollüsk side project with Chris Ballew.'[4]

A review in the *New York Times* mildly criticized the happening for not breaking down the barrier between performer and audience. A valid criticism, perhaps, when compared to the terms laid down by Michael Kirby in his 1968 book *Happenings*: 'Happenings do not focus on an object, but on an event. The artist begins with a plan of action in which the public is brought into an active relationship with the art event. A happening is an eruption into daily space, organized at times and in places where no artistic production is expected [...] An improvisation that breaks the mental habits of the spectator.'[5] But if the happening wasn't in the true spirit of Fluxus, there could be little doubt that Beck, in his music, his art, his very personality, was Fluxus personified. And more importantly, like his grandfather before, was a fly in the ointment of Fluxus, anathema to its less salient exclusiveness and eventual stasis. In an interview with Pedro Gonçalves for *Blitz*, published on the day of release of *Mutations*, Beck embraces the idea of life as unpredictable and in constant flux with an enthusiasm that would have made his grandfather proud: 'Humanity is in mutation, in all aspects we are in mutation. It's obvious that things are in mutation since the universe was created, but the truth is that we live in a time where things change quickly [...] I want to live in my time, I don't want to live in 1945 [...] Mutation can be a negative word, but it is the concept that I am embracing.'[6]

173

The next day Beck was at a book signing for the *Playing With Matches* book at Rizzoli Bookstore. Stern admonishments were issued to the effect that Beck would sign nothing but copies of the book, although as it turned out, he proved willing to pose for photographs and sign whatever was put in front of him. Beck had set up a table with tarot cards, and would have people pick cards at random, frequently writing something relating to their choice along with his autograph. This personal touch endeared him to many present, especially his younger fans.

On 21 September Beck jammed with Sonic Youth's Thurston Moore, and Tom Surgal at the Cooler in New York City. Their composition was entitled 'Kill Any/All *Spin* Personnel', in reference to the infamous *Spin* magazine cover that Beck felt had made him look like a junkie. A tape of the performance was released on the tiny indie label 'freedom from...', which described the collaboration as 'hate/power electronics at their worst.'

On 10 October in San Jose, California, Beck and his band made an appearance at a private benefit party for something called Silicon Planet. Silicon Planet's own website touted the event as 'A High Tech-Meets-Hollywood Trend Show.' How exactly Beck got roped into playing this event is uncertain. Opening with 'Loser', Beck stepped to the stage at the old FMC Defence Factory, basically an old aeroplane hanger, cavernous and filled with computer executives in suits networking and pulling cell phones and filofaxes on each other, paying little attention to the music. Beck chose to première his new album's songs to an oblivious crew of engineers and computer programmers. It was a typically perverse way for Beck to promote *Mutations*, something he seemed to have been corralled into doing. Doubly perverse was his decision to only play 'Tropicalia', instead of debuting the new songs from his next 'official' album which were already worked out, including 'Let the Doctor Rock You', 'Debra' and 'Jockin' My Mercedes'(a.k.a. 'Hollywood Freaks').

Beck's childhood heroes Devo opened and whipped out forty-five minutes of 'Whip It' and 'Mongoloid' wearing their trademark yellow jumpsuits and red planter hats. Beck, in turn, wearing black vinyl pants and a denim jacket decorated with tiger patches, shouted, 'Computer people! I am going to take you all the way round the world tonight!' The private fund-raiser for AIDS research was $100 a ticket, and the free drinks flowed like honey from a broken crock. Despite the formidable distractions of Microsoft multimedia demonstration booths and an over-forties cover band doing Creedence Clearwater Revival songs, this was a significant night: the night irony died. Playing to such an indifferent crowd made it all the more easy to finally jettison all the postmodernist ironical pastiche'n'parody tags Beck had been saddled with in the past. Now the emphasis was on his new electro funk. 'I don't feel ironic at all', he told *Ray Gun* magazine in January 1999. 'I'm dead serious about what I do. If I jump up and down and do the splits, I'm feeling that, you know?'[7]

Beck's engineer on the new album, Tony Hoffer, subbed for Smokey, off on tour with Sean Lennon. The entire eight-piece band, including the Brass Menagerie, highlighting the absurdity of the evening, were dressed in most ridiculous attire, with DJ Swamp in a peaked witches cap and Hoffer wearing a cliché Adidas and Kangol cap, evoking the old skool hip-hop style. The band stuck in a snippet of Van Halen's 'Hot For Teacher' at the end of 'Sissyneck'. For an encore, Beck covered Eddy Grant's 'Electric Avenue'.

On 3 November 1998, *Mutations* was released to critical accolades matched by its high placing on the pop charts (U.S. number 13; U.K. number 24); it went gold one month after its release in the States. If anything, this proved that Beck's artistic aims were resonating in the popular culture. Well marinated and then cooked on a hot charcoal brazier, *Mutations* is assuredly Beck's most palatable album. And this in no way diminishes its flavour. Spiced with the talents of many fine musical minds, it is lightly charred on the outside, pink and juicy in the middle. 'Diamond Bollocks' is like an after dinner liqueur with forty different ingredients, potent and enervating after such a delectable main course. 'You've got to leave space for the song to breathe. I tend to record a song with instruments playing all the way through in every track, and then at the end of the day, it's a matter of subtracting – taking things away and opening up the space. That's why you only hear it in bits and pieces. It's tastier that way.'[8]

Discussing the album in the press after its release, Beck raised the point that it is no longer possible to cut oneself off from pan-global cultural influences at this point in time: '*Mutations* embraces where I come from musically and it embraces the impurity of who we are culturally at the end of the century. We live in a world where so many different kinds of music and ideas have invaded parts of our consciousness, so there's no way to achieve purity because everything's gonna come out in the music in one way or another.' When the inherently fascistic implications of 'purity' are considered, then 'impurity' seems to be a very good thing indeed. Beck's rejection of any form of musical limitation, categories or genres, makes him the perfect pop star for the *fin de siècle*: 'I just think that because there's so much music out there right now, the music scene has become really dense and chaotic. And to deal with the chaos, we categorize the music to make it easier to deal with. But music has never been about fitting in certain boundaries; it's always been mutating.'

'Tropicalia' was the first single released from the album. The European version of the single contained 'Halo of Gold', a cover of a song by the late Alexander 'Skip' Spence, a man plagued by madness and blessed with a devastating ear for melodic invention. The track also appeared on *More Oar: A Tribute To The Alexander 'Skip' Spence* which was released after Spence's death, though he got to hear final mixes of it on his death bed. *Oar*, Spence's only solo album after his troubled tenure in Moby Grape, has that peculiar feeling of addressing events in the indeterminate distance, a space-folk odyssey on three channels. The new remix on Sundazed, which brings *Oar* closer to Earth and gets those three tracks humming, gives an earthy warmth to the songs. Beck's cover of 'Halo of Gold' is extraordinary, capturing the evanescent melody buried in the original, as if he had put himself with Spence in the mental hospital at Bellevue, as he dreamt up his songs in his head, with no paper to write and with no guitar. It is a multi-part piece, with three distinct sections, tempo and key changes galore – radical stuff indeed for pop music of the 1990s. Beck gets some death metal pedal guitar in, harmonies galore, synth pop lines and a shimmering pedal steel guitar lick wrapping up a Johnny Cash quote. Manning's synthetic harpsichord opens the track, later, a vocoded break closer to krautrockers Faust than any of Beck's contemporaries, with a firm Tropicalia *batucada* underlayer.

Even a throwaway like the instrumental 'Black Balloon', the third track on the 'Tropicalia' CD single, is clever and exceptionally melodic. Which points up the fact that this band has a way with melody that is almost immoral.

In Australia and Japan 'Cold Brains' was issued as a single, with two tracks tucked away that are two of the best songs Beck has ever penned. These songs were the first flourishing of an entirely new phase in Beck's career, one hinted at by 'Tropicalia' and 'Diamond Bollocks'. With the mixing and engineering team of Mickey P(etralia) and Tony Hoffer, that would accompany Beck through the recording of *Midnite Vultures*, these two songs are some of the most emotive and expertly recorded work in his catalogue.

'One Of These Days' features just Beck, Meldal-Johnsen and Manning, and takes inspiration from Brian Wilson and the Beach Boys' *Pet Sounds*, tempered with a disarming vocal mixed to the fore. Beck and the others harmonize exquisitely, just avoiding the feyness with which modern bands try and fail to capture a Beach Boys flavour. Other highlights of the track include the great Leslie organ blips and pseudo-Theremin synth lines, with compressed drums beating at a slow tempo. Underneath the surface, Beck does a great job of catching the sometimes fearful undercurrent that pervades all of Brian Wilson's best work. At the tail end of the song, the chords get really sickly, taking a turn toward the atonal. Very interesting and daring of Beck and the band to play with songs like that. The song has a sparkling clarity, with first-rate engineering and mixing that create a great implied spaciousness that is one of the most beautiful aspects of the recordings of pianist and composer Martin Denny.

One of Beck's finest songs, 'Diamond In The Sleaze' features Beck leaning heavily on the tremolo bar for some of his finest playing ever, with twanging Ennio Morricone-meets-Duane Eddy lines. This song also marks the full fruition of the brilliance of sideman Roger Manning.

175

Manning plays the loosest jazz drums heard in any indie song since, oh, say Tortoise's exquisite album *TNT*. Manning has a fluid rolling touch with percussion, reminiscent of Tony Williams playing on Miles Davis' epochal 1968 album *In A Silent Way*. Justin punctuates the low end with tasteful bass, a dab here and there, never too much, and with a warm subsonic punch. It's his most understated and refined bass line bar none, offering a kind of counterpoint to the melody that is so rare in today's music. The lyric, a lament almost French in its emotional openness, feels as direct in its directness as 'Lemonade', that other deep look inside Beck's inner frictions. These two songs are rare in their emotional openness; whereas Beck often sabotages his most emotional songs with noise or deadpan vocals, these reflect not only maturity but also a stylistic leap forward. In a line from the song, Beck sings of 'the doctor' whose patients prove resistant to his cures. The doctor, like the self-mocking jackass, is one of Beck's alter egos, a shaman-like figure who provides a vital service that is often misunderstood or unappreciated.

Probably the strangest Beck contribution ever came in the form of a guest mumble on the *Rugrats* soundtrack, also released on 3 November. The track, 'This World Is Something New To Me' features an astonishing cast of Beck, Jakob Dylan, Patti Smith, Iggy Pop, A Tribe Called Quest's Phife, Lisa Loeb, B-52s, Laurie Anderson, Violent Femmes' Gordon Gano, Lou Rawls, Cypress Hill's B-Real, Lenny Kravitz and En Vogue's Dawn Robinson. Too bad it was totally insignificant; Beck mumbles two quite appropriate lines, "I'm irritated" and "Can somebody turn down the light?" The soundtrack coordinator was Mark Mothersbaugh of Devo, who must have been owed a lot of favours.

On 8 November, Beck and the band appeared on U.S. radio's 'Modern Rock Live' to play a selection of tracks from *Mutations*. Between songs Beck did something rare for him; he became annoyed. It was prompted by a caller asking him what his favourite book was. 'I don't have favourites,' Beck replied, curtly. With the host running interference, Beck avoided answering any of the stupid questions, and even the smart ones, unable or unwilling to commit himself. He sounded put upon, dragging through a promo tour that wasn't even supposed to be, and only became animated when sticking to the music. Moreover, he was a bit alarmed at how careerist the kids' questions were, with fifteen-year-olds asking him 'at what point in your career did you...?', as if it was a trajectory he had sat and planned out one night.

Beck played his fifth session for 'Morning Becomes Eclectic' on 24 November. Along with Smokey Hormel, Justin Meldal-Johnsen, Joey Waronker, Roger Manning, David Brown, and David Ralickie, he performed 'Cold Brains', 'Bottle Of Blues', 'O Maria', 'Sing It Again', 'Nobody's Fault But My Own', 'Dead Melodies', 'Tropicalia', and an impromptu 'Debra'. 'Tropicalia' was prefaced with an explanation that it was not a Tropicalia style song but a bossa nova which, he pointed out, 'Would be like calling a power ballad New Jack Swing'. A super extended jam at the end of 'Debra' had Beck segue into 'Hollywood Freaks', rapping about Norman Schwarzkopf in a Snoop Doggy Dog style, with Roger Manning churning out impressive sparkling keyboard riffs evoking Grandmaster Flash's 'The Message'.

After a three-date tour of radio station sponsored shows in Chicago, Minneapolis, on 20 December Beck played in Detroit, for radio station 98X's 'The Night 98X Stole Christmas'. A more apt title for the multi-band show would have been 'the grinch alterna-fans who stole Christmas'. Headliner Beck came on last, opening with 'Loser'. A riotous crowd booed him mercilessly and hollered abuse. By the time the band began 'Mixed Bizness' the chairs on the ground floor level were torn out and thrown at the stage. Nothing, not even 'The Little Drum Machine Boy', nor an exceptionally valiant and soulful 'Debra' could warm these alternative fans' cold hearts. The band played 'Sexx Laws' for the ingrates, but to no avail, and closed with a perfunctory 'Where It's At' with very low audience call and response action. There was no encore. For a man who naturally embraced so many of Fluxus' principles, and who only got off on stage when he felt the audience were involved in the gig heart and soul, the gig must have been a sore disappointment indeed: 'When I come to a show, the show isn't about me, it's about everybody who is there. If the people aren't there, then the show isn't happening. I've always thought of my career as somewhat of a collaboration.'[10]

1 Morales, Ed. 'Looking Beckward', *Village Voice*, 15 September 1998
2 'Beck Honours His Grandfather's Fluxus Work', MTV, 17 September 1998
3 Smith, Ethan. 'Re: Fluxology – Beck And Yoko Ono Sound Off On Found Art, Family Ties, And Flying Pianos', *New York* magazine, 21 September 1998
4 Flaherty, Adam. Beck-Odelay@worldnet.att.net – http://members.tripod.com/~Beck Mellowgold
5 Kirby, Michael. *Happenings*, E.P. Dutton & Co., 1968
6 Gonçalves, Pedro. *Blitz*, 3 November 1998
7 Gladstone, Eric. 'Musical Mutations', *Ray Gun* magazine, January 1999
8 Siegel, Robert and Wertheimer, Linda. 'All Things Considered', National Public Radio, 1998
9 Wiederhorn, Jon. 'The Many Faces of Beck', *Guitar*, January 1999
10 Kot, Greg. 'Beck's Back', *Chicago Tribune*, 6 November 1998

16

LET THE DOCTOR ROCK YOU

I like to freak it and party, and I like to just disappear out of
the scene regularly too, drop back in after a year or two and
challenge all the quick draw cats and chicks who've been
building up a rep.
Al Hansen, letter to Kristine Stiles, 1980

In February 1999, Beck presented an award to Neil Young and wife Pegi for Young's work with Farm Aid and The Bridge School Benefit concerts. 'Pegi and Neil are amazing people', Beck commented, 'and I'm honoured to be presenting this award, and I just wanna say how important his music is and the world that he's created. It's made a big impact on myself and a lot of people I know.' It was a rare direct acknowledgment of one of his icons. 'Young and his crew [...] are so open. You'd think at the point they're at, how long they've been doing it, they wouldn't have the time of day for the opening band, and it's totally not the case. They completely embrace you. It's inspiring, if anything, that you can do it that long and still be interested.'[1]

In *Rolling Stone* magazine's annual music awards, Beck won Best Male Artist, and 4th Best Album of the Year. Not that *Rolling Stone* has any worth whatsoever. MTV and *Rolling Stone* are the voice of corporate music, assembly line sameness and blandness. In America the boringness of *Rolling Stone* is mirrored by the dogmatic and equally bland extreme of niche magazines like *Flipside* and *Maximum Rock and Roll*, in many ways as conservative in their vapid orthodoxy as *Rolling Stone* is in perpetuating stagnation. In Britain, this stasis is paralleled by *NME*'s bland cynicism and the *Melody Maker*'s often touching if misguided championing of deadbeat bands. In the British music rags, bands are hyped to unrealistic heights only to be demolished within weeks, whereas in American music mags bands are applauded for their mediocrity and encouraged to stay there. Both strategies have stalled so many promising bands from developing a second act to their careers.

On 9 January on *Saturday Night Live* Beck performed 'Nobody's Fault But My Own' and a ragged 'Tropicalia' with a Beefheart fanfare, horns and guitars tangling. The next night was a classic Beck concert at Town Hall on West 43rd Street, in New York City.

Luna opened with their dream pop, and roadies stood wondering what to do with the little harpsichord, which resisted all efforts to be tuned. After great deliberation the offending instrument was hauled off. Beck's band opened with a lovely 'Cold Brains'. 'Bottle Of Blues' was a bit of a fumble, starting unevenly, but soon the band was well into it. For 'Sing It Again' Beck paused, scratched his chin, and asked the band, 'Uh, what key is this song in?' Audience member Chris Reis shouted 'A!' and laughter rippled around the room. Smokey stepped out with a long and luscious solo, taking it back to the Texas twang of Bob Wills and the Texas Playboys. On 'O Maria' Beck sang with *Odelay* too-much-touring hoarseness, without detracting an iota from the feel of the song, rather adding to its Dr John-laced languor. Smokey Hormel unpeeled a shimmering solo on a 12-string guitar. Beck and the band did a waltz time rendition of 'We Live Again' evoking the country dance halls of old. The mirror ball sent light spinning into silver shards, cascading in ellipses round the Town Hall.

After performing every track off *Mutations* bar 'Diamond Bollocks' at the gig, the band bid the album adieu. Beck returned to California to continue work on his new album, which he'd had firm ideas about for some time. 'If anything, the instrumentation is very dumb. It's going back to an older hip-hop where it was really primitive. An old drum machine, a bass line, one or two really bad-sounding samples. We're going to have songs on the new record that match the energy of what we're doing live [...] Somebody will come up with some designated phrase of what it is. But, it's peppy, enjoyable music for all ages.'[2]

The first week of February, both rapper Kool Keith and electro folkist Beth Orton came by Beck's home studio in Pasadena to record vocals for new Beck songs. Keith, a rapper with impeccable credentials dating back to his tenure in the mid Eighties with old skool rap act Ultramagnetic M.C.'s, had become one of hip-hop's most unpredictable and sporadically brilliant MC's. His alter egos of Dr Octagon, Dr Dooom and Black Elvis spouted untrammelled rhymes with imagery and language twists not unlike Beck's own. 'I liked working with Beck because it wasn't a conceptual market scam,' Keith revealed. 'I went up to his house and he had the same types of thing I might have listened to, weird people that you wouldn't expect he would have in his CD case. [...] We could do a record called "Aluminium Foil" and he's laughing and he's with it all the way. He's running with the idea also. '"Aluminium Foil?" Hey, fuck it, let's just call it 'Aluminium Foil.'" He had no boundaries. We have no musical limitations.'[3] Beck was equally enthusiastic: 'When we hooked up, we immediately wrote three songs together. We were completely on the same wavelength. Whatever our musical planets, we're definitely on the same orbit.'[4]

Though Beck ultimately chose to reserve his collaborations with Kool Keith for the follow-up to *Midnite Vultures*, seeing it perhaps as pointing the way to future direction, the collaboration was a success and fulfilled Beck's long standing hope of connecting directly with hip-hop. Hip-hop's more experimental minds had responded to *Odelay*, and respect was beginning to filter through. Prince Paul, one of the finest minds at work in hip-hop, experimental since his days with Stetsasonic and De La Soul, told *Index* magazine, 'Beck is really ill; it's the production. A lot of hip-hop is just one loop that goes through the entire record with a hook, while Beck's production is so intricate.'[5]

Beth Orton, a friend of Steve Hanft's, had found herself very ill with Crohn's Disease, and on Beck's recommendation had travelled to Los Angeles to visit his doctor. Orton's two albums on Heavenly are one of the few to live up to that label's name. Her 1996 album *Trailer Park* was an unexpected revelation, with 'She Cries Your Name''s spiralling Hindustani strings in counterpoint to her plucked acoustic and powerful, unusual voice shaded with the ravishing tonalities of traditional British Isles folk music. 1998's *Central Reservation* saw Orton bring the brilliant arranger Robert Kirby, who had scored two of Nick Drake's albums, out of semi-retirement, to help craft an excellent album full of inspired melodic touches. Orton displayed a sensibility in line with Beck's own when she told the *Observer*, '*Central Reservation* is a very un-ironic album, very straightforward, very honest and open. That in itself was hard. Someone once said to me, "The more embarrassed you feel making your record, the more painful it is, the more you know you're on the right track."'[6]

At Los Angeles club Largo in West Hollywood, on 5 February, multi-instrumentalist and talented arranger Jon Brion's series of shows had some special guests. Beck joined Beth Orton for an hour-long jam session, with Brion drumming. They took requests, bantered with the

179

audience and played a cross section of each other's material, Beck joking 'My songs are all elbows, but your songs are soft cheeks.' Elbows or not, Beck's new song 'Beautiful Way' with harmonies by Orton was enough to raise shivers in the audience. The pair had tried to work on songs two days previously, but Orton's poor health meant that she couldn't put herself under too much strain.

Beck headlined a post-Academy Awards show on 21 March at the House of Blues. He was introduced by Patricia Arquette and played 'Electric Avenue' with a rapid flash segue into 'Loser'. After a cursory overlook of the material they toured *Odelay* with, Beck launched into a glass-shaking 'Debra', testifying and growling like Curtis Mayfield, before playing a track off the new album, 'Hollywood Freaks', followed by an incandescent 'Tropicalia'. The band reprised 'Electric Avenue' before making their exit. But this was just moonlighting from the work at hand, which involved strenuous beat sequencing. Largely forsaking the samples that had provided *Odelay* with part of its structure, the new album was created out of infinitesimal beats sequenced into a whole. Often Beck and Hoffer and Petralia would sample Smokey or Justin and then fragment their playing into small bits that were reassembled in varying order. The technique was in line with concurrent hip-hop and R&B production, which was worlds away from Herc's turntables. With feverish work by Tony Hoffer, Mickey P and Beck, cutting and splicing beats with the patience of bonsai gardeners, work continued on the new album deep into the night for weeks at a stretch. The new album was due for a spring 1999 release, but the sheer work and the legal manoeuvring in the background were threatening to push the release back. Of the recording process, Beck said, 'The first couple months were a blast, I had more fun than I had ever had, and then the last ten have been like paddling across the Atlantic in a canoe with two holes in it. It's like that cliché of one per cent inspiration, ninety-nine per cent sweat, but this was sweat, blood, gristle, manure, foliage and aerosol.'[7]

During a break, Beck split for Japan for an eight-date stand starting on 11 April at Tokyo's Shibuya Kokaido. On a pit stop on his return from Nippon, Beck played on 24 April in Honolulu, Hawaii. Emma Yuen reported, 'Beck was wearing a black tight shirt with gold fringe on the arms and a golden safety pin on the front, and frayed cut apart pinstriped pants for the first half of the performance. The second half, he came out all in pink, with a fairy cape on. The tight pink shirt he had on also had fringe.' A certain pandrogyny had taken hold, which had been building since the tour the year before. Call it Californian glam, but Beck's style involved a fusion of organic and synthetic, with corduroy and vinyl, as if Jackson Browne had suddenly gotten hold of a New York Dolls album in the mid-Seventies and somehow gotten it all wrong.

Yuen wrote, 'Beck's robot moves were so perfect, and he jumped, did splits, and showed off his biceps, joking "they're going to explode, or implode." He was being weird, and attached the bottom of the microphone stand to his scrawny little butt and made farting noises in it between songs. The head of the microphone was in some other guy's crotch, but I'm not really sure what that was supposed to symbolize. After "Debra" and throwing a water bottle hard on the stage like a baby, and singing higher than I could, he stormed out, and Justin sneakily said "This is a little project we've been working on. You guys like reggae?" The band launched into Musical Youth's 1983 lite-reggae hit "Pass the Dutchie". Beck storms back out, and yells, "What the hell are you doing! Are you trying to scare them away?"'[8]

Meanwhile, DGC's parent company, Universal Music Group, had bought out PolyGram, A&M and Interscope, and a huge reshuffle was shaking the organization. Unfortunately, Beck and his management had been attempting a renegotiation of his contract since May 1998, but talks had stalled as the new executives proved to be perhaps less receptive than the previous crew had been. Beck's attorney, Jill Berliner, commented that a new deal is 'not getting made because people who historically are very, very good at their jobs are not free to do their jobs. They could have had a new contract with him instead of a lawsuit if they had closed the deal.'⁹

It seemed every empathetic contact Beck had in the company's sparkling headquarters was packing his or her belongings into boxes after being summarily dismissed. Both chairman/CEO Ed Rosenblatt and president Bill Bennett were ousted. Beck and his management company GAS had opted to wait for the PolyGram acquisition to go through before resuming their push for better terms in January 1999. But progress eluded them and, frustrated, Beck invoked a California labour statute limiting the duration of personal services contracts to seven years as a last-ditch attempt to break the deadlock. Beck informed both Bong Load and DGC that he would no longer render his personal services as of 23 April 1999, under the loophole provided by section 2855 of the California Labour Code.

Both Geffen and Bong Load promptly filed separate motions in a California Superior Court on 26 April against Beck for breach of contract, and seeking that their respective contracts with Beck remain binding, with damages to boot. Bong Load also claimed that Beck had breached a production agreement, and announced that they would be suing for non-delivery of recordings; Jill Berliner announced that Beck intended to file a counter suit. Bong Load and Beck were required to provide masters for three albums to Geffen, which had two options for the delivery of four additional albums. According to the Bong Load suit, the deadline for Geffen to exercise its first option has not yet come due. But Berliner countered that Bong Load was 'ignoring the fact that Beck worked for a good year and a half for Bong Load before he had a contract.'¹⁰

Beck's counter suit was promptly filed two weeks later in a U.S. District Court in Los Angeles, with Beck claiming that Geffen Records improperly wrested control of his most recent album, *Mutations*, from Bong Load. He also claimed that Geffen had not paid him an advance or any royalties for over 430,000 copies of the album which had been sold in the States. It now appeared that *Mutations* had been recorded to fulfil Beck's obligation to Bong Load. He was now seeking $500,000 damages from Bong Load, and wanted to be released from his contract.

On 2 May Beck was at the Dusties' house working out a song with a Latin flavour. 'I'll write the chorus and then we'll build it. We'll usually get about ten melodies, and they'll battle it out for an hour,' he murmured, subdued but intensely focussed. This record was to be the first where Beck had complete creative control: 'I took complete responsibility for every aspect, through to the final mastering and packaging.'¹¹ He sat on the balcony, overlooking Silverlake, in the midst of lush foliage and potted plants, plucking out a mesmerizing bossa nova lick over a computerized beat. Mike Simpson cued up vinyl for some samples. In a distracted moment as Simpson prepared the track for playback, Beck laid out an inspired variation on the riff he had been playing.

The next week the full band was jamming at Beck's house doing a great Booker T style R&B workout, and enthusing about vintage pedals. 'Anything with wood on it, sounds good,' Beck said, commiserating with the lads. Manning jammed out on a Fender Rhodes, with Justin thumping his bass, and DJ Swamp squeaking out scratches. Later Beck and his mates listened to an incredible Uri Geller album, with the famous conjurer intoning over a backdrop of the 101 Strings Symphonia, comically trying to use his will to bend a very unbending spoon.

On 6 May, Beck and the band appeared at the Tropicana Resort and Casino in Las Vegas. Beck pals Tenacious D, a comedic duo armed with acoustic guitars and ribald balladry were the opening act. That the decadent glamour of this new phase in Beck's trajectory was bound by inextricable peals of laughter was compounded by the surroundings, the Tiffany Theatre, a Vegas lounge where the *Best Of The Follies Bergere: Sexier Than Ever* was performed during the week. But the red fleck wallpaper and cut glass chandeliers aside, this was still a theatre, the best venue

181

to see Beck perform in. Theatres work best for Beck; where he achieves the right blend of intimacy and distance with the audience, free to use the empty spaces to mesmerize and the warm acoustics to add vibrancy to the music.

Beck took the stage demanding 'Where's my freaks at?' A thousand fans sat at tables better suited for bingo than rock shows. 'We're just tryin' to adjust ourselves here,' said Beck, relishing the absurdity of the locale. 'We're not used to people sittin' down. Usually Visigoths are gnawing on each other's thighs out there. Blood is flowing. We have to hose ourselves down afterward.'[12] Resplendent in black with hideous white fringe sewn into his shirt sleeves, Beck did lascivious bumps and grinds to 'Novacane', 'Beercan', 'Tropicalia' (Beck thoughtfully dedicating it to the Tropicana, with, 'That's two Trops for the price of one') and 'Hotwax'.

'People are gonna look at all this fringe and say we've gone Vegas,' he told the crowd, 'but we're like this all the time.' During the increasingly briefer acoustic set, Beck seemed adrift, missing cues, his mind already fast at work extrapolating the next fusion. A highlight was Smokey's absolutely entrancing guitar solo on 'Sing It Again'; he drew his own ovation on it. Beck, somewhat subdued himself, momentarily forgot about the harmonica solo section of the song.

Beck bragged shamelessly of his 'seven-octave range' before doing a full Vegas rendition of 'Debra', working the Tom Jones school of macho baladeering to its fullest. The band stretched out with jazz sevenths and ninths, working the changes like Django Reinhardt. At the end Beck, disconsolate, stormed off the stage into the wings.

Justin reprised the vaudevillian 'Pass The Dutchie' schtick, telling the audience: 'that number usually wipes Beck out, but we'd like to introduce ourselves. We're the backing band; we call ourselves Rainbow Warrior. You guys like reggae?' Smokey, alarmed, stage whispered, 'No, no man, that's not cool.' Justin shrugged it off with, 'Oh it's okay, man, he's gonna be gone for awhile', whereupon Beck's head popped out from the wings and he lambasted his band roundly for their behaviour: 'People have come from far and wide, on trains, planes, and bicycles, and here you are playing THIS shit?' After a run through 'Minus', the band finished with 'Electric Avenue'. Beck, now wearing a pink jumpsuit, did the funky worm on-stage before turning over and flipping himself up to his feet; 'We're kicking it Tropicana-style', he cheerfully informed those in the audience.

For the encore the band re-emerged in huge wigs, cowboy hats and purple capes; Justin had found himself a singularly hideous outfit consisting of a neon orange tank top and crimson vinyl pants set off by a pair of handcuffs clipped to his belt. Beck was the last on, with his seaweed green satin shirt and pink pants. What could all this mean? Beck shouted to his band, 'What else am I gonna do?' 'You're gonna bust some beats that you've never busted before!' the band replied. With maniacal fervour, he asked again, 'What else am I gonna do?' The band came right back with, 'You're gonna rock some freaks that you've never rocked before.' And then it was off to 'Make-Out City' for a supreme 'Where It's At' with every last bit of irony plucked from the chandeliers overhead to make the girls (and boys) scream.

On 8 and 9 May, Beck did a two-night stand at the Wiltern Theatre in Los Angeles. The excellence of these two shows, their sheer unbridled brilliance, indicated that Beck was approaching his goal of transcending irony, just in time for the rapidly approaching end of a century full of it. An enormous backdrop of the Grand Canyon and subdued swirling lighting set the scene. Beck, Smokey, DJ Swamp, Justin, Roger were joined by two string players, who played viola and violin, or joined Smokey on sitar and essraj. Supremely intimate, Beck played the hometown crowd for all it was worth, fleshing out every nuance with commendable subtlety. Perhaps the definitive live versions of 'Nobody's Fault But My Own' and 'Debra' were performed at these shows. The band emerged in full Spinal Tap regalia for an encore of 'Jack-Ass' and 'Debra', which was extended to include a drawn out pre-orgasmic build up in which Beck moaned about waiting for Jenny to get off work in the parking structure in his Hyundai, commiserating with her aching legs as she 'restocked the backroom', all the while licking his lips thinking about her stockings and high heels. Saucy and sympathetic, Beck flashed a glimpse of taut stomach at the audience, eliciting swooning sighs and laughter. Tracy Chapman, the folk purveyor, said she had never laughed harder in her life.

In the midst of the legal warfare, work continued unabated on the new album. Like Al with his collages, Beck was keen to pick up on elements that received opinion would argue were devoid of artistic worth and to make art with them, to play with ideas of what can be cool and what can't. 'So far it's a digital orgasm. It's embracing tastelessness in all its finery and apparel. I'm trying to cull the cream of the whole vast vat of tastelessness. I'm going for sounds that are just wrong. In a way it's reclamation of these horrible keyboard sounds and styles that came out in the Eighties. There's a sonic immorality to a lot of music; the music that just hurts to listen to. I tend to gravitate towards that really horrible music and try to rescue it somehow.'[13] His comments in the press made it clear that Beck was enjoying the experience of working creatively in his home studio, writing and programming at his own pace. '"Debra" is the direction this album is going, it's very licentious,'[14] he revealed to *Jam!* As ever, the humour that lay at the heart of all Beck's music – something which is so wanting in Nineties pop culture generally – came to the fore in his discussions of the new album, especially in his dismissal of the idea of making weighty observations on the end of the century and of the millennium: 'I'm sensing that a lot of people are coming out with these millennial statements, especially in the next year, and there's just something gaudy about that: fuck it, I wanna come out with a dumb-ass record. I want to come out with a party record. 'Cos, essentially, life is silly. In these high-charged moments, where time and history are supposedly coming to some cross point, it's not a time to soberly step back and consider all the questions of the universe. It's a time to stick your dick in a gopher-hole. It's a time to head-butt a eunuch.'[15] He later told *NME* that he thought of the album as in some ways his most personal, and that he'd consciously refrained from editing himself.

In Los Angeles, Power 106 was pumping out some of the most genre-defying, loose and experimental music on the entire radio spectrum. The nightly countdown was full of sporadic delights, as the rapid-fire drum breaks of drum'n'bass began to make inroads into hip-hop, what Beck termed 'Timbaland by way of drum and bass'.[16] Colder, technological sounds were also punctuating the increasingly inventive rhyme patterns produced by the rappers, closer to the phrasing of skilled oratory or beat poetry. Both techno and drum'n'bass were helping to liberate hip-hop from its least attractive feature over the last ten years or so – static beats at even tempos. There was a new pulse, and the rippling waves of bass rolling out of cars on Sunset Boulevard affirmed a new sense of motion, of pushing forward into realms as yet uncharted. Beck commented on the new beats, speaking favourably of Busta Rhymes, who could take a sample from the theme from *Knight Rider*, for Christ's sake, and turn it into a cold, technotic tank of a jam. Beck had time too for rapper Mystikal, part of the No Limit Records crew led by producer/owner/rapper Master P., who has created an empire with no help at all from MTV or mainstream media. Beck also praised R. Kelly, whose 140-minute double CD set *R* is a bold and expertly produced collection of jams. Many indie fans might find Kelly's trademark 'emoting' distasteful at first, but on repeated listenings, a paradigm shift occurs and the soulful subtlety, humour and warmth of Kelly's work shines through. 'A lot of people have mentioned that there's a Prince influence on the new record,' Beck told the *Boston Phoenix*, 'but I think R. Kelly was much more of an influence on me.'[17] Beck had hopes that the album would be seen in the context of Kelly and Missy Elliot, though he expressed his doubts at the time that it would be taken that way. A scan down the stations lands one on commercial alternative (a terrible oxymoron if ever there was one) station KROQ 106.7, where the latest flavour-of-the-month band was reiterating the same lifeless stagnation that had pervaded 'alternative music' since Cobain had topped himself. Further down the dial, National Public Radio's KCRW 89.9 FM had wildly eclectic nighttime programming, with the most progressive play list and DJs in the country. They were putting out combinations of everything, echoing the halcyon days of Detroit DJ the Electrifying Mojo back in the early Eighties, or the time when DJ Red Alert regularly blasted uptown and downtown, Bronx and the East Village, with white and black, new wave and rap, on New York's WBLS.

Sex was to be the defining theme behind *Midnite Vultures*, but Beck drew little or no inspiration from white rock for that. 'The slo-jams have this mixture of sensuality and earnestness, this unmitigated, full-on lust, coupled with a devout pledging of love,' he commented. 'You just don't hear that in rock music. You don't hear that humour and ambivalence. That's the one overriding element of this record, the embracing of sexuality in all its different colours, from fuchsia to chromium. We're going for it.'[18] It was exactly the trashiness of the slo-jams, their lyrical absurdity, even more than their high-production values, that appealed to Beck. 'The slo-jams really express a culture and a way of thinking,' he observed, 'and by rejecting that, you're rejecting a whole culture. When people like Alan Lomax went out to gather field recordings of country blues in the Twenties and Thirties, most people, including the musicians they recorded, thought they were nuts. "What do you want to record us for? Our music is trash." People like Robert Johnson and Blind Lemon Jefferson were street musicians. That wasn't perceived as music – it was junk. And the same thing is at play now.'[19]

Beck had long praised the album *ATLiens* by Atlanta based hip-hop group Outkast. Released in August 1996, *ATLiens* was produced by hip-hop mogul Babyface, and is laced with rich textured instrumentation, guitar, violin, bass, organ and one Skinny Miracles on piano, in addition to the usual scratching and computerized beats. Beck was quick to praise the Southern sensibilities of Outkast's work, which he recognized was injected with a little more air and stylistic freedom than its East or West Coast peers. It was albums like *ATLiens* that drew Beck deeper into contemporary hip-hop. Tracks like 'Elevators (Me And You)' unleashed beats closer to Kraftwerk and the more experimental end of abstract hip-hop than anything else in contemporary pop culture. Beck commented, '*ATLiens* is such a perverse union of these almost easy listening soft tracks with heavy gangster lyrics, and their rapping style is so loose, it's almost bebop.'[20] Of course, it was exactly that bringing together of diverse, if not opposing, elements which appealed to him.

The presence of Babyface on records such as *ATLiens* reaffirms that hip-hop is often a producer's world, and recalls the control and influence that producer Phil Spector, who weaved magnificent wall of sound orchestrations and arrangements around singers, achieved. But a tide shift seems to be occurring in hip-hop in more recent times, as the rappers become more technology savvy and are able to start incorporating a host of sounds and textures that marketing wisdom would cite as uncommercial. Outkast's first self-produced single was no less than 'Elevators (Me and You)'. The new pack of producer/artists, like DJ Quik, laced their albums with a fulsome Fender Rhodes, flute, piano and horn flavour over the shuddering beats sampled on an Akai MPC 3000 played live, or scratched in on trusty twin Technics 1200 turntables. Outkast themselves were branching into ever more adventurous territory, with their *Aquemini* album. Even fleeting singles like B.G.'s 'Bling-Bling' were steady rolling beat collages overlaid with cold, electronic melodies. In Los Angeles, the nightly countdown of the new slo-jams and R&B jams continue to grow quickly in terms of experimental phrasing, unusual rhythms. 'There

184

will always be an element of unpredictability,' Beck commented. 'It comes from the street. The music's alive; no matter how you try to package it, it always comes back. Whether it's New York or New Orleans or Atlanta or Seattle or anywhere, it's gonna pop up somewhere.'[21]

As the end of the decade approached, the genre known as 'Alternative' was dead, with lame bands putting out increasingly safe and non-threatening pap. In modern American pop culture, there is a continual need for the restatement of the obvious, and this is largely pushed by MTV and the major labels, and more importantly the marketing teams at work behind the scenes. Hence, although Kurt Cobain blowing his head off causes shock, the palatable 'pain' of bands like Bush will do just fine. Pain in quotation marks is easier to sell. Beck continually challenges the obvious clichés, digging into the dregs of what other people consider trash. So, when it came to the kind of music pumped out from Power 106, Beck delved in to better understand it and found that despite all the slick production and often ludicrous lyrics there was a commitment and passion, utterly lacking in white indie alternative music. In today's music, the only alternative music is the one you don't understand yet. Or more succinctly, as Madonna said in 1989, 'They call it alternative because no one likes it.'

On 3 July, Caetano Veloso performed an instrumental version of Beck's 'Tropicalia' at his show in Los Angeles, before calling Beck up. 'Beck had suggested four songs of mine for us to do, and I found his choices very interesting,' Veloso told *Wire* magazine. '"Coracao Vagabundo", "Super-Bacana" (which is a song from my first solo album), "Baby" and "Maria Bethania", which was my favourite of his choices because it was a song that I wrote when I was living in England and I used to be ashamed of those songs.' Like Beck's performance with Koerner, Ray and Glover this was a vital connection to past traditions. Beck's position as fly in the ointment of popular music paralleled Veloso's own in Brazil, and it was most welcome for Beck to receive this sort of acknowledgment from such a masterful and iconoclastic musician. Like Beck's shows, Veloso's tour had a similar air of suggesting that almost anything was possible, not only in music but in the larger scope of day to day life. 'When all the musicians danced, I invited Beck to dance', Veloso recalled. 'He was very good doing his version of breakdancing [...] it's very interesting that these young guys are interested in what we were doing in the Sixties. It's a way of acknowledging the richness and importance of Brazilian music as a whole.'[22]

On 8 July, Beck played a surprise opening set for Beth Orton's show at the El Rey Theatre in Los Angeles. Billed as 'Silverlake Menza', Beck borrowed a guitar and harmonica from Orton and belted out 'Tropicalia', 'Nobody's Fault But My Own', 'Cold Brains', and 'Lazy Flies'. In late July former Smiths' guitarist Johnny Marr was in Los Angeles on the lookout for a producer and a record deal. On the 24 July Beck's engineer Mickey P took Marr over to NRG Studios, where Beck invited Marr to lay down guitar for 'Milk And Honey' and they worked well into the night on Saturday perfecting the tracks. 'I had him do a Lynyrd Skynyrd guitar lead on "Milk And Honey", Beck revealed with relish to *Rolling Stone*. 'It was fairly surreal watching Johnny Marr play a Skynyrd riff. I don't think he was too enthused, but he said he would do it, but only for me.'[23]

On 5 October, Beck settled his lawsuits, as expected, with improved terms. Beck was no longer contractually bound to Bong Load, though Bong Load would continue to release the vinyl versions of his albums. In the press, Beck did his best to play down the affair. 'Any musician on a record label believes they're not getting what they deserve,' he argued. 'In my case, it was brought to my attention that it was grossly unfair. It was below what any musician off the street would be getting as far as a deal goes. It was all perfunctory legal manoeuvring, and in the end it worked itself out.'[24]

Beck played a surprise show on 6 October, dropping into the food court at the University of Santa Barbara student centre with the band. Announced on the college radio station scant hours before the show, the band rocked a crowd of 200 students. The power blew after the first song; revived, it blew again after the second. After half an hour, the power was restored and the show continued. Opening with 'Sexx Laws', Beck dropped the new 'Pressure Zone' and 'Mixed Bizness' and the crowd went nuts. The next day the band did a similar lightning strike at the Satellite Student Union at CSU Fresno.

On 9 October, Beck closed the first night of the Coachella Festival, held in the desert one hundred and fifty miles outside Los Angeles, past the fake greenery of Palm Springs. Signs pointing to signs pointing to signs led off the Interstate led to a trudge through powdery fine dusted parking lots. Out in a grove of coconut palm plantations, the fifty-seven acres of polo grounds were a marvellous setting save for the unseasonable heat. Not fifteen miles away was the motel room, the 29 Palms Inn, where Gram Parsons died of an accidental overdose, a waste of such a fine talent, and one, who like Beck, never saw a genre as a barrier.

The gig marked a return to the confrontational vibe for Beck, with a huge supporting cast of freaks. Half the crowd were ready to represent, half were along for the ride. They looked like a lost generation, all together in the middle of nowhere, and many of them seemed very much alone in the middle of everyone. Dehydrated hipsters, flush with five-dollar beer, stumbled across the cool grass in the crucifying heat; not one water fountain, but plenty of flush toilets. Everyone looked exhausted, too tired to get up and listen to Perry Farrell sing haunting melismas over jungle beats. But it was nice to hear that voice, which formed an essential part of the backdrop of Nineties youth. It was a comfort to hear that weird, keening voice that sounded so bizarre humming out of the radio right before alternative music hit the pop charts.

People were scattered among the smooth grass underfoot at the polo grounds, under the shadow of purple mountains and thousands of palm trees bristling in the wind. The fall of evening brought a revitalization of energy. Massed block rockin' beats came courtesy of the Chemicals, Morrissey groaned away for his cadre of fans in shorts, knee socks and Smiths T-shirts. Spiritualised provided bel-canto modular space rock. After geometric patterns on the screens dissolved into black, a zebra-headed dummy with a banjo was hoisted into centre stage and the set-up for Beck began. He was the star attraction, closing nine hours of mostly big beat spectacles and tents full of ravers careening to lonely, dub-influenced techno and jungle.

Stark lights overhead beamed down on the crowd of techs and set-up men, roadies and others walking around with walkie-talkies looking fraught. The speakers blasted out obscure DJ Shadow B-sides and Moog fanfares. At long last the band marched on, Beck was splendid in ass-hugger corduroys and fringe bedecked purple shirt, tight on his small wiry chest. His hair was in his face, long and shaggy, his eyes were wild and stern, recalling Roland Alphonso of the Skatalites, scanning the crowd, unsmiling, serious and intent.

From the opening 'Novacane', Beck was plagued with sound problems. Justin Meldal-Johnsen, sporting his trademark Jew-fro, rocked the bass from the groin outward, striking ludicrous poses. Smokey, with sly smirk at stage left, held it down, skirting over the top of the samples and drums. He ripped out country solos and metalloid noise, riffing up and down the neck of his guitar. DJ Swamp, long-haired, stood like Merlin behind the turntables which were set on a cloth-draped table, looking sullen. Joey Waronker on a drum riser in centre stage, beat on an impressive ten-piece drum set with his racing stripe JW logo emblazoned on the bass drum. The show seemed transitional, tentative in spots, rough in others, and sometimes electrifying.

'The New Pollution' rocked, getting the somewhat sceptical crowd on the band's side. For 'Sexx Laws' two black female backup singers percolated to the rhythm, all slow finger snaps and head nods, while layering the choruses with sumptuous harmony. For the banjo solo, the special mannequin of a zebra, outfitted with a customized metallic banjo, span around as Swamp played a sampled version of the solo. 'Deadweight' was a perfect song for the balmy night, with the palms swaying in the distance. 'Sissyneck' followed, and then 'Mixed Bizness', in which Beck was plagued with such mic problems that his words were unintelligible. 'Debra' drove every woman and many men to sexified distraction; Beck's weariness gave the song a perfect air of sexual consumption. The Brass Menagerie at stage right danced in synchronized steps, bleating artfully on sax trombone and trumpet. Beck hits piercingly high notes with commendable clarity and force. Not all were so sure: two concertgoers turned to each other and shrugged. 'Is he making fun of the slo-jams?' one asked the other.

Both 'Jack-Ass' and 'Nobody's Fault But My Own' proved too lulling for the crowd, despite Smokey's excellent twang. For 'Minus', moshers threw themselves at the stage, sending a young girl hand over hand around the crowd, which Beck viewed with noticeable alarm. The set was loose and bordered on the chaotic. Sound problems continued to plague the band as mics went dead and Beck sang dead verses, grimacing. The frustration clearly evident, he slammed a microphone down, kicked the amplifier over.

The new songs bewildered the audience, save for the few who had already downloaded 'Sexx Laws' or had traded it over the Net and memorized the words. Small girls stuck in the crowd yelled out the words and screamed 'Beck, I love you!', while beefy drunk morons bellowed 'Play "Loser"!' in every silent stretch. Beck's off-kilter rhythms circled in and out of the beat, making it difficult to catch a groove on the new songs. There were, of course, blinding moments, as the lights pump and Beck debuts his new sexiness, humping the gel light set into the stage, straddling the mic stand, slamming it into speakers. Beck dropped 'Loser' halfway into the set and the crowd freaked as a collective one. It was a cursory rendition on Beck's part, though the band was rock solid, with Meldal-Johnsen in particular nailing the bass line with dead-on accuracy. Beck looked utterly indifferent as he sang the lines that launched him to unwitting stardom.

'Pressure Zone' was a victory – great stinging glam riffs from Smokey, and tube distortion that must have had Mick Ronson peeking down from heaven in approval. 'Beercan' also suffered from sound failures, but they were remedied in time for the lightning-fast segue, complete with sudden eruption of stage lights, into 'Electric Avenue'. The band closed the set with a pared-down, non-make out city 'Where It's At'. Then, a very solemn DJ Swamp fashioned collaged beats into 'Smoke On The Water' but fumbled and dispassionately broke the record into smithereens. For the encore of 'Devil's Haircut' the band emerged in outrageous get-ups, with the Brass Menagerie in football-player padding.

Neon glow sticks which ravers had been waving inside the tents all day came showering onto the stage, not in anger, but in rabid approval. Soon the ridiculous two-dollar bottles of water started flying onto the stage. The band picked them up and start throwing them back as the encore broke down into Dada theatre. One band member threw a nearly full bottle straight out into the crowd, hitting an audience member dead on the head. People were staggering through the crowd; one guy fell face down in a stupor. It was a panic-filled performance, with Beck and the band seeming so alien to anyone else who played that day. 'Devil's Haircut' dissolved into a total noise overload, with Justin and the Menagerie wrestling all over the stage, and simulated sex as Joey toppled his drums for the last time. It was Joey and Smokey's last show with the band – they were shortly to leave for REM and Tom Waits respectively. Beck's new drummer would be Victor Indrizzo, who had played with Chris Cornell; Lyle Workman, who had worked with Todd Rundgren and Frank Black, would be the new guitarist.

Backstage, after the show, Beck relaxed and hung out in the trailers set up for the musicians. He appeared tired, perhaps pissed off at the sound problems. As he walked back to the tour bus someone ran up and stuck a *Mutations* album cover in his face, stopping him in mid-stride. He squiggled a black pen on it, and then he and the band boarded the tour bus for the 110-mile ride back to Los Angeles. As the bus rolled away Beck looked out the window at the distant purple hills, and the wind picking up now, blowing trash over the trampled green fields. His famous wide blue eyes seemed to be drilling the horizon for clues.

On 23 November *Midnite Vultures*, Beck's eighth album, was released. By turns his most polished work, the album is a study in paradoxes. Pervaded by bursts of noise that lace all his other releases, *Midnite Vultures* is also buffed and polished until all its subtleties shine. Mixed to be played at high volume, the engineering by Beck, Hoffer, and Petralia is closer to contemporary hip-hop production than anything in the indie world, which tends to eschew finesse as smacking of corporate sell-out.

Drawing in with one hand and pushing away with the other, *Midnite Vultures*' lyrics approach the extreme Dada poetry of Tristan Tzara along with the concise and sharp one-liners that are inimitably Beck's own. Drawing from inspirations as diverse as Captain Beefheart and mid-Seventies Rolling Stones albums, along with the contemporary R&B that had been his favoured listening music for the past several years, *Midnite Vultures* is so dense with ideas and inspirations as to act as something of a mirror. A fairground mirror, impenetrable and disorienting in the images it reflected. Almost entirely free of recognizable samples, the album suffers at times from lack of spaciousness, by comparison with *Odelay*. But there is something enervating about the density too as if, echoing Kurt Schwitters, Beck had been able to condense his influences to the point where they had transformed into his own unique style.

On first hearing, the lead-off track and first single 'Sexx Laws' sounds strangely neutered, an anthem of funky insanity with a Sixties tweeness. The first line refers to drums 'hijacking equilibrium', a reference perhaps to the soulless beats of techno? Was Beck doing some Situationist lampooning of the spectacle with this pop monstrosity, or was he doing a take on Sly Stone at his most decadent, recording in a plush-fake-fur-lined anechoic chamber? But there was a horrid catchiness to the song, and after the shock of the new wore off, 'Sexx Laws' sounded inventive and fresh, mixing the conflict between organic and synthetic that was to be this album's central duality with great deftness. 'I think that this record is more direct', he told Belgium's *Humo* magazine. 'Even if you don't like the songs, you'll understand them more or less. There is pumping bass, which makes it sound perfect in your car stereo. It's a more physical record.'[25]

In the mode of Sly, Beck was directing a small orchestra of skilful sidemen. He wrote the horn arrangement for the Brass Menagerie himself, and had Herb Pederson play banjo and Jay Dee Maness on pedal steel for a solo that was truly psychedelic in the unrefined Huxleyian meaning of the word. A bluegrass player extraordinaire, Pederson played with Gram Parsons and Emmylou Harris, as well as with former Byrds-man Chris Hillman in country's Desert Rose Band. However, Pederson is perhaps best known for playing the theme from *The Dukes of Hazzard*. The horn charts had a surprising genesis – Beck revealed, 'I used to watch the L.A. Rams when I was growing up, and it just reminded me of Monday night football in 1978.'[26]

Beck went to great pains to ensure the album's production was immaculate, a reflection of his interest in the sophisticated smoothness of R&B. 'On *Odelay* you could hear all the rough edges, this time there are still all these different pieces, but they're completely glued together and incorporated', he told *Elle*. 'We did "Sexx Laws", and I felt at the time, "People are just going to think this is pastiche, they're going to focus on the retro qualities of it." So without ruining what worked in the song already, I added all these other elements and textures. Ultimately it created a new sound that isn't rock or funk. It isn't folk. It's something else.'[27]

Viscous bass and super-slight guitar scratches underpin the corporate pimp soul of 'Nicotine & Gravy'. David Campbell wrote out a brilliant string break, with discordant violin, viola and cello swirling in sharp counterpoint to the rest of the track's low-end funk. These touches are what distinguish Beck's music in an era when so few songs venture past one key change let alone embrace contradictions. A falsetto punctuation of 'I don't wanna die tonight' laces the track with the undertow of dread that is a characteristic of *Midnite Vultures*. If this is a party album, then it is a strangely disorienting one, with Beck's astringent flat guitar colliding with the banjo deep in the mix here. The strings spiral to a slightly sour crescendo, before being cut short by a sticky bass and drum four on the floor. The beats on *Midnite Vultures* are pervaded with a stickiness close to New Orleans funk scientists the Meters strict syncopation. Beck mocks his own sense of dread, stating in one line 'I think we're going crazy' only to upstage it with a falsetto 'I don't wanna die tonight'. On paper, the lyrics come across as frightening, but the music is so uptempo the effect is one of disorientation. The lyrics also seem to be Beck's most rhythmic, supporting the grooves, a supporting cast for the melodies. Thematically, the lyrics are pervaded by a gender dysphoria, a clever constant inversion of gender roles: 'It's just a revolving door. none of those lines are specific to each other; you don't know whose relationship is whose.'[28]

'Mixed Bizness' continues the album's lack of adherence to the straight-eight chords and four-on-the-floor rhythms, defying verse-chorus-verse and just about every other musical convention, except to invert them. Even the song's up-tempo funk is droll and somewhat distant, as if toying with the structure of funk rave-ups as it's performed. Brass Menagerie horns and wah-wah guitar by Hoffer buttress the rhythm on either side of the stereo spectrum. The track encapsulates the point that *Midnite Vultures* – one of the best-engineered albums outside of the hip-hop world – creates a sonic space that is inviting and cold at the same time. 'Mixed Bizness' is playful on the surface, but with the sinister misanthropy of Mick Jagger's 1968 'Memo From Turner' (which also features the words 'business' and 'leather') itching underneath. Every joke is barbed, every gender role confused. Relationships are incestuous, pimps and prostitutes emerge rain-soaked, and artificially enhanced archetypes roam night time boulevards. Every exhortation is also a cautionary tale.

On 'Get Real Paid' the warmth of the bass is set against an analogue synth that glistens coolly, with the chilliest background vocals this side of the Tubeway Army, and a Kraftwerk sample from 'Home Computer'. This delves straight back to electro's ambivalent soul, its love of cold technological sounds competing with vocals so soulful that they almost become histrionic. But 'Get Real Paid''s strength lies in its Chinatown-meets-techno-taco-shack evocation of driving down deserted Los Angeles streets at night. Though this album has been plagued with facile comparisons to Prince, on 'Get Real Paid' the nod to Wendy and Lisa's brilliant work on albums like Prince and the Revolution's *1999* is apparent. Prince himself spoke warmly of the coldness of some of the songs from albums of that period. 'I've always liked Prince,' Beck told *Select* in late 1999. 'I remember all his early videos and everything. I love "Raspberry Beret", "Darling Nikki" and "Kiss". I remember when he used to perform in the trench coat and a g-string. I liked that because when I was a kid I was really into trench coats.'[29] People forget how subversive Prince was when he started out. In 1981 the diminutive pop genius could be seen on late late night cable television, descending a stage ramp wearing thigh-high purple boots, naked but for briefs with metal studs, with huge flash pots going off and two white chicks licking his chest, all the while singing about fucking a bride on her way to the church to be married. 'Prince

189

kicks ass and he's completely fey at the same time,' Beck observed. 'There's something about that mixture, that cocktail, that I can relate to.'[30]

The Dust-produced 'Hollywood Freaks' is as close to a Power 106 homage as *Midnite Vultures* gets. Evoking nights of sleaze on the scene in Hollywood, and sniping beats inspired by Master P's battalion of hip-hoppers, particularly Beck's favourite, Mystikal, 'Hollywood Freaks' is hardly the 'minstrelry' one of its harsher critics decried it as, but Beck's own play on the vocal phrasing in R&B and hip-hop that functions as a commentary on the beats beneath, wreaks havoc with time, on the beat, behind the beat. Instead of a straightforward lift of 106 fare, however, Beck introduces clever twists, such as the vocals evoking Sly Stone in his ravaged 'Family Affair' mode, echoing repeats on the verses, and double-tracked raps slightly out of synchronization with each other to create the wavering tonalities that make the futuristic R&B on 106 so unusual and progressive. Beck's self-deprecating laughter at the end shows that's he not trying to 'come off legit'. The vocal outburst that punctuates the track derives from a specific source: 'We were listening to an Ice Cube song on the bus, and he's always going "Heemahnunnn!!!!" We thought he was saying, "He's my nun". So on "Hollywood Freaks", I start the song with "Hee-Mah-Nunnn" and you can hear a couple of the guys in the background busting up.'[31] Beck's rap on the track pays homage to his favourite rapper, the late Eazy-E, who like Ice Cube and Dr Dre, was part of Los Angeles rap crew NWA. Beck compared Eazy-E's rapping style to Blind Willie McTell, which is apropos, as Californian raps have more southern flavour than their New York counterparts, with accents on sliding vowels and a distinct after-the-beat slackness.

As well as drawing on the seamier side of life in Los Angeles, the album also satirises the empty bombast of the late Nineties in marketing and media-manipulated America, even more hollow than that of the Eighties. 'This point in time seems more power-oriented,' Beck observed to *Spin*. 'Power workout, power diet, power body parts, power relationships, power steering, power rangers. People are scrubbed and clean, well toned and manicured.'[32]

'Peaches & Cream' uses the sex and religion duality that you-know-who utilized so well in the Eighties, but again Beck's take is not derivative but an extrapolation, with roots as far back as Son House and Skip James' inner battles between sin and sanctity. Beck drops sly references to the Bible and Koerner, Ray and Glover, tying in with the biblical parable on the temptations of pride. The tempo is a woozy West Coast funk, like a War jam after much too much of Eric Burdon's wine has been spilled. The title is a nod to fellow travellers Ween, and also highlights the gastronomic decadence interspersed throughout the album's lyrics. Each song seems to tackle a different deadly sin, with playful exposés of gluttony, lust and envy figuring heavily. 'I've always been interested in decadence,' Beck confessed in late 1999. 'It's part of my nature: I think everyone is curious about looseness and extreme situations. and I don't necessarily mean sexual looseness.'[33] The vocals are credited to the 'Arroyo Tabernacle Men's Chorale', coming off like a cross between Parliament and the Mormons. It's perhaps worth noting here that in informal discussions amongst Beck fans on the mailing lists this track was singled out for particular vilification.

'Broken Train', which was initially entitled 'Out of Kontrol' until the Chemical Brothers launched a pre-emptive strike on the title, fuses Tom Waits-style clanking percussion with some of Joey's loosest and most memorable playing. Manning plays lovely clavinet and acoustic guitar, while Beck plays marimba. The lyrics approach pure cut-up – skewering billionaires, deportees, snipers, and rioters riding an out of control train crumbling on its tracks, leading nowhere. Lyrics like these find Beck at his most caustic but, pointedly, he includes himself as one of their targets. 'We're out of control', Beck sings in falsetto. Songs such as these find parallels in the Rolling Stones' spotty mid-Seventies albums such as *Some Girls* and particularly Sly Stone's dark funk gotterdammerung *There's A Riot Going On*. 'I love the "dumb party sex" feeling,' Beck told *Humo* magazine, 'but on second thoughts I thought it wasn't fascinating enough to fill a complete record with. That's why the second half of the CD goes more towards "rock-instrumental-pop", with a good deal of soul and funk. *Midnite Vultures* was recorded with the *Odelay* tour band, and the soul and funk mainly come from them. It's their 'vibe', when they are there, it sounds like that.'[34]

'Milk & Honey' is a fusion of classic rock overload guitar, perfunctory scratches, video game synth blasts, and some of the most soulless staccato rhyming this side of Stephen Hawking before Beck breaks out into some very soulful singing in the verse, accenting the first syllable to egg on tension with the slight promise of release in the chorus. Johnny Marr does a singularly unconvincing Lynyrd Skynyrd imitation, instead playing a money-shot of a guitar line to the song's promised but delayed crescendo, which gushes from his guitar in the outro. Marr frequently does some of his best work in unexpected collaborations (his superb wah-wah solo in the Pet Shop Boys 'October Symphony' springs to mind). The song fades into acoustic reverberation and a mellotron fade out. The acoustic outro wavers without resolution before segueing into the next track's muted opening.

'Beautiful Way' is to *Midnite Vultures* as 'Diamond Bollocks' was to *Mutations*, a cross link perpetuating the notion of Beck's album being linked together on a non-linear plane. Beth Orton shadows Beck's vocal, but ever so slightly, which is a shame. Smokey Hormel provides characteristically melodic and subtle guitar fills in the bridge, while Greg Leisz and Jay Dee Maness do superb duelling pedal steel guitar accompaniment, giving the song a sort of Key West reverie feel. In the studio videos offered on his website, Beck was seen working out the arrangement for this song with Leisz; it seemed Beck had something specific in mind, but it was temporarily beyond his grasp. Finally, he asked Leisz for 'The classic, poignant sounds, mixed in with the more psychedelic'. The song captures that feel in spades, blending the Velvet Underground's 'Countess Of Hong Kong' with a Louvin Brothers feel. Astute listeners of Beck's music will come across bits of his songs in a variety of other musicians works; mind you, this is not theft, but a return to the principle that guided people such as Jimi Hendrix to use a section from a Donovan song and reconfigure it into his own unique piece. This old skool sampling is as old as time and should be encouraged; a musical cross referencing and cross pollination that dares to let its roots show. Commenting on Beck's eclectic musical appetite, Joey Waronker noted, 'Beck has this incredible gift, where he can pull all these weird pieces together and make it work. I've never seen anyone else who can do it. He's one of the least self-conscious musicians in the studio that I've ever seen.'[35] By the time 'Beautiful Way''s gorgeous harmonica solo by Beck arrives, the respite from the rest of the album's feverish pitch is most welcome. But the respite, like a taste of pickled ginger, is only a palate cleanser before the final build-up.

'Pressure Zone', with its crushing compressed metal chords, was the most electrifying of the new songs in concert, immediately connecting with the audience, largely because, well, it rocked. And in America, any song that rocks has a crack at getting through, witness Blur's throwaway 'Song 2', accomplishing in three minutes what three American tours had failed to achieve. Beck called 'Pressure Zone' 'a Cars-style blueprint of an alternative rock song,'[36] The song is also lyrically as cutting as shrapnel, with lines like 'masterpieces liquidate in fertile tears' underscoring the theme of discombobulated sadness that sabotages even the most upbeat songs on this most ambiguous of all Beck's albums. Conflicting emotions and dualities in fiery contention power the urgency with which the songs on this remarkable record are proffered; ballads of emotional blackmail. In the fade out of the song, Beck and Manning harmonize on a volley of 'la la la's' that recall great Liverpool band the La's' epic track 'Looking Glass'.

191

'Debra' closes the album, and is presented here in a laid-back, Dust-produced, rendition that sounds little like its stage counterpart versions. 'At first "Debra" was kind of funny,' Beck told *NME* in late 1999, 'but now it's acquired a certain amount of soul.'[37] Philly soul seems to be the signifier here, and wafts of MFSB and Gamble and Huff float through the mix, particularly through the Ramsey Lewis sample that loops throughout the track. The Brass Menagerie is oddly absent, but in their place a three-piece horn section provides sharp blasts and rollicking rolls which punctuate every stanza. Smokey is in top form, Manning leans in on the soul notes on his Fender Rhodes and Justin plays upright bass. The horns also reference Jorge Ben's 'Maria Teresa', echoing like a fanfare for a failed romance. 'I think sexuality has to have a sense of playfulness,' Beck observed. 'It shouldn't really take itself that serious. It can have some darkness in there. It can have some of that angst, or frustration, and "Debra" has a little bit of that, but it still should be playful.'[38] At the end of 'Debra' Beck moans 'I'm not afraid to...', and apparently trails off without completing the line. But turning the volume up all the way the listener can hear Beck concluding, with a wink, '... fuck you.'

That *Midnite Vultures* marks something of a transitional phase is affirmed by Beck: 'I wanted to stick a few things on *Midnite Vultures* that really represented where we started out on *Odelay*, some of the things that we never really got to do. This record's sort of torn between that. It's torn between an album I probably should have made two years ago, and an album that I want to be making now, or where I'm going. "Sexx Laws", "Mixed Bizness", and "Debra" are cast from the same mould as *Odelay*. But "Get Real Paid", "Hollywood Freaks", and "Nicotine & Gravy"... that's kind of where I'm launching off to.'[39]

After a minute or two of silence comes a hidden track, a short distillation of the various elements that inform the album – sci-fi clavinet and Moog, synthetic and acoustic percussion, film soundtrack snippets and dismembered voices, along with blasts of guitar and bass reminiscent of the Japanese noise band the Boredoms as well as Cornelius' masterful *Fantasma* album. Like Dylan's Sixties albums, on which the final tracks would map out his next itinerary, Beck's new direction seems to be pointing east, to Japan, where he is a bona fide star. A Japan-only bonus track, 'Arabian Nights', opens with gunfire and roosters crowing, echoing Beck's teenage neighborhood. A Satie-like piano figure anchors the rolling R&B beats, with Beck rapping out a litany of Los Angeles' mutated archetypes, before a melancholy fugue-like organ spirals into silence.

As the public digested *Midnite Vultures*, the restless Beck was already talking about the future. 'There are some bombs, man! There's a whole other record that we're going to try and finish and put out next year. I did some things with Kool Keith and I did a whole bunch of other songs with the Dust Brothers that are all ready to go.'[40]

In November and December of 1999, Beck conducted a short string of dates promoting the release of *Midnite Vultures*. Despite hitting the Top 20 in Britain, the album had only reached number 34 in America, his worst showing yet. He had stiff competition in the guise of interchangeable boy bands, teen heart throbs, and pedantic lite hip-hop. So, off to Europe he went, and appeared on no less than three British television pop shows, before two dates in Amsterdam and Cologne. In Cologne, Beck accidentally struck a photographer from *NME* with his mike stand. *NME*'s Steven Wells graciously responded with, 'You did it on purpose, didn't you? But there's no onstage apology, no statement of regret. And none after, either. Fuck you very much, Beck. You scumbag.' What exactly the *NME*'s photographer was doing lying flat on the stage angling for a photo was left unexplained, but there appeared to be no malice whatever on Beck's part. Wells concluded with, '[Beck's] the Yank equivalent of our own dear Neil Hannon.

A smug dilettante, a jerk with a smirk. A white, male, middle class, middle-of-the-road no-knob milksop – puffed up and pampered by a legion of white, male, middle class, middle-of-the-road rock hacks who see in him, we must presume, a dazzling reflection of their own mediocrity.'[41]

And so the backlash begins, as it inevitably must. It's the surest sign of artistic progress in these strange, desiccated times in popular culture. Hype is certainly no great feat, nor even critical accolades, but a backlash might be the first sign that Beck truly has made an impact in an ever fleeting world of sensation and disposable icons. And just like that night at the Opry when they hissed 'Carpetbagger!' at him, whether they curse him or they love him, he'll pay no mind.

It is inevitable that Beck will come increasingly under attack for trying to bridge hitherto unbridgeable barriers. Seeking nothing less than reintegration at a basic level, Beck's music reflects a duality within himself that is perhaps his central conflict, and which only he fully knows the content of. Beck's brilliance lies in his ability to use his own artistic struggle as a mirror of a struggle in the culture at large.

Beck played a show in Seattle just days after 30,000 protesters took to the streets of the city marching against the ever less subtle incursions of the forces of extreme capitalism, embodied in the sinister guise of the World Trade Organisation, an extra-legal committee which potentially has the power to bring entire nations into line with the threat of sanctions. As the end of the Nineties rapidly approached, the all pervasive apathy of young people in the face of escalating corporate power and dwindling resources seemed to be at an end. The non-violent demonstration was well-organised at a grass roots level, with underpaid stewardesses, steel workers, student activists and environmentalists determined to not allow the eight hundred WTO delegates to meet. The demonstration rapidly broke down into a two-day state of siege, as anarchists smashed windows of corporate chains and cops shot protesters at point blank range with rubber-tipped bullets. As tear gas canisters and concussion grenades flew down Seattle's Broadway, the ugly fruits of twenty years of neo-conservative policies in America and the U.K. were all too apparent at millennium's end.

In his music, Beck is playing the role of a pop shaman, enacting the culture's conflicts and reflecting them back to its participants. The conflicting joy and fear expressed on *Midnite Vultures* point directly at a transitional moment in culture. If embracing flux to kill stasis is at the heart of Beck's music, then he also is tackling some very explosive conflicts in the larger scope of culture. There is the tension between the impoverished working-class bohemians versus their privileged middle-class counterparts in a song like 'Modesto'. The folk versus noise schism in 'Lemonade' pits Beck's own introspection against his explosive extroversion. The ambiguity deployed in his recorded work is more reminiscent of the European avant garde rather than the unalloyed sincerity in America. Beck said, 'Americans believe in a protean spirit that embraces trueness and sincerity, and anything that's dishonest is un-American. But sometimes dishonesty is interesting. It's part of art, it's artifice.'[42] The duality of sincerity against irony is best embodied by the metamorphosis of 'Debra', a track which illustrates the friction point at which pastiche becomes not only tribute, but something inimitably the artist's own. Here, Beck successfully transmuted a joke into an epic.

The duality of the artifice of studio engineering and gloss over the bare bones simplicity of the country blues, (or *Midnite Vultures* versus *The Banjo Story*) shows Beck aiming to present his excursion into hip-hop with finesse and skill, while the lo-fi stylings of his early work were spawned out of the desire to connect to simplicity in the light of all the inflated emptiness of Eighties rock. But Beck has spoken disparagingly of albums such as *Mellow Gold*, complaining that lack of recording tools, necessary engineering skills, and time and money constraints compelled him to record his albums raw. The technological juggernaut of *Odelay*'s samplers and

Midnite Vultures' intricate jigsaw beats stand in sharp contrast to the unvarnished half-incinerated plywood no-name acoustic guitar of lore.

Beck had to contend with 'going electric', quite unintentionally, in the light of 'Loser''s success. As his songwriting progressed Beck began to suspect the purism of folk could lead to a dead end. By extension, in indie rock he found the stasis of angst, whereas in hip-hop he found the freedom of emotion. The pull of preserving tradition in songwriting when the cultural impetus tells him to push to the inexorable release of machine sounds of the future gives an album like *Midnite Vultures* an edginess under its smooth finish, a conflict between organic folk and synthetic electronic funk. 'I did start in this more traditional vein, but it's evolved with all these other ideas and other musical directions over the years', he observed in 1999. 'There's definitely a conflict there. I just love songwriting as a pure form, as a craft. And I have a lot of fun with all these machines and gadgets, but sometimes I just [enjoy] working with a guitar or a piano, just working purely with chords and harmonic structure, without any distraction.'[43]

Also, as the contractual obligations of endless tours and promotion start to weigh on his artistic soul, fired as it was in a kiln of anti-folk's fiercely independent 'we will not be fooled' ethos, will Beck become a cynic? A caustic edge nips at the edges of *Midnite Vultures'* party beats. In interviews, tired of being misrepresented, Beck has become more and more serious, the playful non-sequiturs of his early interviews being increasingly abandoned in favour of careful, considered and somewhat defensive replies.

The accusations of Beck's supposed insincerity, distant irony, casual eclecticism and appropriation of black music forms are all things he roundly refutes. Moreover, Beck frequently finds himself in contention with the increasingly conventional notions of what constitutes 'cool', so often spoon-fed by marketing and media. 'I'm just trying to say there are other ways of expressing ourselves, and whatever's been decided this year is the "cool" way to be isn't the only way to be. To me that's always been the ultimate coolness – not giving a shit. And by expressing that you get to that honesty and vulnerability, and in a way that's the real American character.'[44] In 'Static' from *Mutations*, Beck advocates 'laugh(ing) at yourself' as a means of banishing the oppressive weight and paralysis of ironic detachment. The recurring appearance of the jackass, braying in the songs and used as a prop in the stage shows, mocks pomposity and spectacle, even the sincere sentiments in the song of the same title.

For the most part, Beck seems grimly determined not to take himself too seriously. To embrace his own worst instincts and his guise as a pop saboteur continues to be one of his most intriguing roles and he remains a wryly subversive pop icon. Far from a sell-out to corporate blight, Beck lifts the curtain so the rest of us can see its nefarious workings. After his appearance on Jay Leno's *Tonight Show* to perform 'Sexx Laws', Beck sat on the sofa opposite Leno, and pointedly moved his *Tonight Show* coffee cup so the viewers could see the words printed in white letters on the back of the cup. He smiled beatifically into the camera, his blue eyes blinking with mischief as the credits rolled on this latest spectacle.

The cup read: "GUEST Number 3".

1   Bream, Jon. 'Where It's At: Summer Festivals', *Minneapolis Star Tribune*, 1 August 1997

2   Beck Reveals Plans For Next Album: 'Peppy, Enjoyable Music'. www.ubl.com, 19 November 1998

3   Simutis, David. 'The Man Who Would Be King', *Iron Minds*, 3 September 1999

4   *NME*, 16 October 1999

5   Myers, Christopher. Prince Paul. *Index* magazine, May 1998

6   McLean, Craig. *Observer*, 7 March 1999

7   'I Love The Smell Of Methane And Bananas In The Morning', *Mean* magazine, December 1999

8   Yuen, Emma. (webmaster) Enchanting Wizard Of Rhythm Website
    www.freespeech.org/beck_fishbulb/index.html

9   Morris, Chris. 'Beck Cites California 7-Year Law In Contract Fight.' *Billboard*, 8 May 1999

10 Morris, Chris. 'Beck Cites California 7-Year Law In Contract Fight.' Billboard, 8 May 1999

11 *Select*, December 1999

12 Chonin, Neva. 'Beck', *Rolling Stone*, 24 June 1999

13 Sakamoto, John. 'Music Oddball Beck Gets Mutated', *Jam!*, 8 October 1998

14 Sakamoto, John. 'Music Oddball Beck Gets Mutated', *Jam!*, 8 October 1998

15 Mulvey, John. 'State Of The Mutation', *NME*, 11 November 1998

16 *Spin* Online Chat, www.Spin.Com, 10 November 1999

17 Ashare, Matt. 'Slow Jamming: Beck Reveals His Inner Soul Man', *Boston Phoenix*, 25 November–2 December 1999

18 Rotondi, James. 'Beck: Return of the Mack', CMJ, November 1999

19 Rotondi, James. 'Beck: Return of the Mack', CMJ, November 1999

20 Hansen, Beck. 'The Best Thing I've Heard All Year', *Mojo*, January 1997

21 Loder, Kurt. 'Beck Mutates', MTV Online, 11 November 1998

22 Veloso, Caetano. 'Invisible Jukebox', *Wire* magazine, January 2000

23 Uhelszki, Jaan. Beck Names His "Dumb-Ass Party Record", *Rolling Stone*, 14 September 1999

24 Rotondi, James. 'Beck: Return of the Mack' CMJ, November 1999

25 Interview with Beck, *Humo* magazine (Belgium), 14 December 1999

26 'I Love The Smell Of Methane And Bananas In The Morning', *Mean* magazine, December 1999

27 Schoemer, Karen. 'The Last Boy Wonder', *Elle* magazine, December 1999

28 'I Love The Smell Of Methane And Bananas In The Morning', *Mean* magazine, December 1999

29 *Select*, December 1999

30 Sullivan, Jim. 'You Know He's Not A Loser', *Boston Globe*, 8 August 1997

31 Bliss, Karen. 'Beck On Axl Rose, Ice Cube, But No Millennium Please'. 2 December 1999, *All-star* magazine,
    www.cdnow.com

32 Norris, Chris. 'Return Of The Funk Soul Brother', *Spin*, December 1999

33 Interview with Beck, *Humo* magazine (Belgium), 14 December 1999

34 Interview with Beck, *Humo* magazine (Belgium), 14 December 1999

35 Kaufman, Gil. 'Beck Recorded More Than 20 Songs For *Midnite Vultures*', *Entertainment Weekly*,
    5 October 1999

36 Rotondi, James. 'Beck: Return of the Mack', CMJ, November 1999

37 *NME*, 16 October 1999

38 Basham, David. 'Midnite Cowboy'. December 1999
    http://mtv.com/news/gallery/b/beck99/beckfeature99.html

39 Basham, David. 'Midnite Cowboy'. December 1999
    http://mtv.com/news/gallery/b/beck99/beckfeature99.html

40 Basham, David. 'Midnite Cowboy'. December 1999
    http://mtv.com/news/gallery/b/beck99/beckfeature99.html

41 'Beck: Play That Funky Music White Boy', *NME*, 2 December 1999

42 *NME*, 16 October 1999

43 Basham, David. 'Midnite Cowboy'. December 1999
    Http://mtv.com/news/gallery/b/beck99/beckfeature99.html

44 *NME*, 16 October 1999

EL POSTSCRIPTO

Austin, Texas
25 January 2000

Strange that it should all begin and end here. Ten years ago Austin was a low-rent bohemian enclave, an oasis of liberal mores and harmless misfits in the middle of the vast dry plains of Texas. But that was before then-Governor of Texas, Ann Richards, signed a bill that is slowly but surely killing off the city's offbeat vibe. The legislation, designed to turn Austin into a computer industry powerhouse, the South-east's answer to California's Silicon Valley, succeeded very well. In the process, it quadrupled rents, brought in a flood of white-collar computer start-up companies, clogged the streets with new cars and triggered off a building boom to service the voracious needs of the city's cadre of yuppies. So, the city immortalized in Richard Linklater's 1990 film *Slacker* is no more. Simply put, no one can afford to have any slack in this town these days. Wages are kept low by the formidable presence of Austin's two largest employers, the university and the city. The sheer number of cars, the rise of identical corporate outlets on every block, the deepening division between two cities – one white and prosperous (West) and one poor and Latino and black (East) – have turned Austin into a model nightmare of a modern metropolis. The coffee houses are closing, landmark live music venues are being bulldozed. A coffee shop employee works a twelve-hour shift six nights a week and has little left after rent and food.

In the garish wreck of the Austin Music Hall, the first night of Beck's Midnite Vultures tour begins. My girlfriend Rachel and I are issued an envelope at the box-office window with bracelets reading 'Aftershow' and two VIP stickers, courtesy of a secret benefactor. Thank you. We proceed up to the second-storey platform with a bunch of people who got freebies or won radio competitions for the gig. Hank Williams III is the opener tonight, and he flabbergasts the audience with "honky tonkin' and hillbilly rockin'", a forty-five-minute blast of punk rockabilly twang. He's amazing, yodelling and slamming out brutal riffs on an acoustic equipped with a pick-up. Needless to say, his frame and voice are bound to remind one of his hard-living grandfather, whose car lies at the end of a hall in that museum in Nashville. The guitarist from the Jesus Lizard, a fiddle player, a maniac of a drummer and a stand-up bass player with a NOFX cap support Hank – Hank, with his lean angularity and relentless intensity that make you think he won't live much longer than his legendary forebear. The audience take it in like drunken lemmings, utterly still under the short sharp shock of punkabilly riffs that make the Cramps sound like Conway Twitty. Hank's boots are held together by duct tape. This is significant, though I'm not exactly sure why. He's punk.

The audience is restless, itching. I understand now more than ever what a freak is; the crowd seem to be truly misfits from whatever banner they temporarily find themselves under. There are fraternity louts grunting in the back, never daring to dance, who've drunk themselves silly before Beck's roadies have even set the stage up. Strange girls with extravagant make-up lark through the crowd on some exotic kind of acid that is circulating below. There are Mexican-American kids and a smattering of black bohemian girls. Next to us is a girl with skintight black-and-white striped pants and a knitted top, her boyfriend in undertaker garb. They have the same raven black hair down to the ass. Here a freak, there a freak. None of them fit in back home, or at school, or even among their friends. A lot of unusual, beautiful faces in the crowd, all lit up with animated conversation. Ultimately, none of these people seem to have anything in common other than their freakish uniqueness. But that's not such a bad thing.

When Beck, thin, wiry and explosive as ever, comes barrelling on-stage, the crowd goes collectively insane. The dazzling backdrop of a curtain with sparkling lights sewn into it immediately strikes the right tone – one of almost gaudy glitter. The entire stage is lit up like a high-tech-circa-1983 studio set, with long lengths of rubber tubing in pastel colours running up and down the stage, draped behind the musicians. Roger Manning and DJ Swamp play atop burnished chrome pillars. Lyle, the guitarist, wears a decidedly un-flash red-and-black parachuting outfit reminiscent of a Night Ranger video. The fluorescent light stage props are stacked in triangles and parallelograms around the perimeter of the stage set. It's the dregs, man, the dregs of plastic American pop culture. But like Al Hansen picking up pieces of broken plaster angels toppled from the bulwarks of demolished grand buildings in New York, Beck is practising what art historian Kristine Stiles called 'the aesthetics of recovery', and succeeding beautifully.

From the first song, 'Mixed Bizness', the crowd crushes toward the stage. 'Novacane', with funkbot moves by Beck, elicits screams from the audience, but whether that's because they are being crushed or because of Beck's lean frame is not clear. 'The New Pollution' gets a sizeable portion of the audience in motion, and they sing every word to 'Nicotine & Gravy', suggesting that the album has made headway despite what *Billboard*'s pop charts tell us. (*Midnite Vultures* is number 76 on the charts this week.) 'Pressure Zone' is incendiary, tight and taut, with Beck's new guitarist and drummer professional – perhaps a bit too professional. Rachel and I dance our asses off, though a lot of people just sit through it looking like stunned rabbits. The sound is loose, sometimes disjointed, but played with fervour and abandon. Beckenstein's monster arises with his seams showing. Everyone's instruments seem to be tuned slightly differently, but this doesn't reflect badly at all on the band; in fact, it fits the mood and the crowd much better. Some girl up front throws a plastic zip-lock bag full of marijuana on-stage. Beck pauses for a millisecond to look at it. 'Wow, thanks,' he deadpans, dropping right back into the next verse. Minutes later, the girl's panties fly on-stage as well.

Beck drives everyone insane with tight dance moves, splits and leaps – 'All right, it's time for some breakdancing,' he drawls, launching into superior pop and lock, with elbows, shoulders and hands rippling at odd angles. 'Loser' is dispatched, with much more gusto than at Coachella just a few months ago – the crowd all join in. An uneven 'Deadweight' meanders, there's a radio-friendly aerodyne version of 'Milk & Honey', and then a leaner, more battle-worn 'Debra'. 'You know, there's something going on with music today... and it's not good. So I want you all to do me a favour and go out and do something about it, for me. Go on and fuck shit up!' With that, Beck launches into a riveting version of 'Hollywood Freaks' that sounds as bold and dynamic as it did on the first listen, his ode to Ol' Dirty Bastard rendered with precision, right down to the glorious breakdown. 'Peaches & Cream' is followed by a lovely jangling 'Jack-Ass' with Beck coming as close to acoustic as things get tonight, that is to say, with band accompaniment and an acoustic with a pick-up. 'Where It's At' winds up the set, and then DJ Swamp riffs on 'Louie Louie' and Deep Purple.

The band encore with a brassy 'Sexx Laws'; the Brass Menagerie are now in football gear, swinging from side to side. The Intellabeams flash relentlessly, producing a dizziness akin to the feeling of walking through a shopping mall two days before Christmas. 'Devil's Haircut' dissolves into noise overload; Beck staggers around with an orange mailbag, holding the pastel rubber tubing between his legs like an enormous flaccid cock. Around his neck is the bottom half of a pink mannequin. He waves at the crowd with white gloves, evoking memories of David Lee Roth, that other Los Angeles maverick showman. Lights flash wildly, the band unleashes feedback, Roger Manning does Bach arpeggios on his keyboards, and the drummer beats erratically. The Brass Menagerie let loose fanfares and reveilles. All is panic, and then it's over. The lights come back on; everyone blinks and files to the exit like sheep. I look at myself and my girlfriend, with her blonde hair swept up into a chignon bound with pins, smart black dress and stockings, bohemian kohl-lined eyes and dark red lipstick. A film noir existential beauty. I wear an ancient Doo Rag T-shirt, army fatigue pants, a long black overcoat that kept me warm on London streets so long ago, ragged leather boots and flannel. We're just as freaky as all the others.

The security team push the barrier forward, a solid line of metal grating bearing down on the stragglers. After they clear everyone out, we wait up in our perch, wondering what exactly the meaning of 'Aftershow' is. A Beck aftershow conjures up images of a salon with leather divans and scrawny white aesthetes sprawled out smoking bidis, listening to Pharaoh Sanders; urbane women looking like a cross between a Jacqueline Susann novel and the Bloomsbury Set drinking Diet Coke and talking under potted palms.

We make our way backstage. Rachel tells someone I am writing a book on Beck; that someone tells someone else. Then a woman pipes up with: 'You're Julian? Hi, I'm So-and-So, I work with Beck's management.' She walks into the dressing room. After five minutes she pops her head out and invites us in. Picture a boiler room in a gymnasium, about the size of a closet, with two huge ragged couches. Five or six people in there, some weirdo in a silver winter coat with his back turned to us, two maniacal groupies, Roger Manning on the couch. The silver coat turns around and extends a hand. 'Hey.' It's Beck. He doesn't look like 'Beck'; he's very pale with flushed cheeks, intense blue eyes and fine, fair hair. His demeanour is sharp and angular; he smiles a Cheshire Cat smile and we shake hands. Then the groupie twins pull him round again before he gets to say another word.

The catering team have deposited a rucksackful of horrid vegetables, rutabaga - and okra-looking things, on the table, along with a magnum of bottled water. The two girls, not groupies at all really, but glamour tarts wearing red jump-suits and plastic devil horns, start in with, 'Beck, you shouldn't have gotten your veggies from Whole Foods Supermarket, they're totally corporate, you shoulda gotten 'em from Wheatsville, independently owned....' Beck looks at them blankly. I sit down next to Roger, telling him that the drumming he did on 'Diamond In The Sleaze' was some of the best shit I'd heard this side of Tony Williams. He lights up, nice guy, damned good musician. We talk for ten minutes about clavinets, Mellotrons and prog rock. 'Look,' he says, 'prog rock is like any other musical form, even disco. Ninety-five per cent of it is dross, and five per cent is treasure.' I remember all those amazing interlocking musical pieces that made up his other band, Jellyfish.

Beck ambles over, finally free of the veggie terrorists (who've been expelled more or less politely), 'Hey,' he says again. I show him the cover and the photo contact sheet for the book. '*Beautiful Monstrosity*', eh? Nice.' One feels that Beck rarely expresses things in exclamation marks off-stage. He reminds me of the old adage that all comedians are serious people when they're out of the limelight. He lingers on the contact sheet, soaking up old memories: 'A lot of shows, so many shows.' I try my luck: 'Beck, you look too busy for an interview, but I would like your blessing.' He's amused now. 'Hmm...' he says, smiling that confounded half-smile again, rubbing his chin. After all, an interview is tantamount to authorization.

'Beck, we got dinner waiting on the bus,' his aide informs him. Roger leaves. 'Beck,' I say, seizing my chance, 'I'd like two minutes or so to tell you about the book.' But the aide is impatient: 'We've got to go, Beck.' He cuts her short with 'Let him say his piece, man.' I sit down on the couch and Beck sits down next to me, hands folded in his lap like a calm buddha. He radiates a simple peacefulness brought on by exhaustion. He's not cordial but detached as he was a minute ago when talking to the veggie duo or to my girlfriend who was trying to get him to laugh by asking him questions such as, 'Hey Beck, what's the meaning of life?'

I tell him my take, basically how I felt when he shouted out 'you know that fear when you wake up in the morning? That's one foot in the grave, baby, you gotta r-e-g-u-l-a-t-e'. To me, I explain, his 'regulation' was sort of a call to arms, to embrace flux, and defy the static that paralyses modern culture. 'Wow, that's pretty close,' he responds, nodding and grinning slyly. 'I wanted to undo the media myths about you,' I continue, 'I think they treated you unfairly.' He grimaces, a little defensive, 'Oh, I don't have any problem with the media, I mean, sometimes they don't understand what I do.' He smiles again. Well, of course, he's right – the media adore him now, but what about all those times they called him 'slacker', 'man child', 'a Cheetos-eating channel surfer', 'couch potato', 'voice of Generation X' and forty other inane things? 'I'd be interested to see what you've done,' he adds, winding up now, 'could you send it to me through my management? Put my name at the top and it'll get to me. I'm sorry I can't talk to you more, but I got to get rolling to Dallas, talk to the old lady, ya know.' The way he says 'old lady' makes us both crack up, and his eyes sparkle. In this room, he is the calm at the centre of the storm.

Outside: freezing cold. There are twenty people waiting out past the barriers. Beck signs damn near everything thrust at him, chats briefly, has his photo taken with people; meeting and greeting like a trouper. When he's done, and turns to walk away, I call 'Hey Beck!' and he stops. I give him a hug, sing a snippet of the old Carter Family song 'Will The Circle Be Unbroken' to him and add, 'Beck, whatever you're doing, you're doing the right thing, just keep on doing it. You're getting closer.' He's taken aback, perhaps, but seems moved by my gesture of Zen absurdity. I think of Al Hansen, laughing somewhere – sometimes absurdity is the best reality check. Beck shakes my hand firmly. 'Thanks, man.' Over and out.

199

DISCOGRAPHY

By Martin J Bridges (mjbridges@ndirect.co.uk http://www.mjb.ndirect.co.uk)

(With additions culled from discographies by Truck at http://www.beck.com/discography
and Squeegee at Slo-Jam Central at http://earth.vol.com/~debber//beck/discog1.html)

U.S. SINGLES

Flipside FLIP 46 'To See That Woman
Of Mine'
'MTV Makes Me Wanna Smoke Crack'
('Privates On Parade', 'Rock Scissors
Paper' by Bean)
(7", Split single, clear blue vinyl, 500
only, 1992)

Bong Load BL5 'Loser'
'Steal My Body Home'
(12", 500 only, later re-pressed, 'words of
wisdom' inscribed in the run-out groove,
1993)

Bong Load BL 11 'Steve Threw Up'
'Mutherfucker'
(Cupcake)
(7", sides labelled '2' & '3', last track
untitled, features the girls from that dog,
1994)

Geffen DGCS 7-19270 'Loser'
'Alcohol'
(7", March 1994)

Geffen DGCS-12270 'Loser'
'Alcohol'
(cassette, March 1994)

Geffen DGCDM-21930 'Loser'
'Corvette Bummer'

'Alcohol'
'Soul Suckin' Jerk (Reject)'
'Fume'
(CD, March 1994)

Geffen DM-22000 'Beercan'
'Got No Mind'
'Asskizz Powergrudge (Payback '94)'
'Totally Confused'
'Spanking Room'
Bonus Noise
(CD, 'Bonus Noise' is a 'muzak' version
of 'Loser', 1994)

K iPU 45 'It's All In Your Mind'
'Feather In Your Cap'
'Whiskey Can Can'
(7", foldover p/s, very dark brown vinyl,
later black vinyl, 1994)

Cosmic COSMIC 002 'Twig'
'Lint Cake'
(7", as Caspar & Mollüsk [alias for Chris
Bellew & Beck respectively], actually 4
tracks, 1994)

Mammoth MR 0078 'Jabberjaw No.2'
(7", 1500 only, includes 'Cold Ass
Fashion', other tracks by Hole and
Teenage Fanclub, 1994)

Geffen GED 21911 'Pay No Mind'
'Special People'

'Trouble All My Days'
'Supergolden (Sunchild)'
(CD, jewel case or cardboard slipcase, 1995)

Geffen 'Where It's At' (Edit)
'Where It's At'
(Remix by Mario C. & Mickey P.)
Bonus Beats
(CD, 1996)

Geffen DGC 12-22214 'Where It's At'
(Edit)
'Make Out City'
(Remix by Mike Simpson)
'Where It's At'
(Remix by Mario C. & Mickey P.)
Bonus Beats
'Where It's At' (Remix by U.N.K.L.E.)
(12", 1996)

Geffen DGC 9180 'Where It's At'
(LP Version)
'Make Out City'
(Remix by Mike Simpson)
'Where It's At'
(Remix by Mario C. & Mickey P.)
'Where It's At' (Remix by John King)
Bonus Beats
(12", 1996)

Geffen GED 22175 'Devil's Haircut'
'Dark And Lovely'
(Remix by the Dust Brothers)
'American Wasteland'
(Remix by Mickey P.)
(CD, 1996)

Geffen DGC 12-22222 'Devil's Haircut'
(LP Version)
'Dark And Lovely'
(Remix by the Dust Brothers)
'American Wasteland'
(Remix by Mickey P.)
'Lloyd Price Express'
(Remix by John King)
'Clock'
(12", 1997)

Geffen GED 22204 'The New Pollution'
'Electric Music For The Summer People'
'Richard's Hairpiece'
('Devil's Haircut' Remix by Aphex Twin)
(CD, 1997)

Geffen GED 12-22300 'The New
Pollution'
'The New Pollution'
(Remix by Mario C. & Mickey P.)
'The New Pollution' (Remix by Mikey P.)
'Lemonade'
'Richard's Hairpiece'
('Devil's Haircut' Remix by Aphex Twin)
(12", 1997)

Geffen DGC 12-22303 'Jack-Ass'
'Burro'
'Strange Invitation'
'Brother'
(12", 'Burro' is 'Jack-Ass' in Spanish with
a Mariachi band and 'Strange Invitation'
is an orchestral version, 1997)

Geffen Deadweight
'Erase The Sun'
'SA-5'
(CD, 1997)

Geffen 'Sexx Laws'
'Sexx Laws'
(Malibu Mix by Roger Manning)
(Limited edition 12", 1,000 only, clear
vinyl, sold only through the beckdirect
store, 1999)

201

U.S. ALBUMS

Sonic Enemy (no Cat. No.)
Golden Feelings
(cassette only, early 4-track material,
includes early version of 'Mutherfucker'
[spelt 'Mutherfukka'], January 1993)

Sonic Enemy (no Cat. No.)
Golden Feelings Tour Version
(same as above but with less bassy mix,
no artwork and several titles spelt
differently; tapes duplicated by 52nd
Street and sold at early shows, 1993)

Fingerpaint 02 *A Western Harvest Field
By Moonlight*
(10", 3000 copies, includes
fingerpainting, 1994)

Fingerpaint 02 *A Western Harvest Field
By Moonlight*
(10", reissue, 2000 copies, no
fingerpainting, 1994)

Geffen DGCD-24634 *Mellow Gold*
(CD, with untitled noise after last track,
number 13, March 1994; edited version
sold through K-Mart & Wal-Mart; also
on cassette)

Bong Load BL12 *Mellow Gold*
(LP, with 12" insert and label insert,
March 1994)

Flipside FLIP 60 *Stereopathetic Soul
Manure*
(CD, compilation of early home recordings 1988–1993, some copies with hidden 25th track of noise featuring backward message 'Bend me over in the
clover', April 1994)

K KLP 28 *One Foot In The Grave*
(CD, also on cassette, November 1994;
copies exported to U.K., August 1996)

K KLP 28 *One Foot In The Grave*
(LP, November 1994; copies exported to
U.K., August 1996)

Geffen DGCD-24823 *Odelay*
(CD, adds short bonus noise, June 1996,
number 16; also on cassette)

Bong Load Custom BL 30 *Odelay*
(LP, 180g vinyl, with tri-foldout poster,
label sticker & insert, June 1996; copies
exported to U.K.)

DGC DGCD-A-25309 *Mutations*
(CD, March 1998, number 13)

Bong Load Custom Records *Mutations*
(LP (BL39) + 7" (BL40), on 180 gram
vinyl. Includes bonus 7" with 'Diamond
Bollocks' and 'Runners Dial Zero',
January 1998)

CS 069490485 DGC *Midnite Vultures*
(CD, recorded at Beck's house. Limited
edition of 500,000 pressed in digipak
format, 23 November 1999, number 34)

U.S. PROMOS

Geffen PRO-CD-4613 'Loser'
(1-track CD, 1994)

Geffen PRO-A-4629 'Loser'
(12", stickered title with sleeve, 1994)

Geffen *Mellow Gold*
(10", with bonus track, 'Corvette
Bummer', omits other tracks, 1994)

Geffen PRO-CD-4633 *Mellow Gold*
(CD, for instore use, omits 'Fuckin' With
Head' and 'Truckdrivin' Neighbours
Downstairs (Yellow Sweat)', 1994)

Geffen PRO-CD-4653 Beck Sampler
(CD, 5-track, 1994)

(no Cat. No.) A History Of Beck
(cassette, non-Geffen material, 1994)

Geffen PRO-A-4875 'Where It's At'
(Promo Mix)
'Where It's At' (John King Remix)

'Where It's At'
(Mario C. & Mickey P. Remix)
Bonus Beats
(12", white label, stamped sleeve, 1994)

Geffen PRO-CD-4887 'Where It's At'
'Where It's At' (Radio Edit)
(CD, 1994)

Geffen PRO-CD-1014 'Where It's At'
'Make Out City'
(Remix by Mike Simpson)
(CD, 1994)

Geffen PRO-CD 4939 'Pay No Mind
(Snoozer)'
'Special People'
'Trouble All My Days'
'Supergolden (Sunchild)'
(CD, 1995)

Geffen DGCDA 24823 *Odelay*
(CD album, 1996)

Geffen PRO-CD-1016 'Devil's Haircut'
(CD, 1996)

Geffen PRO-CD-1066 'Devil's Haircut'
(Mike Simpson Remix)
(CD, 1996)

Geffen PRO-CD-1077 'Jack-Ass'
(Butch Vig Mix)
(CD, 2-track, 1997)

Geffen 'The New Pollution'
'The New Pollution'
(Remix by Mario C.)
(12", 1996)

Geffen PRO-CD-1082 'The New
Pollution'
(CD, 1-track, red/green striped sleeve, 1996)

Geffen PRO-CD-1090 'The New
Pollution' (Mikey P. Remix)
(CD, 1996)

Geffen PRCD 7637-2 'Deadweight'
(CD, 1-track, blue stickered case, 1997)

Geffen/Bong Load Custom Records
'Cold Brains'
'Electric Mind And The Summer People'
'Halo Of Gold'
'Runners Dial Zero'
'Diamond Bollocks'
(CD-5, promotional only single
distributed to radio stations, also released
in Australia, March 1999)

U.K. SINGLES

Geffen GFS 67 'Loser'
'Alcohol'
'Fume'
(7", 33rpm, February 1994, number 15)

Geffen GFSJB 67 'Loser'
'Loser'
(7", jukebox edition, February 1994)

Geffen GFSC 67 'Loser'
'Alcohol'
'Fume'
(cassette, February 1994)

Geffen GFSTD 67 'Loser'
'Totally Confused'
'Corvette Bummer'
'MTV Makes Me Wanna Smoke Crack'
(Lounge Act Version)
(CD, February 1994)

Geffen GFS 73 'Pay No Mind (Snoozer)'
'Special People'
(7", April 1994, unreleased)

Geffen GFSC 73 'Pay No Mind
(Snoozer)'
'Special People'
(cassette, April 1994, unreleased)

Geffen GFST 73 'Pay No Mind
(Snoozer)'
'Special People'
'Trouble All My Days'
'Supergolden (Sunchild)'
(12", April 1994, withdrawn)

Geffen GFSTD 73 'Pay No Mind
(Snoozer)'
'Special People'
'Trouble All My Days'
'Supergolden (Sunchild)'
(CD, April 1994, withdrawn)

Geffen GFST 22156 'Where It's At' (Edit)
'Where It's At'
(Remix by Mario C. & Mickey P.)
Bonus Beats
'Where It's At' (Remix by U.N.K.L.E.)
(12", June 1996, number 35)

Geffen GFSC 22156 'Where It's At'
(Edit)
'Where It's At'
(Remix by Mario C. & Mickey P)
Bonus Beats
(CD, June 1996)

Geffen GFS 22183 'Devil's Haircut'
'Lloyd Price Express'
(7", November 1996, number 22)

Geffen GFSTD 22183 'Devil's Haircut'
'Dark And Lovely'
(Remix by Dust Brothers)
'American Wasteland'
(Remix by Mickey P.)
'000.000'
(CD, November 1996)

Geffen GFSXD 22183 'Devil's Haircut'
'Devil's Haircut'
(Remix by Noel Gallagher)
'Groovy Sunday'
(Remix by Mike Simpson)
'Trouble All My Days'
(CD, November 1996)

Geffen GFS 22205 'The New Pollution'
'Electric Music For The Summer People'
(7", February 1997)

Geffen GFSTD 22205 'The New
Pollution'
'Richard's Hairpiece'
('Devil's Haircut' Remix by Aphex Twin)
'Electric Music And The Summer People'
(CD, February 1997)

Geffen GFSXD 22205 'The New
Pollution'
'The New Pollution'
(Remix by Mario C. & Mickey P.)
'Lemonade'
(CD, February 1997)

Geffen GFS 2253 'Sissyneck'
'Feather In Your Cap'
(7", May 1997)

Geffen GFSC 22253 'Sissyneck'
'The New Pollution'
(Remix by Mickey P.)
(cassette, May 1997)

Geffen GFSC 22253 'Sissyneck'
'The New Pollution'
(Remix by Mickey P.)
'Feather In Your Cap'
(CD, May 1997)

Geffen GFS 22276 'Jack-Ass'
(Butch Vig Mix)
'Strange Invitation' (orchestral version)
'Devil Got My Woman'
'Jack-Ass' (Lowrider Mix by Butch Vig)
'Burro'
'Brother'
(7", doublepack, gatefold p/s, 33rpm,
September 1997)

Geffen GFSTD 22276 'Jack-Ass'
(Butch Vig Mix)
'Jack-Ass' (Lowrider Mix)
'Burro'

'Strange Invitation' (orchestral version)
'Devil Got My Woman'
'Brother'
(CD, September 1997)

Geffen GFS 22293 'Deadweight' (Edit)
'Erase The Sun'
(7", October 1997)

Geffen GFSC 22293 'Deadweight'
'Erase The Sun'
(cassette, October 1997)

Geffen GFSTD 22293 'Deadweight'
(Edit)
'Erase The Sun'
'SA-5'
(CD, October 1997)

(no label) 'Clock'
'The Little Drum Machine Boy'
'Totally Confused'
(CD, given away with *Select*,
December 1997)

Geffen GEFDM 22365 'Tropicalia'
'Halo Of Gold'
'Black Balloon'
(CD, 3 March 1998)

Geffen/Bong Load Custom Records
'Tropicalia'
'Halo Of Gold'
(7", limited edition of 1,500, 7
December 1998)

Geffen 'Sexx Laws'
'This Is My Crew' (previously
unreleased)
'Sexx Laws'
(Wiseguys Remix)
(CD-3, 25 October 1999, number 15)

Geffen 'Sexx Laws'
'Salt In The Wound' (previously
unreleased)
'Sexx Laws'

(Malibu Remix by Roger Manning)
(CD-3, 1 November 1999)

Geffen 'Sexx Laws', 'Salt In The Wound'
(7", picture disc, limited edition of
1,500, 1 November 1999)

U.K. ALBUMS

Geffen GED 24634 *Mellow Gold*
(CD, with unlisted track, 'Analogue
Odessey', March 1994, number 41)

Geffen GEC 24634 *Mellow Gold*
(cassette, with unlisted track, 'Analogue
Odessey', March 1994)

Geffen GED 24908 *Odelay*
(CD, adds bonus track 'Diskobox',
June 1996)

Geffen GED 24926 *Odelay*
(CD, adds bonus tracks 'Diskobox' and
[unlisted] 'Clock', June 1996)

Geffen GEC 24908 *Odelay*
(cassette, June 1996)

Geffen GED 25184 *Mutations*
(CD, adds track 'Runners Dial Zero',
11 March 1998)

Geffen CS 069490485
Midnite Vultures
(CD, 22 November 1999)

U.K. PROMOS

Geffen WGFSTD 22156 'Where It's At'
(CD, 3-track, card sleeve, 1997)

Geffen BECK1 'Devil's Haircut'
(CD, 1-track, 1996)

Geffen WGFSTD 22253 'Sissyneck'
(CD, 1-track, card sleeve, 1997)

Geffen WGFSTD 22276 'Jack-Ass'
(CD, 2-track, die-cut buff sleeve, 1997)

Geffen WGFSTD 22293 'Deadweight'
(CD, 1-track, yellow card sleeve, 1997)

SELECTED OVERSEAS
RELEASES

Geffen GED 21891 'Loser'
'Totally Confused'
'Corvette Bummer'
'MTV Makes Me Wanna Smoke Crack'
(Lounge Act Version)
(CD, Sweden, 1994)

Geffen MVCZ-15001 'Where It's At'
(Edit) (Remix by John King)
'Lloyd Price Express'
('Devil's Haircut' Remix by John King)
'Dark And Lovely' ('Devil's Haircut'
Remix by the Dust Brothers)
'Clock'
(CD, Japan, 1996)

Geffen 'Where It's At' (Edit)
'Where It's At'
(Remix by Mario C. & Mickey P.)
Bonus Beats
(CD, Australia, 1996)

Geffen GEFD-24634 *Mellow Gold*
'Mexico'
'Totally Confused'
'Jagermeister Pie'
'Lampshade'
'Rowboat' (1995)
(Double CD Australian Tour version with
bonus disc)

Geffen 'Devil's Haircut'
'Dark And Lovely'

'American Wasteland'
(CD, Australia, with discount voucher for
Odelay, 1996)

Geffen MVCZ-10005 'The New
Pollution'
'The New Pollution'
(Remix by Mickey P.)
'The New Pollution'
(Remix by Mickey P. & Mario C.)
'Richard's Hairpiece'
('Devil's Haircut' Remix by Aphex Twin)
'Thunderpeel'
'Lemonade'
'000.000'
'Feather In Your Cap'
(Japanese Tour CD with booklet, aka
'The New Pollution and Other
Favourites', 1997)

Geffen 'The New Pollution'
'Electric Music For The Summer People'
'Richard's Hairpiece'
('Devil's Haircut' Remix by Aphex Twin)
(CD, Australian, card slipcase, 1996)

Geffen 'The New Pollution'
(CD, Holland, with extra video track, 1996)

Geffen GEFD-24948 *Odelay*
'Sissyneck'
'Burro'
'Dark And Lovely'
'Brother' (1997)
(Double CD, Australian Tour version
with bonus disc)

Geffen GEFDM 22310 'Sissyneck'
'Burro'
'Dark And Lovely'
'Brother'
(CD, Australian Tour edition, 1998)

Geffen *Mutations*
(CD, Germany, adds bonus track 'Halo
Of Gold', November 1998)

Geffen *Mutations*
(CD, Japan, adds track, a new version of
'Electric Music For The Summer People',
November 1998)

Geffen *Mutations*
(CD, Germany, adds 'Tropicalia' single
tracks, November 1998)

Geffen *Mutations*
(CD, Japan, adds 'Runners Dial Zero'
and 'Electric Music For The Summer
People', November 1998)

Geffen/Bong Load Custom Records
'Nobody's Fault But My Own'
'One Of These Days'
'Diamonds In The Sleaze'
(Japanese edition, April 1999)

IMPORTANT COMPILATION
APPEARANCES

No Life/KXLU KXLU 88.9FM *Los
Angeles Live Volume 1*
(U.S., CD, includes live version of
'Whiskey-Faced', 'Radioactive' and
'Blowdryin' Lady', 1993)

Mammoth MR 0074-2
Rare On Air Live Performances
(U.S., CD, includes 'Mexico' from 1993
KCRW Session, 1994)

Geffen GFL 19247 *Geffen Rarities Vol. 1*
(LP, includes 'Bogusflow', also
cassette/CD, 1994)

Geffen *Swag*
(CD, includes 'Corvette Bummer', 1994)

Mammoth MR 00981-2
Good To The Last Drop
(CD, includes 'In A Cold Ass Fashion',
1994)

Yo-Yo YO-YO CD-3 *Periscope: Another
Yo-Yo Compilation*
(U.S., CD, includes 'The World May
Lose Its Motion', 1994)

Brinkman Fast Forward 2
(U.S., CD, includes 'Trouble All My
Days', 1995)

WIN Poop Alley Tapes
(U.S., CD, includes alternate version of
'Girl Dreams', 1995)
Volume 16VCD 16 *Volume 16
(Copulation Explosion)*
(CD, with book, includes different
version of 'Thunderpeel', July 1996)

YoYo *YoYo A Go Go*
(U.S., 2-CD, includes 'Untitled'
[actually 'Satellite Of Love'] and
'Sleeping Bag', 1996)

UNI Distribution *Vans Warped Tour*
(U.S., CD, includes 'Make Out City'
['Where It's At' Remix by Mike
Simpson], 1996)

Geffen *Swagalicious*
(CD, includes 'Clock', 1996)

Geffen GED 25107 *Just Say Noel*
(CD, includes 'The Little Drum Machine
Boy', 1996)

Geffen GED 25121 *Suburbia Soundtrack*
(CD, includes '94 version of 'Feather In
Your Cap', 1997)

No Life KXLU Presents: *Demolisten
Vol. 2*
(U.S., CD, includes 'Untitled', 1997)

Sympathy For The Record Industry
SFTR 1482 *Kill The Moonlight*
soundtrack
(U.S., CD, includes 'Leave Me On The
Moon', 'Last Night I Traded My Soul's

Innermost For Some Pickled Fish' and 'Underwater Music', 1997)

Reprise 9362-46824-2 *The Bridge School Benefits Vol. 1*
(CD, includes 'It's All In Your Mind' [live from 1995 Bridge School Concert], 1997)

Capitol 859 911-0 *Tibetan Freedom Concert* (3-CD, foldout digipak; includes 'Asshole' on 'enhanced' 3rd disc, 1997)
NME BRAT '98 Bratpack '98
(cassette, includes 'Deadweight' [edit], cover-mounted on *NME*, January 1998)

K Records *Selector Dub Narcotic* (CD, double LP, features 'Close to God' from 1993–94, K Records sessions, USA , 1998)

Grand Royal Records GR068 ADV *At Home With The Groovebox* (CD, features 'Boyz', USA, February 2000)

GUEST APPEARANCES/ COLLABORATIONS

Sympathy For The Record Industry *Get Thee Gone*
(U.S. 10", by the Geraldine Fibbers; includes 'Blue Cross', by Beck, Chris Ballew & The Fibbers, 1994)

Matador! OLE 105-2 *Orange* (U.S. CD, by Jon Spencer Blues Explosion; 'Flavor' features Beck rapping, 1994)

Nardwuar The Human Serviette Cleo 8 *Skookum Chief Powered Teenage Zit Rock Angst Presented By Nardwuar The Human Serviette* (CD, LP, 1995)

Cosmic Records COS 002 *Caspar And Mollüsk* (7", Chris Ballew (Caspar) and Beck (Mollüsk) do 'Twig', 1995)

Win Records WIN 010 *Poop Alley Tapes* (Double CD, 'Girl Dreams' redone with that dog, USA, 1996)

Matador! OLE 1112 Jon Spencer Blues Explosion: *Experimental Remixes* (U.S. LP, 'Flavor Pt 1&2' remixed by Mike D & Beck; Beck raps on 'Pt 2'; also on cassette & CD, 1995)

Vast Records *Hear You Me!* (CD, Beck plays banjo on that dog's 'Silently', USA, 27 January 1998)

Supreme/Island Records *Amnesia: Lingus* (CD Ex-Medicine front-man Brad Laner's new project features Beck on harmonica on 'Drop Down', USA, 14 July 1998)

Minty Fresh *Kahimi Karie* (CD, Beck plays harmonica on 'Lolitapop Dollhouse', USA, 8 September 1998)

Nickelbag Records *Can Tribute Album* (as-yet-unreleased) (Beck does a great version of Can's 'I'm So Green')

Interscope Records *The Rugrats Movie Soundtrack* (CD, Beck guest mumbles two lines on 'This World Is Something New To Me', USA, 3 November 1998)

TVT Soundtrax *The Hi-lo Country Soundtrack* (CD, Beck and Willie Nelson do 'Drivin' Nails In My Coffin', USA, 19 January 1999)

Dreamworks *Forest For The Trees:*
The Sound Of Wet Paint
(CD/ECD Beck buried somewhere in
the mix of 'Jet Engine', USA, 9 March
1999)

Birdman Records *More Oar: A Tribute*
To Alexander "Skip" Spence
(CD, Beck's superb version of Spence's
'Halo of Gold', USA, 6 July 1999)

Almo Sounds *Return Of The Grievous*
Angel: Tribute To Gram Parsons
(CD, Beck and Emmylou Harris do 'Sin
City', USA, 13 July 1999)

REMIX WORK

Caroline 'Sexy Boy' by Air
(CD, 12" (also available on AIR: Kelly
Watch The Stars 12"), USA, UK, 1998)

Elektra 'Hunter' by Björk
(CD, France, 1998)

Elektra 'Alarm Call'
(Bjeck Remix) by Björk
(CD, UK, 1998)

Elektra 'Alarm Call'
(Bjeck Remix) by Björk
(12", DJ Club vinyl, UK, 1998)

OTHERS

Fresh Takes On Old Slabs: A Tribute
To Beck
(22 track CD-R compiled by Mr. Chonk,
with versions of Beck's songs done by
fans. Beck commented on it: 'It's great!',
ordering info:
http://members.aol.com/mrchonk,
28 September 1999)

209

BIBLIOGRAPHY

BOOKS

Carlin, Richard. *The Big Book Of Country Music*, Penguin, 1995

Cohn, Lawrence. *Nothing But The Blues*, Abbeville Press, 1993

Hansen, Al. *A Primer of Happenings and Time/Space Art*, Something Else Press, 1965

Hansen, Al. Fluxus. *Playing With Matches*, Smart Art Press/Plug In Editions, 1998

Hansen, Al. *Questions And Answers*, Al Hansen Archive Text, 1976

Hansen, Al. *Why Shoot Andy Warhol?* Illustrated book, Verona, Italy 1984. Reprinted in *Playing With Matches*, Smart Art Press/Plug In Editions, 1998

Rummel, Jack and Rebennack, John 'Mac'. *Under A Hoodoo Moon: The Life Of Dr John The Night Tripper*, St. Martin's Press, New York, May 1995

Kellein, Thomas. *Fluxus*, Thames And Hudson, U.K., 1995

Kirby, Michael. *Happenings*, E.P. Dutton & Co., New York, 1965

McCormick, Carlo. Interview With Beck Hansen. *Playing With Matches*, pp. 57–73, Smart Art Press/Plug In Editions, 1998

Toop, David. *Rap Attack 3*, Consortium Book Sales & Distributors, 15 June 1999

Tosches, Nick. *Country: The Twisted Roots Of Rock And Roll*, Da Capo Press, 1977

Various authors. *Online Diaries: The Lollapalooza '95 Tour Journals*, Soft Skull Press, January 1998

NEWSPAPER AND MAGAZINE SOURCES

Adams, Scott. 'Cry Of Conscience', *Arete* Magazine, 1990

Ashare, Matt. 'Eat Their Dust: Meet The Men Behind Beck And The Beasties', *Boston Phoenix*, 28 November–5 December 1996

Ashare, Matt. 'Slow Jamming: Beck Reveals His Inner Soul Man', *Boston Phoenix*, 25 November–2 December 1999

Babcock, Jay. 'Beck', *Huh*, July 1996

Bam, July 1996

Barber, Nicholas. 'Beck To The Future, Harmonica In Hand', *Independent On Sunday*, 9 March 1997

Bennun, David. 'Beck To The Future', *Melody Maker*, 16 November 1996

Billboard, 27 November 1993

Bliss, Karen. 'Beck On Axl Rose, Ice Cube, But No Millennium Please'. 2 December 1999, *All-star* magazine, www.cdnow.com

Bream, Jon. 'Where It's At: Summer Festivals', *Minneapolis Star Tribune*, 1 August 1997

Breslin, Jimmy. 'The Happening Of A Lifetime', *Newsday*, July 1995

Burnett, Erich. 'Losing The "Loser" Mentality', *Scene*, August 1996

Bush, Melanie. 'History of the Fort', *Village Voice*, 1997

Chonin, Neva. 'Beck', *Rolling Stone*, 24 June 1999

Cigarettes, Johnny. 'Gouda Vibrations', *Vox*, March 1997

Cohen, Scott. 'The Joy Of Beck', *Details*, August 1996

Colliton, Carrie. 'Can A One Man Band Go Solo?', *Music Monitor*, November 1998

'Cool As Fuck!' *Dazed & Confused*, May 1997

Cromelin, Richard. 'Loser Gets Amnesia and Thicker Skin', *Los Angeles Times*, 30 April 1995

Cromelin, Richard. 'Nobody's Fool', *Los Angeles Times*, 21 July 1996

Dark, Jane. 'The Best Albums Of The 90s', *Spin*, November 1998

Davis, Billy. 'Interview With Smokestack', *American Music* zine, 6 August 1998

Bibbe Hansen Interview With Vaginal Davis, *Index* magazine, November–December 1999

Decurtis, Anthony. 'Beck: Q&A', *Rolling Stone*, 26 November 1998

Dedman, Donna. *Gellow Molde* fanzine, 1994–5

Dedman, Donna. Interview with Bibbe Hansen. *Cyanide Breathmint* fanzine, 1995

Deluca, Dan. 'Now A Real Showman, Beck Holds Big Audience In Thrall', *Philadelphia Inquirer*, 1 April 1997

Doss, Yvette C. 'The Chicano Jew Chats About His Life', *Frontera* # 4, 1996

Dunn, Jancee. 'Beck: Resident Alien', *Rolling Stone*, 11–25 July 1996

Farley, Christopher John. 'Beck To The Future', *Time*, 20 January 1997

Ferguson, Troy. 'Beck: Where He's At', *Rip It Up*, January 1998

Ferman, Dave. 'Beck To The Future', *Fort Worth Star-Telegram*, 3 November 1998

Foege, Alec. Reader's Poll 1997, *Rolling Stone*, 23 January 1997

Friar, William. 'Beck's Live Show Defies Judgement, But It's Some Fun', *Oakland Tribune*, 12 October 1996

Friedman, Ken. 'The Twelve Criteria Of Fluxus', *Lund Art Press* magazine, Vol. 1, No. 4, Summer–Autumn 1990

Garelick, Jon. 'Beck Is Better Than The Real Thing', *Boston Phoenix*, 5–12 June 1997

Gilbey, Ryan. 'The Cap Doesn't Fit', *Independent*, 5 April 1996

Ginsberg, Allen. 'A Beat/Slacker Transgenerational Meeting Of Minds', *Shambhala Sun*, 27 September 1999

Gladstone, Eric. 'Musical Mutations', *Ray Gun* magazine, January 1999

Goldberg, Michelle. 'Beck The Untouchable', *Metro Active Music* magazine, 1998

Gonçalves, Pedro. *Blitz* magazine (Brazil), 3 November 1998

Grob, Julie. 'Beck', *Thora-zine*, www.eden.com/thora-zine, May 1994

Hansen, Beck. 'The Best Thing I've Heard All Year', *Mojo*, January 1997

Hansen, Beck. 'Tiny Beck: Your Personal Advice Columnist', *Sassy*, November 1994

Hilburn, Robert. 'Beck's Got A Brand New Bad', *Los Angeles Times*, 14 November 1999

Hilburn, Robert. 'Pop Music "Dream" Deferred No More', *Los Angeles Times*, 16 November 1997

Hilburn, Robert. 'The Freewheelin' Beck', *Los Angeles Times*, 26 February 1997

Hoskyns, Barney. 'The Mix It Up Kid', *Mojo* magazine, March 1997

Hoskyns, Barney. *World Art Magazine*, issue 19, Autumn 1999

Hughley, Mark. 'Beyond The Boundaries', *Oregonian*, 28 August 1997

'I Love The Smell Of Methane And Bananas In The Morning', *Mean* magazine, December 1999

Interview with Beck, *Humo* magazine (Belgium), 14 December 1999

Interview With Jon Spencer, *Magnet*, issue 29, November 1994

Johnson, Calvin. 'Calvin Talks to Beck, Beck Talks Back to the Rocket', *The Rocket*, January–February 1997

Johnson, David. 'Beck and Call: Lighting

Design For Beck's Rock Music Concerts', *TCI* magazine, April 1997

Jones, Cliff. 'Captain Sensible', *The Face*, 1996

Joyce, John. 'Diary Of An LP', *Melody Maker*, 28 November & 5 December 1998

Kemp, Mark. 'Where It's At Now', *Rolling Stone*, 17 April 1997

Kim, Jae-Ha. 'Pop's Golden Boy; Beck On Mantras, Dadaism And Fame', *Chicago Sun-Times*, 30 July 1997

Kot, Greg. 'Beck's Back', *Chicago Tribune*, 6 November 1998

List, Daniel. 'Bibbe's Ma, Audrey', *Village Voice*, 15 August 1968

McCormick, Neil. 'Beck To The Future', *Daily Telegraph*, 6 November 1997

McKenna, Kristine. 'Beck's First Sampling', *Los Angeles Times*, 3 May 1998

McLean, Craig. *Observer*, 7 March 1999

McMillan, Matt. 'Beck', *Exclaim*, 1996

Mehle, Michael. 'Beck's Progressive Risks Pay Off', *Denver Rocky Mountain News*, 18 May 1997

Michel, Peter. 'Summersault '96', *Blah Blah Blah* fanzine, December 1995–January 1996

Mini Interview with Beck. *Select*, September 1996

Mirkin, Steve. 'Old Pollution: Where It's Art Exhibit Shows That Beck's Love Of Pop Garbage Runs In The Family', *Rolling Stone*, 11 May 1998

Morales, Ed. 'Looking Beckward', *Village Voice*, 15 September 1998

Morris, Chris. 'Beck Cites California 7-Year Law In Contract Fight', *Billboard*, 8 May 1999

Mulvey, John. London Brixton Academy Review, *NME*, 4 January 1997

Mulvey, John. 'State Of The Mutation', *NME*, 11 November 1998

Mutant Machine, Unknown Source, 1998

Myers, Christopher. Prince Paul. *Index* magazine, May 1998

Nielsen, Jeff. 'Viva Tropicalia', *Ray Gun* magazine, January 1999

Norris, Chris. 'Moonwalking In L.A.', *Spin*, December 1999

Norris, Chris. 'Return Of The Funk Soul Brother', *Spin*, December 1999

Option, issue 56, May 1994

Parker, Aaron. *Buzzine*, 1997

Perlich, Tim. 'Beck's Trek', *Now*, November 1996

Phalen, Tom. 'Beck's Back: He's A Loser, Baby, Who Knows How To Write Songs', *The Seattle Times*, 1 July 1994

Philbrook, Erik. 'Beck: The New Solution', *Playback*, 1997

Porter, Charlie. 'Beck To The Future', *The Times*, 25–31 October 1997

Powell, Alison. 'The Urge For Serge', *Interview* magazine, April 1997

Robbins, Ira. 'No "Loser", But A Winning Night With Beck', *Newsday*, 25 March 1994

Roberts, Randall. 'Chameleon Of Creativity', *St. Louis Post-Dispatch*, 4 October 1996

Rogers, Ray. 'Loser?' *Interview* magazine, August 1996

Rotondi, James. 'Beck: Return Of The Mack', CMJ, November 1999

Rotondi, James. *Guitar Player*, September 1994

Rubin, Mike. 'Subterranean Homeboy Blues', *Spin*, July 1994

Saunders, Michael. '"Loser" No More: Beck', *Boston Globe*, 23 August 1996

Schoemer, Karen. 'The Last Boy Wonder', *Elle* magazine, December 1999

Simutis, David. 'The Man Who Would Be King', *Iron Minds*, 3 September 1999

Smith, Ethan. 'Re: Fluxology – Beck And Yoko Ono Sound Off On Found Art, Family Ties, And Flying Pianos', *New York* magazine, 21 September 1998

Sprague, David. 'Sudden Change Of Fortune', *Newsday*, 1994

Stevenson, Jane. 'Nice Try, Beck, But You Can't Hide Talent, *Toronto Sun*, 6 June 1996

Stiles, Kristine. (Dissertation) 'Battle of the Yams: Al Hansen, The Anonymous Arts Recovery Society, and Recovering an Aesthetics of Recovery'. Department of Art and Art History, Duke University, August 1997

Strauss, Neil. 'Artist Of The Year', *Spin*, 1996

Sullivan, Jim. 'You Know He's Not A Loser', *Boston Globe*, 8 August 1997

'Super Beck: "Loser", Artist, Rock Star, Genius'. *UHF* # 10, July–August 1996

'The Evolution Of Golden Boy Beck', *Paper* magazine, July–August 1996. www.papermag.com/magazine/beck

Thomas, David. 'It's Good To Be Beck Hansen, Musical Genius', *Daily Telegraph*, 10 May 1997

Thompson, Ben. 'Reasons To Be Cheerful', *Independent On Sunday*, 15 September 1996

Tignor, Steve. 'Beck Beat', *Puncture*, Summer 1996, issue 36

Uhelszki, Jaan. 'Beck Names His "Dumb-Ass Party Record"', *Rolling Stone*, 14 September 1999

Violanti, Anthony. The *Buffalo News*, 21 August 1996

Wahl, Chris. 'Beck Blows Roof Off Varsity Arena', *Toronto Sun*, 3 April 1997

Weisbard, Eric. 'After The Goldrush', *Spin*, 1996

Wiederhorn, Jon. 'The Many Faces Of Beck', *Guitar*, January 1999

Wild, David. 'Beck', *Rolling Stone*, 21 April 1995

Williams, Simon. Live: London Kilburn National Ballroom, *NME*, 15 March 1996

RADIO AND RECORDED MEDIA

BBC1 Evening Session, November 1994

Hanft, Steve. *Kill The Moonlight* soundtrack liner notes, Sympathy For The Record Industry, 1997

'Nardwuar vs. Beck'. *Skookum Chief Powered Teenage Zit Rock Angst Presented By Nardwuar The Human Serviette*, 18 April 1994. LP, CD (Cleo 8 Label, 1995, USA)

Portfield, Nolan. Liner notes, *Jimmie Rodgers: 1932 'No Hard Times'*, Rounder Records, 1991

Siegel, Robert And Wertheimer, Linda. 'All Things Considered'. National Public Radio, 1998

Wolfe, Charles. Liner Notes, *Anchored In Love: The Carter Family*, Rounder Records, 1991

INTERNET ADDRESSES

Alt.music Beck Internet Newsgroup. news://alt.music.beck

'Beck Honours His Grandfather's Fluxus Work'. MTV Online. www.mtv.com, 17 September 1998

'Beck Reveals Plans For Next Album: "Peppy, Enjoyable Music"'. www.ubl.com, 19 November 1998

Basham, David. 'Midnite Cowboy'. December 1999. http://mtv.com/news/gallery/b/beck99/beckfeature99.html

Boots, J., Interview With Beck. http://www.vpro.nl/3voor12, VPRO Radio, Netherlands, 1997

Bornemann, Tim. 'Beck Meets Squeegee'. Slo-Jam Central website. http://earth.vol.com/~debber/beck/mainpg2.html, 2 April 1997

Browne, David. 'Beck In The High Life', *Entertainment Weekly*. www.ew.com, 14 February 1997

Cummings, Sue. 'Beck: Dumpster Divin' Man'. MTV Online. www.mtv.com, June 1996

Dagbladet, December 1999, www.dagbladet.no

Douridas, Chris. 'Morning Becomes Eclectic'. KCRW Radio, Los Angeles. http://www.kcrw.com, 19 June 1996

Exan. 'Beck And Me'. MTV Online,
www.mtv.com, May 1996
Flaherty, Adam. Beck-
Odelay@Worldnet.Att.Net
Godwins, Rupert. Analysis Of 'Runners
Dial Zero'. news://alt.music.beck,
November 1999
Gundersen, Edna. 'Beck In The Saddle
Again'. MSN Entertainment Channel.
http://musiccentral.msn.com, 1998
http://members.tripod.com/~beck
mellowgold
http://www.eyeneer.com/ema.html
Interview With Emmylou Harris.
www.cdnow.com, CDnow, January
1998
Kates, Mark. Geffen Beck Website.
www.geffen.com/beck/bio
Kaufman, Gil. 'Beck Recorded More Than
20 Songs For *Midnite Vultures*'.
Entertainment Weekly, www.ew.com,
5 October 1999
Loder, Kurt. 'Beck Mutates', MTV Online,
www.mtv.com, 11 November 1998
Margetts, Jayne. 'Je Suis Un
Revolutionaire'. www.thei.aust.com/,
Reverberation, 1996
Martin, Richard. 'Beck Hansen May Be
The Hardest-Working Man In Show
Business'. www.wweek.com, 1996
Momus (Currie, Nick).
www.demon.co.uk/momus/, Momus,
London, March 1997
Puttin' It Down website. Webmaster:
Giffoni, Carlos. www.geocities.com/
sunsetstrip/3226/putt.htm
Sakamoto, John. 'Beck Answers His Fans',
Jam!, www.canoe.ca/jam, 5 June 1996
Sakamoto, John. 'Music Oddball Beck
Gets Mutated'. *Jam!*,
www.canoe.ca/jam, 8 October 1998
Scoppa, Bud. 'Dust Brothers Are Where
It's At'. Addicted To Noise online
music website, www.addict.com, 1996
Sessions At West 54th Street,
www.sessionsatwest54th.com,
6 September 1997

Slo-Jam Central website.
http://earth.vol.com/~debber/beck/
mainpg2.html
Veloso, Caetano. 'Invisible Jukebox',
Wire magazine, January 2000
www.beck.com Official Beck Website
(Webmaster: Truck)
Yuen, Emma. (webmaster) Enchanting
Wizard Of Rhythm Website.
www.freespeech.org/beck_fishbulb/

EXHIBITION CATALOGUES
Hansen, Al. *Notes On A Mini-
Retrospective*. Kölnisches Stadt Museum,
Köln, 1995

PAMPHLETS
Hansen, Al. 'An Incomplete Requiem For
W.C. Fields', Great Bear Pamphlets,
New York, 1966

PUBLIC APPEARANCES

1989
The Chameleon, New York City, New York
(First Public Performance)
The Fort, New York City, New York
ABC No Rio, New York City, New York

1990–2
Raji's, Los Angeles, California
Al's Bar, Los Angeles, California
Highland Grounds, Los Angeles, California
Onyx Los Feliz, Los Angeles, California
Jabberjaw, Los Angeles, California
Troy Café, Los Angeles, California
Spaceland Silverlake, Los Angeles, California
Fuzzyland, Los Angeles, California
Pik-Me-Up, Los Angeles, California
Big Oaks Lodge Saugus, California (Ten Ton
    Lid – Beck and Martha Atwell trad
    countryside project)
Various locations (Loser – Beck and Steve
    Hanft metal band side project)

1991
August Sunset Junction Street Fair,
    Los Angeles, California
August Jabberjaw, Los Angeles, California

1993
7 July KCRW Radio, Santa Monica, California
7 July Troy Café, Los Angeles, California
23 July Venue unknown, Pomona, California

1994
1 January Al's Bar, Los Angeles, California
3 January Troy Café, Los Angeles, California
1 March KCRW Radio, Santa Monica,
    California

March (exact dates unkown) SXSW Festival,
    Austin, Texas
20 March Goat's Head, Houston, Texas
22 March the Boot, New Orleans,
    Los Angeles, California
24 March Dark Horse Tavern, Atlanta, Georgia
25 March the Shoebox, Athens, Georgia
26 March Duke University, Durham,
    North Carolina
27 March American University, Washington,
    District of Columbia
29 March Knitting Factory, New York,
    New York
30 March Axis, Boston, Massachusetts
31 March Middle East Café, Cambridge,
    Massachusetts
1 April the Grand, New York, New York
2 April JC Dobbs, Philadelphia, Pennsylvania
4 April the Rivoli, Toronto, Ontario, Canada
6 April Detroit Science, Detroit, Michigan
7 April the Distillery, Columbus, Ohio
12 April Cicero's, St. Louis, Missouri
13 April Rhumba Box, Kansas City, Missouri
15 April Ground Zero, Boulder, Colorado
16 April DV-8, Salt Lake City, Utah
18 April Slim's, San Francisco, California
19 April the Troubadour, Los Angeles,
    California
20 April World Beat Center, San Diego,
    California
22 April McCabe's, Santa Monica, California
8 May Beale Street Music, Memphis,
    Tennessee
3 June Price Center, La Jolla, California
4 June the Roxy Club, Phoenix, Arizona
5 June Huntridge Theatre, Las Vegas,
    Nevada

10 June Shoreline Amphitheatre, Mountain View, California

11 June Venue unknown, Los Angeles, California

13 June DV-8, Salt Lake City, Utah

15 June Ogden Theatre, Denver, Colorado

17 June Deep Ellum Live, Dallas, Texas

18 June Toad's, Houston, Texas

19 June Liberty Lunch, Austin, Texas

21 June Mississippi, St. Louis, Missouri

22 June Bogart's, Cincinnati, Ohio

24 June Eastwood Theatre, Indianapolis, Indiana

25 June Phoenix Plaza, Pontiac, Michigan

27 June The Metro, Chicago, Illinois

28 June The Rave, Milwaukee, Wisconsin

29 June 1st Avenue Club, Minneapolis, Minnesota

2 July Howden Ballroom, Vancouver, Canada

3 July Oz, Seattle, Washington

4 July La Luna, Portland, Oregon

6 July the Fillmore, San Francisco, California

7 July the Whisky, Los Angeles, California

5 August the Playroom, Goldcoast, Australia

6 August the Roxy, Brisbane, Australia

9 August the Herdsman, Perth, Australia

11 August the Old Lion, Adelaide, Australia

12 August Prince of Wales, Melbourne, Australia

13 August Prince of Wales, Melbourne, Australia

14 August Wall Street, Melbourne, Australia

17 August Anu Bar, Canberra, Australia

18 August Newcastle University, Newcastle, Australia

19 August Sydney University, Sydney, Australia

22 August JJJ Radio Session, Sydney, Australia

23 August PowerStation, Auckland, New Zealand

25 August Neptune II, Wanchai, China

27 August Faces, Makati, China

29 August Club Citta, Kawasaki, Japan

31 August Diamond Hall, Nagoya, Japan

1 September IMP Hall, Osaka, Japan

2 September Skala Espacio, Fukuoka, Japan

4 September Club Citta, Kawasaki, Japan

5 September Club Citta, Kawasaki, Japan

6 September Liquid Room, Tokyo, Japan

7 September Liquid Room, Tokyo, Japan

9 September After Dark, Honolulu, Hawaii

19 October Metropol, Pittsburgh, Pennsylvania

20 October Marquee, Buffalo, New York

21 October the Opera House, Toronto, Ontario, Canada

22 October Le Spectrum, Montreal, Quebec, Canada

24 October Middle East Café, Cambridge, Massachusetts

25 October Lupos Heartbreak, Providence, Rhode Island

26 October Irving Plaza, New York, New York

28 October Toad's Place, New Haven, Connecticut

29 October Metropolis, Harrisburg, Pennsylvania

30 October Trocadero, Philadelphia, Pennsylvania

31 October 9:30 Club, Washington, District of Columbia

3 November Salle Des Fetes, Vernier/ Le Lign, France

5 November The Revolver, Madrid, Spain

6 November Estandard, Barcelona, Spain

8 November Crossover, Turin, Italy

9 November Circolo Degli, Rome, Italy

10 November Factory, Milan, Italy

12 November Belmondo, Prague, Czech Republic

13 November Charterhalle, Munich, Germany

15 November Luxor, Cologne, Germany

16 November Grosse Freiheit, Hamburg, Germany

17 November Loft, Berlin, Germany

18 November Vision Boarde, Les Deux Alpes, France

20 November Vera, Groningen, Netherlands

21 November Loppen, Copenhagen, Denmark

22 November Gino, Stockholm, Sweden

23 November Rockefeller, Oslo, Norway

26 November Manchester University, Manchester, UK

27 November King Tut's Wah, Glasgow, Scotland

28 November Astoria Theatre, London, UK

29 November Splash Club, London, UK

1 December Transmusicales, Rennes, France

2 December Arapaho, Paris, France

4 December De Melkweg, Amsterdam, Netherlands

5 December Vooruit, Ghent, Belgium

12 December Spaceland, Los Angeles, California

17 December Slim's, San Francisco, California

18 December the Troubadour, Los Angeles, California

1995

7 January Pantages Theatre, Los Angeles, California

16 January KCRW, Los Angeles, California

21 April Doornroosje, Nijamegen, Netherlands

20 June Catalyst, Santa Cruz, California

21 June Cactus Club, San José, California

22 June Cattle Club, Sacramento, California

24 June World Beat Center, San Diego, California

25 June Music City, Fountain Valley, California
Start of the Lollapalooza tour

4 July the Gorge, George, Washington

5 July UBC Stadium, Vancouver, B.C., Canada

8 July Fiddlers, Denver, Colorado

10 July Sandstone Amphitheatre, Kansas City, Missouri

11 July Riverport Amphitheatre, St. Louis, Missouri

12 July Deer Creek Amphitheatre, Indianapolis, Indiana

14 July Polaris Amphitheatre, Columbus, Ohio

15 July New World Amphitheatre, Chicago, Illinois

18 July Riverbend Amphitheatre, Cincinnati, Ohio

19 July Pine Knob Amphitheatre, Detroit, Michigan

20 July Pine Knob Amphitheatre, Detroit, Michigan

22 July Blossom Music Center, Cleveland, Ohio

23 July Molson Park, Toronto, Ontario, Canada

25 July Great Woods, Boston, Massachusetts

26 July the Meadows, Hartford, Connecticut

28 July Randall's Island, New York, New York

29 July Randall's Island, New York, New York

30 July Blockbuster/Sony Pavilion, Philadelphia, Pennsylvania

31 July Starlake Amphitheatre, Pittsburgh, Pennsylvania

2 August Charles Town Races, Charles Town, West Virginia

3 August Racetrack, Charleston, North Carolina

5 August Lakewood Amphitheatre, Atlanta, Georgia

6 August Walnut Creek Amphitheatre, Raleigh, North Carolina

9 August Southpark Meadows, Austin, Texas

10 August Starplex Amphitheatre, Dallas, Texas

12 August Desert Sky Pavilion, Phoenix, Arizona

14 August Irvine Meadows, Los Angeles, California

15 August Irvine Meadows, Los Angeles, California

18 August Shoreline Amphitheatre, San Francisco, California
End of Lollapalooza tour

25 August Reading Festival, Reading, UK

26 August Pukkelpop, Open Hasselt, Belgium

27 August Lowlands Festival, Dronton, Netherlands

29 August Bataclan, Paris, France

31 August Fri-Son, Fribourg, Switzerland

1 September Winterthürer, Winterthür, Switzerland

2 September Holzstock '95, Ebensee, Austria

9 September El Pop Festival, Badalona, Spain

12 September Elysee, Montmarte, Paris, France

18 October Shoreline Amphitheatre, Mountain View, California

28 October Bridge School Benefit, Mountain View, California

11 November Club Spaceland, Los Angeles, California

29 December Venue unknown, Sydney, Australia

1996

7 January Summersault Festival, Perth, Australia

1 March Fast Forward Festival II, venue unknown, Tilburg, Netherlands

18 March Noorderlicht, Tilburg, Netherlands

27 March Le Bataclan, Paris, France

31 March, Venue unknown, London, UK

3 April Venue unknown, Cologne, Germany

5 June Regency Room, Toronto, Ontario, Canada

16 June Tibetan Freedom Concert, San Francisco, California

16 June *Odelay* release party show

17 June KOME, San José, California

19 June KCRW, Santa Monica, California

27 June Galaxy, Santa Ana, California

28 June Venue unknown, Pomona, California

3 July Quart Festival, Kristiansand, Norway

4 July Venue unknown, France

5 July Venue unknown, France

6 July Les Eurockeene, Belfort, France

8 July Venue unknown, Austria

9 July Backstage, Munich, Germany

10 July Venue unknown, Germany

12 July Feile Festival, Thurles, Ireland

13 July T-In-The-Park, Scotland

14 July Dour Music Festival, Dour, Belgium

16 July Venue unknown, Italy

17 July Vidia Club, Cesena, Italy

19 July Phoenix Festival, Stratford, UK Filmed for UK TV

21 July Paradiso, Amsterdam, Netherlands

23 July Rote-Fabrik, Zurich, Switzerland

24 July Venue unknown, Switzerland

26 July Lollipop Festival, Stockholm, Sweden

27 July Venue unknown, France

2 August Live 105, San Francisco, California

3 August Kitsap Bowl, Bremerton, Washington

4 August Timberbowl, Estacada, Oregon

14 August First Avenue, Minneapolis, Massachusetts

15 August Cabaret Metro, Chicago, Illinois

17 August Sanctum, Pontiac, Michigan

18 August Odeon, Cleveland, Ohio

20 August Ogden Music Hall, Buffalo, New York

21 August Concert Hall, Toronto, Ontario, Canada

22 August Chumcity Building, Toronto, Ontario, Canada Filming for ODEBECK, Much Music TV

23 August La Spectrum, Montreal, Quebec, Canada

24 August Avalon, Boston, Massachusetts

25 August Lupos, Heartbreak, Providence, Rhode Island

27 August Supper Club, New York, New York

28 August WXRK Radio, New York, New York

30 August Trocadero, Philadelphia, Pennsylvania

31 August 9:30 Club, Washington, District of Columbia

1 September Maxwell's, Hoboken, New Jersey

2 September Columbia University, New York, New York

6 September *David Letterman*, CBS TV, New York, New York

20 September Venue unknown, Charlotte, North Carolina

23 September 328 Performance Hall, Nashville, Tennessee

28 September Venue unknown, Tulsa, Oklahoma

11 October Civic Auditorium, Santa Monica, California

12 October Venue unknown, Los Angeles, California

23 October IMP Hall, Osaka, Japan

24 October Diamond Hall, Nagoya, Japan

25 October Skala Espacio, Fukuoka, Japan

27 October Blitz, Tokyo, Japan

28 October Blitz, Tokyo, Japan

30 October Blitz, Tokyo, Japan

31 October Blitz, Tokyo, Japan

1 November Liquid Room, Tokyo, Japan

3 November Bayside Jenny, Osaka, Japan

4 November CK Café, Kyoto, Japan

5 November Forest National, Brussels, Belgium

15 November Revolver, Madrid, Spain

20 November Venue unknown, Stuttgart, Germany

24 November The Cirkus, Stockholm, Sweden

29 November Le Bataclan, Paris, France

9 December Academy, Manchester, UK

10 December Brixton Academy, London, UK

11 December SSX, Dublin, Ireland

14 December KROQ 'Almost Acoustic Christmas Show', Arrowhead Pond, Anaheim, California

15 December Cow Palace, Live 105 Christmas show, San Francisco, California

1997

11 January *Saturday Night Live*, New York, New York

12 January Roseland, New York, New York

13 January Ventura Theatre, Los Angeles, California

20 January Radio Free L.A., Los Angeles, California

6 February UBC Student Recreation, Vancouver, B.C., Canada

7 February Paramount Theatre, Seattle, Washington

8 February Salem Armoury, Salem, Oregon

10 February EMU Ballroom, Eugene, Oregon

12 February Pioneer Theatre, Reno, Nevada

13 February Freeborn Hall, Davis, California

14 February S.C. Civic Auditorium, Santa Cruz, California

15 February Stanford Auditorium, Palo Alto, California

16 February Rainbow Ballroom, Fresno, California

19 February Rimac Arena, San Diego, California

20 February Celebrity Theatre, Phoenix, Arizona

21 February Huntridge Theatre, Las Vegas, Nevada

2 March Kilburn National, London, UK

3 March Cardiff University, Cardiff, Wales

19 March the Edge, Fort Lauderdale, Florida

20 March USF Special Events Center, Tampa, Florida

21 March Florida Theatre, Gainesville, Florida

22 March Classic Center, Athens, Georgia

24 March Ryman Auditorium, Nashville, Tennessee

25 March Reynolds Coliseum, Raleigh, North Carolina

26 March Patriot Center, Fairfax, Virginia

28 March Lefrak Hall, Amherst, Massachusetts

29 March University of Rochester, Rochester, New York

30 March The Spectrum, Philadelphia, Pennsylvania

2 April Metropolis, Montreal, Quebec, Canada

3 April Varsity Arena, Toronto, Ontario, Canada

5 April Rhodes Arena, Akron, Ohio

7 April Music Hall, Cincinnati, Ohio

8 April Stephan Center, South Bend, Indiana

9 April Expo Hall, Indianapolis, Indiana

11 April Branden Auditorium, Normal, Illinois

12 April University of Chicago, Chicago, Illinois

219

14 April Mancuso Theatre, Omaha, Nebraska

15 April Shrine Mosque, Springfield, Missouri

16 April TNT Building, Oklahoma City, Oklahoma

18 April Performing Arts Center, Topeka, Kansas

19 April River Park, Tulsa, Oklahoma

20 April Starplex Amphitheatre, Dallas, Texas

25 April Universal Amphitheatre, Los Angeles, California

2 May Festimad, Madrid, Spain

3 May Heineken Festival, Dublin, Ireland

6 May *Later with Jools Holland*, BBC TV, London, UK

7 May Apollo, Manchester, UK

9 May Aston Villa Leisure Centre, Birmingham, UK

10 May Brixton Academy, London, UK

11 May Rock City, Nottingham, UK

13 May Barrowlands, Glasgow, Scotland

14 May Mayfair, Newcastle, UK

17 May Rock Am Ring, Nürnburg, Germany

18 May Rock Am Ring, Nürnburg, Germany

19 May Pinkpop Festival, Landgraaf, Netherlands

22 May Red Rocks, Denver, Colorado

24 May Apple River, Amphitheatre, Minneapolis, Minnesota

25 May New World Music Theatre, Chicago, Illinois

26 May Marcus Amphitheatre, Milwaukee, Wisconsin

26 May Riverport Amphitheatre, St. Louis, Missouri

28 May Phoenix Center, Detroit, Michigan

30 May Brandeis University, Boston, Massachusetts

31 May RFK Stadium, Washington, D.C.

1 June Blockbuster Amphitheatre, Philadelphia, Pennsylvania

12 June *Kill The Moonlight* Premiere, Los Angeles, California

27 June Glastonbury Festival, Glastonbury, UK

28 June St. Gallen Festival, St. Gallen, Switzerland

29 June Rosklide Festival, Roskilde, Denmark

2 July Imperial Festival, Oporto, Portugal

5 July Torhout Festival, Torhout, Belgium

6 July Werchter Festival, Werchter, Belgium

27 July Mount Fuji Festival, Mount Fuji, Japan

H.O.R.D.E. Festival

1 August River's Edge, Sommerset, Wisconsin

2 August Alpine Valley, East Troy, Wisconsin

3 August New World Music Theatre, Chicago, Illinois

5 August Vernon Downs, Syracuse, New York

6 August the Meadows, Hartford, Connecticut

8 August Great Woods, Boston, Massachusetts

9 August Great Woods, Boston, Massachusetts

10 August Space, Albany, New York

12 August Jones Beach, Wantaugh, New York

15 August Bizarre Festival, Cologne, Germany Filmed for *Rockpalast*

16 August V97 Festival, Leeds, UK

17 August V97 Festival, Chelmsford, UK

27 August Henry J. Kaiser, San Francisco, California

29 August Champoeg Amphitheatre, Portland, Oregon

30 August Bumbershoot Festival, Seattle, Washington

31 August P & E Fairgrounds, Vancouver, B.C., Canada

2 September *Late Show with David Letterman*, New York, New York

4 September MTV Video Music Awards, New York, New York

6 September Sessions At West 54th, New York, New York

13 October Farm Aid, Tinley Park, Illinois

19 November El Rey Theatre, Los Angeles, California

5 December KROQ 'Almost Acoustic Christmas Show'. Arrowhead Pond, Anaheim, California

16 December El Rey Theatre, Los Angeles, California

31 December Bondi Pavilion, Sydney, Australia

1998

3 January Mudslingers Festival, Perth, Australia

4 January Mudslingers, Festival, Perth, Australia

6 January Barton, Adelaide, Australia

8 January Forum, Melbourne, Australia

9 January Forum, Melbourne, Australia

12 January Enmore, Sydney, Australia

13 January Festival Hall, Brisbane, Australia

17 January Logan Campbell Centre, Auckland, New Zealand

18 January Town Hall, Wellington, New Zealand

8 May Santa Monica Art Museum, Santa Monica, California

17 May Galaxy Theatre, Santa Ana, California

23 May Rockshow, Copenhagen, Denmark

24 May Haigh Hall, Wigan, UK

26 May Zeleste, Barcelona, Spain

28 May Lisbon Coliseum, Lisbon, Portugal Filmed by MTV

1 June Blossom Amphitheatre, Cleveland, Ohio

2 June Pine Knob Amphitheatre, Detroit, Michigan

3 June Molson Amphitheatre, Toronto, Ontario, Canada

5 June Foxboro Stadium, Foxboro, Massachusetts

6 June Performing Arts Center, Saratoga, New York

7 June Giants Stadium, East Rutherford, New Jersey

8 June Spectrum, Philadelphia, Pennsylvania

9 June Darien Lakes, Buffalo, New York

10 June Starlake Amphitheatre, Pittsburgh, Pennsylvania

11 June Jones Beach, New York, New York

1 August Mt. Fuji Festival, Mt. Fuji, Japan

21 September the Cooler, New York, New York

10 October Silicon Planet, San José, California

3 November KROQ, Los Angeles, California

24 November KCRW Radio, Santa Monica, California

30 November National Public Radio

18 December Rosemont Horizon, Rosemont, Illinois

19 December Target Center, Minneapolis, Minnesota

20 December Joe Louis Arena, Detroit, Michigan

1999

10 January Town Hall, New York, New York

5 February Largo, Los Angeles, California

21 March House Of Blues, Los Angeles, California

11 April Shibuya Kokaido, Tokyo, Japan

12 April Shibuya Kokaido, Tokyo, Japan

14 April Shiminkaikan, Fukuoka, Japan

16 April Shiminkaikan, Osaka, Japan

18 April Sun Plaza, Sendai, Japan

19 April Sun Plaza, Tokyo, Japan

21 April Kouseinekin, Tokyo, Japan

24 April Andrews Amphitheatre, Honolulu, Hawaii

6 May Tiffany Theatre, Tropicana Hotel, Las Vegas, Nevada

8 May Wiltern Theatre, Los Angeles, California

9 May Wiltern Theatre, Los Angeles, California

16 May E3 Sony Playstation, Culver City, California

6 Oct UCSB Hub, Santa Barbara, California

7 Oct Satellite Student Union, Fresno, California

9 Oct Coachella Festival, Indio, California

1 Nov Galaxy Theatre, Santa Ana, California

6 Nov MTV Studios, New York, New York

12 Nov *TFI Friday*, London, UK

18 Nov *Videotech*, London, UK

19 Nov Shaffy Theatre, Amsterdam, Netherlands

20 Nov *Later with Jools Holland* London, UK (Recorded 16 November)

1 Dec Phoenix Theatre, Toronto, Canada

3 Dec First Union Center, Philadelphia, Pennsylvania

4 Dec *Saturday Night Live*, New York, New York

5 Dec VH1 Fashion Awards, New York, New York

6 Dec 9:30 Club, Washington, District of Columbia

9 Dec Key Arena, Seattle, Washington

10 Dec *The Tonight Show*, Los Angeles, California

11 December Arrowhead, Anaheim, California

11 December KROQ 'Almost Acoustic Christmas Show'. Arrowhead Pond, Anaheim, California

2000

25 January Austin Music Hall, Austin, Texas

26 January Bronco Bowl, Dallas, Texas

28 January Midland Theatre, Kansas City, Missouri

29 January American Theatre, St. Louis, Missouri

31 January Aragon, Chicago, Illinois

1 February Vets Memorial Auditorium, Columbus, Ohio

3 February Hill Auditorium, Ann Arbor, Michigan

4 February Taft, Cincinatti, Ohio

6 February Maple Leaf, Toronto, California

9 February Cepsum, Montreal, California

10 February Orpheum, Boston, Massachusetts

11 February Orpheum, Boston, Massachusetts

15 February Radio City, New York, New York

5 March Coliseum, Lisbon Portugal

6 March La Riviera, Madrid, Spain

7 March Zeleste, Barcelona, Spain

9 March Alcatraz, Milan, Italy

10 March Volkshaus, Zurich, Switzerland

11 March Colosseum, Munich, Germany

13 March E-Werk, Cologne, Germany

14 March Columbiahalle, Berlin, Germany

15 March Grosse Freiheit 36, Hamburg, Germany

18 March KB Hallen, Frederiksberg, Denmark

20 March Cirkus, Stockholm, Sweden

23 March Wembley Arena, London, UK

24 March Apollo, Manchester, UK

25 March Armadillo Theatre, Glasgow, Scotland

27 March Congressgebouw, The Hague, Netherlands

28 March Halles De Schaerbeek, Brussels, Belgium

29 March Le Zenith, Paris, France

17 May Castle-Jo Hall, Osaka, Japan

18 May Aichi Kinro Kaikan, Nagoya, Japan

20 May Zepp, Fukuoka, Japan

21 May Zepp, Fukuoka, Japan

23 May Sun Plaza Hall, Sendai, Japan

24 May Sun Plaza Hall, Sendai, Japan

26 May Zepp, Sapporo, Japan

29 May Budokan Hall, Tokyo, Japan

30 May Budokan Hall, Tokyo, Japan

INDEX

229